H   O   W   D

BOOK OF
POISONS

BOOK OF
POISONS

A GUIDE FOR WRITERS

SERITA STEVENS, RN, BSN, MA, LNC
AND ANNE BANNON

WRITER'S DIGEST BOOKS

www.writersdigest.com
Cincinnati, Ohio

Visit our Web sites at www.writersdigest.com and www.wdeditors.com for information on more resources for writers.

To receive a free weekly e-mail newsletter delivering tips and updates about writing and about Writer's Digest products, register directly at our Web site at http://newsletters.fwpublications.com.

11   10   09   08   07   5   4   3   2   1

Distributed in Canada by Fraser Direct, 100 Armstrong Avenue
Georgetown, ON, Canada   L7G 5S4, Tel: (905) 877-4411; Distributed in the U.K. and Europe by David & Charles, Brunel House, Newton Abbot, Devon, TQ12 4PU, England, Tel: (+44) 1626 323200, Fax: (+44) 1626 323319, E-mail: mail@davidandcharles.co.uk; Distributed in Australia by Capricorn Link, P.O. Box 704, Windsor, NSW 2756 Australia, Tel: (02) 4577-3555

Library of Congress Cataloging-in-Publication Data

Stevens, Serita, 1949-
  Book of poisons : a guide for writers / by Serita Stevens and Anne Bannon. -- 1st ed.
     p. cm. -- (Howdunit)
  Includes bibliographical references and index.
  ISBN-13: 978-1-58297-456-9 (pbk. : alk. paper)
  ISBN-10: 1-58297-456-X
  1. Poisoning--Popular works. 2. Poisons--Popular works. 3. Crime--Fiction. I. Bannon, Anne. II. Title.
  RA1213.S737 2007
  615.9--dc22
                              2006031515

Edited by Michelle Ehrhard
Designed by Claudean Wheeler
Production coordinated by Mark Griffin

DEDICATION

To my daughter Alexzandra for letting me take the time to write.

—SERITA STEVENS

AMDG. And to Michael Holland and Corrie Klarner—you guys are the light of my life.

—ANNE BANNON

ACKNOWLEDGMENTS

Special thanks to:

Kristi L. Koneig, MD, FACEP, Professor of Clinical Emergency Medicine, Director of Public Health Preparedness U.C.I. Dept of Emergency Medicine (Irvine, California). And to Henry Tarlow, RN, MPH for his invaluable contributions to the research.

—SERITA STEVENS

Dr. Ashok Jain, associate professor of emergency medicine at the Keck School of Medicine at the University of Southern California; Dr. Jawaid Akhtar, emergency physician and medical toxicologist at Pittsburgh Poison Center; Daniel Anderson, of the Los Angeles County Coroner's Office; to Gary Klarner, who supported me through the first version of this book; to my friends and the best support system ever: David Waldon, Angela Briscow, Edwina Clay, Della Gallo, Michelle Harris, Carol Modesti, Michael Roy, Tim Clodfelter, Bill Didio, Brent and MaryLou Furdyk, Glen Garvin, Karen Heyman, and Judy Sloane and anyone else whose name slipped me at the worst possible time; and to all the men and women who work in poison centers across America.

—ANNE BANNON

TABLE OF CONTENTS

A GUIDE TO UNDERSTANDING
THIS BOOK

All things are poisons, for there is nothing without poisonous qualities. It is only the dose that makes a thing poison.

—PARACELSUS, 1493–1541

Poisoning is a serious business. Once the preferred method of murder, homicidal poisoning has somewhat fallen in popularity because modern pathologists can detect almost any poison. Of course, the pathologist must know what poison to test for. There are, in fact, very few poisons that are ideal—odorless, colorless, tasteless, quick acting, and nontraceable. Many poisons meet one, two, even three of the criteria, but many drugs have their own built-in clues for the detective.

DEFINITION OF POISON

What is a poison? *Webster's New Collegiate Dictionary* defines a poison as "a substance that through its chemical action usually kills, injures, or impairs an organism" or "a substance that inhibits the activity of another substance or the course of a reaction or process." Anything in a large enough dose can prove toxic. Our concern in this book is feasibly deadly doses.

If death by poison is involved, the writer owes the reader respect for his intelligence. This is why *Howdunit: Book of Poisons* was written. All too often, a writer loses credibility by creating a world very similar to the real one, then shattering it by using an incorrect fact. Poisons are a time-honored part of mystery fiction. Yet, too often a writer will have a victim swallow something and collapse, dying instantly, when in real life the poison would have taken at least twenty minutes to act. Or just as often, the victim's symptoms could not possibly have been caused by the substance given. Many readers would not know the difference, but those who do would find the story ruined because of the error.

Until the first edition of this book, writers had trouble finding correct information about poisons. Agatha Christie had the advantage of working in a hospital pharmacy during World War I. Most other writers must ask questions where they can and go by what little information they have, or struggle through materials written in medicalese, trying to make sense of such technical terminology.

Book of Poisons is written in understandable English. All medical terms are in the glossary. Symptoms, forms, methods of administration, and reactions are cross-referenced, so writers who need a poison that will turn the victim yellow can turn to the symptoms appendix and find which poisons change a person's coloring.

LETHAL POISONS

This book deals with acute poisoning, as opposed to chronic poisoning. Chronic poisoning takes place when an antagonist slowly administers more and more of a given poison and eventually kills the victim. As this process can take years and does not guarantee death, this book focuses on more-certain methods, except in a few cases where chronic poisoning could produce other symptoms helpful to a writer.

The majority of the poisons described are lethal immediately or in short periods of time. Some toxins, however, take more time to work. During that time, the killer must prevent the victim from seeking medical aid.

Taste also presents a problem in trying to poison someone. Most poisons have a bitter taste that needs to be hidden if the poison is to be swallowed. In real life, the old trick of slipping a barbiturate into a cocktail could not work unless the victim habitually gulps drinks or is completely ignorant of how a drink should taste. Admittedly, not all poisons taste bitter, but the people in the best position to know the tastes of many of these substances are no longer around to say what they are. It is best to assume, unless otherwise noted, that the poison in question has a bad taste.

The symptoms and toxicity ratings given in this book vary from person to person. This is because human beings are very different in health, weight, and resistance. Alcoholics do not feel the effects of drinking as quickly as teetotalers do. An old lady with a bad heart can die from a dosage that would only cause a stomachache in her healthier daughter. When writing, it is best to avoid the exceptions to the rules, unless the exception is the whole point of the story. For the purposes of this handbook, it is assumed that the victim is a healthy person weighing approximately one hundred and fifty pounds.

NAVIGATING THE BOOK

The vast majority of the toxins in the book are listed by name with the following headings: Name (and depending on the substance, other names for the same thing or similar substances that mostly react the same way), Toxicity (approximately how poisonous a substance is based on the chart below), Form (gas, liquid, powder, etc.), Effects and Symptoms, Reaction Time, Antidotes and Treatments, Notes (interesting bits of information that don't fit under the above headings, such as what the toxin is used for and where it might be found), and Case History (stories or real incidents involving the poison when applicable).

Some chapters vary because, as in the medical chapter, many drugs are in classes and act similar or go under a variety of names; it would be redundant to list each and every drug separately. However, efforts were made to make notes of drugs that varied within the class. Other chapters, like plants, have various names around the world but really are the same plant or at least the same plant family.

The poisons in this book have been rated in terms of relative toxicity, with six (6) being supertoxic, requiring only a minuscule amount to cause death, and one (1) being practically nontoxic except in immense doses. Actual dosages do not seem to be an issue in current literature; therefore, a more specific rating system was deemed unnecessary. Few poisons in this book are rated one (1) or two (2), as they probably would not be useful to the mystery writer with a plot to advance.

TOXICITY RATING CHART

TOXICITY	PROBABLE ORAL LETHAL DOSE FOR 150 POUND HUMAN BEING	
6 Supertoxic	Less than 5 mg/kg	A taste (less than seven drops)

TOXICITY	PROBABLE ORAL LETHAL DOSE FOR 150 POUND HUMAN BEING	
5 Extremely toxic	5-50 mg/kg	Between seven drops and one teaspoon
4 Very toxic	50-500 mg/kg	Between one teaspoon and one ounce
3 Moderately toxic	0.5-5 gm/kg	Between one ounce and one pint or pound
2 Slightly toxic	5-15 gm/kg	Between one pint and one quart
1 Almost non-toxic	above 15 gm/kg	More than one quart or 2.2 pounds

NOTE: The notations mg/kg and gm/kg can be confusing. They refer to milligrams (mg) or grams (gm) of basic substance to kilograms (kg) of host substance—in this specific case, milligrams or grams of poison required per kilogram of potential victim.

CHANGES IN MEDICAL TREATMENT

It should be noted that, over time, things can change and, indeed, have in the years since the first edition of this book appeared. Most notable is in the arena of the treatment of poisoning. In fact, a change in the approach to emergency treatment of poisoning victims is under way even at the time of this writing. Up until about five years ago, there was an emphasis on emptying the stomach of any ingested toxins through inducing vomiting or by stomach pumping, more technically known as gastric lavage (except in the case of corrosive agents, which would only corrode more of the victim's system on the way back up). Parents of small children were encouraged to keep syrup of ipecac on hand for such emergencies.

Now, the American Pediatrics Association recommends that parents don't even keep ipecac in the house. As for treatment in the emergency department, gastric lavage is being used less and less. Toxicologist and Emergency Physician Jawaid Ahktar of the Pittsburgh Poison Center, in Pennsylvania, flat out said: "It's pretty clear it doesn't work." Numerous journal articles found on www.pubmed.gov question the use of stomach pumping, and one, from the November 2005 *Medical Clinics of North America*, even questioned the use of activated charcoal, a fine tasteless powdered charcoal known for its ability to adsorb or bind to a wide variety of substances, which is sometimes used in treatment.

The interesting thing is that among the many books consulted by the authors, gastric lavage is still listed as a method of treatment. Dr. Ahktar speculated that the books are somewhat behind the actual practice, and that some physicians are still using the older practice. The writer, however, should be aware that stomach pumping reflects an older standard of care—something that would be useful when writing a piece set ten years ago. So if you notice gastric lavage as one of the treatments for a poison in this book, keep in mind that it is only included so that you can accurately write pieces set before the twenty-first century. The current standard of care focuses on supportive treatment, or taking care of the symptoms as they present themselves.

CONCLUSION

It is possible that a particular poison is not included in the book. Given the space limitations, some poisons simply could not be included. And many poisons require such large doses to be lethal that they rarely kill. And some poisons just aren't as poisonous as myth would have them. Tear gas, for example, has not been included, since the worst it can do is give the victim second-degree burns. Many household chemicals are not as toxic to adults as they are to young children.

Remember, in addition to providing correct information about poisons, this book can also be useful for story ideas. Poisonous chemicals are not to be taken lightly in real life, but the right poison can move the plot of a good story along nicely—and how nice it is to have correct facts!

A SHORT HISTORY OF THE
DREADED ART

I love the old way best, the simple way
Of poison, where we too are strong as men.

—MEDEA, IN THE PLAY OF THE SAME NAME
BY EURIPIDES, 480–406, B.C.

The first discovery of poisons came about by trial and error. Foraging for food among different plants, early humans soon found some were deadly. Those who mastered the knowledge of poisons were regarded with respect and fear, and were either venerated as tribal sorcerers or burned at the stake.

Evidence of the sophisticated art of homicidal poisoning, practiced for centuries by the ancient Egyptians, Chinese, Indians, and Greeks, appears as early as in the pre-Christian Roman annals, along with stories of greed, betrayal, and power. Searching for the perfect suicidal poison, Cleopatra, queen of Egypt, experimented on her prisoners and slaves. She remained dissatisfied. Henbane (*Hyoscyamus niger*) or belladonna (*Atropa belladonna*), despite their rapid action, produced too much pain; *Strychnos nux-vomica*, from which strychnine was eventually extracted, caused convulsions that left facial features distorted at death. She finally selected the bite of the asp (a small African

---

cobra), whose venom produced a serene and prompt death. Legend holds that in the second century B.C., the Greek king Mithradates VI habitually ingested small amounts of many known poisons, hoping to build immunity to them. The accuracy of this is doubted, however, since many poisons are fatal, in even the smallest dose.

The use of poisons in trial by ordeal, on arrowheads, or as instruments of state for execution by popes and princes of the Renaissance provided a fund of empirical knowledge that paved the way for the pharmacology of modern times. Such drugs as digitalis, ouabain, and atropine owe their existence to the scientific investigation of plant preparationS used for killing animals and humans.

The best-known poison of the fifteenth, sixteenth, and seventeenth centuries, arsenic, formed the basis of many poisons of the time: *cantarella*, commonly used by the Borgia family, and *aqua toffan,* or *aquetta di Napoli,* used by Catherine de Medici. *Aqua toffan,* a combination of arsenic and cantharides—from a dried beetle, *Lytta (Cantharis) vesicatoria,* used as a counterirritant and vesicant (a blistering agent)—was reportedly created by the Italian countess Toffana. Only four to six drops of this mixture in water or wine caused death within a few hours. Other common poisons of the time, found easily in the woods and meadows, included water hemlock, foxglove, henbane, and the prussic acid of almond trees. It was because of this prevalence of poisons that most royalty employed food tasters. However, they were often ineffective in protecting their masters.

KEY PLAYERS INVOLVED IN POISONS

Italy of the fifteenth century was known for its dynasty of poisoners, the Borgias. The most well known were Cesare Borgia and his father Rodrigo, who later became Pope Alexander VI. However, the whole family was adept at the art. Anyone who crossed a Borgia was apt to be invited to a party, after which he would become quite ill—if he even survived the evening. The food during this era was so highly spiced that often it was impossible to taste alien flavors, and one could easily take a poison without noticing. Sometimes the poisoning was used as a warning or to remove an obstacle; other times, it was simply experimenting with some new combination.

Catherine de Medici, an Italian princess, married France's Henry of Orleans. Upon her marriage, she brought with her to France a train of attendants, including *parfumeurs* and astrologers, two occupations that often hid the production of poison.

As soon as Catherine arrived in France, mysterious illnesses and deaths began. The best-known poison of the time was arsenic and one of Catherine's favorite poisons. Among the French, the word *Italien* soon became synonymous with *empoisonneur.*

Foremost among de Medici's victims was the dauphin François, Henry's oldest brother. His death left her husband as heir to the throne. After an active game of tennis, François asked for water, which was brought him by his *Italien* cupbearer. The dauphin died moments later. Under torture, the cupbearer later admitted the poisoning. Catherine's next victim was the Cardinal of Lorraine, an old enemy of the de Medicis. His death was accomplished by a poison (possibly nicotine, which had just been discovered in the New World) that penetrated his skin pores after he had handled tainted money.

Catherine's favorite poisoner was Rene "the Florentine," known by the city where he had first learned his art. Reportedly he killed Jeanne of Navarre, a political rival, by selling her a pair of gloves laced with poison, possibly *venin de crapaud*. This poison was obtained by feeding arsenic to toads and other creatures and distilling the juices from their bodies upon death; the poison then contained not only the arsenic, but also hydrogen sulfide as a byproduct of the decomposition.

In the early 1600s, notorious poisioner Antonio Exili toured the courts of Europe, from the Vatican, to Sweden and France, to the Baltic countries. His services were welcomed by some and feared by others. Exili boasted he could supply death in any form—lingering, quick, painful, or gentle as sleep. French sorceress Catherine Monvoisin, known as "La Voisin," was one of the main players in the famous poison affair (*affaire des poisons*), which disgraced the reign of Louis XIV. The bones of toads, the teeth of moles, cantharides, iron filings, human blood, and human dust were among the ingredients of the love powders concocted by La Voisin. Among her clients were Olympe Mancini, comtesse de Soissons, who sought the death of the king's mistress, Louise de La Vallière; and Françoise-Athénaïs, marquise de Montespan, another of the king's mistresses, who also performed black masses to curry the favor of the king. La Voison was later convicted of witchcraft and publicly burned.

The poison affair began a period of hysterical pursuit of murder suspects, during which a number of prominent people were implicated and sentenced for poisoning and witchcraft. The furor began in 1676 after the trial of Marie-Madeleine-Marguerite d'Aubray, marquise de Brinvilliers, who had conspired to poison her father and brothers with her lover, army captain Godin de Sainte-Croix, in order to inherit their estates. There were also rumors that she had poisoned poor people during her visits in hospitals. She fled but was arrested in Liège. She was forced to confess, sentenced to death, and on July 17 was tortured with the water cure (forced to drink sixteen pints of water), beheaded, and burned at a stake.

On the other end of the spectrum was Christopher Glaser, a well-known Swiss chemist noted for his poison antidotes. A favorite of many royals, his specialty was *theriaca*, a compound containing a mixture of opium and other drugs that would alleviate the symptoms of poison. Its efficacy was difficult to verify, since the realization that one was being poisoned rarely came until it was too late. Milk was another antidote Glaser espoused, and royals drank that in large quantities for fear of someone slipping poison in their food.

Unfortunately, Godin de Sainte-Croix seduced Glaser into the nefarious business of death by showing him how much more money could be made by killing people than by curing them. Glaser committed suicide when it appeared likely he'd been found out. Sainte-Croix himself died while looking for a poison that could kill with one sniff. He evidently found it, but was unable to pass on the information.

Knowledge of many of the poisons used in the fifteenth, sixteenth, and seventeenth centuries is said to have disappeared with time, but the poisons themselves still exist.

Informally, the isolation of morphine from opium by Bernard Serturner started the study of poison. The beginning of poison as a formal study, however, began in the nineteenth century with Claude Bernard's research on the effects of curare, a vegetable poison used by the South American Indians to poison their arrows.

During the Industrial Revolution, the findings of two scientists, Matthew J.B. Orfila and his colleague Francois-Vincent Raspail, were especially important. Orfila, considered the founder of modern toxicology, experimented with and catalogued poisons and their effects. *Traite des Poisons on Toxicologie General* was published by Orfila in 1814, followed in 1829 by Robert Christison's *Treatise on Poisons*.

Arsenic was able to be detected in minute amounts in the new techniques established by British chemist James Marsh around 1836. So sensitive was the test that it could detect as little as one-fiftieth of a milligram. His findings were written up in The *Edinburgh Philosophical Journal* in 1838.

In 1839, in the world-famous LaFarge case, Dr. Orfila, who had testified in other cases of arsenic poisoning, applied Marsh's test for finding arsenic to biological specimens. Orfila told the judge it would be possible to detect traces of arsenic even in the paint on the arm of the judicial bench. His expert testimony convicted Madame LaFarge.

Madame LaFarge, née Marie Cappelle, was a poor relation to the French royal family. Her marriage to Charles LaFarge was an unhappy one. Despite this, when her husband fell ill in 1839, Marie nursed Charles. Even with her care—or maybe because of it—he became sicker, and subsequently died. Marie was accused of killing Charles after a servant reported seeing Marie mix a white powder into Charles's drink. She insisted the arsenic in the house was for the rats, but Orfila showed there was substantial poison in LaFarge's body. Marie LaFarge was sentenced to life imprisonment and died in 1852 after writing her story.

By 1830, chemical analysis could detect most mineral compounds, but not organic poisons. While investigating a nicotine homicide in 1851, Belgian chemist Jean Servais Stas was the first to discover a technique for extracting alkaloid poisons. He was the first to isolate nicotine from postmortem tissue.

Poisoning as a favorite criminal weapon declined considerably when methods of detection and knowledge of poisons increased. The improved medical care for the victims also put a damper on those using poison as a weapon. Those two facts in place, death by poison could no longer be guaranteed.

With the beginning of the twentieth century, industry increased and so did the chemicals available for poisoning. Many poisons originally from plants were duplicated synthetically, with varying symptoms and degrees of toxicity.

The advent of synthetic poisons added to the problems of toxicologists, who believed they had poisoning well in hand with the control of arsenic, cyanide, and strychnine. After World War II, barbiturate use became widespread, and there was a corresponding increase in suicides. By 1954, the number of barbiturate suicides had increased to twelve times the number for 1938. During the 1950s, people who had taken an overdose of barbiturates died at a rate of about fifteen to twenty-five per hundred, regardless of how quickly they received medical care. Today, the mortality rate, if the patient is hospitalized in time, is negligible.

In a 1997 worldwide survey, poisoning as a cause of death ranked first for people ages one to fourteen; third for people ages fifteen to twenty-three, fifth for people twenty-four to forty-four, sixth for those forty-five to sixty-four, and seventh for those over sixty-five.

The National Clearing House for Poison Control Centers indicates that, in the United States, internal-use medicines are most used for poisoning, followed by medicines for external use, cleaning fluids and other domestic products, pesticides or plant poisons, and vegetable products, with gas and fumes the least used to kill or commit suicide. The *Statistical Abstract of the United States* from 1998 indicates that carbon monoxide and gases still fall last in deaths by poisoning.

For several centuries, people were less interested in antidotes than in poisons for killing, whether for pest control or murder. Therefore many superstitions have risen regarding remedies. One such myth is that milk is a universal antidote. In many cases, milk is merely a dilutent and not an antidote. Salt water, another common first-aid measure, has recently been shown to be dangerous. While intended to dilute and absorb poison in the stomach, large amounts of sodium chloride can bring on fatal heart attacks, especially in victims already weakened.

No antidote should be attempted without medical supervision, as many supposed antidotes cause more harm than the poisons. A dangerous antidote can even be part of the poison plot. Since much of this information is relatively new, the killer trying to get rid of her maiden aunt could say she was only doing what she thought best.

Matthew J.B. Orfila and others who searched for the universal antidote came to understand that no such miracle chemical existed. The use of any antidote depends on the type and amount of the drug taken, how it is administered, and the time delay between ingestion and medical treatment. In many cases, since each poison produces a variety of symptoms depending on the person, all that can be done is to treat the symptoms as they arise.

The science of toxicology is not static. New antidotes and methods of treatment are developed every day, and the network of poison knowledge is expanding accordingly throughout the world.

CHAPTER 2

A DAY IN THE LIFE OF A
CRIMINAL TOXICOLOGIST

It's the running gag on the *CSI* shows—DNA results in minutes, as opposed to the week, if not months, it would take to get results in real life. We buy it because the writers on *CSI: Crime Scene Investigation, CSI: Miami,* and *CSI: New York* have only one hour (usually) in which to tell their stories. It is the convention of the one-hour dramatic television series that time is amorphous, and events are sped up and compressed so that the story can be told within the allotted time.

But one of the reasons the *CSI* franchise has such a huge following is that the science itself is mostly accurate. The machines you see on the sets of those shows were acquired from the companies that make them for real crime labs across the country and even around the world.

But the worlds of the *CSI*s, *Law and Orders, NCIS,* and their most recent clones are still fictional.

To see how it's done in the real world, let's visit the toxicology lab of the Los Angeles County Coroner's office. Please note that, at the time of this writing (spring of 2006), efforts were being made to fund and build a new annex, so the slightly frowsy, 1960s look may not be a part of that office by the time you read this.

But "retro"—intentional or not—is not an uncommon look in civic buildings. In fact, the well-used look of the walls and carpeting in the reception area is probably more real than anything we see on TV. In fact, but for the odd smell and the sign, this is a county-level office identical to countless others. Mood lighting? Not here. It's all washed-out fluorescent.

After a wait in the lobby, you are brought upstairs to the tox department by one of the office workers. He's friendly, but seems preoccupied, which he is, though not, as you might think, with some mysterious new substance that has popped up in a case, but with a mundane computer problem. You are seated next to a copy machine in the crowded antechamber of a set of three offices. Again, there's nothing to distinguish these from any other generic office—except that hanging off the back of one chair is a black windbreaker that says across the back, in large yellow letters, "CORONER." The jacket looks familiar; it's just like those you see on the news, worn by the folks hauling a body from a crime scene.

Daniel Anderson is the criminologist in charge of the toxicology lab. There are two other tox labs in Los Angeles, but this one focuses on postmortem tox screens, while the others are more focused on evidence produced by the living. His lab processes close to six thousand toxicology cases a year. Surprisingly, a significant portion of those analyses are not to find out what killed a victim.

"It's to answer questions later on down the road," Anderson says.

For example, a police officer is "involved in a shooting." It's obvious from the gunshot wound to the victim's chest that he died of a gunshot wound. But when Internal Affairs gets around to investigating the shooting to determine if the officer was firing in self-defense, it will make a big difference if analysis of the victim's blood shows that he was tripping on PCP.

Or, for another example, the driver of the car that causes a multiple-fatality accident is among the dead. Investigators need to know the blood alcohol level of that driver to find out whether she was drunk or made some other fatal mistake.

When actual poisoning is involved in a death, it's almost always a drug overdose, a suicide, or accidental. Intentional poisonings don't happen very often. In fact, Anderson could only recall one such case, and even that was a few years old: A woman had poisoned her husband with oleander tea, then put ethylene glycol (antifreeze) into his Gatorade to finish him off.

The labs in the tox department are in a series of rooms on the perimeter of a block of individual offices. In one room is a series of microscopes. In another, there's a refrigerator and a shelf with some basic blenders just like you'll find in any ordinary kitchen. On a counter across from the fridge is a tray crowded with glass sample jars and some covered paper cups. All are labeled. The sample jars clearly contain blood samples from various cadavers. The paper cups contain milk shakes. But you're not going to want to drink these.

Anderson explains that tox screens can only be done on liquids, such as blood. But there are a lot of reasons why a blood sample may not be appropriate for testing. It could be the suspected substance isn't likely to show up in the blood because of time or the nature of the substance. Other reasons include contamination of the blood sample, insufficient blood, or, if there were multiple bodies at a crime scene, an inability to identify the blood as belonging to a specific cadaver. So Anderson tests the liver. The livers are liquefied in a blender, thus making the "milk shake," a viscous, grayish brown liquid.

Testing for toxins is a time-consuming process of elimination. There are two basic types of machines used, the gas chromatograph and the mass spectrometer. Obviously, they are complicated, but both machines look a bit like eggshell-colored bread machines: large boxes, maybe a little smaller than your average cardboard file box, with controls on the top. Part of the control unit is a carousel like you see in lab shots on TV, with room for lots of little labeled vials containing the samples to be analyzed. Anderson flips down the front cover on a mass spectrometer and shows you the hair-thin tube of wire inside. It's coiled so you can't see how long it is, but the liquids are forced through the tube and the machine "reads" the sample to see if the chemicals it's programmed to find are there.

Surprisingly, there are few anatomical changes in the body that point to poisons, let alone one specific poison. In the case of a suspected cocaine overdose, for example, the pathologist doing the autopsy may find damage to a victim's heart muscle. But many things can cause damage to the heart besides cocaine. There is a whole host of drugs that can cause heart damage, not to mention many different bacteria.

The problem with screening for toxins is that the person doing the screening must have an idea of what he is looking for. And since the anatomy will only provide the most general clues, the first step, Anderson says, is to run the sample through the gas chromatograph. This will determine whether it is positive for one or more of several different categories of toxins, including alcohols, street or pharmacological drugs, and heavy metals.

The machine can say only if these toxins are present, not specifically what they are. For example, a sample may be positive for heavy metals, but the gas chromatograph can't say whether that heavy metal is lead, copper, or mercury. That's when Anderson, or one of his co-workers, such as toxicologist Michelle Sandberg, puts the sample through one of several mass spectrometers, each set to find toxins in a different category.

The process takes time. Some tests take hours, even days, to run. If one machine turns up nothing, then it's time to try another.

There's also some significant interpretation involved. As Anderson puts it, anybody can run the machines. The skill is in interpreting the results. A positive result on trace amounts of arsenic in a sample doesn't necessarily mean that person was poisoned by arsenic, because the toxicologist knows that everyone's system contains trace amounts of arsenic. The toxicologist needs to know how clean the sample was: Did it come from a hospital, or was it obtained from the scene of the crime? Blood samples from the hospital are fairly clean extractions. If the sample came from the scene, then how clean the extraction was is anyone's guess.

Then there's the deep frustration of being unable to isolate a given toxin.

"You don't know who screwed up," Anderson says.

It could have been the cops at the crime scene, or one of the techs or the pathologist during the autopsy. Anderson concedes that even he sometimes screws up in the lab. Or it could be that the substance—heavy metal, for example—is not something the mass spectrometers are programmed to look for.

Because the truth is, there are so many substances out there that no one can test for everything. The machines can only say whether the elements tested for are present, which is not the same thing as identifying what is in a given sample. If a test comes up negative for the presence of *x*, *y*, or *z*, that doesn't mean substances *q* or *v* aren't present—it means only that *x*, *y*, and *z* are not present in that sample.

Which leads to another big myth: Science can prove everything. Well, it can't. Sometimes you can categorically prove that someone died of an overdose of oxycodone (the generic drug that is Percocet and Oxycontin). Sometimes you can't. Maybe the tests show there was oxycodone in the victim's system, but not enough for a lethal dose, and the alcohol levels are inconclusive. Or maybe the sample wasn't as clean as it should have been and there's something weird showing up from the gas chromatograph analysis, but none of the other machines can pick it up.

The process usually takes weeks, not the few minutes we see in shows. Part of it is backlog. In 2002, the last year for which figures were available at the time of this writing, the Los Angeles County Coroner's office took on 9,470 cases, just over half of the questionable 18,665 deaths reported in the county that year. Almost two-thirds of those accepted cases went through Anderson's office for analysis. That's over fourteen cases a day, 365 days a year. If it's Thursday, and you're still running analyses on cases from Monday, cases from Tuesday and Wednesday are starting to stack up in the queue. More likely, you're still juggling cases from the previous Thursday, along with some from Friday, and every day since. One investigator working one case at a time does not happen in real life, at least not in the larger jurisdictions. There are usually multiple criminologists, each looking at different types of evidence and juggling several cases, all at different stages of analysis.

Again, it's a multi-step process. Samples have to be processed, then tested. Then the results have to be interpreted, and possibly run through more tests. And then the reports have to be written. None of this happens in a few short minutes, nor is it terribly interesting to watch, which is why we don't see it on television or film.

As former criminologist Devine has noted, the writers on *CSI* have managed to make the science of crime fighting interesting. So, if they have to compress time, pretend there's no such thing as endless paperwork, and use mood lighting in the labs—well, that's television, and if you're writing a TV or film script, go for it. If you're writing a novel, you have more room to allow for the passage of time, so you may be better off sticking closer to reality. Or maybe not. But at least now, if you're challenged on it, you can say that you made the decision to compress and gloss over mundane details for the good of the story and not because you didn't know better.

THE CLASSIC POISONS:
ARSENIC, CYANIDE, AND STRYCHNINE

MARTHA: Well, dear, for a gallon of elderberry wine, I take one teaspoonful of arsenic, and add a half a teaspoonful of strychnine, and then just a pinch of cyanide.

—JOSEPH KESSELRING, ARSENIC AND OLD LACE

Arsenic, cyanide, and strychnine have been grouped into this chapter more because of their popularity than because of any relation they have to one another. Arsenic is a metal, which in high enough doses affects the digestive system. Cyanide interferes with the absorption of oxygen by the body's cells. Strychnine is a stimulant that works on the central nervous system.

ARSENIC

OTHER: White arsenic, gray arsenic, metallic arsenic, arsenic trioxide, arsenous oxide, arsenic trihydride.

TOXICITY: 5

FORM: Arsenic in its pure, natural state is a gray metal. Most often it is found as arsenic trioxide, a white powder.

EFFECTS AND SYMPTOMS: Though not certain, most experts believe that arsenic interferes with the function of vital enzymes in the body.

The best-known symptom of acute arsenic poisoning is severe gastric distress. In fact, before the poisoning could be diagnosed, Victorian physicians often called it "gastric fever." Other symptoms include burning esophageal pain, hematemesis (vomiting of blood), and watery diarrhea. The skin becomes cold and clammy to the touch, and the blood pressure falls, making the victim dizzy and weak. Convulsions and coma occur, and death usually comes from circulatory failure.

In cases where death is not immediate, the victim develops jaundice, becomes restless, and has headaches, dizzy spells, and an inability to urinate or defecate. Occasionally there will be episodes of paralysis. Because arsenic is an element and does not break down, it remains in the victim's hair, fingernails, and urine. Arsenic is fat soluble and stored in body tissue because it is not eliminated by the kidneys. Low doses over a long period of time do not always result in death. However, rapid weight loss can dump a lethal dose into the blood stream. In the case of immediate death, however, the pathologist will find only an inflamed stomach and possibly some arsenic in the digestive tract. Red blood cells are destroyed in the arteries, and the skin becomes yellow-tinged.

If death is delayed by several days, arsenic will show up in the liver and kidneys. If the victim survives the immediate gastric symptoms, complications can crop up anywhere from one to fourteen days from the acute ingestion. Those include various problems with heart function (one to six days), delirium (two to six days), and anemia (one to two weeks). Survivors can experience symptoms, including anemia and cardiac problems, over a prolonged period of time (sometimes years).

Chronic arsenic poisoning causes numerous symptoms, the severity of which can vary depending on the level of poison and the length of exposure. The victim can experience burning pains in the hands and feet, numbness throughout the body, localized swelling and skin irritations, a flaking rash, hair loss, cirrhosis of the liver, jaundice, nausea, vomiting, cramps, weight loss, visual impairment, and, finally, cardiac failure.

REACTION TIME: Symptoms begin as early as thirty minutes after ingestion. In acute conditions, death may occur within a few hours, or take as long as twenty-four hours.

ANTIDOTES AND TREATMENTS: In acute arsenic poisoning, the first measure is to give activated charcoal, although one source mentions that it is not always effective with metals like arsenic. In addition to supportive care, including maintaining the airway and providing fluids to combat the vomiting and diarrhea, the victim is likely to be given dimercaprol or succimer for two to three days (these are chelating agents, which bind with metals in the blood and tissues, and eliminate it quickly from the body, usually through urine). In the meantime, the physician also treats dehydration, shock, pulmonary edema, anuria (the absence or defective voiding of urine), and liver damage. In cases of kidney damage, the victim may be put on a kidney dialysis machine after the chelation therapy to remove the dimercaprol and arsenic. While the patient may survive the initial poisoning, it can take months to heal the damage done to the organs and circulatory system.

NOTES: Arsenic has a wide range of industrial uses, including the manufacture of opal translucent or opaque glass, ceramics, enamels, paints, wallpapers, and rodenticides, as well as in textile printing, tanning, and taxidermy. It used to be among the more accessible of toxins; however, over the past few years, its use has become increasingly restricted in the United States, probably because of how long it can remain in the environment and because of its highly carcinogenic properties. Ironically, an inorganic form of arsenic, known as intravenous arsenic trioxide (Trisenox) was recently approved by the FDA as a chemotherapy drug in cancer treatment.

Historically, arsenic was the murderer's most popular poison, primarily because it was found in so many common household items. A trip to the pharmacy (chemist, in Great Britain) to get rat poison raised little, if any, suspicion.

Traces of arsenic are present in all human tissues. It is the twentieth most commonly encountered element of 103 naturally occurring elements.

In homicidal or suicidal cases, arsenic is generally swallowed. It can also be inhaled, either as a dust or as arsine gas, with the gas producing somewhat different symptoms than the dust. Inhalation is generally a result of industrial exposure.

Arsenic's primary symptoms of stomach distress are the same as for a number of stomach disorders that are usually lumped together under the catch-all diagnosis of "gastroenteritis."

Humans can develop a tolerance for the poison: There have been arsenic eaters throughout the centuries who made a practice of having arsenic daily. One of the tests of the Hellfire Club of eighteenth-century England was to see how much arsenic and other poisons one could consume without being affected. Given arsenic's carcinogenic properties, it would be interesting to know how many members of the club later developed tumors.

CASE HISTORY

There are numerous cases of arsenic use in history. Modern forensic tests on samples of Napoleon Bonaparte's hair have found more than the usual trace amounts of arsenic. Napoleon did believe he was being poisoned, and there were contemporary rumors to that effect; however, arsenic was a common ingredient in the dyes used in wallpapers of the time. Vapors from this wallpaper could account for the samples.

BOOK OF POISONS

Among other famous cases is that of Mary Ann Cotton, a forty-year-old nurse who, by 1872, had been married five times, and was considered Britain's most notorious mass murderer. She was accused of fifteen deaths, though twenty-one people close to her died in twenty years. Among them were all her children, the children of her five husbands, and several neighbors. The children all suffered from "gastric fever," and suspicion arose when the physician refused to issue a death certificate. All the exhumed bodies showed arsenic. Cotton's defense argued that the children had been poisoned accidentally by arsenic contained in the green floral wallpaper used in their home. But her purchase of soft soap and arsenic—to be used, she said, for cleaning bedsteads and killing bedbugs—proved fatal to her case. Mary Ann Cotton was found guilty and sentenced to death.

Among our favorite literary cases is *Strong Poison* by Dorothy Sayers. White arsenic was slipped to the victim in an omelette prepared at the table by the killer. The book stands out because it also uses arsenic tolerance as the key to its solution.

CYANIDE

OTHER: Potassium cyanide, sodium cyanide, and hydrogen cyanide are the most common forms of cyanide. Prussic acid is hydrogen cyanide or hydrocyanic acid.

TOXICITY: 6

FORM: Potassium cyanide and sodium cyanide are white solids bearing a faint bitter-almond odor. Hydrogen cyanide is a gas. Cyanide, in its various forms, can be swallowed, inhaled, or absorbed through the skin. It is generally released from its host compound by acids, such as the hydrochloric acid found in the stomach. The poison in the seeds is released only if the seeds are chewed.

EFFECTS AND SYMPTOMS: Cyanide prevents the body's red blood cells from absorbing oxygen. Cyanide action has been called "chemical asphyxia."

Smelling a toxic dose of cyanide as a gas can cause immediate unconsciousness, convulsions, and death within one to fifteen minutes. Swallowed a fatal dose can take up to twenty minutes or longer to work, especially if it's been swallowed on a full stomach. If a near-lethal dose is absorbed through the skin, inhaled, or swallowed, the symptoms will include gasping for breath, dizziness, flushing, headache, nausea, vomiting, rapid pulse, and a drop in blood pressure causing fainting. With a lethal dose, convulsions can precede death within four hours, except in the case of sodium nitroprusside, when death can be delayed as long as twelve hours after ingestion.

The victim's blood may appear purple.

REACTION TIME: As little as one to fifteen minutes, depending on the amount. In gaseous forms, cyanide can cause almost instantaneous death.

ANTIDOTES AND TREATMENTS: If a victim is to be saved, treatment must begin within the first thirty minutes after the poison is given. Many patients need nothing more than aggressive supportive care. Testing can be done to confirm cyanide poisoning, but not usually in time to be of any use.

In those cases where cyanide poisoning has been confirmed, amyl nitrite (a vasodilator; it expands blood vessels, thus lowering blood pressure) may be administered. An injection of sodium thiosulfate, which counteracts cyanide's effects, can be used even if it's not certain the patient is suffering from cyanide poisoning.

All cyanide antidotes must be used carefully, as they are poisonous themselves. As such, they could be useful in a plot with a murderous doctor wishing to deflect suspicion by first poisoning the victim, then killing him with the cure.

Victims who live four hours will probably recover, although they may suffer for some time afterward from symptoms, such as headaches and other central nervous system problems.

NOTES: Hydrocyanic acid and its sodium and potassium salts have many industrial uses. Cyanide occurs naturally in a large variety of seeds and pits, including those of the *Prunus* genus, such as the peach, apricot, apple, wild cherry, plum, or jetberry bush. Many other plants have cyanogenetic glycosides, which take longer to react but will have a similar effect. (See chapter five on poisonous plants for more information.)

The gas hydrogen cyanide has many uses, such as a fumigant, insecticide, rodenticide, electroplating solution, and metal polish, and has also been used for execution in the gas chambers. It is called one of the "one-whiff" knockdown gases for its quick action at higher concentrations, which probably explains the concerns about its use as a bioterrorist weapon. To be effective, it would have to be released in a closed environment, otherwise the vapors would diffuse before doing significant harm; however, because of the potential, hospitals are starting to stock up on cyanide antidote kits.

The famous bitter-almond odor of cyanide may be noticeable, but not everyone is capable of smelling it. The ability to smell bitter almond is a genetic trait—something that might make an important clue.

Hydrogen cyanide poisoning is also possible during structure fires, as many substances, when burned, give off the gas. Plastics and man-made fibers release cyanide gas when burned. The gas, along with carbon monoxide, are two complicating factors in smoke inhalation cases.

Some cyanogenetic plants include mahogany, Christmasberry, cherry laurel, chokecherry, pin cherry, wild black cherry, flax, yellow pine-flax, velvet grass, Johnsongrass, Sudangrass, arrowgrass, and small arrowgrass. All of these can cause cyanide poisoning if ingested and chewed in sufficient amounts (most would require fairly large amounts to be poisonous). Please see Elderberry, on page 77.

CASE HISTORY

Lizzie Borden is infamous for the 1892 axe murder of her father and stepmother in Fall River, Massachussetts. Less known is the fact that she was also suspected of poisoning them with prussic acid, a form of cyanide, prior to their dismemberment. Police found traces of the poison in the sugar bowl.

Another cyanide incident involves Roland B. Molineux, a New York City factory worker and member of the famed Knickerbocker Athletic Club. Molineux sought the attentions of an attractive young woman who was interested in another young man, a fellow member of the club, named Henry Barnet. When Barnet died mysteriously in 1898, it was said he had taken a poison he had received in the mail. The young woman married Molineux shortly thereafter.

Some time later, Molineux quarreled with a weight lifter named Harry Cornish who bested him at the club. The following week, Cornish received a bottle of Bromo Seltzer in the mail. When his landlady complained of a headache, Cornish gave her some of the medication. She complained of a bitter taste, went into convulsions, and died. The Bromo contained mercury cyanide, which was later traced back to a purchase Molineux had made for his factory. Molineux was found guilty, but then acquitted on appeal in 1902.

It is believed that Rasputin, the "Mad Monk" of Tsarist Russia, consumed a normally lethal dose of cyanide served to him in a cake in 1916. In disbelief that he had survived the poisoning attempt, his would-be assassins then shot him and dumped him, still alive, in St. Petersburg's Neva River. It was conjectured later that insufficient hydrochloric acid in the monk's stomach prevented a fatal reaction.

During World War II, the Nazis used hydrogen cyanide in their gas chambers. The same gas has also been used to execute criminals and was the prescribed means of death in several states until lethal injection became preferred.

Spy stories abound with secret cyanide pellets, to be used as suicide pills in case of capture.

Richard Brinkley, an English carpenter, used prussic acid (cyanide) in his plot to acquire the estate of widow Johanna Maria Louisa Blume, of Fulham, England, in the early part of the 1900s. He told the seventy-seven-year-old Blume that he was collecting names for a seaside outing, and asked her to sign a paper. Only the paper was a new will that Brinkley had written on her behalf, leaving Brinkley everything she owned. Brinkley got signatures from two "witnesses," Henry Heard and Reginald Parker, using the same ruse.

Blume died two days later—it's not clear if it was a natural death or not—and Brinkley produced the will. Blume's granddaughter immediately challenged the signature and Brinkley apparently decided to cover his tracks by getting rid of the witnesses. While visiting Parker, he left a bottle of stout on the kitchen table so the two could look at a dog Parker had for sale. Unfortunately, Parker's landlord, Mr. Beck, his wife Mrs. Beck and their daughter saw the stout unattended and decided to sample it. Mr. and Mrs. Beck collapsed and died, but the daughter survived. It turned out the stout had been laced with prussic acid. Brinkley was tried, convicted, and hanged at Wandsworth Prison on August 13, 1907.

In 1983, several people died in Chicago when they took cyanide-laced capsules of Extra-Strength Tylenol. With help from the Tylenol company, the Chicago police proved that the capsules had been tampered with. The killer was never found, but Tylenol and other pain reliever manufacturers no longer make capsules. Personal product packaging is now almost tamper-proof.

Agatha Christie frequently did in her victims with poisons, and cyanide was one of her favorites. *Endless Night* featured two cyanide poisonings disguised as riding accidents. The second victim was found almost immediately after her poisoning while the bitter almond scent still lingered, and thus gave the murder away. Emily Brent from *Ten Little Indians* was injected with cyanide after being knocked unconscious with chloral hydrate in her coffee. Tea hid the cyanide in *A Pocket Full of Rye*. In *Remembered Death*, a supposed suicide took place in which the victim drank cyanide-laced champagne.

In Isaac Asimov's *A Whiff of Death*, the fictional killer used potassium cyanide gas. The victim, an unlikable student chemist, was alone in his lab. The killer had previously mixed chemicals, knowing the student would check the experiment and wouldn't ask for help. Even though the room was open, the poisonous vapor was released in an area covered with a metal hood and fan specially designed to contain the poisonous gases created by experiments. When the student leaned over to check the chemical process, he inhaled the gas and died.

In *Sudden Death*, William X. Kienzle killed off an obnoxious football player by combining DMSO, a chemical that opens the skin's pores, with cyanide, and put it in the player's shampoo bottle.

STRYCHNINE

OTHER: Dog button, mouse-nots, mole death.

TOXICITY: 6

FORM: Strychnine is a colorless, crystalline powder with a bitter taste. The substance is usually swallowed but can poison by skin or eye contact. It can also be inhaled as a dust.

The substance occurs naturally in some seeds and plants, in particular the dog button plant, *Strychnos nux-vomica*, which grows in India and other tropical places, such as Hawaii. The fruits resemble a mandarin or Chinese orange in shape and color, and are borne abundantly in March. They are attractive, tempting many people to eat them despite their somewhat bitter taste. The gray, nickel-size seeds resemble velvet-covered buttons. The entire plant contains strychnine, but the seeds contain the greatest concentration. The blossoms have an odor resembling curry powder and are a potential cause of poisoning since they might easily be eaten by a child or even added to food as a condiment.

EFFECTS AND SYMPTOMS: Strychnine attacks the central nervous system and causes exaggerated reflex effects, which results in all the muscles contracting at the same time. The strychnine victim dies from asphyxiation or sheer exhaustion from the convulsions.

Symptoms start with the victim's neck and face becoming stiff. Arms and legs spasm next. The spasms become increasingly worse, until the victim is almost continuously in an arched-back position with the head and feet on the floor or other surface. Unlike with other seizures, the victim is conscious and alert during the painful spasms. Fever can also be present. Rigor mortis sets in immediately upon death, leaving the body in the convulsed position, with eyes wide open and the face set in a grimace.

The symptoms of strychnine poisoning are almost the same as those of tetanus or lockjaw.

REACTION TIME: Approximately ten to twenty minutes, longer if given on a full stomach.

ANTIDOTES AND TREATMENTS: Activated charcoal can be administered if the victim seeks treatment before the symptoms start. If the convulsions are mild, they may be treated with diazepam or other barbiturate, with morphine for the pain. However, these must be used cautiously, as both can depress the respiratory system. If the spasms are more severe, the patient may need to be put into complete muscular paralysis and will require intubation and a respirator. While spasms are occurring, the victim must be kept quiet since any loud noise or sudden light will increase the intensity of the spasms.

NOTES: While strychnine is not the fastest-acting poison, it is certainly one of the most startling. The drama of a victim jackknifing back and forth in agony in the final throes of strychnine poisoning may account for its popularity in literature and film. Strychnine, however, is less popular for real-life homicides.

The convulsive effects were first documented in 1818, and the poison was later developed for medicinal purposes as a stimulant. While some antique medicine chests might have some strychnine-based pills, strychnine no longer has any medicinal use. Currently it's used primarily as a rodent poison, although it is sometimes used to cut heroin, cocaine, and other street drugs.

Doses too small to cause acute poisoning will show no symptoms. South American missionaries reputedly take minute doses of strychnine to rid themselves of intestinal worms.

CASE HISTORY

One of the more infamous cases involves a Chicago doctor who provided the wrong kind of help to a lady suspicious that her husband was cheating on her. It started with the July 14, 1881 death of Mr. Stott from strychnine poisoning. Mrs. Stott was arrested. But Mrs. Stott turned state's evidence and implicated Dr. Thomas Neill Cream, saying that he had given her the strychnine. Cream was convicted and sentenced to life at Joliet State Prison.

In 1924, Jean-Pierre Vaquier, a vain, forty-five-year-old Frenchman, poisoned his lover's husband with strychnine-laced "bromo-salts." After meeting with Mary Jones, his mistress, to plot her husband's demise, Vaquier followed her to London and there went to a pharmacy. He purchased twenty grams of perchloride of mercury and twelve grams of strychnine, saying they were for wireless experiments, and signed the poison book all chemists were required to keep.

Joining his lover and her husband at a party at their London hotel, Vaquier noted the husband drinking heavily. When Mr. Jones needed some Bromo-Seltzer, Vaquier offered him the bottle with a lethal dose. "My God! They are bitter!" Mr. Jones said. Within a short time, Jones had died in agony, and postmortem examination found strychnine. Mary and Jean-Pierre tried to wash out the bottle, but traces still remained. Vaquier was identified by the chemist and hanged in August 1924.

During the same time period, Californian Eva Rablen poisoned her deaf husband, Carroll. Fun-loving and a good dancer, Eva often went to the local parties; Carroll would go along reluctantly, since he could neither hear the music nor dance. One April night, Carroll decided to stay in the car, finding it too much to watch his wife dancing with others.

At midnight, Eva came out, bringing her husband coffee and refreshments. Seconds later, he was writhing in agony. His cries brought several parties to his aid. Before dying, he complained of the bitter taste of the coffee. Eva was accused of poisoning Carroll for the insurance, and a thorough search of the dance hall yielded a bottle of strychnine with the address of a local pharmacy and Eva's name on the label. The coffee cup showed traces of strychnine, and Carroll's stomach contents proved murder beyond a doubt. Pleading guilty, Eva was given life imprisonment.

The Mysterious Affair at Styles, Agatha Christie's first novel, featured a strychnine killing of the lady of the house. The killer hid the bitter taste of the poison by putting it in the lady's evening hot chocolate. Strychnine also does in Mr. Appleton of Christie's *The Mysterious Mr. Quinn*.

HOUSEHOLD
POISONS

The house was blessedly silent as Geri headed up toward the bathroom, ready to begin her cleaning. She wouldn't have to pick Kim up from nursery school for several hours yet. At the tub she stared down at the mess her daughter had made and, taking out the ammonia, she began to scrub. No effect. Well, maybe bleach was needed. The strong odor assailed her in a moment, dizziness had struck. Surprised, Geri sank down on the toilet seat, not understanding what was happening. She was still unconscious when her husband found her several hours later.

—ADAPTED FROM NORTHWESTERN MEMORIAL HOSPITAL EMERGENCY ROOM RECORD, CHICAGO, ILLINOIS, 1973

Given the huge number of chemicals in the home, surprisingly few are lethal. Because they can do severe damage, however, and many will kill small children, these potential poisons should be stored carefully.

In pre-1970s households, lethal products were more common, so characters in a novel set in this time or before would have access to stronger detergents and poisons.

One of the many changes since then is in the type of gas found in the home; Coal gas, which was used in homes from the 1920s through the 1960s, was much more lethal than the natural gas used today. So putting the victim's head in the stove—à la poetess Sylvia Plath—will cause illness, but probably not kill. However, all gases can eventually suffocate, because they replace oxygen. The clever writer, therefore, will find a believable way to seal the room in which the victim is trapped, though death will probably take longer than in previous decades. And an even cleverer writer will instead take advantage of the fact that natural gas burns and can explode to create the wanted mayhem.

Many household poisons turn up in industrial situations as well. Carbon monoxide is often listed in poison texts as an industrial hazard, which it can be. But it's probably better known as a hazard in the home, which is why it is listed here. Phenol is another toxin with many industrial uses that most of us will find at home, though perhaps not in the form we expect.

Most people are likely to have access to boric acid in the home, both in its diluted form as an antiseptic for eye injuries and as good old 20 Mule Team Borax, a laundry and cleaning agent. It can be found in other laundry detergents and stain removers, as well. It's also widely used as an ant poison, but it's listed in the medical poisons chapter because of its many uses in that field.

So household poisons cover a wide range of things; some of those poisons follow in alphabetical order.

ALKALINE CORROSIVES AND INORGANIC SALTS

OTHER: While there are many types of alkalis, those focused on here are potassium hydroxide, sodium hydroxide (better known as lye), sodium phosphates, and sodium carbonate.

TOXICITY: 6

FORM: Because penetration through the skin is painful and slow, fatalities are caused by ingestion.

Potassium hydroxide is found in liquid cuticle remover and in some small batteries. Sodium hydroxide (often sold by its common name, lye) is found in other small batteries, aquarium products, and drain cleaners: Drano, for example, combines several alkalis. Sodium phosphates help give cleansers or abrasive cleaners their punch. Dye removers remove dye with sodium carbonate, which is also found in dishwasher soap.

Furniture polish once contained alkalis but now does not.

These chemicals team up with the proteins and the fats in the body to turn firm, healthy tissue into soft, decayed (necrotic) tissue—not unlike the process of lye and fatty acids becoming soap.

Severe pain immediately follows ingestion, followed by diarrhea and vomiting, at which time the victim collapses and can possibly die. If the victim doesn't die initially, he may improve during the first twenty-four hours after the ingestion, and there may be some blood-tinged vomit. However, more problems can occur anywhere from two to four days later, if the stomach or esophagus was perforated by the corrosion and the treating physician didn't find the perforation, thus allowing peritonitis—a potentially severe infection of the abdominal lining—to set in. The patient has a sudden onset of stomach pain, boardlike abdominal rigidity, a rapid fall in blood pressure, dizziness, headache, blurred vision, and fainting. Survival will depend on how fast and aggressively the patient is treated, although it's not guaranteed.

Death, if it's going to occur, usually happens by the third day, and is painful. Necrotic (dead) tissue is shed in strips through vomiting. An autopsy finds gelatinous, dead areas wherever the alkali went.

Even when a victim survives ingestion of an alkali, the esophagus can constrict weeks or months later, making swallowing very difficult.

REACTION TIME: Immediate. Death, if it occurs, may take several days.

ANTIDOTES AND TREATMENTS: Vomiting is not induced since it brings the poison back up, causing more injury. As soon as possible, the physician puts a specially equipped tube down the victim's throat to examine the injuries. Afterward, antibiotics may be given to patients with fever or other signs of perforation, and surgery may be needed to repair damaged tissues.

NOTES: Strong alkalis are so corrosive that it would be difficult to accomplish even a suicide with such a substance, since one taste would likely give the victim a third-degree burn on the mouth and esophagus. Many people, however, accustomed to their five o'clock martini, will down a drink without even checking it. Since very little poison is needed to damage the tissue, the esophagus and stomach could quickly be perforated by one large gulp, resulting in eventual death.

Sodium hydroxide, potassium hydroxide, sodium phosphates, and sodium carbonate are all corrosive chemicals found in many cleaning products. Acids are generally thought of as the principal corrosives, but alkalis, the chemical opposites of acids, can be just as damaging. Just as there are many weak acids, such as vitamin C (ascorbic acid), that are completely harmless on or in the human body, there are many weak alkalis that people use daily, such as dish detergent and shampoo.

Batteries also contain alkalis, and even small watch batteries, when swallowed, can do considerable damage to the esophagus and upper gastrointestinal tract.

Even though there are several chemicals involved in this category, they are grouped together because they have the same effects and are treated the same way.

Label instructions on Drano clearly read, "Do not mix with ammonia, toilet bowl cleaners, household cleaners, or other drain cleaners. Mixture may release hazardous gases or cause violent eruption from drain." (Wouldn't that be a great sight to write about?) Also, you don't want to follow lye or any other drain cleaner down a drain with hot water, because lye heats up water on contact. If the water is already warm, corrosive steam can escape—perhaps a good trap for your victim.

Because acids and alkalis are chemical opposites, they do neutralize each other, as long as the pH, or strength, of one is balanced against the other. Soap is made on this principle. The alkali, usually a small amount of lye, is mixed with a much larger amount of acid from fats (fats and proteins are actually mild acids). Because we are made up of proteins and fats, this is exactly the reaction that happens when a strong alkali comes into contact with our tissues. The two combine to form glycerine in a process called saponification. So while there is lye in soap, it's no longer lye by the time you wash your face. Making soap at home is an increasingly popular hobby, and soap makers need to keep lye around.

CASE HISTORY:

In the movie *Throw Momma From the Train*, the character Owen Lift (played by Danny De-Vito) tries to kill his mother (Anne Ramsey) by adding lye to her soft drink, but then chickens out and knocks the cup away. It probably wouldn't have done much, however, since the acids in the soda would have neutralized some of the lye.

AMMONIA

OTHER: Ammonium hydroxide.

TOXICITY: 4.5

FORM: Ammonia is an ordinary gas that is inhaled. Ammonium hydroxide, household ammonia, is a solution that is ingested.

EFFECTS AND SYMPTOMS: Both gas and liquid damage cells with caustic action, and painfully irritate mucous membranes.

If swallowed, coughing; vomiting; extreme pain in the mouth, chest, and abdomen; and shocklike collapse occur. The stomach and esophagus may perforate later, which increases the abdominal pain and causes fever and rigidity. After twelve to twenty-four hours, irritation and fluid retention in the lungs occurs. If ammonia is inhaled in high concentrations, the lips and eyelids swell; there is temporary blindness, restlessness, tightness in the chest, and reddish skin color, and the victim's pulse becomes rapid and weak. In the case of ingestion, autopsy findings are identical to those of alkali poisoning; in inhalation cases, there will be pulmonary edema, irritation, and pneumonia.

REACTION TIME: Immediate.

ANTIDOTES AND TREATMENTS: As a temporary measure, water may be given to dilute the ammonia. Activated charcoal is not recommended, as it does not absorb ammonia and can block the view of an endoscope, which will be used to look for injuries to the esophagus and stomach.

NOTES: Real ammonia is a gas at room temperature. It has a number of industrial uses, including as a refrigerant and fertilizer. Colorless and strongly alkaline, it has a characteristic odor. The household cleaner is a frequent source of poisoning around the home; although because the concentration is usually less than 10 percent ammonia, the effects are seldom severe, except in small children.

Ammonia becomes an extremely toxic gas when combined with strong oxidizers, calcium, gold, mercury, silver, or bleaches. The ammonia/chlorine bleach combination is the mixture many people have been warned about—mixing the two substances creates chlorine gas, causing unconsciousness and other symptoms of chlorine gas poisoning (see chlorine, on page 42), especially if the area is small and unventilated. The victim would need to be in the fumes for over an hour for the effects to be severe. Because of the length of time needed to kill, a short duration can be used either as a warning to "get off the case" or as a red herring.

CASE HISTORY

In 1972, one depressed man tried to kill himself by locking himself in a poorly ventilated bathroom and mixing the chemicals ammonia and bleach together. He soon lost consciousness, but was found in time and appeared to have suffered no permanent ill effects from his attempted suicide.

BACTERIAL FOOD POISONING

OTHER: There are several variants, but the best known are salmonella, e. coli, and listeria.

TOXICITY: Highly variable and dependent on the host food, concentrations, and susceptibility of the victim.

FORM: Bacteria. Listeria is mostly found in milk and soft cheeses; e. coli and salmonella can be found in water, meat products, and contaminated vegetables.

EFFECTS AND SYMPTOMS: Bacteria invade and infect the stomach and intestines. Gastroenteritis, or upset stomach, is the basic symptom, including nausea, vomiting, cramping, and diarrhea. Fever is also common.

REACTION TIME: Highly variable. While different sources offer different incubation rates, one can expect listeria to incubate between nine and thirty-two hours. Depending on the strain of e. coli, it can take anywhere from twelve hours to eight days for symptoms to develop. Salmonella usually shows up anywhere from twelve to thirty-six hours after consuming the tainted food.

ANTIDOTES AND TREATMENTS: Most treatment is centered on fluid replacement, since dehydration presents the most serious danger. Medicines to ease the vomiting and diarrhea are sometimes given, although doing so is considered somewhat controversial since stopping the diarrhea will also keep the bacteria in the intestines longer. Since listeria can harm fetuses, pregnant women who have eaten food tainted with listeria are treated more aggressively, even though they may only be suffering mild symptoms.

NOTES: Food poisoning has gotten a tremendous amount of press in recent years. While there is no question that some strains of it can be deadly, deaths are relatively rare and unlikely. The small percentage of fatalities occurs mostly among children and the infirm—which can be useful if your villain is trying to bump off an elderly and infirm great-aunt, or a small child standing in the way of an inheritance, or even someone with a suppressed immune system from an organ transplant or chemotherapy.

Death by food poisoning, however, is a hit-or-miss proposition, even among more vulnerable individuals. Chicken, considered a sure thing for producing salmonella, can be left out all day, then only partially cooked, and still not affect anyone. But this is not recommended: The risk of contracting salmonella from chicken (or any meat) handled this way is great. It's just not guaranteed, which can be a problem for a believable plot line. On the other hand, it may be just the twist you need if you want a frustrated villain.

Another problem with food poisoning is that the vast majority of people infected by listeria, salmonella, or even e. coli will be sick to their stomachs, maybe spend the night vomiting and suffering from diarrhea, but will bounce back after a day or two. This is the reason that food poisoning is a real danger to the very old and the very young, who have the most trouble bouncing back from the shock and dehydration brought on by prolonged vomiting and diarrhea. And because food poisoning is mostly bacterial, immunosuppressed people are more at risk because their immune systems aren't up to fighting the bacteria.

Even so, deaths from food poisoning are relatively rare. Listeria is the most deadly form of these toxins, and is on the rise in the United States, although it is still fairly rare, with only three cases per million people in 2005. However, out of the 2,500 cases reported that year, there were five hundred deaths.

CASE HISTORY

In 1984, the Rajneeshee cult attempted bacterial contamination of the town of Dalles, Oregon, in an attempt to make people too sick to vote. They placed the bacteria on personal drinking glasses, doorknobs, saltshakers, urinal handles, produce at the local supermarket, and salad bars in ten restaurants. It took one year for the health department to determine that the 751 cases of salmonella (none fatal) had been caused by one strain that had reproduced. Cult members had already put dead rats and raw sewage, as well as the salmonella, into the Dallas water supply.

In 1993 there was an outbreak of e. coli in the Pacific Northwest, and in 2006, grocery chains Trader Joe's and Whole Food Markets recalled several batches of guacamole and salsa believed to be tainted with listeria.

In 1993, six hundred people got sick with e. coli after eating undercooked hamburgers at Jack in the Box restaurants in the Pacific Northwest. Of those six hundred, there were four deaths, all children—less than 1 percent of the victims. While no consolation to the families of those children, that figure does demonstrate the relatively low mortality rate of food poisoning.

BOTULISM

SCIENTIFIC NAME: *Clostridium botulinum.*

TOXICITY: 6

FORM: The botulism bacillus is eaten with the contaminated food. It's an anaerobic spore, which means it grows without oxygen, so foods packed in oil can grow it easily. As a spore, it is invisible to the eye.

EFFECTS AND SYMPTOMS: Botulism causes muscle paralysis by keeping nerve impulses from getting to the brain. It also affects the other organs in the body, especially those

---

of the autonomic nervous system. The main symptoms are double vision, muscular paralysis, nausea, and vomiting, and can be delayed twelve to twenty-four hours. An autopsy shows congestion and hemorrhages in all of the organs, especially the central nervous system. The liver and kidneys also degenerate. The corpse looks as if the victim had been very ill.

REACTION TIME: Varies according to source and victim, but can start around eight hours after eating the contaminated food; death occurs as much as eight days later.

ANTIDOTES AND TREATMENTS: Botulin antitoxins are available to bind up whatever toxin is currently circulating in the patient's system and stop the illness from getting worse; however, it is contraindicated in patients allergic to drugs made with horse serum. The patient might also be put on a respirator to alleviate breathing problems. Otherwise, treatment is focused on fluid replacement to combat dehydration.

NOTES: Botulism, the bane of the home canner, kills up to 50 percent of its victims. Low-acid foods such as meat, fish, and some vegetables that have been insufficiently heated and improperly canned are the source of the often tasteless and odorless botulinus toxin. The usual indications that botulism may be present are moldy, leaking, or exploded containers. But since botulism can be present even without these signs, the *USDA Complete Guide to Home Canning* strongly recommends boiling any home-canned food at least ten minutes (longer in higher elevations) unless you are absolutely sure the canning was done properly and that the equipment was functioning as it should.

Babies can get botulism from honey, even if it is processed, which is why honey is not a recommended food until after the age of two. Some adults have retained this sensitivity, but it is very rare. (Honey can be deadly to adults if bees have pollinated on oleander or rhododendron: See chapter five, page 64.)

Deaths from botulism poisoning have actually become very rare, because home canning has gotten very rare.

Doctors initially took advantage of botulism's paralyzing properties to cure eye twitches and help with underarm sweating with a drug made from the bacteria known as Botulinum toxin type A. But when plastic surgeons noticed that the stuff also plumped out wrinkles, Botox, the brand name of the drug, took off, and Botox injections became among the most common cosmetic procedures done.

CASE HISTORY

In *A Pint of Murder,* by Alisa Craig (aka Charlotte MacLeod), an improperly canned jar of food was used to murder the victim.

Sarah Shankman's novel *Then Hang All the Liars* also featured a jar of poorly canned marinated mushrooms. The killer knew the botulism was present because other jars from the batch had exploded.

BROMATE

OTHER: The focus here is specifically potassium bromate.

TOXICITY: 5

FORM: Usually found as 3 percent of a solution with water. To be poisonous, bromate must be taken orally.

EFFECTS AND SYMPTOMS: When ingested, bromates have a corrosive action on the tissues. They can cause vomiting, collapse, diarrhea, abdominal pain, and oliguria (less-than-normal urination) or anuria. Lethargy, deafness, coma, convulsions, low blood pressure, and a fast pulse also occur. Tiny, pinprick red spots can appear on the skin as a later reaction. These will remain on the corpse, and an autopsy will also show damaged kidneys.

REACTION TIME: Within five to twenty minutes.

ANTIDOTES AND TREATMENTS: Sodium bicarbonate can be given within an hour of ingestion in an attempt to prevent hydrogen bromate from forming. Sodium thiosulfate is also given intravenously as an antidote. If this is being used in a period piece, then definitely include gastric lavage (stomach pumping) with sodium bicarbonate as part of the treatment because that was the standard for care before the early to middle part of the twentieth century.

NOTES: Almost unheard of in the home nowadays, bromates were found primarily in the neutralizer solutions of cold permanent waves (perms), popular starting in the 1940s. Home perm kits are widely available pretty much anywhere hair care products are sold and some may still contain bromates.

Bromates are also a part of some bread preservatives, although in a very diluted form. You might be able to add some mayhem to your story by setting it close to where they make the preservative.

Bromate becomes poisonous in the stomach, where the hydrochloric acid found naturally there turns the potassium bromate into hydrogen bromate, which is an irritating acid.

CARBON MONOXIDE

TOXICITY: 5

FORM: A colorless, odorless gas, which is inhaled.

EFFECTS AND SYMPTOMS: Unlike oxygen atoms, which hook up with red blood cells and let go when they arrive where they are needed, carbon monoxide molecules hook up with a red blood cell and hang on permanently. With enough red blood cells unable to carry oxygen to the tissues, the body suffocates.

What makes carbon monoxide so dangerous is that its victims are often unawar of being suffocated. Many survivors first think they've got a bad flu bug. Some even describe the sensation as that of falling asleep.

The symptoms progress as the blood saturates. The victim will first feel a slight headache and shortness of breath. Continued exposure will make the headache worse, and cause nausea, irritability, labored breathing, chest pain, confusion, impaired judgment, and fainting with exertion. Increased concentrations of the gas and continued exposure will cause respiratory failure, unconsciousness, and death. Should the victim survive, the whole range of brain injury symptoms may continue, from problems with memory and concentration, to mood disorders, to a permanent vegetative state. A pregnant woman might survive the exposure, but stands a high risk of losing her baby.

The autopsy will reveal microscopic hemorrhages and dead tissues throughout the body, as well as congestion and swelling of the brain, liver, kidneys, and spleen. The skin is often, but not always, a bright cherry red.

REACTION TIME: Depends on the concentrations of the gas and the level of activity of the victim. Fairly heavy concentrations can cause death within one hour.

ANTIDOTES AND TREATMENTS: The victim must first be removed from exposure, after which 100-percent oxygen is given until there are sufficient red blood cells again. In serious cases, a hyperbaric chamber, such as those used to cure scuba divers of the bends, can be used, as the increased air pressure in the chamber can increase the absorption of oxygen into the blood.

NOTES: Carbon monoxide is often abbreviated to CO, for one carbon atom connected to one oxygen atom.

This silent, odorless killer is the result of incomplete burning of carbon materials. Although CO is relatively rare, a badly vented gas heater can make a small room dangerous in minutes—which is why carbon monoxide detectors became so popular in the mid-1990s. The exhaust from gasoline engines can be 3 to 7 percent carbon monoxide. Tobacco smoke is 4 percent CO.

People breathe it all the time, and every time they do, they diminish the number of red blood cells carrying oxygen to their bodies, and in addition make it harder for the remaining blood cells to release the oxygen they contain. A person who smokes twenty cigarettes a day has at least 6 percent of his or her red blood cells saturated with carbon monoxide.

CO is also a common killer among families—usually in poor neighborhoods—who use charcoal grills to heat their homes without providing adequate ventilation.

CASE HISTORY

Depression Era screen star Thelma Todd died of CO poisoning while in her car, which was left running in her garage. How she got there was a source of considerable controversy and sensational speculation in the papers of the time and even today.

In Harry Kemelman's *Saturday the Rabbi Went Hungry*, an alcoholic scientist was killed when the villain left him knocked out in his garage with the car running.

Robin Cook's *Coma* has CO being fed into the patient via the operating room oxygen line during surgery.

CATIONIC DETERGENTS

OTHER: Benzethonium chloride, benzalkonium chloride, methylbenzethonium chloride, and cetylpyridinium chloride are just a few cationic detergents.

TOXICITY: 4

FORM: Cationic detergents are found in solutions or creams. Benzethonium chloride and benzalkonium chloride are both antiseptics. Cationic detergents are usually swallowed but can be absorbed through the skin after the poison has undergone prolonged heating.

EFFECTS AND SYMPTOMS: Symptoms are the same whether the poison is ingested or absorbed. The body's cells readily absorb the detergents, which in turn interfere with the cells' functions. Cationic detergents will also injure mucous membranes.

Nausea, vomiting, corrosive damage to the esophagus, collapse, low blood pressure, convulsions, coma, and death occur.

An autopsy shows nothing characteristic of cationic detergents.

REACTION TIME: First symptoms take ten minutes to an hour. Death occurs in one to four hours.

ANTIDOTES AND TREATMENTS: First, an airway is established and respiration is maintained as convulsions are treated. Because the esophagus is often injured, gastric lavage and forced vomiting are not advised. Activated charcoal is administered. In cases of skin

---

contact, ordinary soap is a good antidote for whatever cationic detergents have not been absorbed into the body, but there is no antidote once the detergent has been absorbed.

NOTES: Cationic detergents are found mainly in dishwasher soap and fabric softeners. The other major use is as an antibacterial disinfectant on skin, surgical instruments, cooking equipment, sickroom supplies, and cloth diapers.

Many cationic detergents are found in solutions, which means they are usually too diluted to be lethal in a reasonable dose. As always, the elderly, the infirm, or the very young are the most susceptible to these compounds. A villain may work for a diaper service or some other cleaning company, and might have access to stronger solutions used to disinfect cloth diapers.

CHLORINE

OTHER: Hypochlorite.

TOXICITY: As gas, 5; otherwise 3 or less.

FORM: The gas is yellowish green with a very irritating smell. Bleaches and pool cleaners are clear liquids with a yellowish cast to them.

EFFECTS AND SYMPTOMS: Both the gas and the liquid are corrosive. Inhalation will cause immediate coughing and burning in the eyes, nose, and throat. In heavier doses, swelling in the airways will cause constriction, increasing the cough. Wheezing can also occur. If a person swallows poll cleaner or industrial-strength bleach, which is a 20 percent solution, the mouth and throat burns are more severe, causing difficulty swallowing, drooling, and severe pain. There's also the possibility of perforation in the esophagus and stomach. Both the gas and the solution can cause nausea and vomiting.

REACTION TIME: Immediate.

ANTIDOTES AND TREATMENTS: Mostly supportive. In inhalation cases, the patient is removed from the exposure, then treated with humidified oxygen; if there is wheezing present, bronchodilators, such as albuterol, may be used. If the chlorine was ingested, an endoscopy tube is used to look for injuries to the esophagus and stomach, and X-rays may be needed to find air pockets that could signal a perforation.

NOTES: Most of us associate chlorine with the disinfectant we put in our pools that also turns blonde hair green. There's also chlorine bleach, a popular cleaning agent and laundry additive. Both of these are actually hypochlorite, a water-based solution containing the heavier-than-air, yellowish green gas that is real chlorine. The household bleach usually contains 3 to 5 percent chlorine; if swallowed, it only causes minor burns to the mouth and throat. Pool chlorine and industrial strength bleach, which are 20 percent solutions, are more dangerous and can cause more significant damage. The gas is deadly, but is usually only found in industrial situations. It is listed here because it is more accessible as the pool cleaner and bleach.

Since this is a corrosive, it will be very hard to trick someone into drinking a fatal amount of industrial bleach, unless you set up a situation in which the fictional victim cannot reach medical aid. The other option would be to set the dramatic final chase in the pool store, where your plucky heroine can throw pool chlorine into the villain's face and make her escape. The burns do cause a rash, so that might make an identifying mark as well.

CASE HISTORY

Chlorine gas was one of the earlier gases used in World War I. While it did cause some fatalities, like most gases, it ultimately wasn't very effective because of the difficulty getting high enough concentrations to kill people and because it was easy to protect soldiers against it with gas masks. Like the better known mustard gas, it did cause a lot of permanent injury.

ETHYLENE GLYCOL

OTHER: Ethylene glycol is found in antifreeze.

TOXICITY: 3 or 4

FORM: A clear, odorless liquid (the bright green of antifreeze is a dye).

EFFECTS AND SYMPTOMS: Ethylene glycol metabolizes into oxalic and other similar acids, throwing off the body's metabolism. The oxalic acid then combines with calcium in the body and forms calcium oxalate crystals, which can be deposited in the kidneys, leading to kidney failure.

The victim will appear drunk for the first few hours after an acute ingestion. There may be some vomiting. Between four and twelve hours later, respiratory problems set in, including hyperventilation; convulsions can also occur, but they are rare. Death can occur at this point from cardiac symptoms or respiratory problems. Between thirty-six to seventy-two hours after ingestion, as the kidneys are increasingly injured, there is the onset of kidney failure, which, if not treated, results in death.

REACTION TIME: First symptoms can start appearing in thirty minutes.

ANTIDOTES AND TREATMENTS: Activated charcoal is not effective with ethylene glycol poisoning. Supportive care is given and in the presence of kidney problems, the patient is put on dialysis. In acute poisonings, the drug fomepizole is given because it reacts with and neutralizes the ethylene glycol, preventing it from metabolizing into the toxic oxalic acids. If fomepizole is not available, or there is a great deal of ethylene glycol in the victim's system, the physician might instead use ethanol, another name for the alcohol found in beer, wine, and hard liquor. Since ethanol reacts with the ethylene glycol in a similar way to fomepizole, it prevents ethylene glycol from becoming toxic in the system, so a fictional husband trying to poison his alcoholic wife may find his scheme frustrated.

NOTES: Pet owners are routinely warned to avoid leaving antifreeze on their driveways. That's because the primary ingredient of antifreeze, ethylene glycol, has a sweet taste that attracts animals and small children. It's one of the few toxins that is relatively easy to hide and readily available. And since the initial symptoms mimic being intoxicated, it can believably be responsible for delayed medical treatment. Alcoholics will sometimes drink ethylene glycol if they can't get regular ethanol products.

CASE HISTORY

As noted in chapter two (A Day in the Life of a Real Criminal Toxicologist), there was a case in Southern California a couple years ago in which a woman poisoned her husband first with oleander, then with ethylene glycol in his Gatorade.

IRON

TOXICITY: 4

FORM: While iron itself is a black metal that oxidizes (rusts) to the familiar brownish red dust, it is most toxic in its form as a vitamin supplement. Poisoning occurs with ingestion.

EFFECTS AND SYMPTOMS: Iron acts initially as a corrosive, then attacks the cells. Symptoms begin with vomiting and diarrhea, often bloody due to corrosion in the gastrointestinal tract, and abdominal pain. Mild lethargy may also be present. Within hours, the vomiting and diarrhea can reappear, along with coma, seizures, liver failure, and death. Even if the patient survives, scarring from the corrosion in the gastrointestinal tract can cause obstructions as much as six weeks after ingestion.

REACTION TIME: Five to twenty minutes.

ANTIDOTES AND TREATMENTS: Aggressive supportive care is given, along with deferoxamine, a chelating drug that binds with the iron to remove it from the body; if the patient's kidneys are already shutting down, however, deferoxamine is contraindicated. Activated charcoal does not bind well with iron and is not given unless there's reason to believe another poison may have been taken as well. Whole bowel irrigation is also used to get the iron pills out of the colon.

Iron is a common nutritional supplement; without sufficient iron, our bodies cannot produce enough red blood cells. But it is also one of the most common causes of poisoning in small children and, according to one source, the leading cause of fatalities in such cases. Children's vitamins contain up to 18 mg of iron, far below the lethal dose. The trouble happens when a child ingests the whole bottle.

The difficulty with using iron as a weapon in a story would be in finding a way to believably hide the vitamins, especially since large ingestions cause vomiting so quickly. But if your victim wants to commit suicide, iron tablets are not an uncommon choice.

ISOPROPANOL

OTHER: Isopropyl alcohol, rubbing alcohol.

TOXICITY: 3

FORM: Always a liquid at room temperature, isopropanol easily evaporates to a gas. It can be swallowed, inhaled as a vapor, or absorbed through the skin.

EFFECTS AND SYMPTOMS: Isopropanol depresses the central nervous system, leading to coma. Isopropanol poisoning causes symptoms similar to extreme intoxication, though much more acute: persistent and severe nausea, vomiting, abdominal pain, depressed respiration, hematemesis (vomiting blood), oliguria, and excessive sweating. Coma can come on quickly. The autopsy may show hemorrhaging in the trachea and bronchial tubes, and pneumonia, swelling, and hemorrhaging in the chest cavity.

REACTION TIME: Ten to thirty minutes. Just as with drinking alcohol, food in the stomach slows the reaction time.

ANTIDOTES AND TREATMENTS: Treatment is supportive, and activated charcoal can be given. Dialysis is sometimes used if the patient is not getting better.

NOTES: Isopropanol, a colorless liquid with a potent smell, is found in the home as rubbing alcohol and in window cleaners. This brother of ethanol (the alcohol in wine, beer, and other spirits) is two to three times as potent a central nervous system depressant, making it considerably more deadly. Alcoholics deprived of ethanol will sometimes try rubbing alcohol instead.

The residual effects of isopropanol poisoning last two to four times longer than those of the average alcoholic drink.

Physicians once prescribed alcohol sponge baths to reduce high fevers, but it was discovered that besides removing the fever, it sometimes produced a coma. Of course, an elderly grandmother who hasn't caught up with modern medical practices might not know this and might do it by accident—or she might know, and do it on purpose.

Since the effects of isopropanol are so similar to those of intoxication, it can make hiding the poison among liquor a good way for a villain to spring a trap, especially if the bystanders have no reason to suspect that the victim's stupor is not from ethanol.

NAPHTHALENE

OTHER: Mothballs, moth flakes.

TOXICITY: 4 (except in the special case mentioned below)

FORM: A white crystalline solid, naphthalene will usually be ingested.

EFFECTS AND SYMPTOMS: Naphthalene destroys red blood cells by clumping them together and forcing the hemoglobins out, then causes kidney damage. The symptoms are nausea, vomiting, headache, diarrhea, oliguria, hematuria (blood in the urine), anemia, fever, jaundice, and pain while urinating. With more serious poisoning, coma and convulsions can occur.

REACTION TIME: Rapid: five to twenty mintues, depending on whether the poison is inhaled or ingested.

ANTIDOTES AND TREATMENTS: In the past, gastric lavage was performed and sodium bicarbonate given. Nowadays, however, with the emphasis on supportive care, doctors are more likely to give the drug methylene blue to counteract the clumping together of the blood cells. If severe anemia develops, a blood transfusion may be needed.

NOTES: Naphthalene is nowadays mostly used in industry, where it has several uses. But since it used to be a common household product (moth balls and flakes were made of naphthalene), it is included here.

Some people have a hereditary deficiency of glucose-6-phosphate dehydrogenase that can make them more susceptible to naphthalene poisoning. This is very rare, occurring most frequently in people of Mediterranean descent. The same deficiency also makes these people sensitive to aspirin, so unless they were adopted and have never taken an aspirin, it's likely they will know they have the trait. This could be a good clue or a good red herring.

PETROLEUM DISTILLATES

OTHER: Kerosene, paint thinner, gasoline, naphtha, solvent distillates.

TOXICITY: 4

FORM: All petroleum distillates are liquids. While inhalation of fumes is possible in some cases, ingestion is much more common. Injection can also happen, particularly when a painter's hand gets in the way of a paint gun.

EFFECTS AND SYMPTOMS: Petroleum distillates dissolve fat; but before taking them to lose weight, remember they also change the way the nerves work, causing depression, coma, and occasionally convulsions.

Ingestion and retention of an extremely large dose of gasoline (which is possible, though not common) results in weakness, dizziness, slow and shallow respiration, unconsciousness, and convulsions. Smaller doses cause nausea, vomiting, and coughing and spitting up blood. Chest irritation often becomes pulmonary edema and bronchial pneumonia.

While not usually fatal, injection can cause severe scarring and permanent injury from tissue inflammation and necrosis—a useful device should your fictional villain need a way to injure but not kill someone.

REACTION TIME: Five to twenty minutes.

ANTIDOTES AND TREATMENTS: Basic supportive care is given. Oxygen may also be necessary if the breathing is slowed.

NOTES: Kerosene, gasoline, and paint thinner are three of the most common products distilled from petroleum oil. Petroleum jelly is another, but it is about as nontoxic as a compound can be. While people have survived fairly large doses of the toxic distillates, some have died from minuscule amounts, though this is unlikely.

Petroleum distillates can cause mild heart attacks after either ingestion or inhalation. They also cause reddened and calloused skin.

People who pump their own gasoline at self-service stations notice warning signs that indicate gasoline can be harmful or fatal and can cause fetal defects if it is swallowed or if its fumes are breathed for any length of time. While getting someone to swallow gasoline is highly unlikely, especially since the odor is so strong, the noxious fumes could possibly be pumped into a closed room, rendering the victim unconscious.

CASE HISTORY

In *The Palace Guard,* by Charlotte MacLeod, a guard in an art museum was found dead after the liquor in his private bottle had been replaced with paint thinner.

Guerillas in South America were known to inject gasoline into victims' feet as a form of torture.

PHENOL

OTHER: Carbolic acid, phenic acid, phenylic acid, phenyl hydroxide, hydroxybenzene, oxybenzene.

TOXICITY: 5

FORM: A white, crystalline substance that turns pink or red if not completely pure, phenol has a burning taste, a distinct, aromatic, acrid odor, and is soluble in water. In addition to the household uses listed the notes below, it is used in production of fertilizers, paints, paint removers, textiles, drugs, and perfumes. All equally deadly are inhalation of mist or vapor; skin absorption of mist, vapor, or liquid; ingestion; and skin or eye contact. Phenol penetrates deeply and is readily absorbed by all surfaces of the body.

EFFECTS AND SYMPTOMS: Phenol is a corrosive. In high concentrations, contact with the eyes can result in severe corneal damage or blindness. Skin contact, which can occur at low vapor concentrations, causes burns that form white patches.

If a sufficient amount of phenol is ingested (and in most household forms, it is very diluted), the victim will suffer from vomiting and diarrhea. Because of the corrosive effects, burns can injure the gastrointestinal tract; if the phenol is absorbed into the system, it may cause seizures, coma, low blood pressure, irregular heartbeat, and respiratory arrest.

REACTION TIME: Thirty minutes to several hours.

ANTIDOTES AND TREATMENTS: For skin contact, washing for fifteen minutes, followed by mineral oil or olive oil or petroleum jelly to treat the burns. Eyes that have been exposed are flushed repeatedly with water or saline solution. After inhalation, victims are removed from exposure and given oxygen. Activated charcoal is recommended for ingestion; however, one source suggests withholding it if the doctor expects to use an endoscope to check for damage to the gastrointestinal tract.

NOTES: This is another toxin that had widespread household use as a germicide and a local anesthetic until replaced by less toxic substances. Even now it constitutes roughly 4.7 percent of the topical ointment Campho-Phenique, and is used in a variety of sore throat remedies, including lozenges and the spray Chloraseptic. It is also used to cause skin peeling for cosmetic purposes.

Dinitrophenol was formerly used medically as a metabolic stimulator for weight reduction.

Phenol is used in making creosotes (wood or coal tar); phenol derivatives are used in making disinfectants, antiseptics, caustics, germicides, surface anesthetics, and preservatives.

CASE HISTORY

In the past, an anti-mildew agent containing pentachlorophenol was used in the final disinfecting rinse of diapers and nursery linens, until it was discovered that it caused fever and "sweating syndrome." There were two deaths and severe poisoning in at least nine infants in a Chicago day care center.

POTASSIUM PERMANGANATE

TOXICITY: 5

FORM: Potassium permanganate is a violet crystal compound that dissolves in water. It might make a nice gift of bath salts for an intended victim.

Potassium permanganate is usually swallowed but can also be absorbed through mucous membranes, usually the vagina. In fact, many drugs mixed in a petroleum jelly base are given as vaginal suppositories; so if your potential victim is taking one, the killer can substitute the poison dose.

EFFECTS AND SYMPTOMS: Potassium permanganate destroys mucous membrane cells with the same caustic action as alkalis. The main symptom of potassium permanganate poisoning is corrosion. Swallowing will cause brown discoloration and swelling of the mucous membranes in the mouth and throat, coughing, swelling of the larynx, decayed tissue in mucous membranes, a slow pulse, and shock with a drop in blood pressure. Topical application of potassium permanganate to the vagina or urethra will cause severe burning, hemorrhages, and collapse of the blood vessels. The vaginal wall may be perforated, which will cause peritonitis with fever and abdominal pain. An autopsy will show decayed tissue, hemorrhage, and corrosion in the mucous membranes where the potassium permanganate came in contact.

REACTION TIME: Within five to ten minutes.

ANTIDOTES AND TREATMENTS: Washing the affected areas with water is the first emergency step. The victim is treated for shock. If the poison was ingested, the physician will also look into the throat with a laryngoscope to determine damage, and any perforations will be surgically repaired.

NOTES: Potassium permanganate is used in aquariums and by hospitals as a disinfectant and as an oxidizing agent. Usually only available in very dilute forms, it can produce burns in even small concentrations. It has a reputation of inducing abortions when placed in the vagina, but the amount needed to cause an abortion will also kill the victim.

TURPENTINE

TOXICITY: 5

FORM: As is the case with all volatile oils, turpentine is a liquid that evaporates easily at room temperature. Turpentine can be inhaled or swallowed. There is a characteristic odor.

EFFECTS AND SYMPTOMS: Turpentine irritates the skin and any other tissues it comes in contact with. Locally, turpentine will cause an immediate reddening of skin. Coughing, chest pain, and respiratory distress as initial reactions indicate it has been taken into the lungs. Swallowing causes abdominal burning, nausea, vomiting, diarrhea, painful urination, hematuria, unconsciousness, shallow respiration, and convulsions. The pulse is weak and rapid. Breathing the fumes causes dizziness, rapid, shallow breathing, rapid heartbeat, irritation of the bronchial tubes, and unconsciousness or convulsions. Kidney shutdown and pulmonary edema (water on the lungs) can develop; also bronchial pneumonia, which, should the victim survive, may complicate recovery.

An autopsy shows damage to the kidneys and intense congestion and swelling in the lungs, brain, and stomach linings.

REACTION TIME: As an irritant, turpentine works within seconds; if ingested, within minutes.

ANTIDOTES AND TREATMENTS: Vomiting should be avoided since, if vomit is reswallowed, it can go into the lungs and cause pneumonia and other problems. Artificial respiration is sometimes necessary. Skin contact is treated by a thorough scrubbing of the area with soap and water.

NOTES: Many households have some turpentine stored away. A volatile oil, turpentine is a mixture of hydrocarbons, ethers, alcohols, esters, and ketones. It's now banned in many places because it's a hazard to the environment. This venerable old paint remover is a natural product, a plant derivative from the resin of pines, firs, and other cone-bearing trees. It also has several medical applications as a skin irritant. Like other irritants, it's rarely lethal, simply because it's too painful to swallow or breathe enough for a fatal dose, even for a determined suicide.

MISCELLANEOUS HOUSEHOLD HAZARDS

There are other items found in every household that can be poisonous, depending on the amount consumed and the current health of the patient. Salt, monosodium glutamate, baking soda, potassium, calcium, hydrogen peroxide, laxatives, insect repellants, and even wine, water, and cheese can all prove deadly under certain conditions.

Hidden salt can be a problem for people with hypertension and other cardiac problems, as it can be for people suffering from kidney or liver diseases. It seems unlikely that anyone with heart problems would be totally unaware of the effects of an overdose of salt, but if such an intake of salt occurred, it would result in a heart attack.

MSG (monosodium glutamate) used to be fairly common, especially in Chinese foods. It's a rarity in food products today, partly because of the high sodium content, and also because many people were prone to sensitivity reactions including headaches, increased blood pressure, and other cardiac symptoms. Some more traditional Chinese restaurants still use it. You can arrange for a character to have a sensitivity to MSG and have your opportunistic villain take advantage of it. Just be careful about who else has this information, or you may give your bad guy away too early.

An excessive intake of water or other fluids can also be dangerous. Drinking massive amounts of water, perhaps while on a health kick, can cause sodium depletion and death from a heart attack. Loss of sodium (hyponatremia) can cause lightheadedness, dizziness, blurred vision, inability to balance correctly, profuse sweating, palpitations, difficulty breathing, and heart failure.

Sodium bicarbonate (baking soda) can be lethal to heart patients if enough is swallowed, but it would take a very clever writer to believably get someone to swallow the cup or more needed to kill. Mixed with sterile water and injected, much less sodium bicarb is needed for a lethal dose, although you would still need a good-sized syringe. While sodium bicarb is used in hospitals to save patients going into respiratory acidosis (a condition that occurs when the lungs cannot remove all of the carbon dioxide produced by the body), an overdose could swing the body into alkalosis (increased alkalinity of the blood and tissues), which would prove just as fatal.

Excessive potassium (hyperkalemia), perhaps from a vitamin overdose, causes the heart to dilate and become flaccid, and slows the heart rate. Other symptoms are nausea, diarrhea, muscle weakness, and numbness of hands, feet, tongue, and face. Large quantities weaken the heart, causing an abnormal rhythm, and cardiac arrest occurs.

Too little potassium (hypokalemia) can cause respiratory alkalosis (low carbon dioxide in the blood), resulting in cardiac failure. People who take diuretics (water pills) are often prescribed potassium to balance the water loss. K-Lyte, one brand of potassium, comes mixed in an orange-flavored tablet that foams with water. Potassium also comes in capsule or pill form, as well as an orange- or cherry-flavored liquid. Bananas are a popular source of potassium, as well. As with all drugs, the elderly and the infirm are most susceptible to overdoses. Hidden potassium often causes heart problems that can quickly lead to death. The symptoms of potassium depletion and sodium overdose are the same.

Calcium (Ca) is another element crucial to proper heart and bodily function. Excess calcium works opposite from excess potassium, causing the heart to go into spastic contractions. A lack of calcium causes flaccidity of the heart and other muscles, similar to excess potassium. Calcium deficit (hypocalemia) involves such symptoms as tingling fingers, muscle cramps, hyperactive reflexes, convulsions, and spasms of the hands and larynx. This is why calcium pills are given for nightly leg cramps and calming the nerves.

Most medicine chests contain hydrogen peroxide, an antiseptic/acid. This often burns on contact and bleaches the skin. A colorless, unstable liquid with a bitter taste, hydrogen peroxide is quite corrosive. Highly concentrated solutions cause blistering burns and severe eye injuries on contact (used as a method of killing in Diane Mott's book *Dying for Chocolate,* when the victim crashed his car due to eye injury), and inhalation may cause lung problems ranging from bronchitis to pulmonary edema. However, most of the peroxide found in homes today is the very diluted 3 percent concentration.

Wine and cheese can be deadly to those on certain antidepressants known as monamine oxidase inhibitors (MAO inhibitors). Since patients are usually warned about possible interactions with their meds, your villain would have to find some way to circumvent that. Or set it up so that your victim is very forgetful or otherwise disoriented.

Laxatives and purgatives are among other items found in the medicine cabinet. While these will not kill immediately, the resultant diarrhea or vomiting, if severe enough, can cause dehydration. If the victim does not know to seek medical help, the problem can lead to death. The flavored laxative can be used to make a "delicious" chocolate cake for a chocolate lover. The catch will be finding a believable way to keep the victim from seeking medical help once it's obvious there's a serious problem.

Insect repellants for human use sometimes contain N,N-diethyltoluamide, a compound used as a topical insect repellent that may cause irritation to eyes and mucous membranes, but not to the skin. To cause harm from ingestion, a great deal would need to be consumed. While poisonings are rare, eye irritation can occur if sprayed into the face. In the movie *Extremities*, a fictional heroine, running for her life, grabbed a can of insect repellant and sprayed it in the villain's eyes to temporarily blind him. (See chapter nine, pesticides, for information on stronger insecticides.)

CHAPTER 5

POISONOUS
PLANTS

*Someone at the picnic had really given Thea an oleander branch.
With three notches in it ... to let the deadly sap escape?... And she
skewered her frankfurter on it?*

—*LUCILLE KALLEN, THE PIANO BIRD*

Since plants are the poison most accessible to the average poisoner, this chapter covers
a lot of material. In an effort to categorize, the plants have been divided into groups:

- plants that are quickly fatal, like foxglove
- plants that can be mistaken for edible, like castor bean.
- plants eaten by animals who then become food for humans, as in laurel;
- plants that are edible in small quantities, like akee berry
- plants that have certain edible parts, like rhubarb;
- plants that are edible only certain times of the year, as mandrake
- plants used for medicinal purposes, like ergot.
- plants that flower, like rhododendron or azalea.

Around the year 1800, more than 90 percent of poisoning cases were caused by poisons
of vegetable origin. Now, with the increase of medical, industrial, and agricultural poi-

sons, vegetable substances account for a mere 7 percent of the total. (Of course, many medicines today are synthetic re-creations of plants.)

Keep in mind that, unless a specific location is mentioned, the plants can grow virtually anywhere, even if they are not found naturally in the landscape where you've set your mystery, because of hot houses, greenhouses, and artificial means of growing things.

Many plants are poisonous without being fatal; they may cause itching, dermatitis, or vomiting. For several of our entries, references conflicted regarding degree of toxicity, so we chose what the majority reported. This chapter does not include all of the plants that are poisonous. Some were left off the list for reasons of conflicting information or lack of sufficient information. There are also many that are poisonous but not lethal.

Finally, if your villain plans to do in a victim with plants, the taste must be disguised in a credible way. Salads are popular, as are casseroles (but remember that some plant poisons lose their lethality when cooked).

PLANTS THAT ARE QUICKLY FATAL

Since the term "quickly" can mean several things depending on how it is used, we define "quickly fatal" as a plant whose poisonous effects are felt within a few hours. Again, depending on the amount consumed, victim's weight, other foods eaten, and how quickly the victim receives medical treatment, it might take several days for her to die.

BARBADOS NUT

SCIENTIFIC NAME: *Jatropha curcas.*

OTHER: Physic nut, purge nut, curcas bean, kukui haole (Hawaii).

TOXICITY: 6

DEADLY PARTS: All (the American Medical Association, in their *Handbook of Poisons,* lists only the raw seeds). The poison is jatrophin (curcin), a violent purgative that stimulates bowel movement.

EFFECTS AND SYMPTOMS: Difficulty breathing, sore throat, bloating, dizziness, vomiting, diarrhea, drowsiness, dysuria (painful urination), and leg cramps.

REACTION TIME: Fifteen to twenty minutes.

ANTIDOTES AND TREATMENTS: Gastric lavage is often done unless vomiting has been extensive. Barbados nut poisoning is treated much as castor bean poisoning is treated, with bismuth subcarbonate or magnesium trisilicate to protect the stomach.

Within the United States, the Barbados nut is found in Hawaii and southern Florida. It can also be found in Africa, Mexico, Central America, Asia, and South America. Poisonings, especially of children in the tropical areas, are frequent.

The barbados nut is a small, spreading shade tree about fifteen feet high with thick branches and copious, sticky, yellow sap. The small, greenish yellow flowers are hairy. The seeds themselves taste pleasant but they contain at least 55 percent of hell oil. More potent than castor oil, it was formerly given as a veterinary purge. The nut is still used for soap- and candle-making in the tropics and the dangerous seeds are taken as a folk remedy.

In Africa, physic nuts (local name) are ground up and mixed with palm oil to make a rat poison. The poison inhibits protein synthesis in intestinal wall cells, resulting in death.

BELLADONNA

SCIENTIFIC NAME: *Atropa belladonna*

OTHER: English nightshade, black nightshade, nightshade, banewort, deadly nightshade, dwale, sleeping nightshade, belladonna lily, Barbados lily, cape belladonna, devil's cherries, naughty man's cherries, divale, black cherry, devil's herb, great morel, dwayberry, lirio, naked lady lily, azuncena de Mejico.

TOXICITY: 6

DEADLY PARTS: All, especially roots, leaves, and berries.

EFFECTS AND SYMPTOMS: Dilated pupils; blurred vision; increased heart rate; hot, dry, red skin; dry mouth; disorientation; hallucinations; impaired vision; loud heartbeat, audible at several feet; aggressive behavior; rapid pulse; rapid respiration; anuria; fever; convulsions; coma; and death.

REACTION TIME: Several hours to several days.

ANTIDOTES AND TREATMENTS: The poisonous effects of belladonna berries may be prevented by swallowing an emetic to encourage vomiting and by gastric lavage. Some home emetics might be a large glass of warm vinegar, or mustard and water. This is followed by a dose of magnesia, stimulants, and strong coffee. Sometimes artificial respiration is needed. Symptoms special to those poisoned by belladonna are complete loss of voice and continual movements of the hands and fingers, as well as dilated eye pupils.

NOTES: The medical components of atropine, scopolamine, hyoscyamine, and hyoscine are used for sedatives and as antispasmodics, as they work by paralyzing the action at the nerve endings. The poison is eliminated almost entirely by the kidneys, if these are in good working order.

Introduced as a drug plant from England and France, it is found in Central and Southern Europe, southwest Asia, Eurasia, and Algeria. Belladonna is occasionally found in the wilder and uncultivated areas or as an ornamental plant of the eastern United States.

Reddish purple flowers appear June through July and the plants are sprinkled with dark, inky, sweet berries. The dull, darkish green leaves, unevenly sized, have a bitter taste fresh or dried. The young stems have soft, downy hairs. The thick, fleshy, and whitish root grows about six inches long. When crushed, the fresh plant gives an ungodly odor, but that leaves as the plant dries.

Belladonna means "beautiful woman" in Italian. During the Renaissance, women applied an extract of the plant to their eyes to dilate their pupils and give them a wide and beautiful appearance.

Rabbits often eat belladonna and pass the effect on to anyone who might eat them.

A powder made from the leaves and roots of belladonna is used to treat asthma, colic, and an overabundance of stomach acid.

CASE HISTORY

In September 1916, three children were admitted to a London hospital suffering from belladonna poisoning, caused from having eaten berries from large fruiting plants of *Atropa belladonna* growing in a neighboring public garden. The gardener claimed to be unaware of their dangerous nature, yet later, in 1921, the Norwich coroner commented on the death of a child from the same berries.

CURARE

SCIENTIFIC NAME: *Strychnos toxifera* of the family *Loganiaceae*, or *Chondodendron tomentosum* of the family *Menispermaceae*.

OTHER: Succinylcholine, tubocurarine, pavulon, moonseed, flying death.

TOXICITY: 6

DEADLY PARTS: All of the plant is fatal when injected or otherwise applied subcutaneously; however, it is harmless when swallowed, and the vapors have no poisonous effect.

EFFECTS AND SYMPTOMS: Injection or intravenous administration causes paralysis of muscles starting with the eyelids and face, followed by the inability to swallow or lift the head. The pulse drops dramatically. Within seconds of injection, the poison moves to and paralyzes the diaphragm. Death is due to respiratory failure. Autopsy reports show a diagnosis of inflamed liver. Several medical journalists noted that with curare poisoning, even after breathing stopped, the heart continued beating.

REACTION TIME: Almost immediate. Medical journals report "Two minutes for a bird, ten minutes for a small animal, twenty minutes for a larger mammal, and perhaps a half-hour to forty minutes for a human."

BOOK OF POISONS

None. It works too fast. but if artificial respiration is performed throughout the time that the poison is active, the victim may recover and have no ill effects.

NOTES: Curare is sold under different trade names by numerous drug companies.

The drug mimics the effects of heart failure. It's used medically when the lungs are being worked on, as it stops normal breathing and enables the patient to be put on a respirator. Most physicians also use it as a muscle relaxant before surgery because it reduces the amount of anesthesia needed.

The drug is also used to relieve spastic paralysis, for treating fractures or dislocations, and as an anticonvulsant treatment for tetanus.

The horror of curare poisoning is that the victim is very much awake and aware of what is happening until the loss of consciousness. Consequently, the victim can feel the progressive paralysis but cannot call out or gesture.

CASE HISTORY

In fiction, curare is the favorite drug of medical killers. It is known in the tropics mainly as "flying death" because of its use as an arrow poison.

Sir Walter Raleigh was among the early explorers who reported about curare in his South American visits. In 1807, the first eye-witness account of its preparation was recorded, detailing the sweet-smelling, thick, dark resin oozing from a climbing vine, used by the South American Indian tribe, the Orinocos to paralyze animals and enemies. In Guyana the Macusi tribe uses a similar poison called urali; and the Peruvian tribes call it woorar, ourari, urari, or urirarey.

Final Treatment: The File on Dr. X, by Matthew L. Lifflander (1960) described the use of curare by New York's "Dr. X" (Mario E. Jascalevich) as he killed many of his patients. Dr. X decided whether his potential victims would live or die according to what he judged to be their contribution to society. He went from hospital to hospital, making his choices, until, like most killers, he became careless. The drug was discovered in his locker. Dr. X was tried for murder and acquitted, and never admitted to his deeds.

In *The Red Widow Murders,* by Carter Dickson, detective Sir Henry Merrivale mulls over a case in which a murdered man is found in a locked, empty room. During the postmortem examination, curare shows up, and the baffled detective searches the body for a puncture wound. Finally, he realizes the victim had been to the dentist that day. The killer, knowing the victim would drink to dull the pain, had mixed the drug in a flask of whiskey. The drug entered through the cut on his gum as he drank. In reality, of course, the victim would have needed several swallows for the poison to have been fatal; also, curare has a bitter taste, so it is unlikely that the victim wouldn't have noticed, unless he was drinking so fast to get rid of the pain, or perhaps he noticed only after he had drunk enough to kill him.

HEMLOCK

SCIENTIFIC NAME: *Conium maculatum.*

OTHER: Poison hemlock, lesser hemlock, deadly hemlock, poison parsley, muskrat weed.

TOXICITY: 6

DEADLY PARTS: All, especially the fruits at flowering time. The leaves are also poisonous. The root is said to be nearly harmless in spring, but deadly afterward, especially during the first year of growth.

EFFECTS AND SYMPTOMS: The pulse is rapid and weak and there is a gradual loss of movement with significant pain as muscles deteriorate and die. The sight dims, but the mind remains clear until death, which comes from paralysis of the lungs. (This hemlock differs from water hemlock, which causes convulsions. See Plants That Are Mistaken for Edible or Are Eaten by Mistake, on page 67.)

REACTION TIME: First symptoms start within thirty minutes; death takes five to ten hours after ingestion, and the mucus membranes become cyanotic. A mousy odor is said to emanate from those affected.

ANTIDOTES AND TREATMENTS: Gastric lavage works only if done immediately after ingestion.

NOTES: Hemlock contains coniine, which paralyzes the muscles in much the same way as curare. Native to Europe and Asia, it has become common on both coasts of the United States. The plant grows in uncultivated areas and on the edges of cultivated fields around farm buildings, railroad tracks, irrigation ditches, and stream banks.

Animals often eat poison hemlock seeds, especially in spring when there is insufficient forage available. The toxicity increases through the growing season and the roots become most toxic later in the year. Once the plant has been dried, the toxicity is reduced but not eliminated.

Affected animals can become nervous, tremble, and become uncoordinated as heart and respiratory rate slows. The legs, ears, and other extremities become cold and can remain this way for several days. The animals might not die of the poison, but the flesh of one hemlock-poisoned quail reportedly can kill a man. Diarrhea, vomiting, and paralysis appear three hours or longer after eating as one slowly dies.

Humans are also often poisoned when they mistake the roots for parsnips, the leaves for parsley, or the seeds for anise.

The variety known as American musquash root, whose symptoms are the same, is a tuber often confused with its edible counterpart, horseradish.

JIMSONWEED

SCIENTIFIC NAME: *Datura stramonium*

OTHER: Devil's trumpet, stinkweed, thorn apple, mad apple, angel's trumpet, Jamestown weed.

TOXICITY: 6

DEADLY PARTS: All.

FORM: The funnel-shaped flowers are white or purple with purple leaves. The prickly fruit, appearing in autumn, is ovoid or globular, and has wrinkled black seeds. The annual herb can grow up to five feet tall.

EFFECTS AND SYMPTOMS: Headache; vertigo; extreme thirst; dry, burning sensation of skin; dilated pupils; blurred vision; loss of sight; frequent urination; diarrhea; weight loss; involuntary movements; restlessness; rapid thoughts; delirium; drowsiness; weak pulse; convulsions; and coma, which can end in death.

REACTION TIME: Several hours.

ANTIDOTES AND TREATMENTS: Treatment is based on symptoms. A purgative such as magnesium sulfate may be used, and sedatives such as Valium are effective for convulsions.

NOTES: Native to the warmer parts of America and the southern Canadian provinces, it is also found in Europe and Mexico. Though it is not native to Britain, it now grows in many southern English gardens and is found in overgrazed pastures, barnyards, and uncultivated areas with rich soils.

There are several species of jimsonweed; all are poisonous. The fragrance varies between pleasant and unpleasant, depending on the season, with the sweeter smell found during growing season. Mostly it is avoided because of the strong odor and unpleasant taste.

Accidental poisoning is most often caused by the seeds. It has been said that jimsonweed has poisoned more people than any other plant. Both adults and children have been fatally poisoned by tea brewed from the leaves or seeds of this plant.

In the past, this plant was used in various medicinal preparations, especially for asthma. The smoke from the burning leaves would be inhaled. Medicinal and culinary use often resulted in poisoning. The seeds are also often misused for their hallucinogenic qualities.

CASE HISTORY

Jimsonweed was originally called Jamestown weed because the soldiers sent in 1676 to quell Bacon's Rebellion, in Jamestown, Virginia, thinking they were edible, ate the leaves of this plant as a salad when food ran out. Mass hallucination resulted from the poisoning. Another Jamestown man was poisoned after he drank an herbal tea brewed from the leaves.

LILY OF THE VALLEY

SCIENTIFIC NAME: *Convallaria majalis.*

OTHER: May lily, Our Lady's tears, convall-lily, lily constancy, ladder-to-heaven, Jacob's ladder, male lily

TOXICITY: 6

DEADLY PARTS: All, especially the leaves.

FORM: The small, white, bell-shaped flowers are well known. The plant bears orange-red, fleshy berries. Even the water in which the cut flowers are kept is toxic.

EFFECTS AND SYMPTOMS: Symptoms include hot flashes; tense irritability; headache; hallucinations; red skin patches; cold, clammy skin; dilated pupils; vomiting; stomach pains; nausea; excess salivation; and slow heartbeat, sometimes leading to coma and death from heart failure.

REACTION TIME: Immediate.

ANTIDOTES AND TREATMENTS: Gastric lavage is recommended, as well as cardiac depressants like quinidine to control cardiac rhythm.

NOTES: The poison is convallatoxin, which is similar to digitalis, a drug that strengthens the contractions of the heart.

Found in most of the United States and the Canadian provinces, this spring-flowering plant is also native to Britain, especially the eastern parts.

The plant has been mistaken for wild garlic and made into a soup.

CASE HISTORY

An old Sussex legend tells of St. Leonard fighting against a great dragon in the woods near Horsham, vanquishing it after mortal combat that lasted many hours. Wherever his blood

---

dropped from his wounds lilies-of-the valley sprang up to commemorate the desperate fight. The woods of St. Leonard's Forest are still thickly carpeted with them.

Although not as common as the foxglove, lily of the valley is still prescribed for cardiac problems and dates back to ancient times. In Apuleius' fourth-century *Herbal* he states the flower was given to Apollo by Æsculapius.

Russian peasants have for many centuries used lily-of-the-valley for faulty hearts.

MONKSHOOD

SCIENTIFIC NAME: *Aconitum napellus, A. columbianum, A. vulparia, A. lutescens, or A. uncinatum.*

OTHER NAMES AND VARIETIES: Friar's cap, garden wolfbane, wolfbane, aconite; western monkshood; yellow monkshood; wild monkshood.

TOXICITY: 6

DEADLY PARTS: All, especially the leaves and roots, which contain the poisons aconitine and aconine.

EFFECTS AND SYMPTOMS: The drug can be ingested or absorbed through the skin. The first signs appear almost immediately: burning; tingling and numbness in the tongue, throat, and face; followed by nausea; vomiting; blurred vision; prickling of skin; paralysis of the respiratory system; dimness of vision; low blood pressure; slow and weak pulse; chest pain; giddiness; sweating; and convulsions. Some victims complain of yellow-green vision and tinnitus. As numbness gradually spreads over the entire body, with subnormal body temperatures and a pronounced feeling of cold, it's as if there's ice water in the veins. At the end, severe pain occurs, associated with the paralysis of facial muscles. Breathing is at first rapid, then slow; finally there is respiratory arrest or paralysis of the heart. Consciousness often continues until the end.

REACTION TIME: Symptoms start rapidly. Death occurs in ten minutes to a few hours. If a less-than-fatal amount is eaten, recovery occurs within twenty-four hours.

ANTIDOTES AND TREATMENTS: There is no specific antidote. Treatment may include gastric lavage, the administration of oxygen to help breathing, and drugs to stimulate the heart.

NOTES: The Indians of Nepal and Bhutan believe evil spirits reside in the monkshood plants. Common monkshood is located throughout the United States and Canada, as well as on the mountain slopes of Europe and east of the Himalayas. A tall plant with blue blossoms and a slim stem, monkshood grows on wet grassland, stony or rocky slopes, and near forest streams at altitudes higher than 3,600 feet.

POISONOUS PLANTS

The yellow variety is native from New Mexico to Idaho. Wild monkshood can also be found from Georgia to Pennsylvania.

Monkshood root is often mistaken for radish. Its leaves, eaten in a salad, can cause poisoning. Young plants have the highest concentration of poison. Children have been known to become ill if they hold the tubers in their hands for too long.

The process of collecting monkshood root takes several days and is usually done in early October as the root matures. Pulled from the ground, it is spread out in the sun to dry. Since the fumes are noxious, the person in charge of the drying operation covers her nose. Even so, many report symptoms of giddiness and heaviness in the head. The dried roots are taken to market for sale and are popular in the bazaars of Calcutta and elsewhere.

The herb is also used for killing rodents and insects.

CASE HISTORY

In ancient Europe and Asia, enemy water supplies were poisoned with monkshood, and hunters used its sap to poison spears, arrowheads and trap baits.

Because of monkshood's poisonous properties, ancient Greece's legend held that the plant sprang from Cerberus' slobber when he came up from the underworld.

The ancient Roman naturalist Plinius describes friar's cap under the name "plant arsenic." The plant was used for killing panthers, wolves, and other carnivores

In England, the cowl-like shape of the flowers gave it its name, and during the Middle Ages, monkshood was associated with witchcraft. It is still used as an external painkiller in folk medicine.

In one case, cardiac failure occurred due to excessive application of Monkshood liniment.

In December 1881, Dr. George Lamson, an English physician, made use of this then-little-known vegetable poison to kill his brother-in-law and help his wife receive an inheritance. He placed the poison in a Dundee cake, which he served. Before eating the cake, his brother-in-law complained of a headache. Lamson offered some prepared placebo pills (empty capsules with sugar in them). Suspecting trickery, the brother-in-law refused the sugar pills but ate the cake. Then Lamson left, saying he had to catch a train. The brother-in-law became ill within ten minutes and died that night.

At his arrest and trial, Lamson brazenly admitted he had fooled his brother-in-law. The poison had been on the pre-cut pieces of cake and not in the capsules. Lamson was executed in April 1882.

OLEANDER

SCIENTIFIC NAME: *Nerium oleander.*

OTHER: Jericho rose.

TOXICITY: 6

DEADLY PARTS: All, including the nectar of the flower.

EFFECTS AND SYMPTOMS: A cardiac stimulator, the drug causes sweating, vomiting, bloody diarrhea, unconsciousness, respiratory paralysis, and death. (See digitalis in chapter eight on page 193).

REACTION TIME: Immediate.

ANTIDOTES AND TREATMENTS: Prompt vomiting is encouraged. Atropine, used to dry up secretions, is used cautiously as an antidote for many drug overdoses. Gastric lavage is recommended, as well as cardiac depressants like quinidine to control cardiac rhythm. The treatment is similar to that of digitalis poisoning.

NOTES: Native to Asia, oleander has been introduced as an ornamental shrub in the southern United States. In the northern United States, it's grown as a house plant. The poison contains cardiac glycosides, oldendrin, and nerioside. Yellow oleander (*Thevetia peruviana*) works in the same way but has a milky sap. Its seeds are very poisonous and contain digitalis-like poisons. It is just as deadly as *Nerium* oleander. An evergreen summer favorite, it favors such temperate climates as Greece, India, Italy, and California, but it can grow almost anywhere. Oleander is a popular poison in Bengal and Madras, India. In Italy and India, mourners place oleander about the bodies of dead relatives, using the blooms as funeral flowers.

Extracts of the plant have been used in India to treat leprosy, as an abortifacient, and as a means of suicide.

Smoke from the burning plant and the water from the cut flowers are also poisonous. Using the twigs for skewered meat or for children's whistles may result in serious effects.

In Europe, oleander is used as a rat poison. The evergreen shrub has a fragrant smell with white, pink, or red blossoms. When bees use oleander pollen for their honey, the honey may be poisonous.

CASE HISTORY

Oleander is a favorite of many authors, including Lucille Kallen, who skewered hot dogs with oleander branches in *The Piano Bird*.

PATERNOSTER PEA

SCIENTIFIC NAME: *Abrus precatorius*.

OTHER: Jequirity bean, lucky bean, prayer bean, love bean, rosary pea, precatory bean, crab's eyes, bead vine, red bead vine, mienie-mienie, Indian bean, black-eyed Susan, wild licorice, Seminole bead, weather plant, Indian licorice.

TOXICITY: 6

DEADLY PARTS: The seeds.

EFFECTS AND SYMPTOMS: The poison inhibits the digestive process, so autopsy may show undigested food, and ulcers in the mouth. Symptoms include diarrhea; nausea; vomiting; tachycardia; convulsions; and diffuse hemorrhages, with bleeding coming from the mouth, nose, and eyes; coma; and death from heart failure.

REACTION TIME: Several hours to three days.

ANTIDOTES AND TREATMENTS: There is a long latent period associated with this poison, so the killer could be far away by the time symptoms have started. Convulsions and collapse of the circulatory system are treated as they occur. A high-carbohydrate diet is given to minimize liver damage.

NOTES: Abric acid, which contains a tetanic glycoside, is in the seeds of this climbing plant. The poison is not released unless the seed is chewed. This fact was often used in trials by ordeal in the Middle Ages, when a favored participant was privately tipped off beforehand to swallow without chewing.

These peas are used as beads in rosaries, bracelets, necklaces, leis, and sometimes children's toys. In the tropics, the juice from the seeds is used as an arrow poison.

CASE HISTORY

In 1976, a young man died five days after suicidally ingesting a lethal dose of the peas, which he ground up in his blender.

RHODODENDRON

SCIENTIFIC NAME: *Rhododendron ponticum, R. arborescens* (azalea)

TOXICITY: 6

DEADLY PARTS: All.

EFFECTS AND SYMPTOMS: Nausea, physical irritation, drooling, vomiting, increased tear formation, paralysis, slowing of pulse, lowering of blood pressure, diarrhea, seizure, coma, and death.

REACTION TIME: About six hours after ingestion.

ANTIDOTES AND TREATMENTS: Treatment includes gastric lavage and addresses any symptoms as they occur.

NOTES: Evergreen shrubs have bell-shaped, showy flowers but no odor, and grow in Canada, in the Appalachians, and on the Pacific Coast of the United States. The state flower of West Virginia and Washington, they are also common in Britain.

Azalea flowers, another variety, are funnel-shaped, often fragrant.

The Greeks found that honey from bees that fed on azaleas, rhododendrons, oleander, or dwarf laurel was poisonous. Making tea from the leaves of these plants results in poisoning.

All parts contain carbohydrate andromedotoxin, the same poison as mountain laurel (*Kalmia* family). (See Plants That Are Mistaken for Edible or Are Eaten by Mistake, on page 67.)

SAVIN

SCIENTIFIC NAME: *Juniperus sabina.*

OTHER: Savin oil.

TOXICITY: 6

DEADLY PARTS: Entire plant.

EFFECTS AND SYMPTOMS: In small doses, this diuretic reportedly brings about menstruation. At high doses, it causes convulsions. On the skin, the oil causes blisters and sometimes necrosis. When swallowed, the irritant causes gastroenteritis with hemorrhages and vomiting of greenish masses with an ether-like odor. Polyuria (frequent urination) may occur, with blood in the urine, followed by oliguria and anuria, convulsive coma, and acute kidney problems.

REACTION TIME: Symptoms start within the hour, but death from respiratory arrest might take as long as ten hours or several days.

ANTIDOTES AND TREATMENTS: Milk is given to alleviate gastroenteritis, then gastric lavage is needed to remove the material. If kidney function is normal, fluids are encouraged. Other symptoms are treated as they occur.

NOTES: Available everywhere, this plant tastes bitter. Savin oil is the drug version of the plant and is used to combat overdose of cardiac medications.

In ancient times, savin was used to cause abortions. The amount needed to abort, however, was usually fatal for the mother.

STAR OF BETHLEHEM

SCIENTIFIC NAME: *Omithogalum umbellaturn.*

OTHER: Dove's dung (biblical name), summer snowflake, snowdrop, nap at noon, sleepy-dick, eleven o'clock lady.

TOXICITY: 6

DEADLY PARTS: All, especially the bulb, which contains the same poisons as lily of the valley (convallatoxin and convalloside).

EFFECTS AND SYMPTOMS: The first signs are stomach and intestinal irritation, which are followed by abnormalities in the heart's rate and rhythm, and this can progress to fatal cardiac arrhythmias.

REACTION TIME: Immediate.

ANTIDOTES AND TREATMENTS: Gastric lavage and symptomatic treatment.

NOTES: Star of Bethlehem grows wild along roadsides, in fields, and in woods of warm climates especially in the Middle East. It can also be found in the southern and western parts of Indiana.

White star-like flowers are found on a leafless stem. Bulbs, which have a higher percentage of the poison, can be used in meal and mixed into flour, but they have a bitter aftertaste.

STRYCHNOS NUX-VOMICA

SCIENTIFIC NAME: *Loganiaceae.*

OTHER: Nux-vomica, strychnine tree, poison nut, Quaker button.

TOXICITY: 6

DEADLY PARTS: Stem, bark, dried ripe seeds.

EFFECTS AND SYMPTOMS: See strychnine in chapter three on page 28.

REACTION TIME: Immediate.

ANTIDOTES AND TREATMENTS: None.

NOTES: Used by Native American tribes to aid in the treatment of hysteria, epilepsy, prolapsed rectum, chronic rheumatism, cholera, dysentery, palsy, and headache.

TANGHIN

SCIENTIFIC NAME: *Tanghinia venenifera.*

OTHER: Ordeal bean of Madagascar.

TOXICITY: 6

DEADLY PARTS: The seeds are notoriously poisonous, containing the cardiac poison tanghin.

EFFECTS AND SYMPTOMS: Heart palpitations, headache, nausea, blurred vision, delirium, slowed or irregular pulse, and death from ventricular fibrillation.

REACTION TIME: Immediate.

ANTIDOTES AND TREATMENTS: Gastric lavage and constant monitoring of EKG. Electrolytes and potassium chloride can be given, as well as other stimulants, but those too must be monitored to avoid cardiac arrest

NOTES: This fragrant plant has star-shaped flowers and milky, sticky sap. Found mainly in Madagascar, it is also sparsely grown in Hawaii.

CASE HISTORY

In the Middle Ages, forced to drink the poison or be sliced by a soldier's spear, the accused was judged innocent by the ruling regime if he swallowed only a gulp and promptly vomited. This was used for of all kinds of crimes: from murder and conspiracy to witchcraft, stealing, and being in debt. If afraid, the prisoner would sip slowly and die almost immediately. Guilt, of course, was predetermined, since death was related to the strength of the extract. In their colonization of Madagascar, the French destroyed all the tanghin trees they could find.

YEW

SCIENTIFIC NAME: *Taxus baccata* (English yew), *T. brevifolia* (Pacific or western yew), *T. canadensis* (American yew or ground hemlock), *T. cuspidata* (Japanese yew)

TOXICITY: 6

DEADLY PARTS: All, except the red fruit of the plant is toxic, especially the wood bark, leaves, and seeds.

EFFECTS AND SYMPTOMS: Nausea, vomiting, diarrhea, severe gastroenteritis, euphoria, abdominal pain, dilated pupils, weakness, pale skin, convulsions, shock, coma, and death due to cardiac failure. The poison, taxine, can be detected only in gastric contents.

REACTION TIME: Within one hour.

ANTIDOTES AND TREATMENTS: None.

NOTES: It is found throughout North America. In earlier days, pregnant women wanting an abortion took this poison, often accidentally overdosing. Survival after poisoning is rare.

PLANTS THAT ARE MISTAKEN FOR EDIBLE OR ARE EATEN BY MISTAKE

BANEBERRY

SCIENTIFIC NAME: *Actaea alba* (white), *A. rubra* (red), and *A. spicata* (black).

OTHER: Cohosh, doll's eyes, herb Christopher, necklaceweed, snakeberry, black baneberry, western baneberry, European baneberry.

TOXICITY: 5

DEADLY PARTS: The AMA *Handbook of Poisonous and Injurious Plants* 1985 lists all parts as being poisonous, but other references indicate only the berries and roots. The root is a violent purgative, and the plant as a whole affects the heart.

EFFECTS AND SYMPTOMS: Ingested, a small dose is enough to produce burning in the stomach, dizziness, and increased pulse. Increased amounts lead to nausea, vomiting, bloody diarrhea, convulsions, and shock. Prolonged handling of the plant produces skin rashes.

REACTION TIME: Several hours to days. Forty-eight hours is average, but symptoms have started in as little as thirty minutes.

ANTIDOTES AND TREATMENTS: Gastric lavage should be instituted at once. Milk, egg white, or other demulcents (substances that provides a soothing film to mucous membranes) are then given to nullify poison. Often the body electrolytes are depleted, kidney failure may occur, and death may follow if the symptoms are not treated immediately.

NOTES: Eastern baneberry is found in the woods from Maine to New York to Canada. Western baneberry can be found in the forests of the Rocky Mountains to the Pacific Coast. The European baneberry is found in Northern Europe in the forests of Germany and France.

The plants blossom with small white or bluish flowers and have red, white, or black berries that grow summer and autumn in mountain wooded areas. The large sharp-toothed leaves have hairy undersides.

CASE HISTORY

In one case from the 1800s, a victim stated: "At first there was a most ordinary pyrotechnic display of blue objects of all sizes and tints, circular with irregular edges; as one became interested in the spots it felt as if a heavy weight was lowered on the top of the head and remained there, while sharp pains shot through the temples: "Then suddenly the mind became confused and there was a total disability to recollect anything distinctly or arrange ideas with any coherency. On an attempt to talk, wrong names were given to objects, and although at the same time the mind knew mistakes were made in speech, the words seemed to utter themselves independently. For a few minutes there was great dizziness, the body seeming to swing off into space, while the blue spots changed to dancing sparks of fire." This victim survived.

In 1972, one English family was poisoned after they made and ate a pie out of the baneberries they had gathered. All but the mother died as a result of the fatal pie.

CASTOR BEAN

SCIENTIFIC NAME: *Ricinus communis.*

OTHER: African coffee tree, castor-oil plant, palma Christi, koli (Hawaii).

TOXICITY: 6

DEADLY PARTS: The beans are poisonous, and even two beans, well chewed, can be fatal. If swallowed whole, however, poisoning is unlikely because the hard seed coat prevents rapid absorption. The poison ricin is made from the beans.

EFFECTS AND SYMPTOMS: Burning in mouth, nausea, vomiting, cramps, drowsiness, cyanosis, stupor, circulatory collapse, blood in urine, convulsions, coma, and death. The toxin causes hemolysis (breaking up of red blood cells) even at extreme dilution, resulting in severe hemorrhaging. It can also induce labor in pregnant women. Autopsy investigation shows vomit and stool containing blood.

REACTION TIME: The first symptoms may take anywhere from two hours to two days. Death may occur up to twelve days after ingestion.

ANTIDOTES AND TREATMENTS: Gastric lavage should be done, and bismuth subcarbonate (as Pepto Bismol) or magnesium trisilicate is sometimes given to protect the stomach. The diarrhea can cause electrolyte depletion, which must be treated with fluids.

NOTES: The castor bean is native to Eastern Africa and India but has spread worldwide and is now found in most tropical regions in North America on wasteland, near railroads and dump sites. Recently the decorative plant has been seen in parks and other public areas.

Sometimes mingled with linseed to make press cakes, this mixture will poison anyone who eats it unless it is heated first to destroy the ricin.

Dating back to 4000 B.C., Herodotus and other Greek travelers noted the plant in Egypt, where it was used as an oil for lamps and for body ointments. India and China also document use as a lamp oil and laxative (2000 B.C.).

CASE HISTORY

A much-publicized case of homicidal poisoning by ricin took place in 1978. Bulgarian dissident Georgi Ivanov Markov died when a small, perforated metallic sphere containing the poison was forcibly injected into his leg.

CORN COCKLE

SCIENTIFIC NAME: *Agrostemma githago.*

OTHER: Purple cockle.

TOXICITY: 4

DEADLY PARTS: All; the seeds are especially poisonous. The poisons are githagin and saponin glycosides.

EFFECTS AND SYMPTOMS: Raw throat, nausea, acute gastroenteritis, fever, giddiness, headache, delirium, severe stomach pains, weakness, slow breathing, sharp pains in the spine, coma, and death from respiratory arrest.

REACTION TIME: Thirty minutes to one hour after ingestion.

ANTIDOTES AND TREATMENTS: Gastric lavage and symptomatic treatment.

NOTES: Native to Europe but brought to North America. A few varieties are cultivated as an ornamental. It's difficult to screen the seeds from wheat or corn, and the plant is often found in those fields. The flowers are purplish-pink and pink with numerous black pitted poisonous seeds.

In the past, this plkant caused bread poisoning when the seeds got into the wheat, but now the process of sifting mostly eliminates this danger.

DAPHNE

SCIENTIFIC NAME: *Daphne mezereum, D. laureola.*

OTHER: Spurge, dwarf bay, lebruary daphne, flax olive, spurge flax, wild pepper, spurge laurel, wood laurel, copse laurel.

TOXICITY: 5

DEADLY PARTS: All, but the fruit is especially deadly.

EFFECTS AND SYMPTOMS: Severe burning of lips, mouth, and throat; stomatitis; abdominal pain; vomiting; bloody diarrhea; weakness; convulsions; kidney damage; coma; and death.

REACTION TIME: Forty-five minutes to several hours.

ANTIDOTES AND TREATMENTS: Gastric lavage should be instituted with caution, since damage may have been done to the mucous membranes, mouth, and esophageal lining. Often the victims go into shock due to fluid loss, which is treated as it occurs.

NOTES: Recognized as poisonous from ancient times, daphne is native to Eurasia, and found throughout the British Isles as well as in the northeastern United States and eastern Canada. Introduced from Europe, it is widely planted as an ornamental. Purple, rosy-purple, or white flowers blossom in spring with a pleasant fragrance.

The berries of *D. mezereum* are bright red, and those of *D. laureola* are green at first, then bluish, then finally black when fully ripe. The poisons are daphnetoxin and mezerein. The juice from the berries or sap from the bark may be absorbed in torn skin and produce systemic reactions. Heating or cooking will not diminish toxicity.

The poison is not destroyed even after the leaves and fruit wither. Eating only a few berries can be fatal to a child.

CASE HISTORY

One case of poisoning in the 1870s occurred in Toronto, Canada, when a woman presented a fatal pie to her ex-husband. He didn't eat it, but his current wife did, and died.

DEATHCAMAS

SCIENTIFIC NAME: *Zygadenus venenosus.*

OTHER: Alkali grass, black snake root, soap plant, poison sego, water lily, wild onion, squirrel food, hog's potato.

TOXICITY: 4

DEADLY PARTS: The fresh leaves, stems, bulbs, and flowers are poisonous, but the seeds are particularly so. Poisons contained are zygadenine, zygacine, and veratrine.

EFFECTS AND SYMPTOMS: Increased salivation, weakness shown by staggering or complete prostration, difficult breathing, and coma followed by death.

REACTION TIME: At least one hour.

ANTIDOTES AND TREATMENTS: There is no satisfactory antidote. Gastric lavage is recommended if spontaneous vomiting doesn't occur. Other symptoms are treated as needed.

NOTES: Found in most of North America, except in the extreme southeast; also in Hawaii, Canada, and Alaska. Part of the lily family, the plant can be mistaken for an onion since it has an onion-like bulb with a dark-colored coat, but the onion odor is missing, and the plant has greenish-white to yellow-white flowers clustered at the top.

Plants retain their poison properties after being dried. This is mainly a cattle poison, but it can kill humans, too.

CASE HISTORY

There are two cases in recent medical literature of poisoning from this plant. A two-year-old boy ate the flowers and shortly thereafter vomited, became drowsy, and then went into a coma. His respiration became slow and irregular, and his blood pressure dropped dangerously. His pupils became unequally dilated, but he recovered after several days.

The second case also concerned a child, who ate some bulbs that had been roasted on a bonfire. Within an hour, he staggered and vomited before losing consciousness and dying.

FOOL'S PARSLEY

SCIENTIFIC NAME: *Aethusa cynapium.*

OTHER: Dog parsley, "wild parsley," fool's cicely.

TOXICITY: 4

DEADLY PARTS: All. The active poisons are cynapine, which is similar to coniine (hemlock) and cicutoxin (water hemlock).

EFFECTS AND SYMPTOMS: Symptoms are similar to hemlock poisoning (see hemlock on page 58).

REACTION TIME: Several hours to several days.

ANTIDOTES AND TREATMENTS: Gastric lavage and symptomatic treatment.

NOTES: Introduced from Europe, it is found in fields and uncultivated areas in the northeastern United States and in eastern Canada. The plant looks very much like poison hemlock, but the purple spotting is absent. Humans have died after eating leaves or roots mistaken for parsley, anise, or radishes.

MEADOW SAFFRON

SCIENTIFIC NAME: *Colchicum autumnale.*

OTHER: Autumn crocus, fall crocus, naked ladies.

TOXICITY: 5

DEADLY PARTS: All, especially the bulb.

EFFECTS AND SYMPTOMS: Burning in the throat, intense thirst, vomiting, difficulty swallowing, watery or bloody diarrhea, abdominal pain, anuria, cardiovascular collapse, delirium, hallucinations, blurred vision, convulsions, muscle weakness, and respiratory failure. Some symptoms are similar to arsenic poisoning. (See chapter three, page 22.) Sudden death may occur after intravenous administration of a small amount of colchicine. In chronic poisoning, hair starts to fall out in ten to fourteen days. Lab findings include blood and protein in urine. Colchicine is eliminated in feces, sweat, and urine. Fatalities occur in 50 percent of poisonings.

REACTION TIME: Two to six hours. Death may take as long as two to three days to occur. The patient is fully conscious until the end.

ANTIDOTES AND TREATMENTS: Besides gastric lavage, activated charcoal is used. Atropine and hypotensive drugs can combat symptoms.

NOTES: It is primarily found throughout Eurasia, often in damp meadows and woodsy areas of England and Wales as well as in some parts of Scotland.

The crocus-like plant has been mistaken for an onion. Tincture of colchicine is made from the seeds. The plant assisted with abortions in the past and now the drug, colchicine, is used for rheumatism and gout.

The drug can be dissolved in milk. Goats, immune to the poison, eat autumn crocus, and their milk can pass on the poison.

MOUNTAIN LAUREL

SCIENTIFIC NAME: *Kalmia latifolia, K. augustifolia, K. microphylla, K. polifolia.*

OTHER: Calico bush, poison laurel, ivy bush, mountain ivy, sheep laurel, lambkill, narrow-leaved laurel, calfkill, hook heller, swamp laurel, alpine laurel, pale laurel.

TOXICITY: 5

DEADLY PARTS: The leaves, twigs, flowers, and pollen are poisonous.

EFFECTS AND SYMPTOMS: Severe gastrointestinal distress; watering of eyes, nose, and mouth; labored breathing; and slowed heartbeat. Kidney failure can happen, as well as convulsions, paralysis, coma, and death.

REACTION TIME: Symptoms usually start in six hours; death, if it occurs, may take from twelve hours to several days.

ANTIDOTES AND TREATMENTS: Gastric lavage and symptomatic treatment.

NOTES: It is found throughout North America in moist areas. The fruit is a many-seeded capsule. The pollen sometimes results in bees making a very bitter, poisonous honey, so astringent to the taste that it is unlikely that one would ingest enough raw honey to be harmed. A cooked honey cake, however, could mask the taste. The poison in mountain laurel are andromedotoxins. North American hazel hens eat laurel (*K. latifolia*), making their flesh deadly.

POKEWEED

SCIENTIFIC NAME: *Phytolacca americana.*

OTHER: Poke, inkberry, pokeberry, pigeonberry, pokeroot, ombu, American nightshade.

TOXICITY: 4

DEADLY PARTS: Roots, leaves, and seeds are the most poisonous. There is some poison in the stems, with less in the fruit. Poisons are phytolaccine, saponins, and glycoproteins. A small child can be fatally poisoned by eating two to three uncooked berries.

EFFECTS AND SYMPTOMS: This violent but slow-acting emetic causes severe stomach cramps, nausea, persistent vomiting, diarrhea, slowed and difficult breathing, weakness, spasms, severe convulsions, and death.

REACTION TIME: Symptoms begin about two hours after ingestion.

ANTIDOTES AND TREATMENTS: Gastric lavage and symptomatic treatment.

NOTES: Common throughout the eastern United States and southeastern Canada, it's found near open fields, along fences and roadsides, and in uncultivated areas. Occasionally it is found on the West Coast and in Hawaii, as well as in Europe and southern Africa. Imported from the Americas to Britain, it is now commonly found in gardens and fields there, as well as in Australia and New Zealand.

The long, flesh-colored root resembles horseradish, and the plant sprouts pass for asparagus. Immature leaves and stems are often eaten as cooked greens in the South but are edible only if twice cooked in different pots, with the water being thrown out between cookings. Even then the toxin still remains to a degree. The plant is used extensively in preparation of certain drugs and as a household remedy for skin diseases and rheumatism.

The white drooping flowers contrast with the black juicy berries, which yield a red dye formerly used by Native Americans for their decorations. The red juice was used to symbolize blood in the anti-slavery protests.

PRIVET

SCIENTIFIC NAME: *Ligustrum vulgare.*

OTHER: Prim, lovage, hedge plant, Japanese privet.

TOXICITY: 5

DEADLY PARTS: All, especially the blackish berries. The poison is ligustrin.

EFFECTS AND SYMPTOMS: Severe gastroenteritis, frequent vomiting, watery stools, abdominal pain, collapse, kidney damage, and fall of blood pressure all culminate in death.

REACTION TIME: Symptoms start within ten minutes of eating, and a lethal dose can cause death in two hours.

ANTIDOTES AND TREATMENTS: Gastric lavage and symptomatic treatment.

NOTES: Once found only in northern Europe, it now grows almost everywhere, especially in parks and gardens as hedges. Most cases of human poisoning come from eating the ripe berries. Privet can also cause skin rashes or hives.

WATER HEMLOCK

SCIENTIFIC NAME: *Cicuta maculata, C. californica, C. douglasii, C. vagans, C. bolanderi, C. curtissii.*

OTHER: Beaver poison, spotted water hemlock, cowbane, spotted cowbane, California water hemlock, gray hemlock, Douglas water hemlock, Oregon water hemlock, tuber water hemlock, lesser hemlock poison, American musquash root, locoweed.

TOXICITY: 6, though toxicity varies with the season and age of the plant. The younger plants have more poison.

DEADLY PARTS: Roots have the most poison, but the whole plant is deadly.

EFFECTS AND SYMPTOMS: Restlessness and feelings of anxiety, stomach pain, nausea, violent vomiting, diarrhea, dilated pupils, labored breathing, sometimes frothing at the mouth, weak and rapid pulse, and violent convulsions terminated by death by respiratory failure.

REACTION TIME: Twenty minutes to an hour or more for symptoms, and possibly death.

ANTIDOTES AND TREATMENTS: Emetics and cathartics are necessary to get rid of the poison. Intermuscular injections of morphine are sometimes used to control convulsions. Short-acting barbiturates are also used to control convulsions.

If seizures have occurred or appear imminent, gastric lavage should not be attempted without the aid of an anesthesiologist.

NOTES: Small white flowers have split roots and a sweet-smelling yellowish oil. Water hemlock (*C. maculata*) is found in eastern United States and Canada; California water hemlock (*C. californica, C. bolanderi*) is found in middle western California; Douglas water hemlock (*C. douglasii*) is found along the Pacific Coast states and British Columbia; tuber water hemlock or Oregon water hemlock (*C. vagans*) is found in the Pacific Northwest; western hemlock (*C. occidentalis*) is in the Rocky Mountain states west to the Pacific Coast; bulbous water hemlock (*C. bulbifera*) is in the northern United States.

Growing primarily in wet or swampy ground, frequently along streams, roadside ditches, marshes and drainage areas, or in wet, low-lying areas in pastures, water hemlock is noted because it becomes greener before the rest of the pasture. Species of water hemlock occur in various areas over the entire United States, including Alaska and Hawaii.

The brown and sticky resin-like substance contains cicutoxin, and the poison is soluble in alcohol, chloroform, or ether.

Numerous poisonings have been reported from the plant being mistaken for parsnips, artichokes, or similar roots. Most cases occur in the early spring during the early growth. Children have been poisoned by making peashooters and whistles from the hollow stems.

Cows have been poisoned by water contaminated with the juice of the crushed plants, although quite a bit is needed, since the poison is not as soluble in cold water.

PLANTS THAT ARE EDIBLE IN SMALL QUANTITIES, HAVE CERTAIN EDIBLE PARTS, OR ARE EDIBLE CERTAIN TIMES OF THE YEAR

AKEE

SCIENTIFIC NAME: *Blighia sapida.*

OTHER: *Aki, ackee, arbre, fricasse* (Haiti), *vegetal* (Cuba, Puerto Rico), vegetable brain. Other Spanish names are *arbol de seso, palo de seso* (Cuba); *huevo vegetal* and *fruto de huevo* (Guatemala and Panama); *arbor del huevo* and *pera roja* (Mexico); *merey del diablo* (Venezuela); *bien me sabe* or *pan y quesito* (Colombia); *akí* (Costa Rica). In Portuguese, it is *castanha* or *castanheiro de Africa.* In French, it is *arbre fricassé* or *arbre a fricasser* (Haiti); *yeux de crabe* or *ris de veau* (Martinique). In Surinam it is known as *akie.* On the Ivory Coast of West Africa, it is called *kaka* or *finzan;* in the Sudan, *finza.* Elsewhere in Africa it is generally known as *akye, akyen* or *ishin,* though it has many other dialectal names. In the timber trade, the wood is marketed as *achin.*

TOXICITY: 5

DEADLY PARTS: The cotyledons (the first, or "false" leaves of a plant) and the unopened, unripe fruit cause several deaths each year, and the overripe, rotten seed covering is just as poisonous as the unripe one. The fruit capsule and seeds are toxic, as is the water in which the fruit is cooked. However, the ripe fruit is fine.

EFFECTS AND SYMPTOMS: The poison causes hypoglycemia (low blood sugar characterized by irritability, profuse sweating, gnawing hunger, and headache). In more severe cases, nausea and vomiting begin two hours after ingestion. The victim then appears symptom-free for several hours before low blood sugar, fall of blood pressure, coma, and death occur. Convulsions occur in 85 percent of fatal cases.

REACTION TIME: Symptoms may occur within two hours or take more than a day to appear. Death can occur twenty-four hours after eating.

ANTIDOTES AND TREATMENTS: Besides gastric lavage and symptomatic treatment, intravenous glucose is important because of the severe hypoglycemia.

An autopsy will usually find hemorrhages in the brain due to the convulsions and breaking of blood vessels.

The akee was reportedly brought to Jamaica in 1793 by the Captain Bligh (mutiny on the *Bounty*) to feed the slaves. Originally from western Africa; it migrated to Cuba, Jamaica, Puerto Rico, Haiti, Florida, and Hawaii.

It is now popular, in small amounts, as a juice and health food.

CASSAVA

SCIENTIFIC NAME: *Manihot esculenta* Crantz, *M. utilissima.*

OTHER: Bitter cassava, tapioca yuca, juca, sweet potato plant, manioc tapioca, mandioc.

TOXICITY: 5

DEADLY PARTS: The greatest danger occurs when the plant is improperly prepared. The raw root and peelings from the tubers have high concentrations of prussic acid sufficient to cause death from cyanide poisoning.

The tubers are the primary source of poison, but the leaves contain variable amounts. The poison, amygdalin, breaks down into hydrocyanic acid, which can cause cyanide poisoning. There is no danger if the plant is cooked correctly.

EFFECTS AND SYMPTOMS: Severe gastroenteritis, including nausea and vomiting; respiratory distress; twitching; staggering; convulsions; coma; and death.

REACTION TIME: The AMA lists "some hours"; *Plants That Poison,* by Ervin M. Schmutz, lists death within minutes.

ANTIDOTES AND TREATMENTS: Gastric lavage and symptomatic treatment.

NOTES: Popular in tropical parts of the Americas, it is found in Brazil and other warm climates, too. The plant is edible only after cooking. Bitter cassava should not be confused with sweet cassava. Both have cyanide, but bitter cassava has more.

ELDERBERRY

SCIENTIFIC NAME: *Sambucus canadensis, S. racemosa.*

OTHER: American elderberry, black elder, red-berried elder.

TOXICITY: 4

DEADLY PARTS: Although cooked elderberries are safely eaten in jam and pies, the leaves, shoots, bark, roots, and raw berries are poisonous.

EFFECTS AND SYMPTOMS: Dizziness, headache, nausea, vomiting, stomach cramps, gastroenteritis, respiratory difficulty, convulsions, tachycardia, and possible death. The

American Medical Association says it has found no documented cases of cyanide poisoning from this plant, but other sources disagree.

REACTION TIME: Several hours.

ANTIDOTES AND TREATMENTS: Gastric lavage and symptomatic treatment.

NOTES: It is found in the northeastern and central United States and Canada, in woods, uncultivated areas and garbage dumps, and along streams. It reaches heights of six to twelve feet. The poison found in the plant is cyanogenic glycoside which causes cyanide poisoning. The ripe fruit, as used in elderberry wine, is harmless when cooked.

MANDRAKE

SCIENTIFIC NAME: *Mandragora officinarum*

OTHER: Devil's apple, loveapple, mayapple

TOXICITY: 4

DEADLY PARTS: The roots, stem, flower, leaves, and unripe fruit. When completely ripe (yellow and soft), the fruit can be safely eaten in small amounts. The plant contains several hallucinogenic alkaloids, including *hyoscyamine* (atropine) and *mandragorin*.

EFFECTS AND SYMPTOMS: Primary symptoms are severe diarrhea with vomiting, heavy sedation, coma, and death. The atropine, which is also used as a medical antidote and in surgery, tends to dry up the body fluids, decreasing gastric juices and shutting down the intestines. Mandrake also causes pupil dilation, paralysis of the eye muscles, delirium, pain, amnesia, and depresses the central nervous system causing slowed heart rate, coma, and death.

REACTION TIME: A few minutes to a half-hour.

ANTIDOTES AND TREATMENTS: Gastric lavage and symptomatic treatment.

NOTES: Found mainly in the Middle East, the yellow plum like fruit ripens during wheat harvest time, and smells sickeningly sweet.

In biblical times, mandrake was believed to be a fertility drug. In the Middle Ages, mandrake was famous as a love-potion and was used in incantations and considered a charm against evil spirits. Others believed elves would find its strange odor unbearable.

The mandrake has a large root, dark brown and rugged, resembling, to some, the male organ. According to superstition, it would kill a man to touch it fresh, and so a dog was used to pull it out of the ground. Supposedly, the mandrake would shriek and the dog would die.

Mandrake is now regarded as an anesthetic, cathartic, emetic, hypnotic, narcotic, and sedative.

Part of the mandrake family is mayapple (*Podophyllum pelaturn*), which causes severe gastroenteritis, headache, giddiness, and collapse. The poison is especially potent when combined with alcohol, and death can occur in fourteen hours. The taste is rather bitter. Workers handling the root often develop dermatitis. The oil is used externally for removing warts.

CASE HISTORY

In 1630 in Hamburg, Germany, three women were executed for possession of mandrake root, supposed evidence that they were involved in witchcraft.

MOUNTAIN MAHOGANY

SCIENTIFIC NAME: *Cercocarpus Montanus*

TOXICITY: 3

DEADLY PARTS: All parts of the tree are dangerous. The plant contains concentrations of cyanide. But the plant is often below dangerous level except when there is wilting or bruising of the leaves.

EFFECTS AND SYMPTOMS: Initial symptoms are difficulty in breathing as oxygen depletes. Excessive salivation, nervousness, and weakness precede death. Mucous membranes appear pink and redder than normal, and collapse and death quickly follows. The amount of poison taken in also depends on prior food ingestion, which can buffer the poison.

Autopsy shows venous blood is cherry red in color.

REACTION TIME: Signs may start within five minutes, and death can occur within fifteen minutes.

ANTIDOTES AND TREATMENTS: Treatment with sodium thiosulphate is sometimes effective in traditional cyanide poisoning.

NOTES: A member of the rose family, *C.montanus* is not related to the hardwood except in name. Found in Texas, Kansas, South Dakota, Arizona, Montana, and Florida, it grows on ledges and in rocky areas.

MOONSEED

SCIENTIFIC NAME: *Menispermum canadense.*

OTHER: Yellow parilla.

TOXICITY: 5

DEADLY PARTS: The bluish black fruit resembles the wild grape. It is poisonous because it contains alkaloids that make it a central nervous system stimulant. The leaves are also dangerous. The pits, with their sharp ridges, cause mechanical injury and bleeding in the intestines.

EFFECTS AND SYMPTOMS: Bloody diarrhea, convulsions, and shock, followed by death.

REACTION TIME: Several hours.

ANTIDOTES AND TREATMENTS: Gastric lavage and symptomatic treatment.

NOTES: Moonseed is a woody, smooth-stem vine found on the banks of streams and in thickets in the eastern United States and Canada. It is grown artificially in other parts of North America.

The roots are bitter. Several cases of poisoning have occurred from mistaking the plant for wild grapes.

A close relative, also called moonseed (*Cocculus ferrandianus*), is native to Hawaii and used as a fish poison.

NUTMEG

SCIENTIFIC NAME: *Myristica fragrans* (nutmeg), *M. argentea* (Papuan nutmeg), *M. malabarcia* (Bombay nutmeg).

TOXICITY: 3

DEADLY PARTS: Seeds of the tree.

EFFECTS AND SYMPTOMS: Doses of 1 gram or more produce visual disturbances and mild euphoria; 5 grams can cause dry mouth, fast pulse, fever, flushing; 7.5 grams or more can cause convulsions, palpitations, nausea, dehydration, and generalized body pain. Large quantities can cause nutmeg psychosis, which may require hospitalization. This is an acute psychiatric disorder that causes confusion, hallucinations, agitation, and the feeling that death is inevitably coming soon. Nutmeg has been abused by teens wanting a high.

If injected intravenously, it is very toxic and can cause liver damage. It can be fatal if used regularly in large quantities because the drug is cumulative.

REACTION TIME: About six hours after ingestion; effects can linger up to three days.

ANTIDOTES AND TREATMENTS: No specific antidote. Adverse effects wear off in approximately three days, but palliative treatment is often needed.

NOTES: There are several different varieties. One version is found in tropical Asia, Australasia, the Banda Islands of Indonesia, Zanzibar, and Grenada (Caribbean). Another grows in New Guinea and in Bombay, Malaysia, Sri Lanka, and St. Vincent (Caribbean).

The spices nutmeg and mace come from this plant.

Nutmeg is the egg-shaped seed of the tree, and mace is the dried lacy reddish covering of the seed. Traditionally it is found in cider and mulled wine and Indian sweets. The colorless or light yellow oil is also used in the perfume, cosmetic, and pharmaceutical industries and is used externally for rheumatic pain and for toothaches. Alternative medicine uses nutmeg for digestive system illnesses.

Highly prized in the Middle Ages, it was traded by Arabs as a costly spice. In Elizabethan times, it was believed that nutmeg warded off the plague, and a few nutmeg nuts might make one's fortune. In the seventeenth century, the Dutch dominated the nutmeg trade—after they massacred many of the Bamda Island inhabitants in 1621. During the Napoleonic Wars, the British took control of the Islands and planted the trees in Zanzibar and Grenada.

"Wooden nutmeg," a term that came to mean fraud, came about when traders in Connecticut (the Nutmeg State) whittled "nutmeg" out of wood.

Nutmeg contains chemicals used in MAO inhibitors and has a similar chemical makeup to MDMA (ecstasy) but has not made it as a recreational drug because of its strong taste and sandpaper texture.

PASSION FLOWER

SCIENTIFIC NAME: *Adeapnia volkensii, A. digitata.*

OTHER: Passion vine, apricot vine, maypop, maracuja.

TOXICITY: 6

DEADLY PARTS: All parts.

EFFECTS AND SYMPTOMS: Drowsiness, lethargy, and weakness increasing to paralysis and followed by death. The plant is a cortical depressant working on the higher centers of the brain. Minute quantities of *A. digitata* are sufficient to cause death. In smaller amounts it works as a sedative.

REACTION TIME: Fifteen minutes to one hour before symptoms are felt.

ANTIDOTES AND TREATMENTS: Treatments are gastric lavage and symptomatic.

NOTES: Cultivated in the Caribbean, Hawaii, Virginia, and south Florida for fruit and juice, passion flowers are native to tropical and subtropical regions of the Americas and Africa. Maypop, another American variety with an edible apricot, is seen the southern United States. In Japan, they are clock-faced flowers, and have recently become a symbol for homosexual youths.

The flower contains hallucinogens and MAO inhibitors (used for depression) and enhances the effects of mind-altering drugs.

The stems exude sticky fluid, which many insects get stuck on.

The Mau Mau used it in their oathing ceremonies, and other tribes used this plant as poison hyena bait. Native Americans in both Central and North America have used the herb to treat insomnia, hysteria, high blood pressure, and epilepsy, as well as pain. In small doses, its narcotic properties can be used for diarrhea, dysentery, neuralgia, anxiety, sleeplessness and dysmenorrhea (painful menstruation.)

The name comes from Spanish Christian missionaries who felt that the flower looked like the Crucifixion and the crown of thorns, reminding them of the Passion of Christ.

RHUBARB

SCIENTIFIC NAME: *Rheum rhaponticum.*

OTHER: Pie plant.

TOXICITY: 4

DEADLY PARTS: The leaves contain oxalic acid and potassium and calcium oxalates, as well as a variety of other poisons. The leaves, in most varieties, are the only poisonous part of the plant and must be removed before cooking or eating.

EFFECTS AND SYMPTOMS: If a person unwittingly cooks the leaf blades in with the rhubarb, the digestive irritant may cause stomach pains, nausea, vomiting, bleeding from the nose and eyes, weakness, difficulty breathing, burning of mouth and throat, kidney irritation, and anuria, which then leads to a drop in the calcium content of the blood and cardiac or respiratory arrest.

REACTION TIME: Several hours.

ANTIDOTES AND TREATMENTS: Gastric lavage along with encouraging vomiting. Calcium in any form (even milk or lime water) will help to precipitate the oxalate. Calcium salts and calcium gluconate are often given along with extra fluids and supportive care.

NOTES: Originally from Asia, it is now frequently seen in many gardens of the northern United States and Canada and southward to Hawaii.

CASE HISTORY

The *Gardeners' Chronicle* of 1847 records that some people became quite ill after eating the young plants, and mentions a case of severe sickness attacking a whole family after they devoured the boiled leaves.

In 1901, a man died, according to the report of the local coroner, because he ate stewed rhubarb leaves. Verdict at the inquest stated: "Accidental death, caused by eating rhubarb leaves."

The *British Medical Journal* in December, 1910, mentions several cases of rhubarb poisoning.

PLANTS USED FOR MEDICINAL PURPOSES

BRYONY OR WHITE BRYONY

SCIENTIFIC NAME: *Bryonia dioica, B. alba, B. cretica.*

OTHER: Devil's turnip, British mandrake, wild vine, wild hops, wild nep, tamus, ladies' seal, tetterbury, navet du diable (French).

TOXICITY: 4

DEADLY PARTS: The berries and roots contain glycosides, bryonin, and bryonidin.

EFFECTS AND SYMPTOMS: Burning of the mouth after ingestion; nausea; and vomiting. The juice is an irritant and blisters the skin. Other symptoms include violent diarrhea, dehydration, convulsions, paralysis, coma, and death resulting from respiratory arrest.

REACTION TIME: Several hours.

ANTIDOTES AND TREATMENTS: Gastric lavage and keeping the victim warm and quiet. Demulcents such as milk and eggs are given to coat the stomach. Fluids and extra electrolytes are administered as needed. Pain medications are often used.

NOTES: Bryony is a common climbing plant with vine-shaped leaves that are very rough to the touch, with short, prickly hairs and pale scarlet berries. It is found in Wales and southern England, and sometimes as far north as Yorkshire, as well as in most of central and southern Europe.

The berries are filled with a juice that has an obnoxious odor. The greenish yellow flowers bloom in May. There are eight varieties in Europe.

When the berries are distilled like an alcohol, the drink can cause abortions. The bitter juice is nauseating and causes violent vomiting. The ripe fruit is a red berry with a dull surface containing flat, black-and-yellow mottled seeds. The whole plant, but especially the root, has an acrid milky juice, the unpleasant odor of which persists after dying. The thick, fleshy, white roots can become quite large and are often mistaken for parsnips or turnips or even mandrake. Medically, it can be used as a diuretic.

It is still considered useful in small doses for cough, influenza, bronchitis, and pneumonia and has also been recommended for pleurisy and whooping cough, relieving the pain and allaying the cough.

Under the name of wild nepit, the plant was known in the fourteenth century as an antidote to leprosy. Bartholomew's *Anglicus* tells us that Augustus Caesar wore a wreath of bryony during a thunderstorm to protect himself from lightning.

CINCHONA BARK

SCIENTIFIC NAME: *Cinchona ledgeriana.*

OTHER: Peruvian bark, quinine bark, quina, quinine, kinakina, China bark, cinchona bark, yellow cinchona, red cinchona, Jesuit's bark, quina-quina, calisaya bark, fever tree.

TOXICITY: 4

DEADLY PARTS: The bark, but the wood has some poison in it.

EFFECTS AND SYMPTOMS: Nausea, vomiting, hemorrhage, headache, tinnitus, deafness, giddiness, collapse, visual disturbances, coma, death from paralysis with respiratory arrest. Ingestion or injection of large doses causes sudden onset of cardiac depression or heart failure.

REACTION TIME: Several hours.

ANTIDOTES AND TREATMENTS: Gastric lavage; also, the falling blood pressure is treated by injection of norepinephrine.

NOTES: The poison conatined in the plant is quinoline or quinine. Cinchonas produce white, pink, or yellow flowers and grow naturally on the mountain slopes in South America as well as in cultivation in tropical countries like India, Java, East Africa, and Australia. The bitter flavoring is popular in many drinks. Cinchona bark is also used for treatment of fevers.

Methods of harvesting the bark are very similar to those from the sixteenth century. The peeling bark is dried after removal from the tree, which then regenerates several times before the quality begins to suffer. The tree is then replaced by a new one.

It is still used as an abortifacient in third-world countries.

CASE HISTORY

In 1971, a girl from a very strict family in Mexico took numerous quinine tablets, thinking she was pregnant. Six hours later, she suffered severe convulsions, causing respiratory distress, and died.

As early as the 1560s, the plant's curative powers were acknowledged. Legend has it named after the wife of the Spanish viceroy of Peru, the Countess of Chinchon, who, toward the end of the Thirty Years' War, was cured of malaria by this Spanish plant. By 1677, it was listed in the London Pharmacopoeia.

The bark caused controversy when King Charles II of England suffered from malaria. He had heard about a secret potion prepared by a Mr. Robert Talbor. The mixture cured him and the king awarded Talbor a physician's license. Shortly thereafter, the dauphin of France was taken ill with the disease, and Louis XIV summoned the physician with his mysterious formula. The prince was healed and the French monarch tried to find out what was in the elixir. Not until Talbor died was the recipe found in his papers. It consisted of rose leaves, lemon juice, and cinchona bark.

In the nineteenth century, the British and Dutch began smuggling the plants out of South America. The Dutch made whole plantations of the tree in Java, and the British followed suit in India and Ceylon. They were not as successful as the Dutch. By 1918, the Amsterdam headquarter's "kina burea" dominated world production.

In World War II, the Japanese occupied Java and cut off the quinine supply, so the attempt was made to grow the plants in South America again. Despite the fact that the plant originated there, it was not successful in returning. This prompted the development of the synthetic drug.

COLOCYNTH

SCIENTIFIC NAME: *Citrullus colocynthis.*

OTHER: Bitter apple, bitter cucumber, egusi, or vine of Sodom.

TOXICITY: 5

DEADLY PARTS: The pale, yellowish-green, bitter-tasting fruit is most deadly part.

EFFECTS AND SYMPTOMS: Blood-tinged diarrhea occurs on the first day, followed by cramps, headache, oliguria, kidney failure, and death. Death has resulted from a dose of one and a half teaspoonfuls of the powder.

REACTION TIME: Several hours.

ANTIDOTES AND TREATMENTS: Milk will relieve gastric irritation, and atropine will decrease the gastric secretions and work as a stimulant to counter the possible collapse. Pain medications are given as necessary. Victims who live for forty-eight hours will probably recover.

NOTES: Native to the Mediterranean Basin, especially Turkey and Asia, it is now found in Central America. Its lemon-sized, yellowish-green fruit has a bitter taste. A powerful liver stimulant, it also acts as a cathartic and abortifacient. Overdosing on the fruit causes dangerous inflammation with violent, sharp pains in the bowels.

CROTON OIL

SCIENTIFIC NAME: *Croton tiglium.*

OTHER: Mayapple, gamboge, purging croton.

TOXICITY: 6

DEADLY PARTS: Seeds and their extracted oil.

EFFECTS AND SYMPTOMS: A thick oil, it causes skin irritation and blistering when applied externally. This can last up to three weeks. Internally, croton oil produces burning pain in the mouth and stomach, bloody diarrhea, violent purging, tachycardia, coma, and death. Autopsy shows blood in the stool and some blood in the urine.

REACTION TIME: Immediately upon skin contact; within ten to fifteen minutes for ingestion.

ANTIDOTES AND TREATMENTS: Gastric lavage is said to be useless. There is symptomatic treatment of pain and kidney and liver damage. The victim is encouraged to drink as much as possible, and continuous intravenous infusion is used to correct the electrolyte imbalance caused by the fluid loss.

NOTES: Native to India and the Malay Archipelago, it is now found in the southwest United States.

Croton oil is easily identified if mixed with an equal amount of alcohol and shaken. A reddish-brown color forms at the junction of the two liquids. A diluted solution of oil will cause a blister within four hours. Because of its skin-peeling effects, croton oil has become the basis of rejuvenating chemicals, and, in combination with phenol, causes the skin to slough.

CASE HISTORY

In *East of Eden*, by Steinbeck, Faye was murdered using this poison.
It was used as a torture in the Civil War novel *Copperhead*.
John Wayne's film *El Dorado* used croton oil to sober up the drunken sheriff and teach him a lesson (pre-Antabuse—a drug for the treatment of alcoholism).

ERGOT

SCIENTIFIC NAME: *Claviceps purpurea.*

OTHER: Ergot of rye, sansert, St. Anthony's fire.

TOXICITY: 5

DEADLY PARTS: A fungus parasite that infests cereal grain, particularly rye, only a small amount is needed to be fatal. The alkaloids from the fungus disintegrate readily, and rye flour contaminated with the black fungus becomes less harmful toward spring. The poison stimulates the smooth muscles and exerts a paralyzing action on the sympathetic nervous system, which affects heart rate, kidney function, the lungs, and digestion.

EFFECTS AND SYMPTOMS: Nausea, vomiting, severe headaches, numbness, anuria, pulmonary infiltration (an opaque object in the lung that can be benign or cancerous, but in this case probably caused by the fungus), coma, respiratory or cardiac arrest, and death.

It causes the uterus to contract. Coldness of the extremities and a tingling chest pain are caused by the contraction of the blood vessels. Ingestion of the drug tends to cause painful convulsions and permanent contractions of muscles. Psychosis (violent mood swings) can also occur. Gangrene of fingers and toes results when poisoning occurs over several days.

It can also cause hyperexcitability, belligerence, ataxia, and staggering.

Nerve pain may start within two weeks after ergot is first ingested. There may be pain, stamping of the feet, and coolness of the affected areas. If ergot consumption

---

continues, numbness overwhelms the affected areas and a sunken line appears between normal tissue and the dry gangrenous tissue.

REACTION TIME: Several days to weeks.

ANTIDOTES AND TREATMENTS: Amyl nitrate is often used to relieve spasms. Gastric lavage should be followed by activated charcoal.

NOTES: The fungus parasite *Claviceps purpurea* mostly occurs on rye but can be in numerous other plants (wheat, barley oat, etc.). It originated in Europe but is now almost everywhere. The taste of the fungus is fishy.

The drug from the plant parasite is frequently found in obstetrical departments as it helps the uterus contract to normal size. Ergot was used in the seventeenth century by midwives for the same purpose. Ergot is also used on migraine headaches and to relieve the pain of herpes zoster.

North Dakota and Britain have yearly outbreaks despite the screening of cereals for fungus.

Poisoning through ergot can be cumulative.

CASE HISTORY

In the Middle Ages, the disease process caused by ergot often reached epidemic proportions. In 944 A.D., forty thousand people died from ergot poisoning in France. Known as *mal des ardents, feu de Saint-Antoine*, and *gangrene des Solognots*, it appeared in two forms: gangrenous (affecting the lower limbs especially) and convulsive (with hallucinations and sometimes paralysis). Legend has it that only those who prayed to St. Anthony survived, but the true reason they lived was that they were taken to a monastery to be healed while they prayed and were fed bread without ergot.

FOXGLOVE

SCIENTIFIC NAME: *Digitalis purpurea, D. lanata.*

OTHER: Fairy cap, fairy bells, fairy glove, fairy finger, fairy thimbles, witches' gloves, dead men's bells, gloves of Our Lady, bloody fingers, virgin's glove, folk's glove, *revbielde* (Norwegian), *fingerhut* (German).

TOXICITY: 6

DEADLY PARTS: All parts of the plant are toxic, but the leaves are especially so. The leaves contain digitalin, digitoxin, and digitonin. Severe poisoning comes from eating the leaves—either dried or fresh—which do not lose their poison when cooked.

EFFECTS AND SYMPTOMS: Headache, nausea, vomiting, diarrhea, blurred vision, delirium, slow or irregular pulse, inaccurate color vision, high rise in blood pressure, and death, usually from ventricular fibrillation (very fast, irregular heart rhythm in the lower chambers of the heart). Digitalis is used as a heart medication that helps slow heart rate.

REACTION TIME: Twenty to thirty minutes.

ANTIDOTES AND TREATMENTS: Gastric lavage is followed by activated charcoal. Victims must be monitored constantly by electrocardiogram. Potassium chloride is given every hour unless urine output stops. Potassium level must also be monitored to avoid hyperkalemia (elevated levels of potassium in the blood) and cardiac arrest.

NOTES: Cultivated in gardens despite its unpleasant odor, foxglove, with its purple and white flowers, is frequently found in early summer growing wild in the north central and northeastern United States, along the Pacific Coast, and in Hawaii, as well as in much of Europe. In Great Britain, it grows freely by roadsides, in woods, in crevices of granite walls, in hilly pastures, and in rocky places, especially in coastal counties of England.

The taste of both fresh and dried leaves is bitter. The fruit has numerous poisonous seeds. Children have been poisoned by sucking on the flowers and swallowing the seeds

Most poisonings are from therapeutic overdoses rather than from homicidal or suicidal intent.

Digitalis (foxglove's drug) is an antidote in monkshood poisoning.

CASE HISTORY

Dr. Edmond de la Pommerais was the son of a French country doctor with pretensions to the title of count. His medical practice gave him only modest support, so in 1861 he married the rich Madamoiselle Dubisy. With that money, he maintained his mistress, Seraphine de Pawr. He insured de Pawr's life for over a half-million francs. She planned to feign illness and scare the insurance company into paying an annuity as a price for canceling the policy.

According to plan, De Pawr became ill but died. Her diagnosis was cholera, said her physician lover, but the insurance company was suspicious since he had also insured his mother-in-law, who had just died. Madame de Pawr's body was exhumed. It was discovered that she had been given a massive dose of digitalis, as had the mother-in-law.

The doctor was tried for the double murder and guillotined in 1864.

INDIAN TOBACCO

SCIENTIFIC NAME: *Lobelia inflata.*

OTHER: Eyebright, bladderpod, asthma weed, lobelia.

TOXICITY: 5

DEADLY PARTS: All, especially the milky juice. The poisons are lobeline and related alkaloids. Touching leaves, stems, or fruits is a frequent cause of skin rash.

EFFECTS AND SYMPTOMS: Nausea, vomiting, exhaustion, prostration, dilation of pupils, stupor, coma, convulsion, and death. Similar to nicotine poisoning. Convulsions lead to death by respiratory failure.

REACTION TIME: One to several hours.

ANTIDOTES AND TREATMENTS: Gastric lavage is done and valium is given for convulsions. Artificial respiration may be needed. Atropine is an antidote if given in time.

NOTES: Found in uncultivated woodlands and on roadsides, it is common to Connecticut and other parts of the northeastern United States. It grows in the Midwest but thins out until it reaches the Pacific Coast. Then it is again seen abundantly in California and Oregon at elevations up to four thousand feet. The plant grows in much of Canada in the same pattern. Aboriginal Indians smoked its dried leaves but quickly found that it destroyed the lung more than regular tobacco.

Red, white, and blue flowers identify the plant, as do the inflated seedpods.

Medically, Indian tobacco is used in the treatment of laryngitis and spasmodic asthma. Overdoses act as narcotic poisons and lead to fatalities.

Eyebright is one of the herbs from the plant.

IPECAC

SCIENTIFIC NAME: *Cephaelis ipecacuanha.*

OTHER: Emetine.

TOXICITY: 5

DEADLY PARTS: The berries and juice of the plant are the most toxic.

EFFECTS AND SYMPTOMS: The nausea and vomiting caused by the plant's juices was used in medicine to rid victims of poison, but an overdose will lead to fatigue, difficulty breathing, tachycardia, low blood pressure, convulsions, collapse, loss of consciousness, and kidney and liver damage, which means problems with painful and bloody urination, and death from heart failure.

Emetine, the alkaloid extracted from the plant, weakens the heart. The cumulative effect stretches over a month or more; so a fictional killer can use chronic poisoning.

The poison, when given by injection, kills tissue. Vomiting often interferes with oral absorption.

An autopsy shows congestion of stomach and intestine (where fluids build up or back up due to an increase or blockage) and degenerative changes in the liver, kidneys, and heart.

REACTION TIME: Immediate. Death may be delayed twenty-four hours to one week. Recovery may take as long as one year.

ANTIDOTES AND TREATMENTS: Gastric lavage, followed by morphine and complete bed rest.

NOTES: Used as an emetic in syrup form to rid the stomach of poisons, it is still found in many households even though its use is no longer recommended.

The fluid extract from the plant is fourteen times more potent than the syrup sold over the counter and should never be used as a substitute for the syrup.

TANSY

SCIENTIFIC NAME: *Tanacetum vulgare.*

OTHER: Bitter button, cow bitter, golden button, and mugwort.

TOXICITY: 5

DEADLY PARTS: The leaves, flowers, and stem contain the toxic oil tanacetin.

EFFECTS AND SYMPTOMS: Convulsions, frothing at the mouth, dilated pupils, rapid and weak pulse, vomiting, uterine bleeding, kidney problems, and death. Dermatitis (rash) is also caused by touching the plant.

REACTION TIME: Several hours.

ANTIDOTES AND TREATMENTS: Gastric lavage and symptomatic treatment.

NOTES: Commonly associated with witchcraft in the Middle Ages, the bitter-tasting herb grows by the roadsides and is often found in uncultivated peat woodlands and sometimes pastures. Native to Europe, it's now found throughout the eastern United States as well as in the Pacific Northwest.

Oil of tansy is used to kill intestinal worms, to cause menstruation to begin, and as an abortifacient. Humans are often poisoned by taking overdoses of oil or tea made from the leaves.

PLANTS THAT FLOWER

BLACK HELLEBORE

SCIENTIFIC NAME: *Helleborus niger.*

OTHER: Christmas rose, Christe herbe, melampode.

TOXICITY: 6

DEADLY PARTS: The entire plant is poisonous, but especially the roots.

EFFECTS AND SYMPTOMS: The poison has a blistering effect on the mucous membranes of the mouth, and causes severe diarrhea, vomiting, and death from cardiac arrest.

REACTION TIME: Symptoms begin within thirty minutes, but death may take several hours.

ANTIDOTES AND TREATMENTS: Cardiac and respiratory stimulants such as amyl nitrate, strychnine, and atropine are often used.

NOTES: Black hellebore is from the buttercup family and grows in the woods and mountain regions of central and southern Europe (especiallyin Germany, from where many of the roots are imported), Greece and Asia Minor. In the northern United States and Canada it is cultivated as a garden plant. It contains the poisons helleborein, hellebrin, helleborin, saponins, and protoamemonie.

This name black hellebore is because of the dark color of its roots. Traditionally used in magic and witchcraft rituals, the herb is associated with Saturn, water, and Mars, and is used for banishing and in necromancy.

The ancient Greek soothsayer and physician Melampus, 1400 BCE, used tincture of black hellebore (minute amounts) as a purgative for mental illness and mania (since it is a CNS depressent) or to slow a rapid heart. In larger doses it causes death by convulsions and heart failure.

The general name of this plant is derived from the Greek *elein* (to injure) and *bora* (food).

CASE HISTORY

In 1987, a patient came to a Los Angeles emergency room complaining of stomach pains and vomiting. No reason could be found for his distress, however, and he went away. He returned several hours later complaining he could not feel his arms. Before the nurse could check him out, he went into convulsions and died. Only later was it discovered that he had been poisoned with hellebore by a friend, who was angry that the young man had given him AIDS.

BLACK LOCUST

SCIENTIFIC NAME: *Robinia pseudoacacia.*

OTHER: Bastard acacia, black acacia, false acacia, pea flower locust.

TOXICITY: 5

DEADLY PARTS: Inner bark, seeds, and leaves.

EFFECTS AND SYMPTOMS: The poison interferes with synthesis of protein in the intestine. Vomiting, diarrhea, stupor, slowed heartbeat, weakened pulse, gastroenteritis, coldness of arms and legs, various features of shock, possible convulsions, and death can all occur.

REACTION TIME: One hour.

ANTIDOTES AND TREATMENTS: Gastric lavage and symptomatic treatment.

NOTES: The poison contained in black locust is robin, a phototoxin. Found in all of temperate United States, Canada, Europe, and Asia. Children are especially susceptible if they chew on the poisonous parts of the plant.

BLOODROOT

SCIENTIFIC NAME: *Sanguinaria canadensis.*

OTHER: Indian paint, tetterwort, red pucoon, red root, paucon, coon root, snakebite, sweet slumber.

TOXICITY: 4

DEADLY PARTS: All. Contact with the red sap may cause skin rashes. The poison is sanguinarine.

EFFECTS AND SYMPTOMS: The poison reduces the heart's action and muscle strength and depresses the nerves. Death occurs from overdoses after violent vomiting, extreme thirst, intense esophageal burning and pain, heaviness of the chest with labored breathing, dilation of pupils, faintness, coldness of skin, and cardiac paralysis. Painful irritation occurs when the prickles enter the skin.

REACTION TIME: One to two hours.

ANTIDOTES AND TREATMENTS: Gastric lavage and symptomatic treatment.

NOTES: The herb bloodroot displays a white waxy flower with yellow stamens. It has thick roots and orange-red juice. There is little smell and the taste is bitter and acrid; powdered root causes sneezing and irritation of the nose and, unless stored in dry cool places, the poison deteriorates quickly.

It is found in North America south to Florida and west to Arkansas, Texas and Nebraska, and in Canada's woodlands.

CUCKOOPINT

SCIENTIFIC NAME: *Arum maculatum.*

OTHER: Adam and Eve, lords-and-ladies, wild arum, wake-robin, Jack-in-the-pulpit.

TOXICITY: 5

DEADLY PARTS: All. The sweet-tasting berries are the most poisonous, but the sour leaves, flowers, and roots also have poison.

EFFECTS AND SYMPTOMS: Blistering, severe gastroenteritis, hemorrhages, convulsions, dilation of pupils, coma, and death.

REACTION TIME: Blistering occurs fairly rapidly, but the other symptoms may take several hours to appear.

ANTIDOTES AND TREATMENTS: No immediate treatment is known; however, obstructed breathing caused by swelling of the pharynx can be treated.

NOTES: The poisons containted in cuckoopint are aroin, which is related to coniine (hemlock), and calcium oxalate.

Starting in northern Africa and southern Europe, it migrated to England. In southern states, Jack-in-the-pulpit (*Arisaema atroubens*), is seen as a common houseplant.

The flower and red fruits grow to about ten inches long. The root sap has a bitter taste to it.

DOG MERCURY

SCIENTIFIC NAME: *Mercurialis perennis, M. annua.*

OTHER: Herb mercury.

TOXICITY: 4

DEADLY PARTS: All. The poison is mercurialine or oil of Euphorbia.

EFFECTS AND SYMPTOMS: Dog mercury acts as an emetic and purgative. Irritant and narcotic symptoms also appear. The poison is cumulative in its effect, and death can result from depressing of the heart's action.

REACTION TIME: Several hours.

ANTIDOTES AND TREATMENTS: Gastric lavage and symptomatic treatment.

NOTES: The plants are poisonous when eaten fresh, but not when dried or boiled, because heat kills the poison. The fresh plant has a disagreeable odor and an acid flavor.

The creeping root has numerous undivided stems and grows in woods and shady places throughout Russia, Asia, Europe, and Britain, as well as in wooded areas in the eastern United States.

CASE HISTORY

During the Depression era, some folks tried making a soup of this plant, with fatal results.

FALSE HELLEBORE

SCIENTIFIC NAME: *Veratrum alba, V. viride, V. californicum.*

TOXICITY: 5

DEADLY PARTS: All but the roots have high poison concentrations.

EFFECTS AND SYMPTOMS: The main symptoms from ingestion of large amounts are nausea and severe vomiting and a roller coaster of blood pressure levles, creating dizziness, visual disturbances, and severe headaches. Other symptoms are diarrhea, muscular weakness, slowing of pulse (down to thirty or fewer beats per minute), and, as the blood pressure lowers, the victim goes into shock and dies.

Repeated use of small doses may produce tolerance to the blood-pressure-lowering effect, but not to the raising effect.

REACTION TIME: Within twenty minutes.

ANTIDOTES AND TREATMENTS: Gastric lavage and symptomatic treatment.

NOTES: Related to death camas; both are members of the lily family.

Not as toxic as black hellebore, it has nevertheless caused fatalities.

The medication made from the plant helps with muscular spasms and neuropathy, and in the past, false hellebore was used against high blood pressure and rapid heartbeat.

Widely spread, considered a pest plant by farmers because it is so toxic to animals, it is found in wet woods and swamps. Green false hellebore, one of the varieties, is found in the west in Alaska through the Olympic, Cascade, and Rocky mountains down to northern California. In the east, its range is Georgia north to Labrador.

HYDRANGEA

SCIENTIFIC NAME: *Hydrangea macrophylla.*

OTHER: Hortensia, hills of snow.

TOXICITY: 5

DEADLY PARTS: All, especially the flower buds. The poison, hydrangin, is a cyanogenetic glycoside.

EFFECTS AND SYMPTOMS: Gastroenteritis, and symptoms of cyanide poisoning (see chapter three, page 25).

REACTION TIME: Several hours for symptoms to occur.

ANTIDOTES AND TREATMENTS: Gastric lavage and symptomatic treatment.

NOTES: Hydrangea is an extremely poisonous plant that is available throughout the Americas and Asia, including China, Japan, the Himalayas, and Indonesia.

LARKSPUR

SCIENTIFIC NAME: *Delphinium consolida, D. alpinum.*

TOXICITY: 6

DEADLY PARTS: All; however, the young leaves, eaten before the plant has flowered, and the mature seeds contain concentrated doses of toxic alkaloids. The poison decreases with the plant's age.

EFFECTS AND SYMPTOMS: Another member of the buttercup family, larkspur produces symptoms similar to monkshood poisoning, including slowing of the heartbeat, burning in the mouth, dermatitis, nausea, vomiting, respiratory distress, itching, cyanosis, and death.

REACTION TIME: Symptoms begin immediately and death may occur in six hours.

ANTIDOTES AND TREATMENTS: Symptomatic treatment is given. There is no specific antidote aside from gastric lavage, oxygen to assist with breathing, and drugs to stimulate the heart.

NOTES: Larkspur kills many livestock. The blue bud is thought to look like a fat dolphin.

Delphinium, the buttercup family, has approximately 250 species and is often found in the Northern Hemisphere—both in Europe and North America, as well as on the high mountains of tropical Africa. Baker's larkspur (*Delphinium bakeri*) and yellow larkspur (*D. luteum*), are native to certain areas of California and are highly endangered species.

NARCISSUS

SCIENTIFIC NAME: *Narcissus poeticus.*

OTHER: Poets' narcissus, pheasant's eye, daffodil.

TOXICITY: 5

DEADLY PARTS: All, especially the bulbs, which are powerful emetics.

EFFECTS AND SYMPTOMS: Nausea, severe vomiting for several hours, colic, tetanic convulsions (where the muscle contraction is sustained) fainting, paralysis, and death.

Juice from bulbs, when applied to open wounds, has produced staggering, and numbness of the whole nervous system as well as paralysis of the heart.

The bulbs of the poet's narcissus (*N. poeticus*) are a powerful stomach irritant and emetic. The flower scent, especially in a closed room, is said to produce headache and vomiting.

REACTION TIME: Several hours to a few days.

ANTIDOTES AND TREATMENTS: Gastric lavage and symptomatic treatment.

NOTES: Skin rashes occur in growers and others engaged in handling.

The jonquil (*N. jonquilla*) and daffodil (*N. pseudonarcissus*) are varieties of narcissus. All are grown as garden flowers.

First grown by the Romans in Europe (southwestern and central) as well as North Africa, it is popular in Britain, especially in the Channel Islands and Isles of Scilly off the Cornish coast, and is also popular in American gardens.

> **CASE HISTORY**
>
> During World War II, a four-year-old girl in the Isle of Jersey died from sucking the juice from the flower's stem.

PEACOCK FLOWER

SCIENTIFIC NAME: *Caesalpinia pulcherrima*.

OTHER: Peacock flower, Barbados pride, dwarf poinciana, Barbados flower-fence.

TOXICITY: 6

DEADLY PARTS: Seeds.

EFFECTS AND SYMPTOMS: Nausea, vomiting, abdominal distress, and dehydration leading to blurred vision, low blood pressure, and collapse.

REACTION TIME: Symptoms start within minutes.

ANTIDOTES AND TREATMENT: Gastric lavage and supportive therapy.

NOTES: Used to poison criminals—and fish—in the islands around Barbados, the peacock flower is native to tropical America (southern Florida and Central America in Guatemala and Panama). The flower blossoms with showy orange and red flowers.

Many in Africa eat the seeds, but only after the seeds are boiled several times over.

YELLOW JASMINE

SCIENTIFIC NAME: *Gelsemium sempervirens*.

OTHER: Yellow jessamine, Carolina jasmine, Carolina yellow jasmine, evening trumpet flower, Carolina wild woodbine.

TOXICITY: 5

DEADLY PARTS: All.

EFFECTS AND SYMPTOMS: A teaspoonful of the juice is toxic and produces vertigo, tremors, giddiness, double vision, headache, droopy eyelids, dilated pupils, labored breathing, slow and feeble heartbeat, dropped jaw, staggering gait, profuse sweats, loss of articulation, sustained muscle contraction, great muscle weakness, almost complete general anaesthesia, and death by asphyxia (paralysis of muscles of respiration). Consciousness is preserved until near the end.

In death, the pupils are completely dilated and fixed and the face takes on a mask-like expression.

In moderate doses, it causes languor, slowing of the cardiac rate, weakness, impaired senses, lowering of the body temperature, drooping eyelids, and dilated pupils, with some sweating that can last approximately three hours.

REACTION TIME: At high doses, death occurs in ten minutes; at low doses, after several hours.

ANTIDOTES AND TREATMENTS: Gastric lavage, encouraging vomiting, and symptomatic treatment including morphine for pain and digitalis to stimulate the heart.

NOTES: Yellow jasmine fragrance is overpowering. Native to the South, from the eastern part of Virginia to Florida and Texas, the plant is found along the banks of streams; in woods, lowlands, and thickets; and generally near the coast. In fact it can be found everywhere except cold places. The poisons in the plant are gelsemine, gelsemicine, and related alkaloids, which also come as volatile oils and resins.

The drug is used, mainly in liquid form, against trigeminal neuralgia (jaw-nerve pain).

MISCELLANEOUS PLANT POISONS

AFRICAN MILK PLANT

SCIENTIFIC NAME: *Euphorbia lactea*

OTHER: Sodom apple.

DEADLY PARTS: All parts when ingested, but especially the juice when the pods split open. Skin irritation results from handling.

TOXICITY: 6

EFFECTS AND SYMPTOMS: Skin irritation within minutes of handling the plant (burning, redness, blisters, swelling); damage to skin and eyes following contact with milky latex. Ingestion causes irritation of lips, tongue, and throat, delirium, convulsions, and death. The natural resin has digitalis-like compounds that affect the heart.

REACTION TIME: Within several minutes.

ANTIDOTES AND TREATMENT: Gastric lavage and symptomatic treatment.

NOTES: Several varieties of the Euphorbia family (*E. candelabrum, E. grantii, E. neglecta, E. giomgiecpstata, E. systyloides, E. tirucalli*) are found all over Africa. African milk plant is a cactus-like plant with spines. When the spine is broken, the poisonous juice comes out. In west Africa, where the plant originated, it was reportedly used by women to rid themselves of evil husbands. Some versions of the plant are used medicinally (*E. neglecta, E. systyloides*) for complaints such as hookworms, while others (*E. candelabrum)* are used for fish poisons and arrow poisons. The wood also yields ash for making gun powder.

The plant is also found in California, Arizona, Washington, Texas, North Carolina, Hawaii, Florida, and Georgia.

ALBIZIA ANTHELMINTICA

SCIENTIFIC NAME: *Acacia anthelmintica* Baill, *Besenna anthelmintica*, A.Rich

OTHER: Worm-bark false-thorn, worm-cure albizia, monoga mucenna albizia, bisenna, bisinna, bussena, mesenna, musenna, *Musenna* and *Wurmbasvalsdoring* (German), *moucena* (French).

DEADLY PARTS: The roots, stem, and bark of this plant are used as an anthemintic (to destroy intestinal worms) and purgative, but a small overdose is said to cause death.

TOXICITY: 4

EFFECTS AND SYMPTOMS: A strong purgative, it produces violent and bloody diarrhea, severe pains, and severe itching, along with liver failure. Deaths have been reported in the medical literature from using "a moderately large amount."

REACTION TIME: Several hours.

ANTIDOTES AND TREATMENTS: Gastric lavage and coating of the stomach with milk and other soothing foods.

NOTES: In tropical areas like Asia, Madagascar, and Australia, it's used for killing tapeworm by native tribes. It is also found in Southwest Africa and Ethiopia, as well as in Central and South America and in southern North America.

The herb reportedly has a bad smell, but in small doses is popular as a medicine. Roots and stem bark are used to treat numerous conditions, including fever, venereal disease, and rheumatism. The bark is also used for basket weaving.

BETEL NUT SEED

SCIENTIFIC NAME: *Areca catechu.*

OTHER: Betel nut palm, pinang, bing lang, areca nut.

TOXICITY: 5

DEADLY PARTS: Seeds.

EFFECTS AND SYMPTOMS: Vomiting, diarrhea, difficulty breathing, impaired vision, and convulsions.

REACTION TIME: Death can come within twenty minutes.

ANTIDOTES AND TREATMENTS: Atropine is sometimes used as a treatment.

NOTES: Noted for its narcotic effects, this brown, flat, oval seed is popular in central and southeast Asia and is also found in South America. The poisons found in it are arecoline, arecaine and guracine.

CELANDINE

SCIENTIFIC NAME: *Chelidonium majus.*

OTHER: Felonwart, rock poppy, swallow wort, wort weed, fig buttercup, small celandine, figwort, smallwort, pilewort, lesser celandine, greater celandine.

TOXICITY: 4

DEADLY PARTS: All, but especially the leaves and stems.

EFFECTS AND SYMPTOMS: Nausea, vomiting, impaired liver function, coma, and death. Skin reaction includes intense itching and rash.

REACTION TIME: Death takes about fourteen hours.

ANTIDOTES AND TREATMENTS: Treatments are gastric lavage and symptomatic.

NOTES: Leaves are noted for their kidney and heart shapes. Celandine commonly grows in Wales and other parts of southern England as well as Europe, Asia, North Africa, and the United States, both in the Northeast and Pacific Northwest on hillsides up to 2,400 feet. As a weed, it has invaded nine states—Connecticut, Delaware, Maryland, New Jersey, Oregon, Pennsylvania, Virginia, Wisconsin, West Virginia—and the District of Columbia, growing in moist corners of fields, near water, and also beneath the shade of trees, where it gives the effect of a glossy dense carpet.

The blossoms reportedly predict the rain and shut their petals before an approaching storm. They also keep a regular schedule of nine to five and then close up shop for the night. The Celtic name of the plant, *grian* (sun), refers to this habit.

Herbalists use greater celandine as a treatment for warts, piles, and hemorrhoids, and as a folk remedy for cancer, gout, jaundice, and a variety of skin diseases. In eastern Asia, it also is used to treat peptic ulcers.

The poisons found in the plant are celandine and isoquinoline.

HENBANE

SCIENTIFIC NAME: *Hyoscyamus niger.*

OTHER: Insane root, fetid nightshade, poison tobacco, stinking nightshade, black henbane.

TOXICITY: 5

DEADLY PARTS: All parts are poisonous, especially the roots and leaves. The seeds (and juice) have the highest scopolamine content.

EFFECTS AND SYMPTOMS: A central nervous system depressant, it works similarly to belladonna (found on page 55) with such symptoms as dilated pupils, blurred vision, increased heart rate, disorientation, hallucinations, aggressive behavior, rapid pulse, anuria, convulsions, fever, coma, and death.

REACTION TIME: Fifteen to twenty minutes.

ANTIDOTES AND TREATMENTS: Treatments are gastric lavage and symptomatic.

NOTES: A medicinal herb known to ancient Egyptians, it is found from Egypt to India and is now grown commercially in many parts of North America and California. It's most noted for the poisons hyoscyamine and atropine. The *H. reticulatus* variety of the plant grows only in India.

HORSE CHESTNUT

SCIENTIFIC NAME: *Aesculus hippocastanum.*

OTHER: Buckeye, California buckeye.

TOXICITY: 5

DEADLY PARTS: Bark and fruit—a blackish brown conker, or nut.

EFFECTS AND SYMPTOMS: Restlessness, severe vomiting, diarrhea, dilation of the pupils, delirium, and death from respiratory arrest

REACTION TIME: It takes one to two days to work.

ANTIDOTES AND TREATMENTS: Gastric lavage and symptomatic treatment.

NOTES: Northern and central Asia are its main location. In the middle of the sixteenth century, it was introduced to England and now is commonly found there, as well as in the northern United States. Human poisoning occurs when conkers are mistaken for sweet chestnuts, leading people to use the leaves to make tea or eat the seeds.

There is no odor but there is a bitter taste. Honey made from California buckeye is also poisonous and retains the slight bitter taste.

The nuts contain high concentrations of aesculin, which causes hemolysis (destruction of red blood cells). The poison can be eliminated by cooking the pulverized nuts in multiple changes of boiling water, which makes a starchy porridge once popular with Native American tribes.

POINSETTIA

SCIENTIFIC NAME: *Euphorbia pulcherrima.*

TOXICITY: 3

DEADLY PARTS: All parts of the plant contain a milky sap.

EFFECTS AND SYMPTOMS: These include abdominal pain with vomiting and diarrhea. A gastric irritatant, it does not usually kill.

REACTION TIME: Several hours.

ANTIDOTES AND TREATMENTS: Gastric lavage and symptomatic treatment.

NOTES: These popular Christmas plants are bred in Hawaii. There have only been two documented cases of death from poinsettia poisoning found in the medical journals. Cats are often attracted to this plant and are poisoned, but there is a lot of disagreement as to its poisonous abilities. It is mentioned because of the myth of its poison.

SPINDLE TREE

SCIENTIFIC NAME: *Euonymus europaeus.*

OTHER: Fusanum, fusoria, skewerwood, prickwood, gatter, gatten, gadrose, pigwood, dogwood, Indian arrowroot, burning bush, wahoo, fusain, *bonnet-de-prêtre* (French), *Spindelbaume* (German). Chaucer, in one of his poems, calls it gaiter.

TOXICITY: 4

DEADLY PARTS: The root, leaves, seeds, berries, and bark contain evomonoside, a cardiac glycoside.

EFFECTS AND SYMPTOMS: In small doses, Euonymin stimulates the appetite and the flow of the gastric juice. In larger doses, symptoms, which are similar to meningitis, are watery, blood-tinged diarrhea; spasmodic abdominal pains; nausea; vomiting; fever; diuretic effects causing one to urinate frequently; convulsions; and liver enlargement that can lead to death in eight to ten hours.

REACTION TIME: Symptoms start within a few hours.

ANTIDOTES AND TREATMENTS: Gastric lavage and symptomatic treatment.

NOTES: A variety is found in Japan and Southern Europe, but the main source is in Britain, Europe, and eastern America near woods and hedgerows. When boiled, it creates yellow and green dye (the later with the addition of alum).

Toothpicks used to be made of the wood, and it is also employed in the making of gunpowder.

ANOTHER POPULAR POISONOUS PLANT

WHITE SNAKEROOT

SCIENTIFIC NAME: *Eupatorium rugosum.*

OTHER: White sanicle.

TOXICITY: 5

DEADLY PARTS: Leaves and stems, possibly flowers. The roots seem to have a lower toxicity.

EFFECTS AND SYMPTOMS: Trembling, sweating, subnormal body temperature, labored or shallow respiration, muscle tremors, partial throat paralysis, jaundice, passage of hard feces, prostration, depression, stiff gait, heart failure, and death (may be sudden without prior warning or symptoms).

REACTION TIME: Onset of signs is typically within two days to three weeks. Death occurs within one day to three weeks.

ANTIDOTES AND TREATMENTS: Supportive care is required, since there is no specific antidote.

NOTES: The herb exists in the woods of the eastern United States. The toxin is cumulative, so one large dose or multiple smaller doses over time can kill.

The milk of cows that feed on snakeroot becomes poisonous, causing a disease known as milk sickness, which was common in the early colonial days and became one of the most dreaded diseases from North Carolina and Virginia to the Midwest until the early nineteenth century. That changed with the current milk-processing methods.

The toxin of white snakeroot, tremetol, is an unstable alcohol and breaks down.

Drinking milk or eating other contaminated dairy products may result in weakness, nausea, vomiting, constipation, tremors, prostration, delirium, and even death in 10 to 25 percent of victims.

CHAPTER 6

FRAGILE
FUNGI

Their mass rotted off them flake by flake
Til the thick stalk stuck like a murderer's stake,
Where rags of loose flesh yet tremble on high
Infecting the winds that wander by.

—SHELLEY (COMMENTING ON INKY CAPS)

All incidents of death by mushroom poisoning are not fully documented, because the gastrointestinal symptoms caused by mushroom toxins are similar to those of other illnesses. Some sources estimate a hundred deaths a year, while others put the number at over a thousand a year. The vast majority of mushroom poisoning fatalities (over 90 percent) are from having eaten either the greenish to yellowish to brownish mottled death cap (*Amanita phalloides*) or one of the destroying angels (*Amanita virosa*), several overall white *Amanita* species.

Most of the victims are amateur mushroom hunters who think they know what they're choosing, while others are fed mushrooms that seemed safe and were not. Many immigrants, especially those from southeast Asia, are dismayed to find that the edible mushrooms from their native lands have toxic look-alikes in America. In addition, poisonous and nonpoisonous mushrooms often grow side by side; until chemical analysis is done on the fungi or on the stomach contents, it's almost impossible to tell which is which. Whole families have died by making the wrong choice. And to further complicate matters, the mushroom brought in for identification and analysis may not be the only one eaten. The rule is to never eat a mushroom unless you are 100 percent sure of its origin.

It has been estimated that at least one hundred of the approximately five thousand species of mushrooms in the United States are poisonous. All mushrooms (poison or not) are pleasant to taste and can be cooked in many ways. Many of the toxins are heat labile and will be destroyed with cooking, parboiling, or preservation in salt. Some varieties will be fatal if allowed to stand for some time, and others if prepared and rewarmed one or more times. There have been numerous cases of leftover casseroles being served day after day, only to have the consumer hospitalized with severe gastrointestinal problems.

Even the "safe" mushrooms can be dangerous. Many have a slight amount of poison in them, or can cause allergic reactions; others can contain environmental toxins such as heavy metals and pesticides. Mushrooms with high lead concentrations have been gathered near highways, and fungi with high mercury are found near industrial sites.

There are many myths surrounding mushrooms. One is that poisonous mushrooms—commonly called toadstools—can be detoxified by adding vinegar to the water they are boiled in and then pouring off that water.

The second is to have dogs or pigs root out the mushrooms, and if they are unaffected, then the mushroom is safe for human consumption. This is an especially dangerous myth, since a lethal dose for the animals differs greatly from a human dose, and what is edible for them might be fatal for a human. In addition, many mushrooms have a delayed response time.

Yet another myth suggests checking for poison by slicing the fungus and rubbing a silver coin against the open surface. Supposedly the coin will darken from the hydrogen cyanide or sulfide formation in the mushroom. This reaction, however, occurs with both edible and inedible mushrooms, while some poisonous mushrooms give no reaction at all.

Other myths for identifying poison mushrooms are that they have bright flashy colors (some of the most toxic species are white like the destroying angel), that snail or insect infestation means they are safe to harvest (a fungus can be harmless to insects and toxic to humans), that poisonous mushrooms taste bad (according to one who made a whole meal of destroying angel, spitting out the pieces after he'd eaten them, it tasted quite good), and lastly, that any mushroom becomes safe after being cooked enough (the chemical compounds of some toxins are stable even at high temperatures).

Most good field guides will tell mushroom hunters what poisonous look-alikes an edible mushroom has, and what differences to look for (cap color, gill color, season, and habitat).

There are reliable and fairly simple tests that can tell whether a given specimen is safe, reasonably safe, or very risky. The mushroom seeds (spores), found in the mushroom's gill (under the cap), are the chief means of identification. The color of the spores gives the family type. (A close-up look at the spores requires a microscope.) The spore color can be tested and the mushroom identified using dark and light paper as contrast. Cut the mushroom, place it gill-down on a half-dark, half-white piece of paper, then place a cover or a jar over the mushroom. Leave it for a short while and then lift the jar, checking to see the color left on the paper. Spores can also be stained with Melzer's reagent (a solution of iodine and chloral hydrate), which detects certain starches in the cell walls. Starches that stain blue, for example, can be identified as amyloid, and thus from the *Amanita* family.

Symptoms of mushroom poisoning range from mild indigestion to severe nausea, vomiting, and diarrhea to death from hemorrhage, hemolysis, and liver failure. As with all toxins, individual response varies, with children, the ill, and the elderly more likely than a healthy adult to have fatal attacks with less of the fungus. The quicker help is reached, the better the chance of recovery. Symptoms occurring four or more hours after ingestion commonly end in fatality.

The toxins don't have to be ingested to be dangerous. The poison from a mushroom can sometimes be extracted and mixed with alcohol. Spilling infected alcohol on exposed body parts will often lead to absorption through the skin with almost the same effect as the mushroom being eaten.

The killer can never be assured what effect the mushroom will have, making death by mushroom far from a certain thing. That does not, however, mean it has not been attempted, as is evidenced in the case history sections in this chapter.

The families of mushroom known to be toxic are *Amanita, Cortinarius, Galerina, Lepiota, Inocybe,* and *Gyromitra.*

AMANITA FAMILY

Dried mushrooms are often considered harmless, and in some cases this might be true, but not for the *Amanita* family. While there are a few amanitas that are safe, the rule with amanitas is: Never eat one.

In fact, never eat any mushroom that even might be one, unless you're an expert and are absolutely certain of your identification.

The most certain means of quick identification—short of studies at the microscopic level—are spore print, gill type, and base type. In the earliest, or egg sac, stage, amanitas might be confused with small, edible puffballs. Simply cutting open the specimen will reveal whether the fungus in question is a gilled mushroom (and possibly an amanita) or a solid, cheese-like puffball.

The spores vary within the *Amanita* species, but they are distinct from those of the edible mushroom. Field mushrooms (*Agaricus campestris*) have brown spores with pink gills turning tan, then chocolate with age. The gills are attached to the stem and are visible when the mushroom is cut lengthwise.

Mushrooms can be determined also by the season of growth—autumn for *Amanita* and spring for *Gyromitra*.

Amanitas have white spores and white to very pale gills. The gills are not attached to the stem. When dug carefully from the ground, with dirt gently brushed off, Amanitas reveal a small swollen or cup-like bag (volva) at the base of the stem. In the early (button) stage, the entire mushroom is covered with a membrane (universal veil) from crown to base. Remnants of this veil may cling to the cap, appearing as a ring, a little skirt beneath the cap, or in patches along the stem.

DEATH CAP

SCIENTIFIC NAME: *Amanita phalloides.*

TOXICITY: 5

FORM: The cap color varies: pale green or yellow-olive in Europe and some places along the two coasts of the United States, with colors ranging from white to light brown in the rest of the United States. Particularly dangerous are the beautiful snow-white to pale green or tan death caps. Another death cap, *A. mutabilis*, has an anise-like odor and reddish granules on its cap; its poison, though not as deadly as that of its other family members, can still do serious damage if not caught in time.

EFFECTS AND SYMPTOMS: The two main poisons involved are slow-acting amanitin, which produces hypoglycemia and is responsible for the major symptoms; and longer-acting phalloidin, which produces degenerative changes in the kidney, the liver, and cardiac muscles.

Amanitin can be detected in the blood almost immediately. Phalloidin takes a bit longer, but it starts to work on the target organs almost from ingestion. The first physical symptoms are usually nausea, vomiting, and bloody diarrhea. After an early feeling of slight discomfort, there is sudden onset of extreme stomach pains, violent vomiting, intense thirst, and cyanosis of extremities. If the liver is badly affected by the phalloidin, jaundice occurs in the eyes and skin, but this will take several hours to days before it appears. The sufferer remains conscious almost to the end, with only brief periods of unconsciousness before lapsing into a final coma. Low potassium levels brought on by severe dehydration ultimately cause cardiac arrest.

REACTION TIME: Symptoms usually develop six to fifteen hours after ingestion; sometimes, however, there may be no symptoms for as many as forty-eight hours. The longer the delay, the more dangerous the results, since the toxin attacks the liver almost as soon as the toadstool is digested. Without symptoms, people do not know to seek medical attention. In the absence of any ill effects, the subject will probably have eaten most of the fungus, thus increasing the dose. Death may occur on the fourth or seventh day—or recovery may take up to two weeks.

ANTIDOTES AND TREATMENTS: There are no known antidotes for Amanita poisoning. The first recourse is gastric lavage, and some victims have survived after receiving liver transplants.

For amanitin-type poisoning, thioctic acid has been suggested, since it is used in Europe, but it has not been approved in the United States. The drug has some unknown side effects and so the medication awaits FDA approval.

NOTES: Abundant in America and Europe and known in ancient times (Pliny's writings ascribe numerous cases of poisoning to the fungi), Amanitas are usually found in the mid-Atlantic states down to Florida and west to Texas. They flourish between October and December. The death cap Amanitas prefer to grow singular in woods and like damper, sandy soil at medium and lower elevations. Other versions of Amanita prefer dry pine woods. The smaller death angel likes mixed woods but can be found in wooded lawns, especially near oaks, and grows from May through October.

Amanita phalloides is the most dangerous species. Because of disagreements among mycologists in classification, and because of the close similarities between the related species, this general description also includes close relatives: *A. verna* (fool's mushroom), *A. virosa* (destroying angel or death angel), and *A. bisporiger* (smaller death angel).

Poisoning by death cap is often associated with complete disruption of the metabolism, since the symptoms often mimic hypoglycemia or cholera.

CASE HISTORY

In 1850, one Marie Landau of Wisconsin washed her feverish husband in an alcohol-based solution to reduce his elevated temperature, only to have him die of dehydration because of his gastrointestinal symptoms. An analysis of the body determined mushroom poisoning, but since it was winter and no mushrooms had been harvested recently, her crime was left undiscovered until she confessed on her deathbed.

In 1991, Wilhelm Winter, a Marin County, California, amateur mycologist, "tasted death and found it delicious." Using an encyclopedia of mushrooms, he and his friend hunted and prepared to eat. Later he denied the severe gastrointestinal symptoms could be from the plants. Positive his symptoms would go away shortly, he told his friend not to worry. She, however, sought medical attention. Even so, both lapsed into comas, and liver transplants were necessary before they recovered.

The 1971 movie *The Beguiled* showed a young girl switching poisonous mushrooms for good ones so she could kill her chosen victim.

Agrippina, mother of Nero, an emperor of ancient Rome, poisoned anyone in her or her son's way. When her husband Claudius tried to name someone else his heir, Agrippina fed Claudius poison mushrooms. He died within twelve hours and was subsequently deified, causing Nero to decide that mushrooms must be the food of the gods, since that is what Claudius became.

LEPIOTA

SCIENTIFIC NAME: *Lepiota cristata, L atrodisca, L. magnispora,L. L. roseifolia, L. roseilivida, Leucoagaricus rubrotinctus.*

OTHER: Parasol mushroom, haggy parasol.

TOXICITY: 5

FORM: Spores are white. The stems turn orange then saffron when they are broken or cut. These mushrooms typically have rings on the stems.

EFFECTS AND SYMPTOMS: Small lepiotas contain the same deadly toxins as *Amanita phalloides* (death cap). The first physical symptoms are usually nausea, vomiting, and bloody diarrhea. See page 106 for more information on symptoms reaction time, antidotes, and treatment.

REACTION TIME: Symptoms usually develop six to fifteen hours after ingestion; sometimes, however, there may be no symptoms for as many as forty-eight hours. Death may occur on the fourth or seventh day—or recovery may take up to two weeks.

ANTIDOTES AND TREATMENTS: There are no known antidotes. Gastric lavage and liver transplant are possibilities.

NOTES: It is found near trees; especially the mixed hardwoods of California. The small (1-5 cm cap) is white with reddish brown scales; often with a fragrant or distinctively foul odor.
　　Some of the larger ones can be edible but it's best not to take any chances.

PANTHER MUSHROOM

SCIENTIFIC NAME: *Amanita pantherina.*

OTHER: Fly agaric (*A. muscaria*) is similar.

TOXICITY: 3

FORM: The fly agaric and the panther mushroom are related; the panther, because of its color variations, is sometimes confused with the agaric. Resembling the "good luck" mushroom (red with white flecks) that is seen in many paintings, the panther mushroom was considered harmless until recently.

In the United States, the two related varieties come in an assortment of colors, and all have distinctive white patches on the caps, though these disappear with age. All have the *Amanita* family's unattached, whitish gills with white spores. Preferring a poor soil of sand or gravel, these mushrooms often grow in arcs or "fairy rings" in hardwood or mixed forests during the late fall.

Other varieties of the fly agaric include alba (white, growing only in northern North America); americana (yellow-orange cap found all over the Americas); flavivolvata (red with yellow spots sprouting from southern Alaska to the Columbia Andes); formosa (orange yellow European variety); guessowii (yellow to orange with the center cap being more reddish orange; found in North America); persicina (pinkish to orange melon with barely visible stem, found in the Gulf Coast states of the United States north to the coastal plains of eastern Long Island, New York); and the regalis (liver brown with yellow warts; European)

EFFECTS AND SYMPTOMS: Nothing is certain as far as symptoms and rate of reaction. Symptoms depend on the amount consumed, but different individuals react differently to the same dose. Small amounts can cause nausea, vomiting, twitching, drowsiness, low blood pressure, excess salivation and sweating, tearing, excessive urination, visual problems, light headedness, convulsions, dehydration from the water loss, mood changes, delusions and hallucinations, staggering, and possible coma. The fly agaric also causes copious mucus in the throat and closing of the throat, which needs mechanical ventilation before respiratory failure occurs. Near fatal doses cause swollen features, and mania intermingled with quiet paranoia.

The poison level varies with season and region and effects can last up to ten hours. Symptoms may subside spontaneously in six to twenty-four hours.

Death from fly agaric is rare. The poison can be nullified through boiling.

Most deaths were in victims with other diseases or who digested a large amount of the mushroom.

REACTION TIME: The symptoms associated with these mushrooms occur in as little as fifteen to thirty minutes, up to three hours after ingestion. Most deaths occur within the first twelve hours as a result of cardiovascular collapse or respiratory failure.

ANTIDOTES AND TREATMENTS: Gastric lavage. Atropine is often used to dry up the secretions.

NOTES: It is found in woodlands throughout west Asia, Europe, and North America.

The panther mushroom is more poisonous than the fly agaric, which is often left open in dishes to kill flies.

The chief poison is ibotenic acid, which affects the central nervous system, but also present is the psychoactive alkaloid muscimole as well as the poisons muscarine and choline.

Muscarine, discovered in 1869, was thought to be the active hallucinogenic agent in *A. muscaria* until the late 1960s, when scientists recognized the hallucinogenic agent as ibotenic acid and muscimol. Some users cook the mushroom before ingestion, which supposedly removes side effects.

A few other mushrooms with muscarine: *A. gemmata, A. pantherina, A. parcivolata; Boletus calopus, B. luridus, B satamis; Clitocybe aurantiaca, C. dealbata, C. nebularis; Hebeloma crustuliniforme; Inocybe fastigiata, I. geophylla, I. napipes, I. patouillardi, I. pudica; Mycena pura.*

The toxic substances of *A. muscaria* are water soluble and susceptible to temperature. The mushroom can be detoxified by cooking in boiling water.

Some authorities believe that this striking mushroom was the mysterious God-narcotic "Divine Soma" of ancient India.

The *Amanita basii* (similar to *A. caesarea* of Europe) in Mexico is considered edible.

CASE HISTORY

Panther mushroom's deadly powers were noticed in Berlin, Germany, where fifteen hundred people were poisoned in 1946 after the war when food was still scarce. Many did not survive.

Count de Vecchi, an Italian nobleman during the late 1800s, died after eating fly agaric late in the season. He probably confused it with royal agaric (*Agraicus caesarea*), a highly edible mushroom similar in appearance to fly agaric. His diary notes his agony before death.

Buddhist adepts may have used *A. muscaria* to achieve enlightenment because of its hallucinogenic properties.

CORTINARIUS FAMILY

DEADLY WEBCAP

SCIENTIFIC NAME: *Cortinarius orellanus, Cort. rubellus.*

OTHER SIMILAR: Fool's webcap.

TOXICITY: 6

FORM: The family name comes from the cobwebby veil that often covers the gills of the young mushrooms. Cap colors vary from shades of blue-violet. As the cap starts to turn redder, it becomes more poisonous. Shades of brown or reddish-brown are the most deadly.

EFFECTS AND SYMPTOMS: The poison, orellanin, acts silently against the liver and kidney. The first symptoms often do not appear for two to three days after ingestion and may be as long as three weeks. Symptoms mimic the flu, and include nausea, vomiting, stomach pains, headache, rapid heartbeat, and dizziness. These are followed by the early stages of renal failure: immense thirst, frequent urination, pain on or around the kidneys, hematuria, jaundice, oliguria, weakness, convulsions, coma, and eventual death.

REACTION TIME: It can take from three days to three weeks for the symptoms to show. By that time, the liver and kidneys are so damaged that very little can be done to save the victim.

ANTIDOTES AND TREATMENTS: Gastric lavage is helpful if the victim is given emergency treatment immediately after ingesting the mushroom. However, because of the delay between ingestion and first symptoms, kidney and liver transplants are often the only lifesaving measures. There is no known antidote.

NOTES: *Cort. Limonius* and *Cort. callisteus* and have similar effects. Deadly webcap (*rubellus*) is found in central Europe (largely Poland), and the temperate parts of Northern Europe, but has been found as far north as Finnish Lapland in pine woods. The fool's cap (*orellanus*) is found throughout southern Europe but has been seen in southern Norway.

For a long time, it was thought that only the *Amanita* family of fungi were lethal, but *Cortinarius orellanus* and *rubellus* have now been proven to be just as deadly. These two mushrooms often get confused with one another and with the edible mushroom *chanterelle*, which shares the same locations. Unlike some mushrooms that can be identified by tasting a small portion, these are so poisonous that one becomes ill even after spitting out what has been tasted.

Any person with unexplained acute renal failure should be questioned about eating wild mushrooms.

GALERINAS

SCIENTIFIC NAME: *Galerina autumnalis, G marginata, G venenata.*

OTHER: Deadly galerina, deadly lawn Galerina, deadly mycoflora.

TOXICITY: 6

FORM: These fungi, with cap colors ranging from brown to reddish-brown, are all lethal. Spores are rusty brown.

EFFECTS AND SYMPTOMS: The poison amatoxin (similar to that in amanitas), causes acute or chronic kidney failure. Other, unidentified toxins may be involved, as those poisoned show severe damage to intestines, reproductive organs, liver, heart, nervous system, and kidneys.

The first symptoms come late—six to twenty-four hours after ingestion. They start with sharp abdominal pains followed by violent vomiting and persistent diarrhea, often with blood and pus in it. These symptoms subside and the victim seems to improve. Three or four days later, his condition worsens as liver and kidneys fail. Death comes in seven days.

Autopsy results show marked gastrointestinal edema (swelling), fatty degeneration of heart and liver, necrosis (dead tissue) in the kidneys, and swollen brain with multiple sites of bleeding.

REACTION TIME: It takes six or more hours for the symptoms to appear, and sometimes there are no symptoms for as long as twenty-four hours after ingestion.

ANTIDOTES AND TREATMENTS: None known.

NOTES: *Galerina venenata* occurs commonly throughout the United States, especially in lawns of the Northwest (United States and Canada) as does deadly galerina (*G. autumnalis*).

Galerina autumnalis frequently grows together with *Psilocybe cyanescens, P. stuntzii,* and several other *Psilocybe* mushrooms. Their size is roughly the same, and the typical darkening at the base of the stem of Galerinas can be mistaken for the bluing reaction of psilocybes (hallucinogenic mushrooms). The spore colors are similar.

INOCYBE

SCIENTIFIC NAME: *Inocybe napipes, I. rimosa I. fastigiata., I. patouillardii.*

OTHER: Caesar's fiber head, torn fiber head, scaly fiber head.

TOXICITY: 5

FORM: Various shades of brown; some lilac or purplish species exist. The cap often appears fibrous or frayed, giving the mushroom its common name of fiber cap, and they give off a musty or spermatic odor.

The dangerous red-staining variety is capped with irregular, broken edges and rough texture. The reddish-pink gills are far apart, with a dark red-pink stem and pink flesh. The color fades in direct sunlight.

EFFECTS AND SYMPTOMS: Persons present classic symptoms, starting with profuse sweating, salivation, stupor, and rapid loss of consciousness. The face takes on a bluish tinge; the lips swell and become darker in color as the blood vessels dilate. There is some twitching, but the muscles become unusually flaccid and the pulse becomes difficult to detect. Death occurs only 4 percent of the time, as medical attention is usually reached.

Victims remain mentally clear and can usually give appropriate history. Often spores can be obtained from vomit or bowel samples.

As quickly as one hour after ingestion.

Gastric lavage is the first recourse, then atropine, as it is an antidote for muscarine. A high-protein diet helps recovery.

NOTES: There are over one hundred variations of inocybe. They grows under hardwoods in all parts of the United States. The poisons found in them are muscarine, which affects the autonomic nervous system and the liver, and orellanin.

Of the *Inocybe* group, the most dangerous are the *red-staining inocybe* (Inocybe *patouillardii*). Two other deadly ones are *I. napipes* and *I. fastigiata*. Microscopic characteristics are the only certain means of identification.

GYROMITRA FAMILY

MAGIC MUSHROOMS

SCIENTIFIC NAME: *Psilocybe semilanceata.*

OTHER: *Teonanácatl* (divine flesh).

TOXICITY: 2

FORM: The smooth cap becomes sticky or slippery when wet. With gray to purple-gray gills, it has nearly black spores. When cut, the flesh turns blue or greenish. They are often mistaken for the poisonous galerina or inocybe.

EFFECTS AND SYMPTOMS: The mushroom produces altered states of consciousness and vivid hallucinations lasting from ten to thirty minutes or as long as three hours after ingestion. The amount of mushroom needed to have a noticeable effect is highly variable.

REACTION TIME: Within a few minutes.

ANTIDOTES AND TREATMENTS: The poison reacts quickly, so treatment can include gastic lavage, and it is also essential to treat any symptoms.

NOTES: Hallucinogenic mushrooms are prevalent in Central America. They are available in the wild and as spores through mail-order catalogues.

Having been used for centuries, they appear as small, stone mushroom icons in Meso-American ruins from 3,500 years ago.

Honey with psilocybe can be purchased at Dutch coffee shops. Compared to LSD, the mushroom high is short-lived, and flashbacks are rarely reported, but occasionally they precipitate mental crises. *Psilocybe cubensis* is variable in potency. Mushrooms bought on the street may be mushrooms adulterated with some other drug.

In 1958, Albert Hofmann first identified psilocin and psilocybin as the active compound in these mushrooms. Psilocybin and psilocin are found in many species of *Psilocybe, Stropharia,* and *Panaeolus,* plus in a few species of *Conocybe, Inocybe, Gymnopilus, Pluteus, Mycena,* and *Psathyrella.* Timothy Leary traveled to Mexico to experience hallucinogenic mushrooms firsthand.

CASE HISTORY

Hallucinogenic *Psilocybe* were known to the Aztecs as *teonanácatl* (divine flesh) and were reportedly served at the coronation of Moctezuma II in 1502. After the Spanish conquest, the use of hallucinogenic plants and mushrooms, like other pre-Christian traditions, was suppressed.

SMOOTH CAP MUSHROOM

SCIENTIFIC NAME: *Coprinus atramentarius, Coprinus comatu.*

OTHER: Inky cap, alcohol inky cap, shaggy mane, mica cap.

FORM: Inky caps are any mushroom having gills that dissolve into a dark liquid after spores mature. Bell-shaped, it breaks up into coarse, white-and-brown curved scales.

TOXICITY: 2

EFFECTS AND SYMPTOMS: Drinking alcohol after ingesting this mushroom (or within forty-eight hours after eating the mushrooms) results in tingling sensations; nausea; vomiting; heavy sweating; respiratory difficulty; flushing, redness, and swelling in the face; and even tachycardia (abnormally rapid heartbeat).

Recovery can occur within a few hours, but if enough of the ink cap mushroom is taken in combination with alcohol, low blood pressure and sometimes cardiovascular collapse can occur.

REACTION TIME: Within minutes upon mixing the mushroom with alcohol.

ANTIDOTES AND TREATMENTS: None needed, as the symptoms go away in a few hours.

NOTES: Alcohol inky caps grow clustered in wood chips and grass throughout North America (and much of the temperate world), from spring to fall in the east, late fall to early spring in California near hardwoods.

The smooth inky cap mushroom mimics the effects of Antabuse, a drug used to cure alcoholics.

Mica cap is the smallest of the inky caps, all of which become watery when you boil them. Mica cap has a mild odor and is edible in soups, stews, and sauces. It is found growing on dead wood, often in California.

TURBANTOP

SCIENTIFIC NAME: *Gyromitra esculenta, G. infula.*

OTHER: False morel, red mushroom, beefsteak mushroom, lorchel.

TOXICITY: 2 to 5, depending on the variety and how it is prepared.

FORM: False morel is brown and looks like a folded brain with a solid stem. False morels resemble true morels in that both are brown and wrinkly. False morels are darker than true morels and shaped irregularly, resembling a brown brain; the true morel is more symmetrical and looks like a sponge.

EFFECTS AND SYMPTOMS: Vomiting, diarrhea, convulsions, hemolysis, and coma. Malfunction of the liver causes death in 20 to 40 percent of the cases. Gyromitrin is a volatile, water-soluble hydrazine compound that decomposes in the body into methyl hydrazine and acts as a hemolytic toxin, damaging the liver and the central nervous system.

Reportedly even the presence of fresh false morels in a poorly ventilated space, like the trunk of a car, may cause headache, dizziness, and nausea. The poison is also cumulative.

REACTION TIME: Symptoms start from two to twelve hours after ingestion.

ANTIDOTES AND TREATMENTS: Vitamin B6 seems to help gyromitrin-type poisoning. If the victim can keep fluids and food down, activated charcoal is successful, as well as vitamin K to control the bleeding from the damaged liver.

NOTES: Gyromitra is common in central Europe, England, Scandinavia, and North America. A few of the European varieties can be eaten safely. The eight to ten species existing in North America are almost all deadly. Gyromitra mushrooms contain the poison monomethylhydrazine (MMH).

False morel is deadly when raw, but in Scandinavia, it is parboiled and eaten as a delicacy and gives off a chocolate odor. Consuming raw or incorrectly prepared false morels can result in catastrophic liver failure and death.

During boiling, the gyromitrin poison dissolves in the water, which must be discarded. Some of the gyromitrin will also evaporate, producing toxic fumes. It is possible for sensitive people to be affected eating even properly prepared mushrooms.

Turbantop and false morel contain compounds similar to a common component of rocket fuel.

American false morels contain more toxin than the Scandinavian specimens.

Between 1885 and 1988, only four cases of fatal gyromitrin poisoning were recorded—all of them caused by eating the mushrooms raw.

CHAPTER 7

SNAKES, SPIDERS, AND
OTHER LIVING THINGS

With thy sharp teeth this knot intrinsicate
Of life at once untie: poor venomous fool
Be angry and dispatch.

SHAKESPEARE, ANTONY AND CLEOPATRA

When most people think of poison, they forget the deadly zoological toxins. However, evaluating the killing power of these poisons is tricky because there are many variables involved that affect toxicity. For the purposes of this chapter, only the most fatal will be discussed. There are many creatures whose bites or stings can be toxic and even fatal. But when it comes to poisonous animals, snakes are at the top of the list for most people, even though many snakes aren't harmful at all.

SNAKES

Cleopatra remains history's most famous snakebite suicide. Poisonous snakes were also used in ancient Egypt to provide a prompt and reasonably painless death for select political prisoners. In several North American native tribes, snake venom or the pulped head of a snake was used as an arrow poison. The venom was often obtained by causing the snake to bite the liver of a deer or other animal. The poisoned organ was then allowed to putrefy in a mix of toxic leaves and other purportedly lethal substances, and arrows and darts were dipped in this mixture. While the natives may have had the right idea, most unintentionally diluted the toxicity of their arrow poison by heating the mixture.

The Bushmen of the Namaqualand region of southwestern Africa take the resin from a plant of the *Buphane* family and smear it on a stone. They then place the rock in the mouth of a snake—usually a spitting cobra—until its venom mixes with the resin. Carefully removing the stone, they dip their arrows in the resultant lethal gum.

Other African poisoned-arrow techniques include the use of a toxic brew of puff adder heads, resin, beetles, and leaves of poisonous plants. This mixture is quite diluted, but still effective. East Bengal natives prepared their arrows by securing bits of cobra venom-soaked wadding to the tips—a foolproof and quite deadly arrow poison.

The majority of snakebites are not fatal because most attacks are by nonvenomous snakes. While snakes have often been used in murderous attempts, there is no guarantee of death, since snakes don't always use all their venom in one strike. With the exception of the dangerously aggressive snakes, they seldom bite unless provoked and are secretive and timid, eager to avoid encounters with humans; further, they are quite as likely to bite the would-be murderer as the chosen victim.

All snake venoms are complex proteins that affect the nerve center for the senses, motor skills, heart, and lungs, attaching to the neural tissues even before symptoms occur. The venom harms the red blood cells; affects the heart, kidney, and lung muscles; and prevents clotting.

While poisoning by bite is the most common, snakes can also be milked for their yellowish venom. It can then be injected with equal effect, with an injection into a vein or artery being the most deadly. The victim can also accidentally drink the venom; however, symptoms and toxicity are usually lessened with oral administration. A few African cobras spit rather than bite. The jet of venom is toxic and can blind, but seldom kills unless it comes into direct contact with the victim's bloodstream, for example, through injections, cuts, or scratches.

In most cases, unless the bite connects with a major vein or artery, the snakebite victim will usually survive if medical care is administered quickly. Left untreated, even the most minor of bites can prove fatal. Snake venom itself can cause allergies, and for someone allergic to the venom, the result is exaggerated and often deadly. Some cases of sudden death following snakebite are believed to have been caused by anaphylactic shock.

Reaction time can be anywhere from ten minutes to several days. Physical activity, or lack of it, also affects the victim, as movement spreads the venom quicker.

A newly devised technique in Britain can show the exact type of snake venom present in the body. It is also possible to determine the type of snake by examining the bite and measuring the distance between the two punctures.

Traditional snakebite kits at one time contained a sharp knife and a small hand-suction pump. Until recently, common practice was to make a shallow knife slit from fang-point to fang-point, and then attempt to suck out the venom. An incision through the fang marks by an untrained person is both inadvisable and dangerous even as an extreme emergency measure. In most cases, more damage is inflicted, and at best only about 20 percent of the venom will be removed—and those removing the venom orally may cause themselves serious harm.

Today, antivenin is the only specific antidote for snakebite, but between 1830 and 1870, alcohol—in the form of a straight whiskey—became the most popular snakebite remedy in the United States. During the last months of the Civil War, a Confederate quartermaster officer became incensed when the physician administered, in a short period of time, a full gallon of whiskey to a snakebitten soldier. The quartermaster argued that the barrel of whiskey, then priced at $450 in inflated Confederate currency, was worth more than the soldier himself.

In the American Old West, hard-liquor cures for snakebite were prevalent, and some people even believed whiskey or brandy made the imbiber immune to snakebite. One frontier physician reported in a prestigious medical journal how he had prescribed a pint of whiskey every five minutes until a quart had been consumed. In another case, he administered a gallon and a half of whiskey over a thirty-six-hour period. The physician complained in all seriousness that when the patient was fully recovered, he actually went out looking for another rattlesnake to bite him.

In ensuing years, science found alcohol of little use in combating the effects of snakebite. In fact, medical experts discovered that drinking liquor is bad for the snakebite victim because alcohol, in moderate to large quantities, accelerates circulation and hastens the system's absorption of the venom. Only in the smallest amounts can alcohol be beneficial, since it then acts as a tranquilizer to reduce the fear and anxiety that can quicken the venom's spread.

While there are antidotes for most snake venoms, several factors play a crucial role in saving the victim of any venomous animal injury: 1) correct identification of the snake—*Crotalinae*, some *Elapidae*, and tropical *Viperidae* are the most dangerous; 2) the location of the bite—the more vascular the area, the more severe the reaction; 3) the amount of time lapsed between bite and antiserum administration; 4) the amount of venom injected—as they bite, snakes inject anywhere from 0 to 75 percent of the venom stored in their glands (younger snakes are more likely to inject all of their venom than adult snakes); 5) depth of the bite and penetration of the fangs; and 6) the age, size and health of the victim. Most fatalities are because the bite is attributed to the wrong type of snake or because too small a dose of antivenin is administered.

Antiserum itself can cause heart or respiratory problems, and if someone who has not been bitten receives the antiserum, the result could be as dangerous as an actual bite. Only the specific antiserum will help. Before it is administered, the victim should be tested for serum sensitivity, since the antiserum itself can be life-threatening. Often the physician will wait for clear evidence of systemic venom toxicity before beginning treatment. Cardiopulmonary measures should be kept ready. And the victim should be calmed and reassured. The victim should lie flat and avoid as much movement as possible. If possible, the bitten limb should rest at a level lower than the victim's heart. In some regions of the world, clothing is wrapped around a bitten extremity proximal to the bite site. However, prolonged use of arterial tourniquets is unwise and has caused loss of limb function. A completely occlusive tourniquet is reasonable when a victim has been bitten by a highly toxic snake, such as a cobra, and is a short distance from medical care.

The basic snake families are the *Colubridae, Viperidae, Elapidae, Boidae, Hydrophiidae and Leptotyphlopidae*, many of which are poisonous. The family *Colubridae* has both poisonous and non-poisonous members. The most common are listed below.

ADDER

SCIENTIFIC NAME: *Vipera berus*.

OTHER: Common adder, puff adder, night adder

FAMILY: Viperidae.

SUBFAMILY: Viperinae.

TOXICITY: 4 to 6

EFFECTS AND SYMPTOMS: Victims of adder bites show symptoms similar to those of cobra bites, in addition to bleeding from the gums and chills and fever. Severe poisoning is indicated by swelling or petechial hemorrhages extending above the elbows or knees within two hours of the bite.

Following a bite on the hand, the whole arm can become swollen within a half-hour and skin will become purple. The victim perspires heavily, vomits blood, and collapses within an hour. The nose and eyes bleed and loss of vision occurs, with subsequent loss of consciousness. Death is inevitable, unless the antiserum is administered quickly, and usually comes from cardiorespiratory failure. The venom's powerful hemolytic effect breaks down the red blood cells and liberates hemoglobin, which can appear in the urine.

REACTION TIME: The venom kills quickly, directly affecting the heart and lungs.

ANTIDOTES AND TREATMENTS: Antiserum is given. Heart failure can rapidly occur; cardiovascular resuscitation is kept available.

NOTES: The *Viperidae* family is found throughout the world, with the majority in Africa. The common adder or European adder (*Vipera berus*), makes its home throughout Europe and Asia, even north of the Arctic Circle in Norway, and grows to about three feet. Its body markings are gray with black zigzag bands on the back and black spots on the sides. The adder is the only poisonous snake listed with a natural habitat in the U.K.

Some other similar snakes in the *Viperidae* family follow.

- The thick-bodied puff adder (*Bitis arietans*), found in Africa and the Arabian peninsula, is quite venomous. Its name comes from the warning it gives when it inflates its body and hisses loudly, sounding like air going out of a balloon. With gray to dark brown skin tones, it has thin yellow chevrons on the back. When approached, it will become aggressive rather than flee.

- The boomslang is a tree-living predator making its home in the scrublands and forests from the Amazon Basin as far north as Costa Rica. Lying in trees or bush, the front of its body extended in midair, it can remain motionless for long periods time. A master of camouflage, its body and eyes change color to match the surroundings. When threatened, it inflates its neck, displaying the dark skin beneath its scales. Its fangs are at the rear of the upper jaw. Even in the smallest quantities the venom is lethal.

- The longest pit viper in the Western hemisphere is the Central and South American lethal bushmaster. Pink or tan body spots contrast with the diamond-shaped blotches on its skin.

- Found in sandy parts of central and sub-Saharan Africa, the gaboon viper (aka the king puff adder) is among the largest of the venomous snakes. A nocturnal species, the snake becomes active toward sunset. Colorfully marked with rectangles and triangles of brown, yellow, and purple, it is thick-bodied and broad-headed with two hornlike projections coming from its snout. Though the snake is huge, its bite can still go unnoticed until pain draws the victim's attention to it, and by then the administration of antivenin may be too late. On a whole, its nerve poison is less toxic than that of the puff adder, but is more toxic when injected intravenously.

- The levantine viper or mountain adder (*Macrovipera lebetina, M. lebetina obtusa, M. lebetina turanica*) is extremely dangerous and found in Lebanon, Pakistan, southern Turkmenistan, and Uzbekistan, as well as in northern Eurasia and Africa. In Zimbabwe, Africa, it prefers stony, semi-arid country with sparse scrubby vegetation. The large fangs seem huge since the head is short. Markings are gray, gray brown, or yellowish, with a gray underside. Appearing placid, it remains alert and strikes quickly.

- The Russell's viper, tic polonga, or daboia is extremely venomous. Its bite is the major cause of snakebite death in the open country from India to Taiwan and Java. Growing only about five feet in length, its bright markings stand out with its three rows of reddish-brown spots encircled by black and then outlined in white.

- The aggressive saw-scaled viper is a relatively small snake, often no more than two feet, but its bite is almost always fatal. Gray or sand-colored with rows of white spots and pale zigzag lines as markings, its rough scales are rubbed together as a warning, produce a hissing sound. It prefers to hide under rocks and is found mainly from northern and western Africa to the drier regions of India and Sri Lanka. The venom causes internal and external hemorrhages. Death may occur twelve to sixteen days after the bite if antivenin is not given in time.

CASE HISTORY

In *Death in the Air* by Agatha Christie, a boomslang snake was indirectly responsible for the death of a French moneylender. The snake's venom was put on a blow-gun dart, which was then shot into the victim in the middle of a plane ride.

BEAKED SEA SNAKE

SCIENTIFIC NAME: *Enhydrina schistosa.*

FAMILY: *Hydrophidae.*

TOXICITY: 6

EFFECTS AND SYMPTOMS: The extremely toxic venom of sea snakes weakens muscles. The first symptom is pain in the skeletal muscles, especially during motion, even though there is little pain at the bite site, which appears to be an innocuous pinprick. The victim's tongue and mouth become paralyzed, vision blurs, and there is great difficulty swallowing. The eyelids droop and the jaw stiffens, as in tetanus. Weakness and paralysis increases. Myoglobin and potassium from the damaged muscles stain the urine red, injure the kidneys, and cause irregularities of the heart.

REACTION TIME: The victim is symptom free for thirty minutes to eight hours. Death may come within hours of the bite but is usually delayed a few days.

ANTIDOTES AND TREATMENTS: There is no specific antivenin, so treatment is symptomatic.

This shallow-water snake is found over both mud and sand bottoms in the Pacific Ocean, Indian Ocean, and throughout Vietnamese, Philippine, and Malaysian waters. It also lives at the mouths and deltas of rivers, such as the Ganges and Indus. The snake has also been found in channels many miles from the open sea, and is often taken in fishing nets. While awkward, it is not completely helpless on land.

Compared to most snakes, it has a distinctive lower jaw. The usual wide shield of the chin tip is, in this snake, reduced to a splinter-like shield buried between the lips. This gives the lower jaw greater flexibility to seize and swallow large prey. A little under five feet, the snake is dull olive green or pale greenish gray with dark crossbands. The belly and sides are cream to dirty white, while the tail is mottled with black.

Some of the varieties are yellow-lipped sea krait (*Laticauda colubrina*), olive-snake (*Aipysurus laevis*), yellow sea snake (*Pelamis platurus*), spiculated sea snake (*H. cyanocinctus*), Hardwicke's sea snake (*Lapemis harwickii*), and the Pelagic sea snake (*Pelamis platurus*).

Sea snakes are true reptiles with lungs and have forked tongues and body scales. They are not fish-like eels. Bites are possible in warm water where fishermen catch the snakes with their hands. The beaked sea snake is the variety responsible for most fatal bites.

The yellow sea snake has its habitat in the eastern Pacific. Its toxicity is lower than that of most sea snakes since it produces very little venom. Nevertheless, several deaths have been reported.

The annulated sea snake, which lives in reefs, has a higher toxicity than the yellow sea snake and causes numerous deaths.

Hardwicke's sea snake, found usually during the rainy season in tropical areas, also yields very little venom, but is still potentially fatal.

The pelagic sea snake, the most widespread of the species, can be found on the west coast of Central and South America but with few fatalities. Toxicity is about one-quarter that of the beaked sea snake.

COBRA

FAMILY: Elapidae.

TOXICITY: 6.

EFFECTS AND SYMPTOMS: Symptoms are characterized by pain within ten minutes. General paralysis, weakness, stumbling gait, pain around the bite, nausea and vomiting, impaired swallowing, convulsions, abdominal pain, and fever can occur quickly. Even with treatment, lung paralysis can occur up to ten days after the bite and be accompanied by a slow onset of swelling. Blood pressure falls and convulsions may occur. Drooping eyelids are a sign of systemic toxicity. Necrosis of the tissue occurs within forty-eight hours. Death is caused by respiratory failure.

Spitting cobras can spit venom into a person's eyes. Immediate and intense pain results, with eye spasms, tearing, and blurring of vision. Systemic toxicity does not occur with eye exposure, but corneal ulcerations, uveitis, and permanent blindness have been reported in untreated cases.

If you are bitten by a black mamba, these are the symptoms you will have: slight local swelling and/or burning pain, drooping or heavy eyelids; drowsiness; blurred vision and dilated pupils; loss of control of tongue or jaw; slurred speech; mental confusion; paralysis of all muscle groups with loss of reflexes; and respiratory distress. Should these appear within the hour after having been bitten, the bite will be life threatening. Respiratory distress, convulsions, and coma come before death. A king cobra's bite may not affect the tissue around the bite site, but respiratory and cardiac systems are directly affected. A drop of the venom is not that potent, but the snake injects so much venom in one bite that enough poison is released to kill twenty people.

The king cobra can stand in an upright threatening posture (with its hood out) as high as six feet and even move in an upright stance; it can stare an average human in the eye. Black-and-white banded baby king cobras (eighteen inches in length) can be just as deadly even from day one.

REACTION TIME: The venom paralyzes the nervous system (sometimes within a matter of minutes) and causes death (sometimes within two hours) if the antitoxin is not given. After a delay of four hours, the antiserum loses effectiveness; after twenty-four hours, it's useless. All this depends of course on the human variables of age, health, weight, amount of venom, and the location of the bite.

ANTIDOTES AND TREATMENTS: Specific antiserum only.

NOTES: These snakes expand their neck ribs to form a hood when disturbed.

The cobra family is found from Africa through Asia and Australia as well as North America. The king cobra (*Ophiophagus hannah*) is found in southeast Asia, India, Indonesia, China, Malaysia, and the Philippines. The largest of the venomous snakes, it can measured up to eighteen feet long. Its bite is lethal 10 percent of the time.

The highly lethal Indian or Asian cobra, or spectacle cobra (*Naja naja*), which can be as long as six feet, reportedly kills well over thirty thousand people a year worldwide but favors the area of Iran and eastward. The cobra often goes into homes seeking its food source, rats. What looks like black-and-white spectacles on its large hood stand out as the markings on its yellow to dark brown body.

The Egyptian and North African cobra (*Naja haje*) was known in ancient times as the asp. This deep-hooded narrow snake grows to at least six feet.

The ringhals, or spitting cobra, (*Hemachatus hemachuatus*) in southern Africa has keeled (ridged) scales. It prefers to spit or spray venom into the eyes of its victims, often causing blindness.

The black-necked cobra (*Naja nigricollis*) found throughout Africa is another aggressive snake that prefers to spit, it is very accurate and can shoot venom into the eyes of a victim from seven feet away. The venom, while harmless to intact flesh, damages the eyes and causes blindness if not washed away immediately.

The tree cobra (*Pseudohaje*) found in equatorial Africa is, along with the mambas, one of two climbing elapids.

There are snakes similar to cobras that do not have a hood. Some of these are:

• The nocturnal-feeding Indian or blue or common krait (*Bungarus caeruleus*) grows to about five feet and is found in open country from Pakistan and India to China. Markings include shiny scales and strongly patterned yellow-and-black or white-and-black bands. It seldom bites unless provoked, but its powerful venom kills 50 percent of those bitten—if they are not treated with antivenin.

• The banded krait or pama (*B. fasciatus*) in Indochina appears docile, but its venom is lethal.

• The black mamba (*Dendroaspis polylepis*) in sub-Saharan Africa hunts its prey in trees. Marked by gray or greenish brown colorings, this slender snake grows to about fourteen feet and has long fangs. It rears up to strike aggressively and can land a bite on a human's head or torso. Without antivenin its bite is 100 percent fatal. Just two drops of venom can kill a person. A mamba can have up to twenty drops of venom in its fangs. Black mamba venom contains neurotoxins and cardiotoxins.

• The green mamba (*Dendroaspis angusticeps*) is a smaller, less aggressive version often found in the trees of eastern Africa, but is equally as dangerous.

• The taipan (*Oxyuranus scutellatus*), also a lethal snake, lives around Queensland, Australia, and is the largest Australian snake of the cobra family. Marked by a yellow underside and brown top, it's extremely aggressive and attacks without warning, inflicting numerous bites in succession with its unusually long fangs. Its venom contains a clotting agent that proves fatal to humans within minutes.

• The death adder (*Acanthophis antarcticus*) is found all around Australia and on nearby islands. While related to the cobras, it has a thick body, a short tail, and a broad head. Its coloring is gray or brownish with dark crossmarkings. Its bite is fatal 50 percent of the time if untreated.

• The Australian tiger snake (*Notechis scutatus*), small but lethal, has yellow-and-brown bands and remains under four feet in length. When about to strike, its head flattens just as its cobra cousin's does and the snake appears to be jumping when it strikes.

Preferring swampy regions of Australia, Tasmania, and islands in the immediate vicinity, the tiger snake is the most dangerous snake of southern Australia.

• The Australian black snake (*Pseudechis porphyriacus*) is a small-headed snake with blue-black body and a red underbelly, and prefers marshy areas. It's the most common of the Australian venomous snakes, and its venom possesses a powerful anticoagulant. Others in this group include the spotted black snake (*P. guttatus*) and the mulga (*P. australis*), which is reddish brown on top and pink underneath.

• The nasty-tempered brown snake (*Demansia textilis*) is fast-moving and slender, adapting to the color of its surroundings, going from light brown to dull green. Growing up to seven feet in length, it can rear up to strike, and has lethal venom. Making its home in New Guinea and eastern Australia, it reportedly has caused more deaths in all of Australia than any other snake. Antivenin from the Australian copperhead (*Denisonia superba*) can be used for counteracting the brown snake's bite. Even though the brown snake is also called a copperhead, the North American copperhead (*Agkistrodon contortrix*) antivenin is useless against the brown snake.

• A nocturnal, burrowing snake, the eastern coral snake, or harlequin snake, (*Micrurus fulvius*), grows about three feet in length and makes its home from North Carolina to Missouri and down to northeastern Mexico. Quite a lot of venom—or a good bite in the right place—is needed for death to occur. This snake has wide bands of red and black separated by yellow bands. Because there are also nonvenomous coral snakes, a folk rhyme reminds people which one to stay clear of: "Red touching yellow, dangerous fellow." However, this rule is not always binding, and caution should be taken with all these snakes.

• The small Arizona coral snake (*M. euryxanthus*) is reluctant to strike at people, but still has dangerous venom. It makes its home in the deserts of the southwestern United States and western Mexico. The best way to identify a coral snake is by: 1) a very blunt head that is black to behind the eyes; and 2) bands that completely encircle the body, along with the yellow or white bands occurring on both sides of the red bands.

• The African coral snake (*Aspidelaps lubricus*), found in South Africa, is quite small, with black-and-white bands over bright orange.

• Other coral snakes include the black-banded coral snake (*M. nigrocinctus*), found in southern Mexico to northern Colombia. (Two fatalities were reported in Costa Rica within the past five years.) The Brazilian giant coral snake (*M. frontalis*), found in Argentina, southern Brazil, Bolivia, Paraguay, and Uruguay, is responsible for quite a number of deaths.

All of these snakes are very lethal.

The venom of the cobra family is chemically different from that of other families. A neurotoxin, it brings on progressive paralysis, causing death when the poison spreads to respiratory muscles. These venoms are more heat resistant than those of any other vipers and have the same toxicity as the yellow scorpion of the Middle East (*Leiurus quinques-triatus*). Cobra venom is also twice as toxic as strychnine, nearly five times as toxic as that of a black widow spider, and seven times as toxic as the mushroom toxin amanitin.

Some coral snake venoms have powerful hemolytic effects—breaking down the red blood cells and liberating the hemoglobin, both of which appear in the urine. The autopsy will reveal gross hemorrhage, necrosis, cloudy swelling in the cells of the other organs, and destroyed kidney tubes.

The venom of the Wagler's pit viper is unique in that it remains almost fully toxic after heating in a sterilizer and causes rapid collapse and death without local swelling or hemorrhage.

CASE HISTORY

Carl Kauffeld, in his 1969 book *Snakes: The Keeper and the Kept,* gave the following account of his symptoms, which occurred approximately six minutes after his nonfatal cobra bite: "I was sinking into a state that could not be called unconsciousness, but one in which I was no longer aware of what was going on about me. ... I felt no anxiety; I felt no pain; it didn't even strike me as strange that the darkness was closing in on the light. ... I am certain I did not lose consciousness entirely at any time; I only felt a complete and utter lassitude in which nothing seemed to matter—not at all unpleasant if this is the way death comes from cobra poisoning."

A scientist in Texas who had been immunized against cobra venom some months before he was bitten suffered no neurotoxic or other generalized symptoms, but developed a gangrenous patch requiring skin grafting.

In Florida in the 1950s, a young man was bitten by a coral snake and rested quite comfortably under hospital observation for about seven hours. Then he began having trouble breathing and moving his eyes. Soon almost all his muscles became paralyzed and he could respond to questions only by raising his eyebrows. Despite administration of antivenin and use of an iron lung, he died in a few hours.

COTTONMOUTH

FAMILY: Viperidae.

SUBFAMILY: Crotalinae.

OTHER: Water moccasin.

TOXICITY: 4 to 6

EFFECTS AND SYMPTOMS: Cottonmouth and water moccasin venom literally dissolves the tissue it contacts. The injection site is dark and oozes bloody fluid while swelling spreads outward. The region turns itchy and will cause the victim to scratch and rub and become irritable and hyperactive. After being bitten, a victim may experience a short period of near-normal activity, followed by another quiet state that eventually terminates in collapse and death. An autopsy shows the injection site as gangrenous and often liquefied.

There will be extensive hemorrhage under the swollen area and small hemorrhages in the heart, lungs, and other organs, causing the victim to die of internal bleeding. The heart fails not because of direct injury but because it can no longer pump effectively through the damaged vascular bed.

REACTION TIME: Within ten minutes.

ANTIDOTES AND TREATMENTS: Antivenin is available in most hospitals if the victim survives long enough to get there.

NOTES: Aquatic pit vipers, as the cottonmouth or water moccasin (*Agkistrodon piscivorus*), are found primarily in low marshlands of the southeastern United States. These threaten with their mouth wide open, showing its white interior.

The copperhead or highland moccasin (*A. contortrix*) variety, a reddish-colored pit viper with a copper-colored head and reddish-brown bands, is found in swampy, rocky, and wooded regions of the central and eastern United States.

The third variety is the cantil or Mexican moccasin (*A. bilineatus*), a brightly colored, poisonous snake that lives from the low regions of the Rio Grande to Nicaragua.

FER-DE-LANCE

SCIENTIFIC NAME: *Bothrops atrox.*

FAMILY: Viperidae

SUBFAMILY: Crotalinae.

TOXICITY: 6, depending on the variety of snake and other factors. On average, a fer-de-lance injects enoiugh venom in one bite to kill a human.

EFFECTS AND SYMPTOMS: Local pain, bleeding from the bite, gums, nose, mouth, and rectum. The blood cannot coagulate and hemorrhages into muscles and the nervous system. Shock and respiratory distress come before death.

REACTION TIME: Symptoms begin within an hour. They can develop sooner depending on how active the person is. Activity creates more blood flow and disperses the venom throughout the body faster.

ANTIDOTES AND TREATMENTS: Antivenin is available for most of the species but the key is identifying which snake has bitten the victim.

NOTES: From central Mexico south into South America, through tropical America, this pit viper makes its home in the forests of Bolivia, Brazil, Venezuela, Peru, Colombia, Ecuador, northern Argentina, as well as Central America and the West Indies. The fer-de-lance—French for "lancehead"—is called *barba amarillo* (yellow chin) in Spanish. Markings are gray or brown with black-edged diamonds on a lighter border. Some of the varieties are habu (*Trimeresurus flavoviridis*), jararaca (*Bothrops jararaca*), wutu (*B. alternus*), jumping viper or tommygoff (*B. nummifera*), Wagler's pit viper (*T. wagleri*).

Other *Bothrops*, and even some Asian *Trimeresurus* living in the tropical Americas, are often called fer-de-lance. Frequently, it's confused with jararaca (a cousin), which has similar markings of olive or gray-brown on darker blotches and which also inhabits the grassy areas of Brazil.

Another dangerous South American pit viper is the wutu. Its marks are dark brown semicircles outlined in yellow over a brown body.

In Central America, another aggressive cousin is the jumping viper. Its skin is brown or gray with diamond-shaped crossmarkings.This viper, not as dangerous as its cousins, lives up to its name, often attacking its victims so vigorously that it lifts itself clear off the ground.

The Okinawa habu, a large, aggressive—but not quite as lethal—cousin, is found on the Amani and Okinawa groups of the Ryukyu Islands, and can wander boldly into homes and cars. Dark green blotches on its body form a wavy lengthwise band.

RATTLESNAKE

FAMILY: Viperidae.

SUBFAMILY: Crotalinae.

TOXICITY: 4 to 6, depending on the type of snake.

EFFECTS AND SYMPTOMS: Rattlesnake venom causes excessive thirst, nausea, vomiting, shock, numbness, drowsiness, sweating, blurred vision, weakness and paralysis, swelling of lymph nodes, respiratory distress, anemia, drooping of the eyelids, pain and necrosis (dead tissue) at the site of the bite, and possible kidney shutdown, resulting in death.

A rattlesnake bite, like that of most vipers, is painful and resembles a hot needle jab. Sometimes the area around the fang puncture is temporarily numb, which means a large injection of venom and a serious bite. Tingling around the mouth and a sensation of yellowish vision are other indications of severe poisoning. Vomiting and violent spasms can shake the entire body, which will show small red spots (petechial hemorrhages) and extensive bleeding at the wound site. One or more puncture wounds or toothmarks will be found. The skin will be discolored, with local swelling.

Death from rattlesnake bite in the United States is rare, since medical help is usually given immediately.

REACTION TIME: Fifteen minutes to an hour. Severe poisoning is indicated by hemorrhages or by swelling above the elbows or knees within two hours.

ANTIDOTES AND TREATMENTS: Rattlesnake antivenin is available in most places.

NOTES: The heat-sensing pit between each eye and nostril has given rattlesnakes the name pit vipers. Found in the desert sections of the Americas (North and South) and Canada, each variety has a distinct rattle (sounding like a hissing or buzzing) created by their tails. Coming from the Crotalus genus, rattlesnakes in North America include the eastern diamondback (*Crotalus adamanteus*) found in coastal plains from North Carolina to Mississippi; the western diamondback (*C. atrox*), located from Arkansas to Southern California and Mexico; the timber rattlesnake (*C. horridus horridus*), found from Minnesota to central Texas; the canebrake rattlesnake (*C. horridus atricaudatus*), which makes its home in the southwestern United States; the Pacific rattlesnake (*C. viridis*), located in Southern California and Baja California; and the Mojave rattlesnake (*C. scutulatus*), living in west Texas to Southern California, and in northern and central Mexico.

The sidewinder, or the horned rattler, (*C. cerastes*) is known for its sideways motion and found in the desert of the southwestern United States and northeastern Mexico. From the genus Sisrurus, the massasauga (*Sistrurus catenatus*) lives in the Great Lakes area and southwest Arizona and Mexico; and the pygmy rattlesnake (S. *miliarius*), with an ineffective rattle, inhabits the southeastern United States west to Missouri and eastern Texas.

In Central and South America, the cascabel rattlesnake (*C. durissus*) goes by the name of the tropical or South American rattlesnake and is a dangerous rattler almost equal in poison to the Mexican West Coast rattlesnake (*C. basiliscus*) living in western Mexico; the Brazilian (*C. durissis terrificus*) is found in southeastern Brazil, Argentina, and Paraguay.

Of all the snakebites in the United States, 98 percent are from rattlesnakes and related species. While the reason for the rattles on the tail has never been proved, the theory is that they evolved to warn grazing herds of their presence, so the snakes could avoid being trampled.

Acetylcholinesterase is the most active toxin in rattlesnake venom, but in Brazil, the tropical rattler also has a poison called crotamine—a toxin known to cause convulsions and to relax the muscles so severely that the head lolls as if the neck is broken.

CASE HISTORY

Representatives of Synanon, the drug rehabilitation program turned cult, attempted to kill an opposing lawyer by putting a rattlesnake, minus its rattles, into the victim's mailbox. The lawyer was bitten on the hand and wrist, sought immediate medical attention, and survived the attack.

In a recent suicide, a despondent exotic dancer who used poisonous snakes and spiders in her act provoked a rattlesnake into biting her. She died four days later.

OTHER REPTILES

Though no deaths have been reported in recent centuries, another poisonous North American reptile is the Gila Monster.

GILA MONSTER

SCIENTIFIC NAME: *Heloderma suspectum, H. horridum.*

OTHER: Mexican beaded lizard

TOXICITY: 6

EFFECTS AND SYMPTOMS: Severe pain at the site of the bite. Systemic symptoms include blue-tinged skin; respiratory problems, such as shallow, rapid breathing; erratic heartbeat; tinnitus; faintness; nausea; vertigo; and weakness. If a fatal dose is taken in, respiratory arrest causes death. Human fatalities are rare, but they do happen.

REACTION TIME: Fifty minutes to a few hours after the bite. As with snakebites, the degree of severity varies with the amount of venom injected, the site of the bite, and the victim's general health.

ANTIDOTES AND TREATMENTS: No specific antiserum is known. Treatment is symptomatic.

NOTES: The Gila monster is found in the desert areas of the southwestern United States and northern Mexico, while the Mexican version is found in dense forests of southern Mexico.

The lizard does not bite unless provoked, but once it bites it is tenacious. Often the victim must be cut free from the animal.

This thick-tailed lizard grows to twenty inches. The stout body has black and pink or orange blotches or bands and beadlike scales. The Mexican version is slightly larger and darker.

The deeply grooved and flanged teeth conduct the venom, a nerve poison, from the glands to the lower jaw.

The amount of venom to produce a fatal dose is not known, but toxicity is compared to snake venom, since a small scratch from the teeth of the Gila monster can produce severe symptoms similar to rattlesnake poisoning.

Prior to 1900, the whiskey antidote that was popular for snakebites was used for Gila monster bites as well and was probably more responsible for the deaths of victims than the actual bite.

AMPHIBIANS

Amphibians, including numerous salamanders, newts, and toads, secrete a venom toxic to humans. Because they have no means of injecting it, however, they rarely cause fatalities unless the venom comes in contact with a wound or sore, or passes into the body via a mucous membrane. A large dose of venom would be needed to cause death. However, one type of highly poisonous amphibian is the poison dart frog.

POISON DART FROGS

SCIENTIFIC NAME: *Dendrobates Azureus.*

OTHER: Dart frogs, dendrobatid frogs, blue poison frogs.

TOXICITY: 6 (Only the snake *Leimadophis epinephelus* is immune to the frog poison.)

EFFECTS AND SYMPTOMS: The poisons have unique effects on the nerves and muscles, paralyzing the victim almost immediately.

REACTION TIME: Immediate.

ANTIDOTES AND TREATMENTS: None.

NOTES: These frogs inhabit the tropical and subtropical zones, going from central Mexico to the southernmost tip of South America. Several varieties exist, including the blue poison frog, which comes in a variety of blue colors with black spots on its head. These are found in the southern part of Suriname, South America. Other species live in tropical South America and from Costa Rica to southern Brazil. Though they are land creatures, they stay near a water source, such as pond or stream, and prefer dark, moist environments, like tropical rainforests. Their diet includes termites, crickets, ants, and fruit flies, which are synthesized into skin poisons. (Those bred in captivity do not ingest the same chemicals and so are much less toxic.)

When house bred, young cannibalistic frogs are territorial and aggressive and so are housed separately from the parents and siblings as the tadpole emerges. It takes twelve weeks to metamorphose from a tadpole to a frog.

The toxins in the skin of these blue frogs are used to poison arrows. The frogs are pinned to the ground by natives, who coat the tips of their arrows by wiping the arrowheads on the skin.

Those frogs with a less deadly toxin are skewered over a fire, and the heat helps excrete large quantities of the poison, which is concentrated for use.

There are four main groups and over 170 species of poison arrow frogs. The main groups include: *Dendrobates, Epipedobates, Minyobates,* and *Phyllobates.* They vary in length from 1.5cm to 7cm with the *Dendrobates minutus* being the smallest. Males can be distinguished from the females by their larger front toe pads.

As a family, the poison arrow frogs are brightly colored: red, green, yellow, and blue, as well as patterned with spots and stripes.

The skin stays sticky from mucus and the poison is secreted through the skin, and even a lick can be fatal. So look, but don't touch, because the poison can enter the bloodstream through an open wound in the skin.

Frogs bred in captivity often lose their poison.

A new pain killer called ABT-594 has been discovered at Abbot Labs in Chicago involving the poison arrow frog *Epipedroates tricolor* from Ecuador. The National Institute of Diabetes and Digestive and Kidney Diseases found that the extract from the skin could block pain two hundred times more effectively than morphine. The compound, epibatidine, appears to have none of the serious side effects of morphine, such as hindered respiration or digestive movement.

The frogs are being threatened by the destruction of the rain forests.

SPIDERS

As with snake bites, the toxicity and reaction time of spider bites depend on how vascular the area bitten is (a bite in the genitals is far more serious than one on the lower leg), the weight of the person, and how much venom is injected. All the venoms are administered by bite but can also be singled out and given as intramuscular injections as well.

The movie *Arachnophobia* made light of some of these little monsters (not so little in the movie), but the bite of a spider can be deadly.

BLACK WIDOW

SCIENTIFIC NAME: *Latrodectus mactans.*

OTHER: Hourglass spider, button spider (South Africa), red back (Australia), *katipo* (New Zealand), *malmignatte* (Mediterranean region), *karakurt* (Southern Russia).

The brown widow (*L. geometrieus*; found in all the tropics) has the same marks as the black widow but is brown and it is reluctant to bite humans. There are no widows, black or brown, in central or northern Eurasia.

TOXICITY: 4

EFFECTS AND SYMPTOMS: The bite is often not felt. Only later does the victim realize there is a problem. Flu-like symptoms will occur for several days. Abdominal or chest muscles become rigid. Anuria, chills and sweating, and nausea and vomiting occur. If the bite proves fatal, death will be from cardiac failure.

REACTION TIME: Symptoms begin within an hour. Most bite victims recover without serious complications.

ANTIDOTES AND TREATMENTS: Antiserum is available. Other treatment is symptomatic.

NOTES: Black widow spiders may be found throughout the United States and in parts of Canada, but mostly populate warmer regions. Other members of the *Latrodectus* family are common through temperate and tropical zones. The spiders inhabit woodpiles, outhouses, brush piles, and dark corners of barns, garages, and houses, and they also hide under upholstery, cushions, and toilet lids. The latter explains why biting of the genital organs is the most common and deadly. Only the shiny, jet-black female with its bulbous, orange-hourglass-marked abdomen is dangerous.

The danger of the famed female black widow "hourglass" spider causing instantaneous death is exaggerated. While both male and female can be deadly, the male's fangs are smaller and seldom penetrate human skin. In fact, of the six species of black widow, all are venomous, but only rarely fatal.

BROWN RECLUSE

SCIENTIFIC NAME: *Loxosceles reclusa.*

OTHER: Violin spider, fiddle-back spider, brown spider.

TOXICITY: 6

EFFECTS AND SYMPTOMS: The initial bite is often painless, but within eight hours the victim may be in agony.

Within two to eight hours, there is a noticeable red ring or bull's-eye surrounding the bite area. The center area will then often blister, which over twelve to forty-eight hours can sink, turning bluish and then black as this area of tissue dies. The untreated lesion increases in size for up to a week. Symptoms also include fever, chills, joint pain, skin rash, hematuria, nausea, vomiting, cyanosis, and delirium. Blisters will form and drain. There may be large areas of necrosis near the bite. Death, if it occurs, usually comes within the first forty-eight hours due to renal failure from coagulation of the blood, but medical help is usually sought before this.

REACTION TIME: Two to eight hours.

ANTIDOTES AND TREATMENTS: There is no specific antiserum known. The venom is deadlier than that of many snakes. Adrenocortical steroids, excision of the bite area, and exchange blood transfusion might be done.

NOTES: The female of this group is the most dangerous of the spider family. The brown recluse lives in twenty-five states (rimarily from New Jersey to Illinois and down to Texas and Hawaii). Fawn-colored to medium-dark brown, the spider has a darker, violin-shaped patch on its back and likes dark, undisturbed places.

CASE HISTORY

Cleaning out her closet in California, a young woman did not notice the bite until the itching was intense. Only then did she see the necrosis around the leg wound. Recalling the spider, she still dismissed it. The symptoms continued rapidly until she sought treatment a few days later, and then massive intravenous antibiotics were needed to save her life.

In 2002, a man in Alaska was bitten on the arm by a brown recluse when he was moving firewood. Supposedly brown recluses don't live as far north as Alaska, but that is where the incident occurred. The immediate reaction was what appeared to be a water blister. When he touched the blister it popped. For the next thirteen days, the area where the blister was became red, constantly increasing in size until it was a five-inch by ten-inch spot that covered most of his arm. Because brown recluses aren't supposed to be in Alaska, he was misdiagnosed at first. After doing some research and reaching the right diagnosis, he was treated with Zithromax, and by day fifteen was much better. He had very little tissue damage. But in the process he did learn of other brown recluse bites in Alaska. These other victims had to have decayed tissue removed from places around the bite. The spiders got to Alaska in boxed shipments. They tend to live in boxes or other storage areas.

OTHER DEADLY SPIDERS

The brown spider (*Loxosceles laeta*), found in Chile; *Ctenus nigriventer,* found in Brazil; and the funnel-web spider (*Atrax robustus*), found in Australia, are all other types of poisonous spiders.

The tarantula or wolf spider (*Lycosa tarentula*), once thought to be fatal, belongs to a species of large, hairy spiders that are only mildly toxic. The largest tarantulas may kill small vertebrates, but their food is usually other spiders. The bite can be painful but is seldom dangerous to humans, although in southeastern Europe it was assumed to be the cause of a nervous condition characterized by hysteria. An Italian superstition dictated that the best cure was dancing the *tarantella* (a lively folk dance) to throw off the poison.

SCORPIONS

Poisonous scorpions of the United States—*Centruroides gertschii, C. vittatus,* and *C. sculpturatus*—live mainly in the arid Southwest (especially Arizona) and other warm areas. In Mexico and Brazil, the poisonous varieties are *Tityus bahiensis* and *T. serrulatus*. In dry areas of Africa, India, and Pakistan, the most deadly are *Androctonus australis* and *Buthus occitanus*. While most prefer warm regions, these species are also found in Mongolia and parts of Europe. Only New Zealand, Antarctica, the colder parts of Canada and Alaska, and southern parts of Chile and Argentina are free of the creatures. Scorpions live near homes and like the dark warmth of shoes and other dark places.

The pale yellow desert scorpion, with its slender claws, is more dangerous than the big black scorpion. The red ones are not lethal. Not aggressive toward humans, scorpions attack only when disturbed suddenly or annoyed. The scorpion's large front pincers grab its victim, and the venomous tail is flung forward to sting once or repeatedly.

COMMON STRIPED SCORPION

SCIENTIFIC NAME: *Centruroides vittatus, C. gertschii* (brown scorpion), *C. sculpturatus* (sculptured scorpion), *Vejovis spinigerus* (devil scorpion), *Hadrurus arizonensis* (giant hairy scorpion).

TOXICITY: 4

EFFECTS AND SYMPTOMS: The sting creates a burning sensation at the site of the wound, and the area might become immediately swollen and discolored. A blister often forms where the skin is pricked. Effects last for eight to twelve hours.

The more dangerous scorpions gives little local evidence of the sting, except for mild tingling at the sting site. This tingling may progress up the extremity, but swelling and discoloration do not occur. The tingling produces intense pain. The victim will also have nausea, extreme irritability, tachycardia, and diarrhea. In severe cases, throat spasms; thick tongue; restlessness; muscular spasms; stomach cramps; trembling; convulsions; extremes of high or low blood pressure; poor cardiac rhythm; internal hemorrhages of the stomach, intestine and lungs; pulmonary edema; and respiratory failure occur along with cardiac collapse. Symptoms starting as soon as four hours after a sting indicate a poor outcome. Most persons stung exhibit anxiety and agitation.

REACTION TIME: Swelling and discoloration occur immediately. The duration of symptoms is ordinarily twenty-four to forty-eight hours, but fatalities have occurred four days after the sting.

ANTIDOTES AND TREATMENTS: Antiserum is available but helpful only if used within minutes after the bite. Other treatments consist of applying a tourniquet close to the bite to limit absorption, and then symptomatic treatment once the victim reaches medical care.

NOTES: A popular belief holds that the sting of any scorpion means death, but that is not necessarily true. Very few species have poison strong enough to kill an adult human. Only one out of a thousand stings is fatal, so scorpions are not as deadly as feared. While scorpion venom is more toxic than that of many snakes, the amount released in a sting is usually minute; and if absorption is delayed, serious symptoms can be avoided. However, the venom can be collected separately and injected intramuscularly, making it quite deadly.

OCEAN-DWELLING CREATURES

There are two types of ingested fish poison: ciguatera and scombroid. These are usually the result of spoiled fish, and while they can make the victim quite ill, they are seldom fatal.

Besides the natural fish poisons, our society must contend with the increase in mercury poisonings. Toxic mercury levels, deposited into the oceans by air pollution and runoff, are accumulating in fish. This is especially true of swordfish, shark, and tilefish, which live longer and feed on smaller fish, thereby increasing their exposure. Women of childbearing age are advised to limit consumption of these fish, as exposure to mercury in the womb can harm the nervous system of the developing baby. Potentially, someone can get mercury poisoning by eating too much mercury-loaded fish.

Some sea dwellers, however, contain their own, home-grown toxins.

BIVALVE SHELLFISH

TOXICITY: 6 during the toxic season (May to October). During the winter months, toxins may rate a 3 or 4.

EFFECTS AND SYMPTOMS: A nitrogenous compound in the shellfish produces curare-like muscular paralysis. Initial signs of poisoning from this toxin are tingling in the lips and extremities followed by a reduction of motor abilities and difficulty breathing. Nausea and vomiting follow. Convulsions may occur. Symptoms progress to respiratory paralysis and death.

REACTION TIME: Symptoms start within thirty minutes. If the victim survives for twelve hours, recovery is likely. Fatalities occur in 10 percent of the cases.

ANTIDOTES AND TREATMENTS: If these symptoms occur after eating shellfish, the standard medical treatment is to give victims oxygen or place them on a respirator. No antidote exists. The only hope is to keep the person alive until the toxin has passed from the system.

NOTES: Shellfish thrive in many marine locations, such as California, Mexico, and Alaska. Mussels, clams, oysters, scallops, cockles, and other shellfish can become poisonous with potent nerve poisons during the warm months of the year, when they feed on certain dinoflagellates—microscopic cellular beings such as *Gonyaulax catenella*—that carry the poison.

Paralytic shellfish toxins (PSTs) are potent neurotoxins produced by some strains of dinoflagellates. When passed through the marine food web, these toxins can lead to human disease through consumption of contaminated shellfish. There are often warnings issued by government agencies telling people not to eat particular shellfish at certain times of the year. The morbidity rate of those consuming toxic shellfish is high. Mussels produce the highest death rate of all the bivalve shellfish.

Another of the toxic dinoflagellates is *Karenia brevis*, formerly *Gymnodinium breve*, that occur periodically in the Gulf of Mexico. Blooms of these algae are referred to as red tides because their presence discolors the water making it a reddish-brown that affects fish mortality. They accumulate in the fish digestive tracts, causing the bivalves—oysters and clams—to be dangerous for human consumption.

BLUE-RINGED OCTOPUS

SCIENTIFIC NAME: *Hapalochlaena maculosa, Octopus maculosa, H. lunulata* (Australian spotted octopus), *Octopus apollyon* (North American West Coast octopus).

TOXICITY: 6

EFFECTS AND SYMPTOMS: The poison affects the central nervous system, with gradual weakness of the muscles progressing to paralysis of the whole body, starting with a prickly sensation around the mouth and lips and continuing until breathing has stopped. The victim is conscious until the very end and has difficulty talking. Convulsions and vomiting are also sometimes seen.

REACTION TIME: Immediate.

ANTIDOTES AND TREATMENTS: Maintaining respiration immediately with mouth-to-mouth resuscitation. Death comes in a high percentage of cases due to the neuromuscular poisons.

NOTES: The brown-speckled octopus is distinguished by the blue bands around its tentacles, which give it its name. This small animal can be dangerous—when the bands around the tentacles glow blue, poison is about to be released. The octopus seldom bothers humans unless it is bothered first, but since it's so small, many humans think it harmless. Barely six inches across, it has a true octopus shape.

Also found in North America from Alaska to Baja California is the *Octopus apollyon*, nearly as deadly.

The Australian spotted octopus is found in Australia near Queensland, New South Wales, Sydney, and Victoria, and also in the Indian Ocean, Indo-Pacific (the Indian Ocean, Pacific Ocean, and the minor seas between the two in the general area of Indonesia), and Japan. The creature likes bays and reefs.

The octopus has killed at least two humans in recent years, both times because the person was playing with the creature.

CASE HISTORY

In 1967, a young soldier held an octopus on the back of his hand for a minute or two and had no sensation of a bite, but after putting the creature down, he noticed blood on his hand. A few minutes later he felt a prickling sensation around his mouth, which rapidly became generalized; within fifteen minutes he was almost completely paralyzed and hardly able to breathe. After an hour, he vomited and began convulsing. One hour after the bite, he was taken to the hospital, still breathing. He was fully conscious but completely paralyzed, with no muscle tone, no reflexes, and no ability to talk. In another hour, he had quit breathing and was put on a heart-lung machine and did, eventually, survive.

A lone fisherman, using the octopus for bait, was barely aware he'd been bitten. Going into the water, he didn't realize his paralysis until it was too late, and he drowned. When the body was later found, there was no sign of the fast-acting toxin in his body. The bite, hard to find under the best of conditions, was nearly impossible to locate in the water-swollen body. Only the telltale signs of flaccid paralysis was a clue to the cause of his death.

CONE SHELLS

SCIENTIFIC NAME: *Conus geographus*

OTHER: Geography cone, conch shells.

TOXICITY: 6

EFFECTS AND SYMPTOMS: At the very least, the cone shell poison causes temporary paralysis of the limbs and prolonged difficulty in breathing. A numb feeling starts with the lips and continues over the whole body. The victim complains of dizziness, tightness in the chest, and pain when breathing. The pulse is rapid. Death occurs from respiratory arrest.

REACTION TIME: Immediate first symptoms. Death can occur quickly. If the victim survives the first ten hours, the prognosis is good.

ANTIDOTES AND TREATMENTS: No antiserum is available. Supportive measures are given as needed.

NOTES: Cone shells are small venomous mollusks within spotted or brightly colored shells. The shell is one to eight inches long, conical shaped with a large aperture. There are three types of cones: worm-eaters, mollusk-eaters, and fish-eaters, all of which are deadly to humans. Their slug-like heads contain harpoon-like teeth that are a half-inch long and strong enough to pierce thin cloth. There are over seventy different species, including *C. magus, C. purcens, C. catus*, tulip cone (*C. tulipa*), and striated cone (*C. striatoxicity*).

Depending on the species, the venom can be white, gray, yellow, or black. The mollusks inhabit the tropical waters of Australia (near Queensland), New Guinea, and near the Barrier Reef, as well as the subtropical waters of the Indo-Pacific, and a few species live in the waters of the Mediterranean, Southern California, and New Zealand.

All human victims in recent years were handling the shell before being stung. The mollusk usually comes out of the smaller end to sting, but it's best to handle the cone with forceps or not at all. There have been several instances in which the mollusk stung through cloth when being carried in a bag swinging against the victim's body.

CASE HISTORY

An Australian fatality occurred on Hayman Island in 1935. The victim, a young man in good health, held a cone shell in his hand as he scraped it with a knife. The mollusk inside extended its fangs and stung him on the palm. Although just a small puncture wound, it caused almost immediate numbness. His lips became stiff, then his vision blurred. Within thirty minutes, his legs were paralyzed; within the hour, he had lost consciousness, drifting into a fatal coma.

Mentioned in *Jurassic Park*, cone shell poison was used in the darts to kill the dinosaurs.

JELLYFISH

SCIENTIFIC NAME: *Chironex fleckeri, Chiropsalmus quadrigatus, Craspedacusta*

OTHER: Cube jellies, sea wasps, box jellyfish, cubomedusae.

TOXICITY: 6

EFFECTS AND SYMPTOMS: In the dangerous varieties, the venom varies from mildly irritating to lethal. Symptoms are severe chest and abdominal pain, difficulty swallowing, extreme pain at the site of the bite, skin necrosis, and respiratory and cardiac depression leading to death. The American jellyfish (*Aurelia*), the flattened jellyfish common along North American coasts, will cause sickness, but probably not kill unless the victim already has a weak heart or other problems. Many Australian swimmers have been found floating in the water, and drowning was thought to be the cause of death until it was realized the victim had been stung by a jellyfish.

The initial pain and shock of the sting makes the victim wrench away and this, in turn, stimulates the tentacles to release more poison, increasing the severity of the dose. On the beach, if the victim attempts to rip off the sticky threads where the poison comes from, more toxin is released. Victims look as if they've been beaten with a cat-o'-nine-tails made of barbed wire. On people who survive, the welts become disfiguring red blisters and may be permanent scars.

REACTION TIME: The deadly variety is fatal in minutes.

ANTIDOTES AND TREATMENTS: An antiserum exists but must be administered immediately, and a tourniquet must be applied to all affected limbs. A copious amount of alcohol should be poured over the sticky tentacles to inactivate the nematocysts (stinging capsules within the sticky threads) and shrivel the tentacles so they can be brushed off without releasing more venom. If the action is slowed, the body can cope.

NOTES: Jellyfish are bluish, rosy, violet, or transparent open umbrellas with four, eight, or more tentacles dangling from the rim. There are numerous species of jellyfish. They float on or near the surface of the waves and often go unnoticed by humans until there is a rash of stings.

Jellyfish often invade beaches around the world in vast numbers. They inhabit cool waters as well as tropical and are seen as far north as the central Atlantic seaboard in the United States.

The dormant nematocysts are capable of discharging poisons for months after being beached if they are regularly moistened by sea water. Even air-dried nematocysts may contain considerable potency after several weeks.

The Australian sea wasp (*Chironex fleckeri*) is possibly the most dangerous of all marine animals. Named in 1956 for Dr. Hugo Flecker, who determined that this species had caused the death of many swimmers, it is considered one of the most deadly organisms anywhere. Rather boxlike in shape, it is often quite small and has tentacles in clusters at the corners of its body. The nematocysts each contain a minute amount of one of the most deadly venoms ever discovered.

PORTUGUESE MAN-OF-WAR

SCIENTIFIC NAME: *Physalia physalis, P. utriculus* (Australian bluebottle).

TOXICITY: 4

EFFECTS AND SYMPTOMS: The sting causes severe chest and abdominal pain, difficulty in swallowing, hives, stinging pain, fever, swelling of the lymph nodes, long welt lines, and shock. The venom is 75 percent as strong as the cobra's. Chest pains can cause problems swimming, so drowning may be the actual cause of death.

The painful lesions can last for weeks.

Since these creatures usually float in groups of a thousand or more, it's rare that the victim will receive only one sting. Therefore, enough venom can be administered to cause respiratory arrest.

REACTION TIME: Immediate.

ANTIDOTES AND TREATMENTS: Symptomatic.

Visible tentacles are removed with the aid of towels or other implements, not with the bare hands. The affected area is then rinsed with fresh or salt water—not vinegar, as is sometimes recommended. When pain is severe, heat or cold may be applied, whichever feels better to the victim.

NOTES: This jellyfish-like creature inhabits the surface of the sea and is found in warm waters around the world. The man-of-war's body looks like an ancient Portuguese soldier's helmet. It consists of a translucent—tinted pink, blue, or violet—nitrogen-filled bladder and blue thread-like tentacles that may be from three to twelve inches in diameter.

The *P. physalis* is most common in the gulf stream of the Atlantic and the subtropical and tropical regions of the Indo-Pacific.

The creature moves by means of its crest, which functions as a sail. Beneath the gas-filled float are clusters of polyps from which hang tentacles of up to 165 feet in length. These tentacles bear stinging nematocystic (coiled thread-like) structures that paralyze small fish and other prey. They attach to the immobilized victim and spread over it, digesting it. The Portuguese man-of-war will eat basically anything that comes in contact with its stinging tentacle polyps.

PUFFERFISH

SCIENTIFIC NAME: *Arothron meleagris.*

OTHER: Toad-blowfish, swellfish, balloonfish, globefish, toado.

TOXICITY: 6

EFFECTS AND SYMPTOMS: Tetraodontoxin affects the nervous system in such a way as to prevent the propagation of nerve impulses. While it does not cross the blood-brain barrier, it inhibits the ability of nerves to send messages to other parts of the body. The first sign that something is awry is a slight numbness in the lips and tongue. This numbness soon increases and spreads to certain parts of the face and throat. Some reported initial symptoms also include involuntary muscle spasms, weakness, dizziness, and loss of speech. There is excessive salivation and sweating, along with slowed heart rate and a drop in body temperature. Victims soon experience respiratory distress, marked by rapid, shallow breathing.

The secondary stage of the poisoning involves increased paralysis, to the point that even sitting becomes difficult. After another increase in paralysis, mental impairment and convulsions ensue. This is followed by an inevitable case of cardiac arrhythmia. There have been reports from survivors that they were completely lucid during the entire event, finally recovering to tell the tale.

There is a mortality rate of over 50 percent for those poisoned by pufferfish.

REACTION TIME: Symptoms start in ten minutes, or can be delayed up to eight hours. Survival past twenty-four hours is a sign of recovery.

NOTES: This fish is commonly found in warm or temperate regions around the world, including the west coast of Central America, throughout the Indo-Pacific, around Japan, and from Australia to South Africa. There are over ninety species of pufferfish, eleven of which belong to the family *Tetraodontidae*. When disturbed, the fish inflates itself and becomes globular in form.

The poison tetraodontoxin is found in the fish's ovaries and liver. But the fish is usually harmless if the poisonous organs and poison sacs are removed before cooking.

One hundred to two hundred people become ill each year after eating pufferfish. Roughly half of these poisonings are fatal, even with immediate treatment.

In Japan, where it is called fugu and is considered the ultimate gastronomic experience, the fish must be cleaned and prepared by a specially licensed chef. The training includes a two-to three-year apprenticeship, after which the chef must pass several written and practical exams, including preparing and eating his own fugu. Because of this rigorous examination procedure, it is generally safe to eat the fugu served in Japanese restaurants.

Ten thousand times more lethal than cyanide, tetraodontoxin is also present in other animals besides pufferfish, including the blue-ringed octopus, harlequin frogs, and rough-skinned newts. Tetraodontoxin has also been isolated from certain strains of algae, and from other marine life, such as some snails, crabs, and even a type of flatworm.

This toxin is the main ingredient in zombie-making rituals in Haiti and West Africa. Some patients who have taken the poison exist in zombie-like states of suspended animation for days before experiencing complete recovery.

A tiny Canadian company is attempting to develop the poison into a drug that can help cancer patients suppress pain, or wean heroin addicts off their habit. Early surveys indicate that it works against pain that no other pain medication has overcome. The drug would be called Tectin.

CASE HISTORY

From 1955 to 1975, of the three thousand people poisoned in Japan by eating fugu, over fifteen hundred died.

This toxin was used in the movie *The Serpent and the Rainbow* to slow the respiration of the victim so that it appeared he was dead. After a quick burial, the victim was dug out and continued to be fed the drug at a lesser dose so that, while his body functioned, his mind did not. He became a zombie or the living dead.

SCORPIONFISH

SCIENTIFIC NAME: *Scorpaena guttata, Pterois volitans* (lionfish), *Synanceja horrida* (devilfish).

OTHER: Stonefish, zebrafish, butterfly cod, turkeyfish, firefish, rockfish.

TOXICITY: 5

EFFECTS AND SYMPTOMS: Marked swelling, convulsions, and intense pain may continue for hours, disabling the victim and even causing unconsciousness. Convulsions and unconsciousness, incredible pain, and paralysis of limbs can cause swimmers to drown. Respiratory distress often leads to cardiac failure. If the victim survives, secondary infection is common and gangrene can occur. A fluctuating fever with sharp highs and lows can lead to collapse and death due to cardiac failure.

REACTION TIME: Instantaneous. Recovery is a slow and painful process of weeks and months. There may be a permanent scar.

ANTIDOTES AND TREATMENTS: Stonefish antivenin is available, but in remote or tropical areas this may be unobtainable.

NOTES: The scorpionfish can be found in the Pacific from central California to the Gulf of California. Other varieties of this fish are found in most seas. The zebrafish is found in the Red Sea, the Indian Ocean, and the western Pacific from Japan to Australia. The stonefish inhabits the Indo-Pacific and the waters around China, the Philippines, and Australia.

The scorpionfish is about four to eight inches long with a large head, big mouth, and bright bands in reddish brown and white. Reef-dwellers, they are often found upside down in coral caves and other shelters. When annoyed, the fish tend to stand their ground and may actually approach the intruder, dorsal spines erect. All spines contain venom. The scratch is extremely painful and can cause a swimmer to be incapacitated. There are eighty different varieties of scorpionfish.

The stonefish looks like an irregular lump of flesh. It has a large, upturned mouth to suck in prey. Closely related to the scorpionfish, it is sedentary, usually lying partially buried in the debris of a coral reef or in mud flats. Colors are subdued, matching their background to some extent. The spines and venom glands of these fish are large. The dorsal fins become erect at the least disturbance, so if an unlucky swimmer or diver steps on the fish, there is an immediate sting.

The zebrafish is a beautiful variety with vivid colors and elegant fins like wings of a butterfly.

The most familiar aquarium species are among the most venomous. Stonefish spines can penetrate flippers and thin tennis shoes as well as gloves.

STINGRAY

SCIENTIFIC NAME: *Dasyatis pastinaca, Urobatis halleri* (round stingray), *Aetobatus narinari* (spotted eagle ray).

OTHER: California stingray.

TOXICITY: 4

EFFECTS AND SYMPTOMS: The venom affects the heart muscle and causes erratic heart rhythm that sometimes brings on a fatal heart attack. The intense pain from the tail barb's penetration of the skin starts a fall in blood pressure, nausea, vomiting, dizziness, profuse sweating, stomach pain, cramps, weakness, convulsions, and collapse. In some victims, there are multiple lesions from the sting that can become necrotic.

REACTION TIME: Immediate. If medical attention is received quickly, recovery can occur in twenty-four to forty-eight hours.

ANTIDOTES AND TREATMENTS: The wounds are surgically debrided and treatment is symptomatic.

NOTES: The stingray is found in the northeastern Baltic Sea, the Mediterranean Sea, and the Indian Ocean. The spotted eagle ray inhabits the tropical waters of the Atlantic, Red Sea, and Indo-Pacific. The round stingray is found from Point Conception in California to the Panama Bay.

CASE HISTORY

In Colombia, over a five-year period (1912–1917), there were eight fatalities, twenty-three amputations of lower limbs, and one hundred and fourteen victims laid off from work while the coast line was repeatedly cleaned.

In September 2006, famed "Crocodile Hunter" Steve Irwin was killed by a stingray barb while filming an underwater episode of his television program for Discovery. While the poison affected him, what killed him was the eight-foot-long barb that pierced his heart.

OTHER POISONOUS FISH

In tropical oceans, especially around Hawaii, there are poisonous fish, such as porcupine fish, mukimuki, triggerfish, parrot fish, moray eel, surgeonfish, moon fish, filefish, goatfish, trunk fish, crown-of-thorns starfish, and box fish. These are all poisonous only part of the year, usually in the warmer months.

CHAPTER 8

MEDICAL
POISONS

If anyone ever gets a real dose of this, he's on his way to the next world.

—KEN BARLOW, 1957, JUST BEFORE CONVICTION
FOR THE INSULIN MURDER OF HIS WIFE

In the eighteenth century, when medical science first stumbled forward, many doctors were reluctant to accept and use folk/plant lore for curing their patients. But the so-called scientific remedies they gave often killed the patients they were trying to help. Now, many of the old folk remedies are used as a starting point in developing new drugs and are the foundation of homeopathic medicine.

There are always new drugs being developed. While the FDA has very strict regulations for new medications, sometimes drugs slip through the process with side effects going unnoticed until the drug is well established in general use.

Of course, just because a drug is being investigated for deadly side effects does not mean that everyone will have the same symptoms when taking the drug. The conditions, and combinations with other drugs that interact with the offender, have to be right.

But even drugs with no known side effects can be deadly. As has been said before, anything, if taken in the right circumstances and right quantity, can cause mayhem.

The amount of a drug needed to cause the desired effect—the regulation of blood sugar, relief of pain, or, in the case of the fictional killer, death—can vary from individual to individual. Generally, no doctor will knowingly prescribe a lethal overdose (except in the rare case of an assisted suicide). However, many fatalities result from a combination of drugs, such as one doctor prescribing a barbiturate and another, not knowing the patient's medications, prescribing a second barbiturate. Drug seekers and addicts take advantage of doctors' inability to check on the number or type of prescriptions an individual has filled.

How the drug is taken can increase its lethal potential. For example, time-release capsules are designed to dissolve in the body slowly at a predetermined rate. But when taken with an accelerant, the medication is released rapidly, dumping the whole amount into the body and causing an overdose with potentially fatal effects. Death can also occur when a drug is withdrawn too suddenly.

Many drugs, when used over time, cause the patient to become dependent (addicted), requiring increasingly larger doses to produce the desired effect. For example, if a victim is taking Valium, and becomes addicted to the drug, and the poisoner wants to use an overdose of Librium to kill the victim, he will require a much larger dose for the drug to be fatal. The two drugs are related, and the victim, by taking Valium, has developed a tolerance to both.

It is important to remember that over-the-counter (OTC) drugs can also be fatal. For example, taking a number of OTC cold products containing acetaminophen (Tylenol) can easily cause an overdose. Even Pepto Bismol (bismuth), a salicylate, can have a negative effect when taken with other drugs, especially things like Coumadin.

Homeopathics, herbs, and vitamins are real drugs but are unregulated by the FDA, as they are treated as food supplements and not drugs. Many seemingly benign alternatives, herb supplements, and vitamins (such as ginkgo, ginseng, and St. John's wort), or foods (such as garlic, grapefruit juice, green tea, milk, carrots, and even spinach), interact with certain medications. For specific information, consult the caution label on the bottle or the drug insert that comes with the medication. Never believe an herbal that claims to have no harmful side effects or drug interactions.

It should be noted that the potency of these drugs is erratic, since there is no FDA regulation of them. The amount can vary from bottle to bottle, and pill to pill, by as much as 50 percent. (In Europe the homeopathic industry is more defined and controlled.)

Another source of poisons is veterinary supply houses, as they are a lot more lax, available to breeders without many restrictions. Some can even be found in mail-order catalogs or online.

The medications listed in this chapter are grouped into categories. All of these have a safe dosage. Symptoms relate in general to the group and apply to overdoses of the drugs, or side effects that need to be watched out for if you are taking that medication.

Symptoms, or other information specific to a particular drug within that category, will be noted, as well as some drugs that are especially interesting. It is impossible to note every available medication in detail, so many drugs here are grouped in categories even though there are minute differences between them.

The amount of the drug needed to cause a fatal overdose varies from person to person.

ASPIRIN

SCIENTIFIC NAME: Acetylsalicylic acid.

OTHER SIMILAR: Buffered forms of acetylsalicylics as Bufferin, Ecotrin, Bayer aspirin, Ascriptin, choline, salicylate, methyl salicylate, and oil of wintergreen

TOXICITY: 4

FORM: Oral (tablets, caplets, and enteric-coated): A white powder with a slightly bitter taste, aspirin is too unstable to be stored as a liquid.

EFFECTS AND SYMPTOMS: Aspirin stimulates the central nervous system and causes an accumulation of organic acids. It also interferes with vitamin K utilization.

Symptoms include burning pain in the mouth, throat, and abdomen; lethargy; hearing loss; ringing in the ears; fever; dehydration; restlessness; incoordination; dizziness, cerebral edema; ecchymoses (black and blue marks); pulmonary edema; convulsions; cyanosis; oliguria; uremia; coma; and respiratory failure. Chronic poisonings cause gastric bleeding or hemorrhages. Lab results show blood and protein in the urine, as well as acidity in the blood.

REACTION TIME: Four to six hours.

ANTIDOTES AND TREATMENTS: Vomiting is generally not encouraged because often poisons are corrosive. In addition, when vomiting, the victim can aspirate (breathing in the vomit, blocking the lungs and damaging the lining of the lungs) if respirations are weakened. Abnormal bleeding may have to be treated with whole blood or platelet transfusion.

NOTES: An anti-inflammatory, aspirin's analgesic and antipyretic (fever reducing) properties are also well known. Aspirin causes bleeding not because it is an anti-coagulant but because it increases the acidity, and attacks the gastric lining of the stomach, which is why there are buffered versions.

Enteric-coated pills such as Ecotrin are made to dissolve in the lower intestine so as not to irritate the lining of the stomach. They take much longer to be effective and must be taken whole to dissolve properly.

Aspirin may greatly increase the liver toxicity of acetaminophen (Tylenol). It also decreases the clotting time of the blood when combined with warfarin. So if someone is taking warfarin and receives a dose of aspirin, there is a greater chance he might bleed to death.

BOOK OF POISONS

Aspirin deteriorates rapidly with moisture and must be stored in an airtight, dry container; therefore there is no liquid version of the drug. Decomposed aspirin smells like acetic acid.

Vitamin C in large doses taken with aspirin can cause a dangerous, but not usually fatal, reaction.

Aspirin is not recommended for younger children and teens, since it may cause Reye's syndrome, a disease affecting the organs, especially the liver and brain.

Many heart patients are given a regimen of low-dose (81mg) aspirin to prevent heart attacks.

While people are told not to take aspirin before surgery because it decreases the blood clotting properties, increasing the amount of aspirin will not significantly increase the blood clotting difficulties.

ATOPHAN

SCIENTIFIC NAME: Phenylquinoline carbonic acid.

OTHER: Cinchophen, Atochinol. Composite preparations in which atophan is hidden and which are particularly dangerous are Uro-Zero, Arkanol, and Gorum.

TOXICITY: 6

FORM: Oral.

EFFECTS AND SYMPTOMS: The drug promotes uric acid excretion in the body and does general liver damage. The victim's urine has a very yellow color. Symptoms are vomiting, jaundice, and poor clotting time, as well as hemorrhages throughout the body. Deaths are usually from acute liver atrophy.

REACTION TIME: Several days.

ANTIDOTES AND TREATMENTS: Medication must be discontinued immediately. No other treatment is known.

NOTES: It is widely used to treat rheumatic disease and podagra (gout).

CASE HISTORY

The father of a twenty-six-year-old man in India noticed that the whites of his son's eyes were somewhat yellow. It was learned that the boy had been taking eight atophan tablets a day for the relief of rheumatism, which had followed an attack of tonsillitis three months before.

CINCHOPHEN AND NEOCINCHOPHEN

SCIENTIFIC NAME: Cinchophen methyl ester, neochymotrypsinogen.

OTHER: It is sold under such names as Acitrin, Agotan, Artamin, Atochinol (atoquinol), Atophan, Atophanyl, Atophanurotro pine, Biloptin (diiodo-atophan), Cass rheumatism treatment, Chloroxyl, Cinchophen (many brands), Fantan, Farastan (mono-iodo-cinchophen, Harrell's rheumatism cure, Hexophan, Iriphan, Isatophan, Leukotropen, Lytophan, Neocinchophen, Novato pan, Oxyliodide, Paratophan, Phenylcinchoninic acid Phenoquam (phenoquin), Quinophan, Renton's rheumatic tablets, Synthaline, Siilphatophan, Tolysin, Van Ard's rheumatism remedy (sanatorium treatment).

TOXICITY: 5

FORM: Oral or injectable.

EFFECTS AND SYMPTOMS: Among the symptoms are gastrointestinal irritation, epigastric discomfort, anorexia, diarrhea, vomiting, hyperventilation (rapid breathing), hyperthermia (fever), delirium, convulsions, coma, and death. Since the drug damages the liver, autopsy findings include yellow atrophy of liver and fatty degeneration of heart and kidneys.

REACTION TIME: Six to twelve hours.

ANTIDOTES AND TREATMENTS: The treatment is the same as with salicylate poisoning. The damaged liver must be treated, and sometimes a liver transplant is necessary.

NOTES: Cinchophen is an analgesic and antipyretic used in the treatment of gout by controlling the buildup of uric acid. Numerous fatalities have been reported due to overdoses. It is now recognized as a dangerous drug, especially when people self-medicate, or even when used in the dosage recommended on the bottle, without medical advice.

NORFLEX

SCIENTIFIC NAME: Orphenadrine citrate.

OTHER: Disipal, distalene, orpadrex, tega-flex, Exotag, Flexon, banflex.

TOXICITY: 6

FORM: Oral or injectable. A white, crystalline powder, sparingly soluble in water and slightly soluble in alcohol. It is practically odorless, but has a bitter taste.

EFFECTS AND SYMPTOMS: The drug possesses anticholinergic actions and is used for relief of muscle pain. Adverse reactions include dry mouth, pupil dilation, blurred vision, tachycardia, weakness, nausea, vomiting, headache, dizziness, and drowsiness. Coma, convulsions, and cardiac arrest frequently occur in acute poisoning.

REACTION TIME: Symptoms start within thirty minutes, but it takes from three to six hours for coma and heart failure.

Treated as atropine poisoning, the drug must be removed from the stomach immediately, since it is rapidly absorbed. Convulsions are usually managed with Valium, since barbiturates will dangerously slow the respiratory and cardiac systems.

NOTES: First found in 1951, it works as a sedative and reduces spasms of smooth muscles, quieting jerking nerves. Its primary use is in Parkinson's disease; to control the side effects of psychiatric drugs; and it is also used as a muscle relaxant. Mentioned in the literature from the Hemlock Society as one of the best ways for "helping yourself or a loved one over," the drug is available over the counter in Mexico and is readily available in Holland. A bitter taste is often hidden by orange juice. Barbiturates deepen the coma.

Of course, membership of the Hemlock Society indicates a person may be terminally ill or may be contemplating suicide—and would allay suspicions that the victim had been murdered.

TYLENOL

SCIENTIFIC NAME: Acetaminophen.

OTHER SIMILAR: Panadol, Paracetamol, Anacin, Emprin Compound.

TOXICITY: 4

FORM: Tablets, capsules, liquid, and rapid-dissolve strips.

EFFECTS AND SYMPTOMS: Tylenol's method of pain relief still has not been documented, but too much of it will injure the liver, kidney, heart, and central nervous system.

Nausea, vomiting, drowsiness, confusion, liver tenderness, hypotension (low blood pressure), cardiac arrhythmias, jaundice, and hepatic and renal failure have resulted from overdoses. After three days, evidence of liver damage is seen. Deaths have occurred from liver necrosis up to two weeks after ingestion.

REACTION TIME: Thirty minutes to four hours.

ANTIDOTES AND TREATMENTS: Vomiting is induced unless respiration is depressed. Activated charcoal is given, but efforts to remove the drug are useless after four hours. N-acetyl cysteine is an antidote if given within fifteen to twenty hours after ingestion. Fresh transfusions of plasma or clotting factors may be necessary.

NOTES: There are two types of overdose: acute (a large dose in a short time) and chronic (a smaller amount over a long time that builds up to fatal amounts in the liver). With acute, it takes a very large amount to kill with Tylenol alone, but in combination with other drugs or a central nervous system depressant, it could be fatal. Often the nausea experienced with the initial dose sends the victim to medical care.

Because it is commonly available, Tylenol, like aspirin, is often used for suicidal overdoses.

Many compounds like Emprin, Excedrin, or Anacin, contain aspirin, Tylenol, and caffeine as well as other painkillers piggybacked on to enhance the properties. Caffeine added to any painkiller enhances the effect.

SCHEDULE II CONTROLLED DRUGS

Schedule II drugs, so-designated by the Drug Enforcement Administration (DEA), require special prescriptions and accountability at all levels of distribution. All schedule II drugs are required to be under lock and key, be it in the hospital, pharmacy, or doctor's office. In the hospital, medication nurses carry the "narc" keys and must sign them in and out, accounting for each drug and dose at the end of each shift. This makes it difficult (though not impossible) to steal the drugs.

Even doctors do not often have access to the narcotic box at the hospital, and have to ask the nurse if they want to obtain a drug. Some physicians who do surgical procedures in their office keep schedule II drugs at their private offices—again, under lock and key. (Despite common perception, most doctors' offices do not carry narcotics. From the physician's office, the best a villain can do is steal a prescription blank.)

All schedule II drugs are very addictive, and individuals often become addicted through legitimate, long-term use due to injury and pain management. Once addicted, they will become drug seekers, visiting many doctors and emergency rooms and complaining of nonexistent pain in order to get drugs. The drugs can also be purchased on the black market. It is not unusual for an addict to take thirty to forty pills a day—a lethal dose for a normal individual, though for an individual who has been taking painkillers over a long period of time, much more is needed to cause a fatal overdose.

Most narcotic analgesics come in oral and injectable form, and some can be inhaled. The oral version is usually a white powder. All are used to control severe pain, and work by depressing the central nervous system. Death from respiratory failure may occur immediately after intravenous overdose, or within two to four hours after oral or subcutaneous (under the skin) injection.

General symptoms from ingestion or injection are unconsciousness, pinpoint pupils, slow, shallow respiration, cyanosis, weak pulse, hypotension, spasm of gastrointestinal tract, pulmonary edema, spasticity (a disorder in which certain muscles are continuously contracted), and twitching of the muscles. Convulsions may accompany codeine, meperidine, apomorphine, propoxyphene, or oxymorphone.

Antidotes and treatments include use of the drug Naloxone, which binds up the narcotics and helps eliminate them from the body. Treatments must be started within two hours of administration. In cases of injection, sometimes the drug absorption can be delayed by use of a tourniquet.

CODEINE

SCIENTIFIC NAME: Methylmorphine.

TOXICITY: 6

FORM: Powder, tablet, or liquid.

EFFECTS AND SYMPTOMS: An addictive sedative and analgesic, codeine's symptoms include sleepiness, a floating sensation, giddiness, unbalanced gait, slowing heartbeat, respiratory difficulty, coma, and death. Since it suppresses reflexes, it is often used as an anti-cough medication.

REACTION TIME: Immediate for injections; within twenty minutes for ingestion.

ANTIDOTES AND TREATMENTS: Naloxone is used, and other symptoms are treated as they occur.

NOTES: Codeine is a nearly transparent, odorless substance with a fairly bitter taste that comes in combination with many drugs, such as acetaminophen (Tylenol), aspirin, caffeine, other painkillers, or cough suppressants. Canada has an OTC drug that contains one-fourth grain of codeine.

Codeine is a dangerous fire hazard when exposed to heat or flame.

MORPHINE

OTHER SIMILAR: Laudanum, narcotine, protopine, meconidine, laudanoisine, and lanthopine.

TOXICITY: 6

FORM: Morphine is a white crystalline alkaloid; it can be taken orally (as a liquid or tablet) or injected.

EFFECTS AND SYMPTOMS: An addictive sedative and analgesic, it's symptoms include sleepiness, sense of physical ease, quickening of the pulse, a floating sensation, giddiness, unbalanced gait, dizziness, heaviness of the head, nausea, slowing heartbeat, contracted pupils, loss of muscle power, respiratory difficulty, unconsciousness, coma, and death.

REACTION TIME: Twenty to forty minutes when ingested; five to ten minutes for injection. If the victim survives forty-eight hours, the prognosis is favorable. Death occurs between six and twelve hours and is almost always due to respiratory failure.

ANTIDOTES AND TREATMENTS: If Naloxone is used, recovery can be as quick as one to four hours.

NOTES: Morphine is refined from raw opium and has been used as a painkiller since 1886, though it is no longer dispensed in the U.S. Liquid morphine, a bluish syrup given to cancer patients for pain, can be mixed with like-colored liqueurs, like crème de menthe, to strengthen the effects of the drug.

Morphine increases the effects of sedatives, analgesics, tranquilizers, antidepressants, and other narcotic drugs. If mixed with alcohol or other solvents, it works faster.

CASE HISTORY

On May 27, 1947, Dr. Robert Clements called a second physician to his Southsea, Hampshire, house to attend his fourth wife, who had fallen into a deep coma. Dr. Clements told his colleague that Mrs. Clements suffered from myeloid leukemia. The disease was listed on the death certificate when Mrs. Clements died the following morning.

Two other physicians, the coroners, were unhappy about the situation, for they noticed that Mrs. Clements's eyes had retracted into the typical pinpoint state associated with narcotic poisoning. A third medical man performed the autopsy and pronounced the cause of death as leukemia. Still, the coroners were not happy. They reported their suspicions to their superiors.

The police began inquiries and noted the couple had not been getting along. In addition, Mrs. Clements had been subject to bouts of unconsciousness—which her husband always seemed able to predict. He had also recently had their telephone removed from their home, a rather odd action for a busy physician with a chronically ill wife. Her health had deteriorated over a period of time, she had vomited regularly, and her complexion had the yellowish tinge associated with jaundice, indicating some form of liver damage. She was also lethargic, a sign of morphine overdosing.

It was then discovered that Dr. Clements had prescribed a high dose of morphine for a nonexistent patient, and a second autopsy was ordered. Before the results could be released, Dr. Clements himself died of morphine poisoning. His suicide note read, "I can no longer tolerate the diabolical insults to which I have recently been exposed." Clements was found guilty in absentia of killing his fourth wife, an heiress, and inquiries showed his three previous wives had also been rich. All three had died of illnesses diagnosed by Clements himself—and he had signed all their death certificates.

PERCODAN

SCIENTIFIC NAME: Oxycodone.

TOXICITY: 5

FORM: Oral or injectable.

EFFECTS AND SYMPTOMS: A central nervous system depressant, Percodan can cause drowsiness, constipation, unsteady gait, light-headedness, dizziness, sedation, nausea, and vomiting. Like other narcotics, this drug is capable of producing stupor, coma, muscle flaccidity, severe respiratory depression, hypotension, and cardiac arrest. With long-term use, the patient can become dependent.

REACTION TIME: Within thirty minutes.

ANTIDOTES AND TREATMENTS: Naloxone—a drug used to counter life-threatening complications to the central nervous system.

NOTES: It is often available in combination with aspirin, phenacetin, caffeine, or other pain relievers. Sedation may increase when taken with tranquilizers, antihistamines, antidepressants, sedatives, alcohol, or other narcotics. Combining this drug with phenytoin (Dilantin) may decrease brain function and cause brain death. Percodan is often prescribed to control coughing.

CASE HISTORY

A man took Percodan for a toothache and then went scuba diving. He died while in the water, drowsy as a result of the drug.

OTHER PAIN-KILLING DRUGS

Unless otherwise mentioned, the toxicity here is 5.

Vicodin, a popular painkiller, combines hydrocodone bitartrate (a variation of codeine) and acetaminophen. It causes sedation, lethargy, anxiety, fear, mood changes, unhappy feelings, urinary spasms, and breathing problems. Drug dependence can result. When used with MAO inhibitors or tricyclic antidepressants, the effects of this drug can be increased. Easily abused, it is often shared among friends.

Fentanyl or Sublimaze (toxicity 6) causes muscle rigidity before death, much the same as strychnine.

DFP or diisopropylphosphate is an eyedrop.

Lorfan (levallorphan) and Numorphan (oxymorphone) cause restlessness before death.

Dilaudid (hydromorphone) is an analgesic.

Hycodan or Dicodid is hydrocodeine, and is often used to control coughs. A derivative of codeine, it causes tremors when overdosing and can be fatal if enough is taken, as it depresses the central nervous system.

Levo-Dromoran (levorphanol) is injectable.

Darvon (propoxyphene) is an addictive painkiller (classed as a mild narcotic analgesic) that is sometimes mixed with aspirin, acetaminophen, and/or caffeine to enhance its analgesic properties, as in Darvocet, Darvon Compound 100, or Darvon 65. An odorless, crystalline powder with a bitter taste, it is freely soluble in water. This is always given orally as a pill or capsule. Among the overdose symptoms are nausea, vomiting, drooping of the eyelids, convulsions, coma, and respiratory depression. Sedation may increase when Darvon is taken with tranquilizers, antihistamines, antidepressants, sedatives, alcohol, or narcotics. A warning in the *Prescription Drug Encyclopedia* indicates it should not be given to suicidal people, as it will increase their depression. Of course, this could aid the killer if he wants the death to look like suicide.

Talwin (pentazocine) (toxicity 6) is an addictive painkiller that is usually injected or given intravenously. It can be given in oral form, but can cause extreme nausea when taken orally. Talwin causes withdrawal symptoms when stopped cold turkey. Sedation increases when taken with tranquilizers, antihistamines, antidepressants, sedatives, alcohol, or narcotics. It's often sold on the black market.

Flexeril (cyclobenzaprine) is used as a muscle relaxant and for pain caused by muscle spasms. It causes drowsiness, dizziness, increased heart rate, weakness, fatigue, nausea, and should not be used by those recovering from recent heart attacks, congestive heart failure, or those who have taken MAO inhibitors (a type of antidepressant) in the past fourteen days.

Demerol (meperidine) and Dolantin (pethidine) (toxicity 5) will cause generalized edema (swelling), coma, and hypertension in addition to all of the symptoms above in the general listing. Sedation increases when taken with tranquilizers, antihistamines, antidepressants, sedatives, alcohol, or narcotics. Serious reactions can occur if MAO inhibitors are taken within fourteen days of Demerol.

Some drugs that are low-toxicity, but still dangerous in combination with another depressant or barbiturate, are Nisentil, Leritine, Apodol (anileridine), Stadol (butorphanol), and Norvad (levopropoxyphene); Romilar (dextromethorphan), which causes dizziness, is a widely used cough suppressant.

Sometimes given to cancer patients, the "Brompton cocktail" or "Brompton mixture" included a variety of drugs like morphine, heroin, alcohol, chloroform, a tranquilizer, and/or an anti-emetic (as Tigan) mixed into a syrup. Invented in London's Royal Brompton Hospital in the 1800s for terminal cancer patients, the original formula was one-quarter each morphine, heroin (obviously no longer easily—or legally—obtainable), gin, and marijuana.

Many painkillers, like Fiorinal, which is used also as a muscle relaxant, increase sedation when taken with tranquilizers, antihistamines, antidepressants, sedatives, alcohol, or narcotics. Fiorinal combined with codeine becomes more dangerous.

Norgesic, a muscle relaxant and pain reliever made up of orphenadrine, aspirin, and caffeine, has side effects such as excitation, hallucinations, increased bleeding, lightheadedness, and blacking out. Confusion, anxiety, and tremors can result from the combination of this drug and propoxyphene (Darvon). Many over-the-counter drugs for colds, coughs, and allergies also interact with Norgesic. This drug often increases sedation when taken with tranquilizers, antihistamines, antidepressants, sedatives, alcohol, or narcotics. Norgesic also increases the action of anti-clotting drugs, making it more likely for the patient to bleed.

ANTI-INFLAMMATORY PAINKILLERS

On their own, anti-inflammatory drugs are of low toxicity. Individuals with gastrointestinal tract disease, peptic ulcers, poor heart function, or those taking anti-clotting drugs are at risk. Many of the drugs mentioned above also have some anti-inflammatory properties, but not enough to primarily class them here.

Some of the anti-inflammatory drugs—diflunisal (Dolobid), ibuprofen (Motrin, Rufen, Advil, Haltrain, Medipren, Nuprin, Trendar), fenoprofen (Nalfon), meclofenamate (Meclomen), naproxen (Anaprox, Naprosyn)—should not be taken in combination with aspirin or other non-steroid analgesic drugs, or with warfarin or other oral anti-clotting drugs, because clotting time may be prolonged. Antacids, however, may sometimes reduce the effects of anti-inflammatory drugs. So if the victim of an anti-inflammatory drug overdose is surprisingly still alive, an antacid could be the culprit.

Anti-inflammatory drugs can become toxic when given to those with renal problems, because the kidneys cannot cleanse the blood and the toxic by-products. Overdoses can cause renal failure and severe liver reactions, including fatal jaundice.

Ibuprofen also inhibits diuretics taken to rid the body of excess fluid. A moderately large dose of ibuprofen, combined with a diuretic like Lasix, increases the chance of congestive heart failure.

Taken with lithium (to control bipolar symptoms), ibuprofen produces an elevated blood level of lithium, which itself is quite toxic and must be constantly monitored. In the wrong concentration, this could be a fatal combination.

It's not wise to take Anaprox (*naproxen sodium*) with Naprosyn (*naproxen*), as they both circulate the same chemical in the blood and the mixture could cause a fatal over dose. Naproxen also tends to increase the effects of anti-diabetic drugs, so a person taking these medications could easily go into hypoglycemic schock and die.

ANESTHETICS

Local anesthetics work outside the central nervous system, meaning that (in normal doses) they do not affect the brain, whereas general anesthesia anesthetizes the entire body, including the brain. With overdosing, they get into the general system and become systemic. No two anesthetics act the same, and the effect also depends greatly on the physical makeup of the person taking them and on the way the drug is administered.

ANESTHESIA GASES

Most of the gases act the same way and so have been lumped together.

SCIENTIFIC NAME: Diethyl ether, ethyl ether, divinyl ether, ethyl chloride, halothane, methoxyflurane, fluroxene.

OTHER SIMILAR: Ether, chloroform, Vinethene, Fluothane, Penthrane, Fluoromar, ethylene, cyclopropane, nitrous oxide.

TOXICITY: 6

FORM: Stored as a liquid or gas; administered as a gas.

EFFECTS AND SYMPTOMS: Unconsciousness and respiratory failure. All functions of the central nervous system are depressed; excessive use causes liver damage and interferes with the autoimmune system. Cyanosis and cardiac irregularities are seen. These later symptoms may be present even without overdose because of oxygen deprivation to the brain.

Liver damage caused by chloroform may progress to cirrhosis and death. Cyclopropane and halothane increase the effect of blood pressure medications and, taken together, can cause the blood pressure to fall dangerously low.

REACTION TIME: Immediate.

ANTIDOTES AND TREATMENTS: Gas is stopped, ventilation forced, and respiration maintained. The body is kept warm; if fever occurs, body temperature is lowered by the application of wet towels. For malignant hyperthermia (a genetic response that occurs in about 10 percent of the population during or after anesthesia, driving body temperature up over 110 degrees), dantrolene sodium and procainamide are often used.

NOTES: These gases are rapidly metabolized out of the body and short-lived effects make them ideal for anesthesia.

Most of these gases are highly flammable and explosive.

NITROUS OXIDE

OTHER SIMILAR: Laughing gas.

TOXICITY: 5

FORM: A highly flammable, odorless gas.

EFFECTS AND SYMPTOMS: The gas, a central nervous system depressant, can cause heart palpitation, irregular heart rhythms, brain damage, and death. Headache, cerebral edema, and permanent mental deficiency can also result if a fatal dose is not used.

REACTION TIME: A few seconds to several minutes.

ANTIDOTES AND TREATMENTS: Oxygen is given and symptoms are treated as they occur.

NOTES: It was discovered in 1776, but the first time it was used as an anesthetic was in 1799 when it was discovered that it did not produce complete anesthesia. In 1860, it became widely accepted by the medical profession. Now it is used as an adjunct to the potent agents and as an analgesic. It is also inhaled by teens for the euphoric effect.

Other uses are to increase speed in race cars and for rocket fuel.

CASE HISTORY

In 1960, a dentist in Utah purposely suffocated several of his clients with nitrous oxide.

PROCAINE AND LIDOCAINE

OTHER SIMILAR: Marcaine, monocaine, nesacaine, nupercaine, duranest, xylocaine, caro-caine, oracaine, unacaine, citanest, and novocaine. All are related to cocaine, and are synthetic versions of the coca bush alkaloids.

TOXICITY: 5

FORM: Colorless liquids or thick gels, these drugs are given by injection or used topi-cally. As a general, it can be given intravenously.

EFFECTS AND SYMPTOMS: These drugs are rapidly distributed in the body and numbness occurs locally.

At first giddiness develops, then feelings of oppression, followed by severe collapse of the body organs, coma, convulsions, and respiratory arrest. After injection or large surface application, circulatory collapse comes about by direct depression of blood vessel tone or by effect on the central nervous system. Dizziness, cyanosis, fall of blood pressure, muscular tremors, convulsions, coma, irregular and weak breathing, bronchial spasm, and cardiac standstill are other symptoms. Rapid intravenous injection causes cardiac arrest.

Hypersensitivity (allergic reaction brought on by repeated exposure) occurs with re-peated topical applications; reactions include itching, redness, edema, blistering. A person allergic to the drug can go into anaphylactic shock.

REACTION TIME: Immediate. Efforts to remove the drug after thirty minutes are useless. After survival of one hour, the victim usually recovers.

ANTIDOTES AND TREATMENTS: The injected drug is stopped and absorption from the injec-tion site limited by tourniquet and ice pack. Airway is maintained and artificial respiration given with oxygen until convulsions and central nervous system depression are controlled.

NOTES: Procaine is considered the most dangerous of all the derivatives and has caused numerous fatalities. As with cocaine, states of shock with a possible fatal outcome can occur with very small doses of procaine. Procaine and other similar drugs also enhance the effects of muscle relaxants.

CASE HISTORY

A scandal occurred in the 1960s when patients at a VA hospital were given overdoses of procaine as a form of euthanasia.

SODIUM PENTOTHAL

OTHER SIMILAR: Truth serum, thiopental, sodium thiopental, thiopentone sodium, or trapanal.

TOXICITY: 6

FORM: Injectable and through IV.

EFFECTS AND SYMPTOMS: It slows heart rate and lowers blood pressure. The depression of the central nervous system can also produce apnea and airway obstruction. Headache, delirium, nausea, and prolonged sleepiness are other side effects, which can last as long as thirty-six hours.

REACTION TIME: Immediate: A person counting backward from one hundred will be asleep by ninety-seven.

ANTIDOTES AND TREATMENTS: Symptomatic only.

NOTES: Sodium pentothal, a barbiturate, decreases higher cortical brain functioning. Since lying is more complex than truth, suppression of these higher cortical functions may lead to the divulgement of the truth, hence the name truth serum.

Ernest Volwiler and Donalee Tabern, working for Abbott Labs in the 1930s, discovered the anesthesia. They first experimented on human beings, March 8, 1934. Three months later, the ultrashort-acting barbiturate was used as general anesthesia by Dr. John Lundy at the Mayo Clinic.

Numerous anesthetic deaths from sodium thiopental occurred after the attack on Pearl Harbor in 1941. Witnesses were given the truth serum so they could communicate details they had supressed. However, the scientists did not take into account that the victims were more sensitive to the drug as a result of trauma, and therefore lower doses should have been administered.

Those who are put into a relaxed state by the drug are more susceptible to suggestion and are easier to interview. So the drug is often used for interrogations. But while the drug makes people gabby, it does not guarantee the truth. Tested in comparison to LSD, this proved a better way of producing short-term anesthesia, but the medical community stopped using it for surgical procedures because it had a prolonged recovery period before return to consciousness. It has, however, been used to induce medical comas when the patient needs to be kept sedated.

It is also one of the three drugs, along with potassium chloride and pancuronium bromide, that is used for lethal injection executions. The megadose places the patient into a rapidly induced coma, and within ten to fifteen minutes he is dead. Thiopental alone would cause death in forty-five minutes.

Some of the other drugs used as truth serum have been scopolamine and alcohol since, as sedatives, they interfere with higher cognitive functions and judgment. The former was used by Dr. Josef Mengele as an interrogation drug, but it was found that, due to the hallucinations caused by the drug, the truth was often distorted.

CASE HISTORY

In an episode of the TV show *MacGyver,* a prisoner is given the choice of confessing freely or using sodium pentothal.

In the show 24, Jack Bauer (played by Kiefer Sutherland) tells a medic to stand by with hyocine pentathol, another form of truth serum.

The show *Alias* makes several references to truth serum.

The films *True Lies, Terminator 2, Meet the Fockers,* and *Jumpin' Jack Flash* all used truth serum.

HYPNOTICS

The word *hypnotic* (from the Greek *hypnotikos,* "causing one to sleep"), encompasses a wide variety of drugs. Some are merely grouped as sleeping pills; others are barbiturates, and still others are narcotics. As a general rule, they are anything that will slow down the central nervous system and put you to sleep. This even includes alcoholic beverages, which is why alcohol, when mixed with one of the other drugs, increases its effects and can be fatal.

Barbiturates, derived from barbituric acid, were first marketed by Bayer Pharmaceuticals in 1864. They are a key factor in 2,500 derivatives, 50 of which are used medically. Accidental overdose of barbiturates is a common cause of death. Marilyn Monroe's autopsy report showed a lethal level of barbiturates in her system when she died.

Many barbiturates are used for sedation: Veronal or Carbutol (barbital), Luminal (phenobarbital—purple hearts, goof balls, or downers), Amytal (amobarbital—blue heaves),

---

Butisol (butabarbital); Nembutal (pentobarbital—yellow jackets), Seconal (secobarbital—reds, red devils, red birds), Pentothal (thiopental), Dialog (allobarbital), Alurate (aprobarbital), Medomin (hexobarbital), Mebaral (mephobarbital), Brevital (methohexital), Gemonil (metharbital), and Surital (thiamylal).

Toxicity depends on whether the barbiturate is long-, medium-, short-, or ultrashort-acting, but they fall within the 4 to 5 range. Ill effects from overdose, such as severe shock or respiratory failure, tend to be more frequent and serious with medium- and short-acting barbiturates than with the long- or ultrashort-acting. Combination drugs such as Tuinal contain a short-acting barbiturate (quinalbarbitone) combined with a medium-acting form (amylobarbitone).

The majority of sleeping pills were not developed until the late 1940s or early 1950s, so if you're doing a period piece you'll want to check the dates on the following drugs. All are central nervous system depressants, so symptoms are the same as those of chloral hydrate. Reaction time is usually from ten to thirty minutes, depending on the dose and the weight of the person. Almost all are found only in pill or capsule form and are easily available.

Those who use sleeping pills often build up a tolerance and can become dependent. Every day pharmaceutical companies are releasing their "new and improved" sleeping aids, each with fewer side effects than the last, but when the fine print is read it is hard to tell the difference. Some manufacturers, to prevent overdose, have added a variety of drugs to the chemical composition that cause vomiting when too many pills are taken at once. This additive has no effect at normal doses.

Depending on the drug, hypnotics can be administered orally, by injection, intravenously, or rectally. The reaction time is a few minutes to a half-hour, depending on how it is administered, the amount of food in the stomach, and the body composition of the victim.

All cause loss of consciousness, either in sleep or surgical anesthesia. The major symptom is sedation, but dizziness, headache, irritability, confusion, irregular heartbeat, shallow breathing, and hypotension can also be a problem. Intravenous injection of any hypnotic may cause severe respiratory depression, as well as rapid fall of blood pressure, leading to death because no oxygen is circulated. Gastric secretions may be decreased, and intestinal muscles and kidney function may also be affected.

Many of the drugs, when taken in small, repeated doses, may accumulate in the system and act as if a larger dose has been given. All hypnotics are easily absorbed in the gastrointestinal tract, so gastric lavage must be started immediately. Other treatment is symptomatic.

Sedation may increase when hypnotics are taken with tranquilizers, antihistamines, antidepressants, sedatives, alcohol, or narcotics.

The effects of these drugs also depend on the liver's ability to metabolize and use them, so someone with liver disease should be careful when using sedatives, hypnotics, or barbiturates. Patients with acute hepatitis (liver damage), because the drugs are not properly eliminated, develop sedation sooner, especially during intravenous administration.

Over-the-counter drugs now use antihistamines, which have a side effect of drowsiness, rather than true hypnotics, which proved to be too dangerous for OTC use.

In small doses, barbiturates may actually increase sensation of pain.

Sudden withdrawal from hypnotics may increase emotional disturbances and can prove fatal.

Ultrashort-acting thiobarbital, used also as an intravenous anesthetic, has the quickest effects on the brain. According to *The Prediction of Suicide*, by Drs. Aaron Beck, H.L.P. Resnick, and Dan Lettieri, this drug is the most widely used of all drugs for suicide among doctors.

AMBIEN OR AMBIEN CR (CONTINUOUS RELEASE)

SCIENTIFIC NAME: Zolpidem tartrate.

TOXICITY: 4

FORM: Tablets.

EFFECTS AND SYMPTOMS: Extreme fatigue, blurred vision, dizziness. Adverse affects include headache, hangover feeling, confusion, seizure, lapse of memory, gastrointestinal upset, depression, anxiety, nightmares, suppression of REM sleep, hallucinations, and coma.

REACTION TIME: A few minutes to a half-hour.

ANTIDOTES AND TREATMENTS: Use of barbiturates may be necessary to prevent dangerous withdrawal symptoms in long-term patients or as a result of an overdose.

NOTES: One of the most commonly prescribed of the new sleeping pills, it is frequently used for short-term insomnia. It is mildly addictive after prolonged use, and withdrawal must be gradual. Aggressiveness has been reported in people who have quit cold turkey. Warnings indicate that it should not be given to suicidal or depressed patients, as there is a greater risk of suicide. There have been recent news articles about people sleepwalking, and sleep-*driving*: victims finding themselves in their cars, still in pajamas, after having taken the drug the night before, not knowing where they are or how they got there. It is not the drug of choice for overdosing, since it takes more than thirty (in most cases) to do serious damage.

Those with renal (kidney) and liver dysfunctions should not take it, because it stresses the liver and kidneys.

It passes through mother's milk, and breast-feeding infants can get the same symptoms as those taking the medication.

CHLORAL HYDRATE

OTHER SIMILAR: Triclos, triclofos, Mickey Finn, Mickey, knockout drops.

TOXICITY: 5

FORM: Clear liquid, capsules, powder (from broken capsules), and suppositories.

EFFECTS AND SYMPTOMS: The central nervous system is depressed. Symptoms include sleepiness, mental confusion, and unsteadiness, followed rapidly by coma; slow, shallow respiration; flaccid muscles; hypotension; cyanosis; hypothermia or hyperthermia; and absent reflexes. Duration of coma is dependent on the amount of medication taken. In prolonged coma, moist rales (a bubbling sound present when there is fluid in the bronchial tubes) are heard in the lower lung fields and can be an indication of pulmonary edema. Carbon dioxide retention under these conditions causes acidosis. Death occurs from pneumonia, pulmonary edema, persistent hypotension, or respiratory failure.

Chronic poisoning from ingestion causes skin rash, mental confusion, ataxia, dizziness, drowsiness, hangover, depression, irritability, poor judgment, neglect of personal appearance, and other behavior disturbances.

REACTION TIME: Symptoms begin with thirty minutes. Death may occur in a few hours.

ANTIDOTES AND TREATMENTS: Gastric lavage; airway is maintained and oxygen intake increased.

NOTES: With the introduction of chloroform as an anesthetic by James Young Simpson in 1847, interest in painkillers increased. Chloral hydrate, discovered in 1832 by Justus von Liebig, is a derivative of chloroform but it has few analgesic properties and was found not to completely sedate patients. It was further found that nursing mothers passed the drug to their infants.

A popular drug of abuse in the late nineteenth century, it becomes fatal when mixed with alcohol. Chloral hydrate has lost its status to more of the newer street drugs, but it is still a schedule IV controlled substance and available now only with a prescription.

CASE HISTORY

The oldest of the hypnotic depressants, chloral hydrate was common in mystery stories of the 1930s as knockout drops or Mickey Finns. In Agatha Christie's *The Secret Adversary* and *The Clocks,* Mickey Finns were used to poison the victims.

Her famous *Ten Little Indians* also used chloral hydrate in Emily Brent's coffee to render her unconscious. (Though it was the injection of cyanide that finally did her in.)

DALMANE

SCIENTIFIC NAME: Flurazepam.

OTHER SIMILAR: Nitrazepam and similar benzodiazepines (Dalinane, in Britain).

TOXICITY: 5

FORM: Powder and liquid.

EFFECTS AND SYMPTOMS: A muscle relaxant and anticonvulsant, it is also used to relieve anxiety. Dalmane is less potent than diazepam (Valium), more like chlordiazepoxide (Librium). Because the victim's central nervous system is affected, breathing is impaired, and the victim doesn't take in enough oxygen and becomes groggy.

Drowsiness, sleep, and unconsciousness are the primary symptoms. Alcohol or other central nervous system drugs will increase the effect of the drug.

REACTION TIME: Ten to twenty minutes.

ANTIDOTES AND TREATMENTS: Gastric lavage; the airway is maintained, oxygen is given, and blood pressure is monitored and maintained.

NOTES: Those attempting suicide often use Dalmane in conjunction with other methods, such as gassing, hypothermia, or drowning. Withdrawal psychosis (paranoia) is possible.

Large amounts of the drug are detected in the blood, with decreasing amounts up to twenty-five hours after ingesting. The drug can be detected in the urine for up to six days after ingesting.

DILANTIN

SCIENTIFIC NAME: Diphenylhydantoin.

OTHER: Phenytoin.

TOXICITY: 5

FORM: Tablets, capsules, and colorless liquid.

EFFECTS AND SYMPTOMS: Symptoms include swelling of gums, fever, liver and kidney damage, anemia, pulmonary changes, lymph gland enlargement, epidermal necrosis, cardiac irregularities, peripheral nerve damage, tremor, psychosis, and muscle rigidity. Additional symptoms include slurred speech, confusion, dizziness, mild nervousness, excessive facial hair growth, and low blood sugar. The later can cause insulin shock and death.

REACTION TIME: Fifteen minutes to an hour, depending on administration.

ANTIDOTES AND TREATMENTS: Gastric lavage.

NOTES: It is often used with phenobarbital for suppression of seizures in epilepsy; also used as a sleep aid. This drug should be discontinued gradually. Barbiturates may increase this drug's action. Blood thinners, antidepressants, or alcohol will reduce its effectiveness.

PARAL

SCIENTIFIC NAME: Paraldehyde.

TOXICITY: 5

FORM: Oral as tablets or liquid; injectable. It is an aromatic liquid at room temperature, but it slowly decomposes to an acetic acid upon exposure to air.

EFFECTS AND SYMPTOMS: Believed to work in the liver and to oxidize into acetic acid, Paral has produced hypotension, tachycardia, cyanosis, rapid and shallow breathing, coughing, confusion, decreased urination, muscle tremors, restlessness and irritability, respiratory distress, weakness, coma, and death. Chronic use can result in addiction, which resembles addiction to alcohol.

REACTION TIME: Immediate.

ANTIDOTES AND TREATMENTS: Giving oxygen and maintaining respiration, and symptomatic treatment.

NOTES: First used in 1882 in obstetrics to calm the anxious mothers, it is used also in the treatment of alcoholism withdrawal and delirium tremors (DT's) and in the treatment of nervous and mental conditions, to calm or relax patients who are nervous or tense and to produce sleep. It is a schedule IV depressant/sedative. It's administered in small doses, and the taste is unpleasant. Even so, many alcoholics became addicted to it after treatment. It is seldom used in the United States.

There is an unpleasant breath odor which lasts twenty-four hours after the medication has stopped.

VERONOL

SCIENTIFIC NAME: Barbital.

OTHER: Phenobarbital.

TOXICITY: 5

FORM: Pills, a colorless liquid for injection, or inhaled gas.

EFFECTS AND SYMPTOMS: Chills and lowered blood pressure, unconsciousness.

REACTION TIME: Immediate.

ANTIDOTES AND TREATMENTS: Gastric lavage and symptomatic.

NOTES: Veronol is often given to control epileptic seizures. It is also a respiratory depressant, affecting the nerve impulses, the victim's responses to lack of oxygen, and blood acidity.

Phenobarbital reacts with many drugs to speed up their half-life (the amount of time the drug remains active in the body), and causes them to be eliminated more quickly.

Other Common Sleeping Pills

Mogadon (nitrazepam) is commonly used in European countries.

Soma (carisoprodol) causes momentary paralysis, visual disturbances, excitement, skin rash, asthma, fever, and high blood pressure.

Placidyl (ethylorvynol) causes fatigue, headache, confusion, nausea, vomiting, pulmonary edema, hemolysis, liver damage, and acidosis (an acid imbalance in the body).

Valmid (ethinamate) causes hemolysis, cyanosis, and liver impairment.

Doriden (glutethimide) and Restoril (temazepam) are often prescribed in hospitals and for post-surgical patients returning home. Doriden was first introduced clinically in 1954 and causes nausea, increased white blood cell count, numbness in the limbs, toxic psychosis, dry mouth, dilation of the pupils, swelling of the brain tissue, and convulsions. Restoril, which is commonly used to relieve insomnia, most frequently causes dizziness, confusion, lethargy, loss of balance, an awareness of the heartbeat, hallucinations, and excessive anxiety, and can be addictive.

Halcion (triazolam), physically and psychologically habit-forming, is rarely used now and has generally been replaced by Ambien. Its side effects include lighted-headedness, nervousness, incoordination, nausea, vomiting, increased heart rate, an excessive feeling of happiness, memory loss, cramps, visual disturbances, altered taste, dry mouth, tingling sensation, tinnitus, poor urinary control, changes in sex drive, liver failure, and hallucinations. This drug is no longer prescribed on a large scale because so many people were experiencing hallucinations. Sudden withdrawal can cause psychosis and paranoia.

Tegretol (carbamazepine) is classed as an anticonvulsant and pain reliever, but is also used for insomnia and treating epilepsy when other drugs have failed. Sometimes it's also used to treat neuralgia in the facial region (TMJ). The symptoms of Tegretol, overdose include urinary retention, skin rash, iron deficiency, upset stomach, jaundice, hypotension, and heart failure. People taking MAO inhibitor antidepressants should not be taking Tegretol since it drastically increases the blood pressure. Victims with high blood pressure, active liver disease, kidney disease, or serious mental or emotional disorders will be adversely affected by Tegretol.

The sleeping drugs Ethotoin (peganone) and Mesantoin (mephenytoin) promote infections in the lymph glands.

Milontin (phensuximide) in overdose causes hematuria and kidney infections, as well as muscle weakness.

Celotin (methsuximide) and Zarotin (ethosuximide) cause edema of the limbs, liver failure, and fatal bone marrow aplasia. There is a delay of one to several days in the onset of the coma.

Phenurone (phenacemide) causes liver damage, a decrease of white blood cells, behavioral effects, kidney impairment, skin rash, and psychotic breaks.

Mysoline (primidone) causes painful gums and excessive fatigue.

There is no specific antidote for sedative and hypnotic drugs. Drugs like caffeine and amphetamines, which are sometimes administered, can complicate overdoses by adding further problems such as irritability and hypertension, even death. Sometimes special problems like hypothermia or hyperthermia develop; in which case, rapid warming or cooling of the victim should be avoided.

The ever-popular Seconal (secobarbital) is another commonly prescribed drug. Most Seconal overdoses go comatose. Seconal and its relatives, such as Tuinal and Nembutal, are highly abused, and high tolerances are not unusual. Withdrawal can cause fatal side effects.

COLD MEDICATIONS

The amount of OTC decongestants that contain ephedrine you are allowed to purchase has been severely restricted. This is because ephedrine is a key ingredient in the manufacture of methamphetamine. Diet pills and sports enhancers that used to have ephedrine have been reformulated without it or discontinued. It is still found in some OTC decongestants, such as Sudafed.

There are no antihistamines that are fatal on their own. Most have a toxicity of 3, but in combination with other drugs, or with specific health problems, they may cause fatal reactions. Dimetapp and Entex, for example, are combinations of antihistamines and decongestants. A large dose can lead to a severe rise in blood pressure, which may then produce a stroke and problems for those with thyroid or heart disease. Some (for example, Coricidin HP) are designed not to affect blood pressure.

Antihistamines will put you to sleep, and sedation increases when these drugs are taken with tranquilizers, other antihistamines, antidepressants, sedatives, alcohol, or narcotics. Decongestants, on the other hand, do not cause sedation and act rather as uppers.

If MAO inhibitor antidepressants are taken concurrently or within fourteen days of taking some of these antihistamines, the blood pressure may rise dramatically, increasing risk of stroke.

Benadryl (diphenhydramine), an antihistamine, is often used for insomnia but is best known for combating anaphylactic shock caused by severe allergic reactions. It comes in liquid, pills, and injectable and topical form.

Optimine or Azatadine (trinalin), Dimetane (brompheniramine), Chlor-Trimeton (chlorpheniramine), Claritin, Allegra, Tavist (clemastine), and Zyrtec (cetirizine HCL) are among the many others that come in all forms, from tablets to liquid, injectable, and capsules. Some of these can be found in single-tablet, twelve- and twenty-four-hour timed-release pills, so it can be easy to overdose.

Many of these cold and flu antihistamines contain acetaminophen. Someone unaware of it who takes the Tylenol Extra Strength for a headache, as well as DayQuil for a cold, and Robitussin Cold and Cough (or store-name equivalents), could easily overdose, causing acute liver failure.

Another drug in this category is Naldecon (a combination of phenylpropanolamine, phenylephrine, phenyltoloxamine, and chlorpheniramine) that, when combined with MAO inhibitors, causes a rise in blood pressure.

Phenergan is generally used to treat nausea. It can lower the convulsion threshold of anticonvulsants drugs causing an increase in the severity of convulsions. It is available as an oral liquid, as pills, as an injectable, or as suppositories. Effects of atropine and related drugs may be increased when using Phenergan.

Most of the OTC drugs for allergies and colds interact negatively with phenergan.

Phenylpropanolamine is used as a decongestant, antihistamine, and appetite suppressant. This drug has been recalled and is no longer used in OTC medications in the United States. Prior to its recall, many OTC drugs for colds, allergies, coughs, and diet aids contained phenylpropanolamine. If the recommended dose is exceeded, there may be a sharp rise in blood pressure. If a person takes a diet aid such as Acutrim (now reformulated without phenylpropanolamine in the United States) and then something for a cold, chances are good for an adverse reaction. People sensitive to epinephrine, ephedrine, terbutaline, and amphetamines may also be sensitive to phenylpropanolamine. Taking this drug can increase the effects of epinephrine and decrease the effects of anti-hypertensives so that victim taking a blood pressure reducer might still have a fatal stroke. If phenylpropanolamine is taken with digitalis preparations, the blood pressure might rise dramatically.

Tussi-Organidin, an expectorant (phlegm-loosener) and antihistamine, and Tussion-ex, an anti-cough medication, can both cause major problems with overdose. Convulsions, low breathing rates, sedation, and loss of consciousness can occur with the former. The latter may increase the thyroid hormone, lowering the effects of anti-thyroid hormones as well as the drug lithium (used to treat bipolar disorder).

DEXTROMETHORPHAN

OTHER: DXM.

TOXICITY: 3

FORM: Available as a powder, it is mostly ingested as a liquid cough syrup.

EFFECTS AND SYMPTOMS: Stumbling, dizziness, blurred vision, restlessness, hallucinations, stupor, coma, and respiratory depression can occur. Deaths usually occur when other drugs, particularly ethanol, are combined with it.

REACTION TIME: Fifteen to thirty minutes.

ANTIDOTES AND TREATMENTS: Activated charcoal is given; care is supportive.

NOTES: Widely available as a cough suppressant, when this substitute for codeine has caused trouble in the past, it was usually with small children drinking too much cough syrup. However, dextromethorphan is increasingly being abused by teens for its hallucinogenic effects at large doses.

The cough suppressant was patented in the 1950s and has been abused ever since. What is causing alarm is the rapid increase in abuse cases since 2000: One *Los Angeles Times* article from 2004 quoted California state poison control center officials as handling four times as many calls since 2000.

DXM is in a host of cold remedies, frequently combined with other medications. In a case of overdose of one of these combined drugs, it's usually the other drug in the medication.

Because causing death is only a possibility, rather than a probability, with dextromethorphan, a believable use of it as a weapon in your story will be difficult. It might be useful to cause hallucinations rather than death. Your fictional villain could mix up an overdose of grape cough syrup and soda water for the proposed victim.

CASE HISTORY

The *Los Angeles Times* article noted above reports two deaths from dextromethorphan, one involving a youth who died from an overdose, and the other when a young man, under the influence of that and other drugs, attacked and killed another man.

DYPHYLLINE

SCIENTIFIC NAME: 7-dihydroxypropyltheophylline.

OTHER SIMILAR: Dilor, Lufyllin, Neothylline, glyphylline.

TOXICITY: 5

FORM: Time-released tablets or syrup for oral use.

EFFECTS AND SYMPTOMS: Dyphylline is a bronchial dilator. Symptoms include headache, nervousness, trembling, insomnia, nausea, dark or bloody vomit, tachycardia, hypotension, convulsions, and heart failure.

REACTION TIME: Peak concentration is reached within one hour.

ANTIDOTES AND TREATMENTS: Gastric lavage and symptomatic care.

NOTES: Relaxing the lung muscles, it makes the air passages more resistant to irritants. Used for people with COPD (Chronic Obstructive Pulmonary Disease) or emphysema, and for infants with breathing problems, Dyphylline is water soluble. Introduced in 1946 as a bronchodilator, it should not be taken by those with an overactive thyroid or those who consume a lot of caffeine. Other stimulants should be avoided, as well. An autopsy reveals the drug through an analysis of the blood and mucous membranes.

VENTOLIN

OTHER SIMILAR: Proventil (albuterol), Alupent (metaproterenol), Aminophylline, Theolair (theophylline), Choledyl (oxtriphylline), and Slo-Phyllin.

TOXICITY: 4

FORM: Stored as a liquid; administered as atomized liquid (fine spray).

EFFECTS AND SYMPTOMS: Large doses can cause bronchial inflammation with fluid buildup, pounding heartbeat, dizziness, nervousness, bad or unusual taste in the mouth, dry mouth, headache, insomnia, anxiety, tension, a sharp rise in blood pressure, flushing of the skin, sweating, and angina-type chest or arm pain.

Fatalities have been associated with excessive use of inhalers. An overdose may cause convulsions, hallucinations, serious breathing problems, fever, chills, vomiting, and cold perspiration. Stroke or external bleeding may result from the sharp blood pressure change. Serious side effects can occur if the drug is taken with or soon after taking another bronchial-tube relaxer or decongestant in pill or liquid form.

REACTION TIME: Immediate.

ANTIDOTES AND TREATMENTS: Oxygen is given; other treatments are symptomatic.

NOTES: These are used as bronchial tube dilators to provide relief during asthma, bronchitis, tightness in the chest, and emphysema. These drugs are often administered into the air by nebulizers or handheld inhalers.

These drugs can be dangerous for people with heart disease, congestive heart failure, high blood pressure, or diabetes, since they often interfere with the rhythm of the heart, especially when taken with rauwolfia drugs (used to reduce high blood pressure; for example, Enduronyl, Rauzide, Diupres, Hydropres, Regroton, Ser-Ap-Es, Salutensin, rauwolfia serpentina, deserpidine, and reserpine).

Lithium levels can be rapidly decreased by these drugs, causing a manic or depressive attack in which a patient may have a suicidal depression or grandiose ideas.

ANTIANXIETY DRUGS, ANTIDEPRESSANTS, STIMULANTS, RELAXANTS, AND PSYCHOTROPIC AGENTS

Most of the drugs in this category are used to treat schizophrenia, bipolar (manic-depressive) illness, and psychotic manifestations like paranoia. They're also used before surgery to relieve apprehension, for the treatments of tetanus, and to treat behavior disorders in children. The symptoms and effects of these drugs are essentially the same, and only a few of the more common ones are mentioned.

DEPAKENE

SCIENTIFIC NAME: Valproic acid.

OTHER SIMILAR: Depakote (sodium valproate or divalproex).

TOXICITY: 4

FORM: Tablets, colorless liquid, injectable, and long-acting liquid injection.

EFFECTS AND SYMPTOMS: A central nervous system depressant, Depakene causes symptoms such as gastrointestinal disturbances, hair loss, psychosis, slower blood clotting time, and hepatic failure leading to death.

REACTION TIME: Within thirty minutes.

ANTIDOTES AND TREATMENTS: Gastric lavage; symptoms are treated as they occur.

NOTES: Used as an anticonvulsant drug since 1967, it is a colorless liquid at room temperature, with a characteristic sweet odor. It is also used as an antipsychotic and for seizures.

ELAVIL

SCIENTIFIC NAME: Amitriptyline.

TOXICITY: 5

FORM: Oral (tablet and liquid) and injectable.

EFFECTS AND SYMPTOMS: Symptoms begin with tingling sensations, tremors, seizures, ringing in the ears, dry mouth, blurred vision, urinary retention, changed sex drive, weight gain, jaundice, drowsiness, dizziness, fatigue, headache, and loss of balance. They continue with hallucinations, delusions, anxiety, agitation, insomnia, manic behavior, and end with changes in blood pressure, skipped or pounding heartbeat, heart attacks, congestive heart failure, stroke, and death.

REACTION TIME: Fifteen to forty minutes.

ANTIDOTES AND TREATMENTS: Gastric lavage. Airway is established, and blood pressure is maintained.

NOTES: Elavil is used to treat illnesses such as depressive neurosis, manic-depression, and anxiety associated with depression. Sometimes Elavil is given to alcoholics to relieve their withdrawal depression. Taking this drug may increase the number of seizures for those who are prone. Elavil can significantly increase the effect of blood pressure medicine, possibly causing a stroke. Blood levels of this drug, and possible toxicity from tricyclic antidepressants, are increased by the use of aspirin, chioramphenicol, haloperidol, chlorpromazine, perhenazine, and diazepam.

Amitriptyline enhances the effect of anticoagulants, so it is possible that someone might have a stroke or excessive internal bleeding from the combination.

This class of drugs, tricyclics, alters catecholamine levels in the brain, interacts dangerously with MAO inhibitors, and may cause agitation, tremor, coma, increased convulsions, and death.

CASE HISTORY

A patient at an Illinois state hospital in 1970 who was mistakenly given a high dose of Elavil meant for another patient (who had developed a tolerance and was getting larger than normal doses) developed psychotic symptoms and killed himself.

HALDOL

SCIENTIFIC NAME: Haloperidol.

TOXICITY: 5

FORM: Tablets, syrup, injectables, and suppositories.

EFFECTS AND SYMPTOMS: A central nervous system depressant, Haldol is used for psychotic states and is a major tranquilizer. Adverse reactions include drowsiness, blurred vision, extrapyramidal symptoms, tachycardia, hypotension, muscle rigidity, coma, and collapse. Other symptoms can be depression, hypotension, headache, confusion, grand mal seizures, rapid heartbeat, exacerbation of psychosis, skin rash, pain in the upper respiratory tract, excessively deep breathing, and sudden death. It can cause psychotic reactions in normal individuals.

REACTION TIME: If a large enough overdose is given, death can come immediately, but chronic poisoning takes several days. However, this is a cumulative action and it builds up quickly.

ANTIDOTES AND TREATMENTS: Artane or Cogentin is used to combat the extrapyramidal symptoms, but the only other way to treat this is to stop the drug. Sudden withdrawal after a high dose, however, can cause psychosis or death.

NOTES: In recent years numerous patients have died while using Haldol. No explanation could be found.

First used in the United States in 1967 as an antipsychotic drug, it's also used to treat Tourette's syndrome and severe behavioral problems in children.

The cocktail used often at the Los Angeles County Hospital for patient control now is Haldol (5mg), Ativan (2mg), and Benadryl (50mg).

LIBRAX

SCIENTIFIC NAME: Chlordiazepoxide hydrochloride, clidinium bromide.

OTHER SIMILAR: Librium (chlordiazepoxide hydrochloride).

TOXICITY: 3

FORM: Pill, capsule, liquid, injectable.

EFFECTS AND SYMPTOMS: A tranquilizer, Librax is also given to control nervous effects of a spastic colon. Symptoms include drowsiness, incoordinated movements, skin rashes, confusion, menstrual irregularities, unsteady standing, fainting, and blurred vision.

REACTION TIME: Thirty minutes or more.

ANTIDOTES AND TREATMENTS: Gastric lavage and symptomatic treatment.

NOTES: While Librax and Librium can be habit-forming, they are seldom fatal; however, mixed with other drugs, they can be deadly.

Withdrawal symptoms include nervousness, tremor, and convulsions. Suicidal tendencies can surface in depressed patients. If the drug is taken with MAO inhibitors, extreme sedation and convulsions can occur.

LITHIUM

SCIENTIFIC NAME: Lithium carbonate (pill) or lithium citrate (liquid).

TOXICITY: 5

FORM: Pills, liquid, injectable, and suppositories.

EFFECTS AND SYMPTOMS: Toxic levels are quickly reached, leading to fatal acidosis or alkalosis. First-noted symptoms are tremors, muscular twitching, apathy, difficulty speaking, confusion, exaggerated reflexes and jerking upon noise or light stimulation, and finally coma and death.

REACTION TIME: Fifteen minutes to an hour for symptoms to start, several hours or even days for death.

ANTIDOTES AND TREATMENTS: The drug is stopped. Sodium chloride is used to counteract it and is given as an intravenous drip, but that means the potassium level must be checked and adjusted as well.

NOTES: Lithium is given orally in the treatment of bipolar cases. Absorption of lithium ions may cause disturbance in the sodium and potassium levels. This is especially the case if the victim is on a low-salt or salt-free diet.

The blood level must be monitored constantly. Patients on this drug will have their blood drawn every few days to make sure that they do not overdose, since this drug accumulates rapidly in the body.

Lithium should not be used with Moduretic (a blood pressure reducer) since it causes a severe decrease in blood pressure. Lithium increases the toxicity of Haldol.

Lithium was first tested in the 1960s.

NORPRAMINE, PERTOFRANE, APO-DESPRAMINE, PMS-DESPRAMINE

SCIENTIFIC NAME: Desipramine.

OTHER SIMILAR: Tofranil (imipramine), Vivactil (protriptyline), Aventyl (nortriptyline).

TOXICITY: 5

FORM: Tablets, syrup, injectable.

EFFECTS AND SYMPTOMS: Used as antidepressants and sedatives. The side effects include seizure, coma, hypotension, and EKG abnormalities. Overdose shows coma, hypothermia, clonic movements (repeated jerking) or convulsions, fall of blood pressure, respiratory depression, dilation of pupils, disturbances of cardiac rhythm and nerve conduction. Cardiac arrest may occur after apparent recovery, giving the fictional killer an alibi.

REACTION TIME: Symptoms usually appear within an hour, but death may take several hours to several days.

ANTIDOTES AND TREATMENTS: Gastric lavage.

NOTES: A central nervous system depressant, Norpramine was first used in 1963 and is supposed to be faster acting and better tolerated than others in this class.

These drugs should not be given within two weeks of MAO inhibitors.

Abrupt withdrawal can precipitate psychosis.

PERMITIAL

SCIENTIFIC NAME: Fluphenazine.

OTHER SIMILAR: Serentil (mesoridazine), Levoprome (methotrimeprazine), Trilafon (perphenazine), Sparine (promazine), Dartal (thiopropazate), Mellaril (thioidazine), Navane (thiothixene), Versprin (triflupromazine).

TOXICITY: 5

FORM: Pills; injectable liquid.

EFFECTS AND SYMPTOMS: These drugs cause prolonged dizziness and orthostatic hypotension (fall of blood pressure when one stands suddenly). Marked sedation occurs with all of these drugs. Other symptoms include severe postural hypotension, hypothermia, tachycardia, dryness of mouth, nausea, ataxia, anorexia, nasal congestion, fever, blurring of vision, stiff muscles, urine retention, coma, and death.

Hypotension and ventricular arrhythmias are the most common causes of death. Prolonged effects at high doses include a purple pigmentation on face, hands, and neck. Lab tests show poor liver function. Phenothiazine compounds can be detected by adding a few drops of tincture of ferric chloride to urine; urine acidified with nitric acid will turn violet, revealing the effects of the drug.

Extrapyramidal symptoms from an overdose of a psychiatric drug (as mentioned before) include spasmodic contractions of face and neck muscles with swallowing difficulties, intolerable motor restlessness, salivation, convulsions, and endocrine disturbances like abnormal milk production in someone not lactating (even a male), interference with menstruation, and increase in thyroid activity.

Abnormal weight gain is often noticed as well, despite increase in thyroid.

REACTION TIME: Twenty minutes to several hours.

ANTIDOTES AND TREATMENTS: Benadryl is often used to reverse the extrapyramidal signs. Phenytoin is given for ventricular arrhythmias.

PROLIXIN, PROLIXIN DECONOATE

SCIENTIFIC NAME: Fluphenazine hydrochloride/deconoate.

TOXICITY: 6

FORM: Oral tablets, elixir, injectable.

EFFECTS AND SYMPTOMS: Early symptoms are dry mouth, flushed face, nausea and vomiting, anorexia, fever, drowsiness, sore throat, unusual bleeding, weakness, tremors, dark urine, pale stool, or rash. Extrapyramidal symptoms are commonly seen. Hypertension, tachycardia, cardiac arrest, congestive heart failure (CHF), cardiomegaly (enlarged heart), pulmonary edema, and irregular heartbeats are also seen, as well as bronchospasm, dilated pupils, suppression of cough reflex, aspiration, and death due to asphyxia or cardiac arrest. A fatal but rare side effect is neuroleptic malignant syndrome, or hyperthermia, in which fevers spike at 104 degrees and higher.

REACTION TIME: Several minutes to a half hour depending on administration.

ANTIDOTES AND TREATMENTS: Gastric lavage and symptomatic treatment.

NOTES: Used as an anti-psychotic drug, it depresses the RAS (reticular activating system—the brain stem core—and especially parts of the brain involved with wakefulness and behavioral responsiveness and muscle tone). Damage to this area can lead to permanent coma.

The drug exacerbates glaucoma and urinary tract problems as well as respiratory distress. Daily doses greater than 20mg orally should be given with caution. The injectable dose is 10mg daily. Someone who is sensitive to aspirin or to Phenothiazine, who is in a coma, who has an imbalance in white or red blood cells, who is having respiratory or liver problems, or who is suffering from glaucoma should not receive this. It lowers seizure thresholds in epileptics, elevates prolactin in breast cancer patients, and increases sensitivity to the sun.

The long-acting version lasts one to three weeks in the body.

False positive pregnancy tests are also seen in women taking this drug.

PROZAC

SCIENTIFIC NAME: Fluoxetine hydrochloride.

OTHER: Apo-Fluoxetine; Novo-Fluoxetine, Prozac Weekly, Sarafem.

TOXICITY: 3

FORM: Capsules (daily and time-release).

EFFECTS AND SYMPTOMS: Should not be used by pregnant women or people with upset stomach or impaired hepatic function, or those who have made serious suicide attempts. People do not generally overdose on this drug alone, but it reportedly makes them more suicidal. It does not make them more depressed; rather it makes them less depressed, but unless the underlying cause of the feelings of hopelessness and worthlessness are attended to, Prozac can give them the mental strength to proceed with their plan.

Side effects include headache, nervousness, insomnia or drowsiness (affects people differently, depending on their personal chemistry), anxiety, tremor, dizziness, sweating, rash, itching, diarrhea, anorexia, dyspepsia (gastric upset), sexual dysfunction, painful menstrual periods, urinary frequency, weight changes, and fevers.

REACTION TIME: The oral doses may take several weeks to build up in the system before effects are seen.

ANTIDOTES AND TREATMENTS: Gastric lavage and symptomatic treatment.

NOTES: Used as an anti-depressant, it is widely prescribed for manic-depression, OCD (obsessive-compulsive disorder), and bulimia. It takes up to four weeks for the effect to be achieved, and the drug is not recommended for those under the age of eighteen.

Given with MAO inhibitors, it can cause severe problems.

The version Sarafem is often confused with Serophene (clomiphene).

QUAALUDE

SCIENTIFIC NAME: Methaqualone.

TOXICITY: 5

FORM: Pill and injectable liquid.

EFFECTS AND SYMPTOMS: Quaalude is used to relieve anxiety and tension as well as to induce sleep. Symptoms include nausea, gastric irritation, vomiting, parasthesia (tingling, pins-and-needles sensation), pulmonary edema, convulsions, and death.

REACTION TIME: Five to thirty minutes—depends on route and amount,

ANTIDOTES AND TREATMENTS: Gastric lavage and symptomatic treatment.

NOTES: Quaaludes were commonly abused in the 1980s but have since been taken off the American market. They can still be found overseas.

SINEQUAN

SCIENTIFIC NAME: Doxepin hydrochloride.

OTHER SIMILAR: Adapin.

TOXICITY: 5

FORM: Liquid and tablets.

EFFECTS AND SYMPTOMS: Overdose causes agitation, hallucinations, drowsiness, tachycardia, hypertension, dizziness, and coma.

REACTION TIME: Within an hour.

ANTIDOTES AND TREATMENTS: Gastric lavage and supportive therapy.

NOTES: In the past few years, at least seventeen fatalities have been reported.

First used as an antidepressant in 1963, it is a derivative of amitriptyline.

STELAZINE

SCIENTIFIC NAME: Trifluroperazine.

TOXICITY: 5

FORM: Tablets, syrup, injectables, and suppositories.

EFFECTS AND SYMPTOMS: A central nervous system depressant, Stelazine produces somnolence, agitation, convulsions, fever, coma, hypotension, and cardiac arrest.

REACTION TIME: Immediate, if injected; twenty minutes or longer if taken orally.

ANTIDOTES AND TREATMENTS: Cogentin is used to remove the extrapyramidal symptoms, and gastric lavage is done. The rest of the treatment is symptomatic.

NOTES: Stelazine is used in the treatment of psychotic anxiety and agitated depressions. It is infrequently used.

THORAZINE

SCIENTIFIC NAME: Chlorpromazine.

TOXICITY: 5

FORM: Tablets, syrup, injectables, or suppositories.

EFFECTS AND SYMPTOMS: A central nervous system depressant, Thorazine is used in the treatment of psychotic anxiety and severe behavior problems in both children and adults. Since Thorazine reduces the cough reflex, the sedated victim can choke on vomit. Overdose causes drowsiness, fainting, hypotension, tachycardia, tremor, dizziness, EKG changes, coma, and convulsions. A syndrome known as phenothiazine sudden death has been noted among psychiatric patients who receive large doses of Thorazine or other phenothiazines. This is often due to suffocation during a seizure.

Signs of overdose include extrapyramidal symptoms (or EPS, neurological side effects of antipsychotic drugs—such as unsteady gait, slobbering, stuttering or slurred speech, rigid back muscles, restlessness, contraction of the face and neck muscles, and hand tremors).

REACTION TIME: Ten minutes to one hour.

ANTIDOTES AND TREATMENTS: Artane, Benadryl, and Cogentin are some of the drugs given to combat EPS. For severe overdose, gastric lavage is done, followed by symptomatic treatment. Severe hypotension is treated with fluids.

NOTES: First used in 1952, Thorazine was found effective in treating psychotic disorders. At one time, this was used almost exclusively for patient management, but it fell into disuse because too many patients were receiving it who did not need it. When thorazine is used, the patient builds up tolerance to the drug, since acutely disturbed patients can receive large amounts, but using it with a comatose victim or combining with barbiturates or alcohol can be dangerous.

The liquid form has a bitter aftertaste.

VALIUM

SCIENTIFIC NAME: Diazepam.

TOXICITY: 5

FORM: Tablets; injectable. It is only slightly soluble in water.

EFFECTS AND SYMPTOMS: Used as an antianxiety agent and for alcohol withdrawal, Valium is a muscle relaxant, sedative, and anticonvulsant. Symptoms include drowsiness, ataxia, muscle weakness, tinnitus, excitability, rage, sores in the mouth, yellowing of skin and eyes, hallucinations, coma, and cardiac arrest. It increases the effectiveness of other antidepressants.

REACTION TIME: Five to thirty minutes.

ANTIDOTES AND TREATMENTS: Symptomatic.

NOTES. This drug can be abused and is addictive, yet it is widely prescribed. Tolerance develops. Most reported abuses or fatalities have been with Valium combined with other drugs, most notably alcohol and barbiturates. It should not be taken by someone with respiratory problems.

Traces can be found in the urine.

Other Psychotropic Drugs

The following are all common drugs in the realm of psychiatry. Used for psychosis, they each have their own niche but react in much the same way.

- Paxil (paroxetine hydrochloride) is another antidepressant/antianxiety, especially for social phobias, panic disorder, and post-traumatic stress. Given as pill or suspension, it can cause ejaculatory disorders and urinary frequency, headache, tremors, dizziness, sleepiness, nervousness, dry mouth, flatulence, upset stomach, and abdominal pain. It interacts with warfarin, and also reportedly gives patients the strength to commit suicide and is not recommended for teens. The pills should not be crushed or chewed. If used with another SSRI such as Prozac, it can cause serotonin syndrome (hypertension, fevers); used with St. John's Wort, it increases sedative effects.

- Ritalin, a stimulant and antidepressant, can be quite addictive and is usually kept locked up. While it is a stimulant, it seems to have the opposite effect on hyperactive children and adults, and is commonly given to them to calm them down. Tolerance or drug dependence may develop with long-term use. A central nervous system stimulant for most adults, overdoses can cause nausea, vomiting, tremors, coma, and convulsions. Toxicity level is 4. Blood pressure can be greatly increased if this drug is taken with MAO inhibitors. If taken with anticonvulsants, changes in seizure patterns may occur. The effects of anti-clotting medications and antidepressants are also increased when taking Ritalin. It is also used now in veterinary medicine for hyperactive dogs.

- Chlorpromazine and related drugs are synthetic chemicals derived from Phenothiazine and used as anti-emetics and tranquilizers. They increase the effects of analgesic and hypnotic drugs.

Antianxiety Drugs and Selected Antidepressants

The benzodiazepine class of drugs is used to relieve short-term anxiety caused by trauma or stress. They're also used to relieve agitation and delirium in alcohol withdrawal, as muscle relaxants, and to help patients sleep.

Most of these drugs can be addicting, all of them increase the effects of the others, and all are affected by alcohol. All are available in oral or injectable varieties; some are available as suppositories. The *Physician's Desk Reference* (PDR) or the *Merck Manual* can give exact details on those not elaborated on here.

The general symptoms include drowsiness, weakness, nystagmus (crossed eyes), diplopia (double vision), and incoordination, progressing to convulsions with coma, cyanosis, and respiratory distress. Chronic symptoms include a skin rash, gastric upset, headaches, and blurred vision. Reaction time on all of these is a few minutes to several hours. Toxicity level is 5.

Taking Tagamet (an ulcer medication that is now OTC) with these drugs can moderately increase their effect.

Among them are Xanax (alprazolam), a fast-acting drug that is a mild antianxiety. Other commonly prescribed, are Librium (chlordiazepoxide), Tranxene (chiorazepate),

Valium (mentioned already), Dalmane (flurazepam), Seraz (oxazepam), Centrax (prazepam), and Halcion (triazolam).

Trancopal (chlormezanone) causes, in addition to the other symptoms common to this class, vertigo, flushing, and depression.

Clonopin (clonazepam) causes hair loss and contradictory hirsutism (excess hair growth), gastrointestinal disturbances, sore gums, and painful urination.

Ativan (lorazepam), often used for anxiety and for calming aggressive patients, is given before surgery, too. Overdoses causes nausea, change of appetite, headache, and and sleep disturbances. It is very addicting, but very good for calming aggressive patients.

Dantrium (dantrolene) can cause liver damage, upset stomach, and bleeding.

Equanil (meprobamate) is used to tranquilize and induce sleep. It causes incoordinated movements, loss of balance, headache, hypotension, palpitations, fluid retention (edema), fever, wheezing, and shock.

Inapsine (droperidol) causes symptoms such as hallucinations, hypotension, and respiratory depression, especially when used with narcotics. Drug dependence can easily result with either of these. Sudden withdrawal from Equanil can trigger severe anxiety, tremors, hallucinations, convulsions, and possible stroke. If taken with anticonvulsants, Equanil will alter the seizure patterns.

Monoamine Oxidase Inhibitors (MAOI)

A different class of psychiatric drugs than tricyclics, MAOI drugs work on the central nervous system and liver. Primarily a central nervous system stimulant, these drugs, like the other antidepressants, change the chemical composition of the brain. They come in oral or injectable forms and are used for hypertension as well as depression. General symptoms include nausea, vomiting, lethargy, dry mouth, ataxia, stupor, drop in blood pressure, fever, tachycardia, acidosis, convulsions, liver damage, and jaundice. Death is usually from cardiac or respiratory failure.

Very few American physicians use these drugs now because of the many side effects and the many drugs that cannot be used with them, but they can still be found overseas.

Some common names are Parnate (tranylcypromine), Nardil (phenelzine), and Eutonyl (pargyline).

The toxicity is 4, but the reaction time is immediate. Since they do not mix well with other drugs, any combination with MAO inhibitors causes problems. For example, if these drugs are combined with Tofranil (imipramine) or an opium derivative such as morphine, they are more likely to cause extreme reactions like fatal hyperpyrexia (a body temperature of 104 to 106 degrees).

In addition, eating cheese or drinking alcohol while taking MAO inhibitors can cause severe hypertension, leading to stroke and possible death. Included in the individual notes of many drugs are cautions against combining them with MAO inhibitors.

Unfortunately, many patients who take this medication outside the hospital are not fully informed of the dietary restrictions or, if they are, don't understand just what the ramifications of going to a wine-and-cheese party could be.

MAO inhibitors increase the effects of barbiturates, antihistamines, antidepressants, merperidine, morphine, and aminopyrine classes of drugs, as well as others.

MUSCLE RELAXATION DRUGS

Neuromuscular blocking agents are given as intramuscular or intravenous injection. They are used to promote muscle relaxation during surgical anesthesia and occasionally to control convulsions. An effective dose of any of these is potentially fatal if respiration is not properly maintained by artificial means.

Other names include Tracium (atracurium); Flaxedil (gallamine triethiodide)—not to be confused with Flexeril, also a muscle relaxant but much milder; and Norcuron (vecuronium bromide); Valium can be listed here as well.

The general effect is to block the neuromuscular transmissions and depress respiration, as in respiratory failure and circulatory collapse. Symptoms include heaviness of eyelids; diplopia; difficulty in swallowing and talking; and rapid paralysis of the extremities, neck, intercostal (rib) muscles, and diaphragm. Death comes from asphyxia. Reaction time is usually immediate. Symptoms will continue for one to ten minutes after the injection is discontinued.

Antidotes can include either edrophonium (Tensilon) or neostigmine (Prostigmin).

The chance of death is greatly increased if several neuromuscular blocking agents are used at the same time.

As previously stated, all central nervous system depressants—including alcohol—increase the effects of one another, and tolerance to one indicates tolerance to others. Hypnotics, antihistamines, and narcotic analgesics slow intestinal absorption.

As a group, these drugs have been used for centuries. As a pre-anesthetic medication, they reduce salivary and bronchial secretions; relax the gastrointestinal tract in certain spastic conditions; and they are used as an antidote to cholinesterase inhibitors.

ANECTINE

SCIENTIFIC NAME: Succinylcholine.

TOXICITY: 6

FORM: Liquid, administered intramuscularly or intravenously; it is also a white, odorless, slightly bitter powder and very soluble in water.

EFFECTS AND SYMPTOMS: Respiratory paralysis.

REACTION TIME: Immediate.

ANTIDOTES AND TREATMENTS: None.

NOTES: Often used in the operating room and for homicidal poisonings. When patients on digitalis are given succinylcholine, because of the extra potassium often prescribed for them or given at the same time, they often have irregular heartbeats that can lead to heart attacks.

An ultrashort-acting drug that affects the skeletal muscles, the drug is unstable in alkaline solution but relatively stable in acid. Solutions should be stored in the refrigerator to protect potency.

Cardiac arrest has occurred during succinylcholine administration after a head injury.

ATROPINE

SCIENTIFIC NAME: Dl-hyoscyamine.

OTHER SIMILAR: Hyoscine, hyoscyamine, belladonna, scopolamine.

TOXICITY: 6

FORM: Tablets, capsules, injectable solutions, inhalants, and eye solutions.

EFFECTS AND SYMPTOMS: The effect is to paralyze the parasympathetic nervous system by blocking acetylcholine release at nerve endings. Kidney function must be normal to eliminate the drug.

The signs and symptoms of atropine poisoning develop quickly. One victim described it as being "hot as a hare, blind as a bat, dry as a bone, red as a beet, and mad as a wet hen." The first symptom is felt immediately as a sensation of dryness and burning of the mouth, followed by intense thirst. Talking and swallowing become difficult or impossible. Dilated pupils cause blurred vision and light sensitivity. There is a loss of sense of reality, possible aggressive behavior, and disorientation as well as paranoia that may occur in a few hours or days. Also found are rapid pulse and respiration, urinary retention, muscle stiffness, fever, convulsions, and coma. A rash sometimes appears, followed by the breakdown of skin, especially in the region of the face, neck, and upper trunk. The circulatory and respiratory systems collapse, causing death.

REACTION TIME: Minutes. A patient who survives twenty-four hours will probably recover.

ANTIDOTES AND TREATMENTS: Physostigmine salicylate can sometimes be given intravenously. Oxygen is often needed, and Valium helps the convulsions.

NOTES: Patients taking atropine are especially susceptible to heat exhaustion.

Twice as much oral atropine is required to achieve the same effect as the injected drug. Hallucinations occur in 50 percent of users.

These potent anticholinergic agents are sold by prescription. However, there are a number of over-the-counter treatments for colds, hay fever, gastrointestinal diseases, and asthma that use small amounts of atropine. And yet despite its poison, it can be a lifesaver. (See chapter twelve, Chemical Biological, and Radiological Weapons.)

Scopolamine has been used as a date rape drug since it causes retrograde amnesia (forgetting what happened just before the rape). Police often think that victims of this are having a psychotic episode. A sign of poisoning from this is fever without sweat. Overdoses of this cause delirium, delusions, paralysis, stupor, and death. A mixture in Columbia and Venezuela containing the drug is called *Burundanga* and used in numerous criminal activities. Because of the paralysis of the eye muscles it can be used in ophthalmology procedures; it's also used when patients have to be intubated. It has been found effective against motion sickness and is used by deep sea divers, but it causes pain in the eyes if the diver goes below fifty to sixty feet. (That pain reportedly subsides when the diver rises to forty feet below.)

CASE HISTORY

A notable Victorian case of hyoscine poisoning is that of Dr. Crippen. He had apparently sacrificed a great deal to his wife's ambition, while she openly flaunted affairs. He purchased the vegetable drug hyoscine hydrobromide (now used in treatments of motion sickness). He knew from working with psychiatric patients in the United States that it dampened the sexual ardor of those who took it, and it's supposed he bought it to stop his wife's philandering. However, he accidentally killed her instead. The hyoscine traces were found at postmortem examination. He appears to be the first recorded murderer in history to use the drug.

Mystery author Charlotte MacLeod used atropine eye drops to poison the victim in her book *The Family Vault.*

In Henry Wade's *No Friendly Drop,* the sudden death of a lord is caused by hyoscine. Hyoscine is also used in Agatha Christie's play *Black Coffee.*

EPINEPHRINE

SCIENTIFIC NAME: Adrenaline.

OTHER SIMILAR: Norepinephrine, naphazoline, amphetamine, ephedrine, eppie, oxymetazoline, tetrahydrozoline, xylometazoline.

TOXICITY: 6

FORM: Injection; inhalation; topical; intramuscular or intravenous injection.

EFFECTS AND SYMPTOMS: Symptoms are nausea, vomiting, nervousness, irritability, tachycardia, cardiac arrhythmias, contracted, pinpoint pupils, blurred vision, hallucinations, chills, pallor or cyanosis, fever, suicidal behavior, spasms, convulsions, gastrointestinal ulceration, hypertension, pulmonary edema, gasping respiration, coma, and respiratory failure.

REACTION TIME: Immediate.

ANTIDOTES AND TREATMENTS: Treatment is directed at relieving the cardiac problems and other systemic reactions.

NOTES: Epinephrine can also be applied to mucous membranes. Used for severe asthma attacks and for allergic reactions, epinephrine is a natural vasoconstrictor (it constricts the blood vessels). Gas inhalation can cause hallucinations and paranoia. Subcutaneous (under the skin) injection causes necrosis and shedding of skin.

Ephedrine is found widely in OTC drugs like cough syrups and nasal decongestants. Continued use of the drug often leads to acidosis and death.

A victim who survives will have continued life-threatening hypertension.

The combination of epinephrine and grapefruit juice is not recommended.

PAVULON

SCIENTIFIC NAME: Pancuronium.

TOXICITY: 6

FORM: Injectable; usually administered intravenously.

EFFECTS AND SYMPTOMS: Eighty percent paralysis has been noted with only a small amount of the drug. Pavulon works most quickly in patients with kidney or liver problems.

The dose is eliminated in the urine as an unchanged drug, and can be detected in autopsy only if the pathologist acts quickly.

REACTION TIME: Immediate.

ANTIDOTES AND TREATMENTS: Endrophonium and neostigmine are antidotes.

NOTES: Developed in 1964 as a neuromuscular blocking agent, it used as an alternative to tubocurarine. It is often used in the operating room and is one of the three drugs used in lethal injections.

PHYSOSTIGMINE

OTHER: Pilocarpine, neostigmine, methacholine.

TOXICITY: 5

FORM: Ingestion, injection, topical cream.

EFFECTS AND SYMPTOMS: Respiratory difficulty is the main symptom. Others include tremor, marked peristalsis with involuntary defecation and urination, pinpoint pupils, vomiting, cold extremities, hypotension, bronchial constriction, wheezing, twitching of muscles, fainting, slow pulse, convulsions, and death from asphyxia or cardiac slowing.

REACTION TIME: Immediate.

ANTIDOTES AND TREATMENTS: If atropine is given, recovery is immediate.

NOTES: Repeated, small doses may reproduce the symptoms of acute poisoning. Autopsy findings include swelling of the brain, pulmonary edema, and congestion of the gastrointestinal tract.

Used for treatments of myasthenia gravis, atonic conditions of bladder in which there is a lack of muscle tone, and certain heart irregularities, these drugs work on the parasympathetic nervous system.

Other varieties include acetylcholine, urecholine, Tensilon, stigmonerne, and mecholyl, which are given by injection, as are Mytelase, muscarine, and Prostigmin, Humorsol, phospholine, and pilocarpine. Miostat can be applied topically or injected.

TUBARINE

SCIENTIFIC NAME: Tubocurarine chloride

TOXICITY: 6

FORM: Injectable, supplied as liquid and powder.

EFFECTS AND SYMPTOMS: Accidental overdose causes hypotension and respiratory failure. Concentration of the drug remains in the liver for a short time after death.

REACTION TIME: Immediate.

ANTIDOTES AND TREATMENTS: Endrophonium or neostigmine are antidotes.

NOTES: This is a popular poison for medical personnel and those who have access to hospital drugs. The drug is supplied as a chloride salt in ampules that must be mixed with sterile water before injection.

It is a curare alkaloid derived from the South American plant. (See curare in chapter five, page 56.) Quinidine and procainamide increase the victim's susceptibility to curare poisoning. Quinidine, procainamide, lidocaine, propranolol, and phenytoin reduce cardiac contraction and thus increase the possibility of heart failure during anesthesia.

CASE HISTORY

The use of tubarine as a homicidal poison was suspected in a series of eastern United States hospital deaths. The patients supposedly all had heart attacks, but when an empty vial of the drug was found in an intern's locker, the bodies were checked. The drug was detected in decomposed tissue.

BLOOD THINNERS

These drugs are used to slow down the clotting process by interfering with clotting enzymes.

COUMADIN

SCIENTIFIC NAME: Warfarin.

OTHER SIMILAR: Dicumarol, ethyl biscoumacetate, heparin, phenindione, diphenadione, acenocoumarol, Valone, Talon, Racumin.

TOXICITY: 4

FORM: Oral or injectable.

EFFECTS AND SYMPTOMS: Warfarin inhibits the formation in the liver of a number of the clotting factors whose formation is dependent on vitamin K.

Symptoms include hemoptysis (blood suddenly arising from hemorrhaging of the larynx, trachea, or lungs; characterized by a salty taste and bright red, frothy blood), hematuria, bloody stools, hemorrhages in organs, widespread bruising, and bleeding into joint spaces. Repeated use leads to acute poisoning. Clotting time is prolonged, so with an overdose the victim can bleed to death from a severe cut. Jaundice and liver enlargement may be seen. Skin rash, vomiting, bloody diarrhea, orange-stained urine, kidney damage, and fever are also found. The kidney and liver injuries, because of the amount of blood traveling through those organs, are often fatal.

REACTION TIME: Fatalities have been reported after repeated daily doses of anticoagulants. Death may occur up to two weeks after discontinuing the drug.

ANTIDOTES AND TREATMENTS: Mephyton is given, along with transfusions and absolute bed rest to prevent further hemorrhages and internal bleeding. Vitamin K brings the prothrombin level back to normal within forty-eight hours. PTT is the blood test.

Coumarin anticoagulants enhance the effects of the thyroid hormone. Therapeutic range of the drug is very narrow and the patient requires constant monitoring. Many other drugs and foods interact with warfarin, causing the effect increase or decrease. It's quite easy for someone taking it to bleed to death.

Bromadiolone, Talon, Racumin, and coumachlor are used as rodenticides.

POTASSIUM (K), CALCIUM (CA), AND SODIUM (NA)

These are several of the body elements, called electrolytes, and their balance is very important to maintain health. Too much or too little can stop the heart. The balance is maintained by the kidneys, so that when one goes into kidney failure, these electrolyte levels become erratic. When one has kidney problems, electrolyte balances should be monitored closely. When one goes to the hospital with difficult breathing or heart pain, electrolytes are always checked, along with blood gases.

One electrolyte alone can throw off the body function to such a degree that respiratory acidosis can occur, leading to cardiac arrest and death. Some of the drugs that contain potassium are potassium alum, potassium bichromate, potassium bromate, potassium carbonate, potassium chlorate, potassium chloriese, potassium cyanate, potassium cyanide, potassium iodide, potassium permanganate, and potassium thiocyanate.

K-Lyte, or potassium bicarbonate, which comes sometimes as a liquid and sometimes as an orange-flavored pill that dissolves quickly in water, is given to patients who are on diuretics such as Lasix. Other forms of potassium come as Kay Ciel, K-Lor, Klotrix, K-Tab, Micro-K, and Slow-K (potassium chloride).

Some of the calcium drugs are calcium arsenate (similar to arsenic), calcium carbimide (similar to cyanamide), calcium disodium edetate, calcium hydroxide, calcium oxide, and calcium phosphate. A calcium blocker drug will prevent calcium from linking up with the other chemicals in the body.

The most famous sodiums are sodium chloride, or table salt, and bicarbonate of soda. While salt has a definite taste, sugar can sometimes be used to mask the flavor, and enough salt in a susceptible person can raise blood pressure high enough to cause a stroke. Withholding salt on a hot day can cause heatstroke and death.

Variations of these drugs can be injected, taken orally, or given as suppositories.

The first symptoms are slight paralysis of the limbs, nausea, abdominal discomfort, vomiting, diarrhea, mental confusion, unusual weakness, shortness of breath, and then respiratory failure, since the action is quick. Consciousness is fully preserved until the end. The toxicity rating for potassium, calcium, or sodium is 4. In a kidney patient, quite a bit less would be needed. People taking salt substitutes are already getting a large dose of potassium.

Spironolactone or triamterene (Dyrenium, a blood pressure reducer), when taken with potassium supplements, may cause an excessive rise in blood potassium levels that can be fatal.

CASE HISTORY

In one episode of *Murder She Wrote,* a heart attack was induced by giving too much sodium. When the patient was taken to the ER, she was given bicarbonate of sodium as a standard ER treatment for heart attack, which killed her.

ASTRINGENTS AND ANTISEPTICS

These drugs, when not used to poison, remove microorganisms that cause disease, fermentation, or putrefaction.

Phenol, featured in Household Poisons, chapter four, is used in carbolized Vaseline as well. A dangerous poison, it is the basis of all antiseptics and is what surgeon Joseph Lister used when he was discovering sterilization.

M131 is not a secret agent but the pharmacopeia listing for everyday Listerine. Made with eucalyptol, menthol, methyl salicylate, and thymol, the amber original version (not the minty kind) is an all-around topical that can be used for burns, bug bites, and rashes—and is listed as a poison by the National Poison Control Center with the warning that medical attention is to be sought immediately if it is swallowed.

BORIC ACID

OTHER SIMILAR: Sodium borate, borax, *Pentaborane, decaborane,* and *diborane* are used as repellents.

TOXICITY: 5

FORM: A white compound, boric acid dissolves slightly in cold water and decomposes in hot water. It can be ingested or absorbed through skin or mucous membranes.

EFFECTS AND SYMPTOMS: Concentrated boric acid is toxic to all cells. The effect on an organ is dependent on the concentration reached in that organ. Highest toxicity usually occurs in kidneys.

Boric acid dust is irritating to mucous membranes and can cause excitability, unconsciousness, vomiting, diarrhea of mucus and blood, lethargy, and twitching of facial muscles and extremities, followed by convulsions, cyanosis, fall of blood pressure, collapse, coma, and death.

In chronic poisoning, the victim will suffer weight loss, vomiting, alopecia (hair loss), convulsions, anemia, and skin rash, as well as the other symptoms.

Autopsy findings in fatal cases are gastroenteritis, fatty degeneration of the liver and kidneys, cerebral edema, and congestion of all organs.

REACTION TIME: Immediate. Deaths occur frequently following the swallowing of or excessive skin exposure to concentrated boric acid powder or solution.

ANTIDOTES AND TREATMENTS: Boric acid is removed from skin or mucous membranes by washing. Internal poison is removed by ipecac emesis and by gastric lavage.

NOTES: Boric acid is also used in industry and in a very diluted form as an eye wash. An environmentally safe insecticide, it is especially effective on ground-walking insects, such as beetles and roaches. It was formerly used as an antiseptic and to make talcum powder flow freely. Sodium borate (borax) is used as a cleaning agent. Sodium perborate is used as a mouthwash and dentifrice (teeth cleaner).

IODINE

OTHER: Iodoform, iodochlorhydroxyquin, chiniofon, betadine (povidone), iodides. There are numerous other "dines" that are used topically. Betadine is water-based rather than alcohol-based and does not sting.

TOXICITY: 5

FORM: A bluish-black powder soluble in alcohol and slightly soluble in water. Iodoform, a slightly yellowish powder or crystalline material with a penetrating odor, is insoluble in water but soluble in alcohol. Sodium and potassium iodides are white crystals soluble in water.

EFFECTS AND SYMPTOMS: Iodine acts directly on the cells by precipitating proteins. The affected cells are often killed. The effects are similar to acid corrosives. Iodine depresses the central nervous system.

On the skin, in a concentrated form, it can cause burns.

Ingestion causes severe vomiting; frequent, liquid stools; abdominal pain; thirst; a metallic taste; shock; fever; anuria; delirium; stupor; and death from uremia (poisoning of the body from toxic wastes the kidneys cannot expel). A patient who recovers might have esophageal stricture. Nausea, respiratory distress, and circulatory collapse have also been reported. Application to the skin may cause weeping, crusting, and blistering.

Iodine dyes are used in many different radiological studies. If an individual is allergic to iodine, it may cause sudden, fatal collapse (anaphylaxis) as a result of the injection. Symptoms are shortness of breath, cyanosis, fall of blood pressure, unconsciousness, and convulsions leading to death.

REACTION TIME: Immediate. Survival is likely if the victim lives one hour.

ANTIDOTES AND TREATMENTS: Sodium thiosulfate will immediately reduce iodine to iodide.

NOTES: In autopsy, the kidneys show necrosis.

Shellfish allergy is an indicator of iodine hypersensitivity. Iodines are also used to stain cells in laboratories and for turning garments brown.

It is used prior to surgery to sterilize large areas of the body.

Iodine crystals combined with ammonia hydroxide make a very unstable explosive called nitrogen triiodode.

You might recall using iodine on cuts as a child, but that is no longer recommended since the antiseptic destroys the healthy cells at the margins of the wound and interferes with the healing process. Of course, in an emergency you would still use it, since getting rid of the infection is more important than avoiding scars.

SILVER NITRATE

TOXICITY: 5

FORM: A water-soluble salt that is fatal if ingested as a salt or a liquid. Also available in stick form; the end is moistened to apply to skin lesions.

EFFECTS AND SYMPTOMS: Ingestion damages the kidney and liver and causes the victim to have pain and burning in the mouth; blackening of the skin, mucous membranes, throat, and abdomen; increased salivation; vomiting of black material; diarrhea; anuria; collapse; shock; and death from convulsions or coma. Repeated application or ingestion causes a semi-permanent, bluish-black discoloration of the skin and mucous membranes, especially those of the eyes.

REACTION TIME: Immediate.

ANTIDOTES AND TREATMENTS: This drug is diluted with water containing table salt; the drug is removed from the intestines via an enema; and milk and pain medication are given to relieve gastric distress.

NOTES: Recovery has been reported at higher than the usual fatal dose. It varies greatly with individuals.

Silver nitrate solution is used for the treatment of newborn eyes and in dermatology.

CARDIAC DRUGS

There are some twenty-five commonly used drugs for treating heart-related diseases. Most of them are available by prescription only.

The three types of cardiovascular drugs are cardiac glycosides (used to treat heart failure), vasodilators (used for angina), and catecholamines (used for abnormal blood pressure, discussed under Antihypertensives on page 197.)

Physicians order cardiac glycosides for patients who have congestive heart failure. Among them are digoxin, digitoxin, digitalis, deslanoside, and ouabain. These are used to strengthen the contractions of the heart. As a result, the heart pumps stronger and more blood flows to the kidneys, leading to elimination of more salty fluids. In turn, venous congestion decreases, easing the workload of the heart. Patients taking digoxin and digitoxin may have exaggerated problems with hypokalemia (an inablilty to retain sufficient amounts of potassium). These cardiac glycosides are also used to treat irregular electrical impulses from the heart and help to stabilize the heart rhythms.

Those used mainly to prevent and treat angina are nitrates, such as nitroglycerin and isosorbide dinitrate. These vasodilators expand the veins and venules (small veins between the capillaries and the veins) so that more blood flows through the vessels before returning to the heart. It takes less energy for the heart to pump; therefore the heart is less likely to develop a myocardial oxygen deficit that causes angina or myocardial ischemia. These drugs are given sublingually (under the tongue.)

A few other cardiac drugs are Isordil, amyl nitrate, nitrostat, nitrospan, nitrobid ointment, and tridil.

Strophanthin, another cardiac drug, similar in effect but found mainly in Europe, was used in Christie's *Verdict* to dispose of the burdensome wife.

DIGITOXIN, DIGITALIS

OTHER: Lantoxin, Crystodigin (oral), Purodigin (intravenous).

TOXICITY: 6

FORM: Tablet or liquid.

EFFECTS AND SYMPTOMS: Used for congestive heart failure to regulate the heart rhythm, all the cardiac drugs work on the heart muscle to increase contractions and reduce fluid retention.

Overdose causes nausea, vomiting, diarrhea, blurred vision, and cardiac disturbances such as tachycardia, uneven heart beats, and other electrical changes in the heart that result in cardiac imbalance with an inability to pump the blood smoothly.

REACTION TIME: Immediate.

ANTIDOTES AND TREATMENTS: The stomach is washed with tannic acid or strong tea and the victim is kept lying down. Stimulants such as caffeine, ammonia, or atropine are given.

NOTES: Derived from the plant foxglove and used by Native Americans to treat heart problems for centuries, digitoxin can be given orally, intramuscularly, or intravenously.

Intake of food affects the oral absorption time. The risk of toxicity from digitalis is increased by administration of reserpine or succinylcholine, by laxative abuse, or by calcium and potassium loss induced by diuretics.

Digoxin (Lanoxin) has the same symptoms as digitoxin and is also used in treatment of congestive heart failure. Alone, the toxicity level is 5, and reaction time is six hours. Digoxin is potentiated by mixing with quinidine or quinine.

CASE HISTORY
_____

Agatha Christie's *Appointment With Death* and *Postern of Fate* used digitoxia, a drug of the digitalis series, as the cause of death. The overdose slowed the pulse, retarded the heart contractions, and increased the amount of blood flowing to the heart, giving the person a heart attack.

Marissa Piesman, in her book *Unorthodox Practices,* had her victims killed with digitalis powder in the food.

In England, during the early 1970s, when several patients of one doctor mysteriously died, digitoxin was identified by bioassay (a chemical-checking process) and found in the skeletal muscle of nine out of fourteen victims, all dead for seventeen to forty months. The doctor had accidentally replaced estradiol with digitoxin.

LASIX

SCIENTIFIC NAME: Furosemide, chlorothiazide, hydrochlorothiazide.

OTHER SIMILAR: Diuril, Hydrodiuril, Hygroton, Esidrix, Enduron, Zaroxolyn, OTC diuretics.

TOXICITY: 4

FORM: Tablets or liquid; or injectable.

EFFECTS AND SYMPTOMS: The drug works on the kidney tubules and decreases the fluid in the body, thus lowering blood pressure. Symptoms of overdose include nausea, vomiting, frequent urination, dizziness, headache, hypotension, blurred vision, tingling sensations, weakness, bleeding under the skin, photosensitivity (sensitivity to light), fever, difficulty breathing, pulmonary edema, shock, hyperglycemia, kidney failure, dehydration, muscle spasms, tremors, and death.

All patients receiving these are fragile and have other problems, so they are usually monitored for fluid and electrolyte depletion. An I & O record (intake and output flow chart) is done if the patient is in the hospital, measuring how much liquid is taken in compared to how much urine is excreted. Too much of the drug can cause acidosis or alkalosis and subsequent heart failure. Patients using Lasix must be watched especially closely, as they are most affected by any slight electrolyte change.

REACTION TIME: One to eight hours if ingested. Five minutes or more if injected.

Electrolytes are given to combat fluid loss.

NOTES: Lasix is a diuretic and antihypertensive. It is usually given in cases of congestive heart failure, pulmonary edema, liver problems, or other swelling to help the tissues release fluid. In general, it eliminates excess fluid from the body. It also affects electrolyte balance.

It's quite possible to faint and become quite ill with just a little too much Lasix. Most people who take diuretics on a regular basis also have a supply of electrolyte replacements in the house (pills, or a liquid such as Pedialyte or K-Lyte). Those who have poor kidney function or liver disease must be careful, as Lasix does not leave the body quickly. People taking diuretics are more prone to sunburn.

Some people abuse diuretics for rapid weight loss and overdose that way.

Diuretics, when combined with other blood-pressure reducers, can create unstable reactions in some patients. It's important to keep electrolytes in balance, and patients on diuretics often have drugs like spironolactone, triamterene, or amuloride in the house. Pain relievers and barbiturates may increase their effects.

Lithium taken in combination with these drugs can quickly reach a poisonous level.

This drug received the name Lasix because its effects last six hours.

NITROGLYCERIN

SCIENTIFIC NAME: Glyceryl trinitrate.

OTHER SIMILAR: Nitrobid, Nitrostat, Nitropaste, amyl nitrate, ethyl nitrate, sodium nitrate, mannitol hexanitrate, pentaerythritol tetranitrite, isosorbide dinitrate, and trolnitrite phosphate.

TOXICITY: 4 by itself; much higher when mixed with things like Viagra.

FORM: Tablets (Nitrostat or Nitrobid), aerosol spray (nitrolingual), or liquid.

EFFECTS AND SYMPTOMS: The drug dilates blood vessels throughout the body by direct relaxant effect on smooth muscles. It also causes headache, flushing of skin, vomiting, dizziness, collapse, a marked fall in blood pressure, cyanosis, coma, and respiratory paralysis.

REACTION TIME: Immediate.

ANTIDOTES AND TREATMENTS: Gastric lavage.

NOTES: Used medically to dilate coronary vessels and reduce blood pressure. Any person taking nitro has a cardiac problem and is already in a fragile state.

Ethylene glycol nitrate and nitroglycerin are highly explosive and unstable by themselves. Dynamite is nitro mixed with cellose, which stabilizes it.

Lab results will show chocolate-colored blood due to conversion of hemoglobin to methemoglobin, and a buildup of fluids in all organs. The exam must be done quickly, since methemoglobin disappears in standing blood.

When taken with alcohol or blood pressure reducers, nitroglycerin can cause a severe drop in blood pressure. Yet, since blood pressure problems many times occur simultaneously with heart problems, doctors often give the drugs together without realizing the problems, or in spite of the danger, knowing that high blood pressure is more life-threatening.

Nitroglycerin (glyceryl trinite), amyl nitrite, ethyl nitrite, mannitol hexanitrate, sodium nitrite, isosorbide dinitrate, and trolnitrate are used medically to dilate the coronary vessels and reduce blood pressure.

Nitrites are used to preserve the color of meat in pickling or salting. The allowable residue in food is .01 percent. There are nitrosamines used in fertilizer, plastics, toiletries, and pesticides. They also occur in surface water near industrial parks.

Drugs like Viagra and other ED (erectile dysfunction) drugs are contraindicated with nitrates as they can cause a sudden drop of blood pressure, and on some occasions death has occurred.

CASE HISTORY

Several movies and television shows have had people taking nitro, needing it suddenly for angina. The villain sits by and watches the victim die, withholding the medicine. This is not accurate, as angina is painful but rarely fatal.

PERSANTINE

SCIENTIFIC NAME: Dipyridamole.

TOXICITY: 5

FORM: Tablets. Persantine is an odorless, yellow crystalline powder with a bitter taste. It is soluble in dilute acids, methanol, and chloroform, but insoluble in water.

EFFECTS AND SYMPTOMS: Headache, dizziness, nausea, flushing, weakness, blackouts, severe chest pain, seizures, heart attack, temporary stroke, severe difficulty breathing, and death.

REACTION TIME: Immediate.

ANTIDOTES AND TREATMENTS: Aminophylline is given, and the patient lies down to avoid a more severe drop in blood pressure; if necessary nitroglycerine is given. Caffeine and ergot, which are sometimes used to dilate the blood vessels, stimulate the central nervous system. Gastric lavage is done, and all other symptoms are treated as they occur.

NOTES: A blood vessel dilator, Persantine is used to dilate or enlarge the coronary arteries and increase the blood flow to the heart. Given orally, it is used to prevent the pain of angina pectoris, but does not stop an acute angina attack. In cases of low blood pressure, it will make the pressure fall even lower. It is used with other drugs to reduce the risk of blood clots after heart valve replacement. It works by preventing excessive blood clotting.

There will be altered—decreased or increased—effects when taken with drugs like Aricept, Cognex or Exelon (used for Alzheimer's), Coumadin, Indocin, certain heart medications like adenosine, and valproic acid (Depakene.)

ANTIHYPERTENSIVES

Antihypertensives are used medically to lower blood pressure and come in many types. Some (epinephrine and norepinephrine) are classed as catecholamines, which lower blood pressure by depressing the stress response of the central nervous system.

A change in blood pressure medication can cause confusion and delusions, as well as fainting. The elderly are especially susceptible and are many times misdiagnosed as suffering from dementia or Alzheimer's. Correcting the dose or medication causes symptoms to disappear, and normality returns.

There are two distinct classes of these drugs: alpha, such as Minipress (prazosin hyrochloride) or phentolamine mesylate; and beta, such as Sectral, Tenormin, Lopressor, Visken, Inderal, and Timolide. Both work by preventing responses to the sympathetic nervous system. If the blockers are suddenly withdrawn, heart failure may result, especially in people with aorta problems. They all have similar symptoms and toxicity ratings.

There is another variety of antihypertensives that are centrally acting sympatholytic drugs. Some of them are Aldomet (Methyldopa), Dopamet (CN), Clonidine, Guanabenz, Guanfacine, and Tizanidine.

There are also calcium channel blockers such as Norvasc, Amlodipine, Diltiazen, Nicardipine, Felodipine, Isradipine, Nifedipine, Nimodipine, and Verapamil.

ALDOMET

SCIENTIFIC NAME: Methyldopa.

TOXICITY: 3

FORM: Liquid or tablet.

EFFECTS AND SYMPTOMS: Drowsiness, headache, dizziness, weakness, tiredness, lightheadedness, skin rash, joint and muscle pains, impotence, reduction of white blood cells, fever, and nightmares.

REACTION TIME: Twenty minutes to one hour.

ANTIDOTES AND TREATMENTS: Stimulants like caffeine or atropine are used.

NOTES: If taken with alcohol, the sedation effect is increased and the blood pressure is lowered excessively. The effects of other blood pressure pills are increased if taken with Aldomet, as are effects of anticoagulant drugs like Coumadin and warfarin. Tolbutamide or lithium also quickly reaches a dangerous level in the body. If the drug is taken with Haldol, behavior disturbances could result. If it is taken with MAO inhibitors or tricyclic antidepressants, the blood pressure will rise dramatically. The effects of other medications are also increased with diuretics. Check the individual drug insert or PDR for more information.

CATAPRES

SCIENTIFIC NAME: Clonidine.

OTHER SIMILIAR: Hyperstat, Apresoline, Loniten, Regitine, phentolamine, minoxidil, hydralazine, captopril, Capoten, prazosin, dopamine, Intropin, dopastat.

TOXICITY: 6

FORM: Tablet or injectable.

EFFECTS AND SYMPTOMS: Symptoms include slow heartbeat, drowsiness, gastrointestinal upset, possible hepatitis, heart failure, rash, increased sensitivity to alcohol, coma, hypotension, and depressed respiration.

REACTION TIME: Within a few minutes if taken by injection; thirty minutes if taken orally.

ANTIDOTES AND TREATMENTS: Atropine is indicated. The cardiac and respiratory system must be observed carefully. The victim must be kept lying in a supine (face-up) position. Kidney function also must be monitored.

NOTES: Catapres is a white, crystalline powder, slightly soluble in water, and is given either by tablet or injection.

A hypertensive crisis can occur with an abrupt withdrawal of the medication. This can also trigger hyperexcitability (anxiety), psychosis, cardiac arrhythmias, and death.

INDERAL

SCIENTIFIC NAME: Propranolol.

TOXICITY: 5

FORM: Pills.

EFFECTS AND SYMPTOMS: Inderal reduces or blocks cardiac and bronchial response to excessive stimulation. It affects the central nervous system and causes hypotension.

Symptoms include slow pulse, nausea, vomiting, numbness in the limbs, orthostatic hypotension (faintness on rising), dryness of mouth, diarrhea, fall of blood pressure, hallucinations, headache, sleeping abnormalities, disorientation, hypoglycemia, shortness of breath, respiratory depression, convulsions, coma, catatonia, rigidity, stupor, delirium, and death.

REACTION TIME: Within thirty minutes.

ANTIDOTES AND TREATMENTS: Isoproterenol.

NOTES: Heart attack can occur after abrupt withdrawal.

If the victim is being treated for overactive thyroid, low blood sugar, diabetes, or kidney or liver disease, Inderal should be carefully monitored, since serious complications, including many of the side effects, could be exacerbated. Asthma or hay fever patients may experience more problems with breathing and a dangerously low heart rate. If alcohol is consumed, the blood pressure may drop. The properties of antidiabetic drugs are increased when taking this medication or when taking herbs such as fenugreek or garlic, and so the patient's blood sugar should be monitored to prevent the possibility of insulin shock.

PROCAINAMIDE

SCIENTIFIC NAME: Prazosin hydrochloride.

TOXICITY: 5

FORM: A clear liquid administered intravenously.

EFFECTS AND SYMPTOMS: The pulse becomes irregular and suddenly disappears (straight-lines) and, with a total collapse of the circulatory system, the patient fails. Almost immediately, there is an onset of convulsions and death.

REACTION TIME: Immediate. Death caused by hypersensitivity or rapid injection.

ANTIDOTES AND TREATMENTS: Treatment is the same as for cardiac arrest.

NOTES: Procainamide is given for irregularities of ventricular contraction, including tachycardia or fibrillation.

QUINIDINE

OTHER: Conquinine, Pitayine.

TOXICITY: 6

FORM: Tablets; injectable liquid.

EFFECTS AND SYMPTOMS: Quinidine depresses the metabolic activity of all the cells, but its effect is mostly on the heart. Principal effects are fall of blood pressure, and nausea. Poisoning from ingestion includes tinnitus; headache; nausea; diarrhea; hypotension with the circulatory system collapsing; involuntary, rhythmic movement of the eyeball; brady-cardia; and respiratory failure. Sudden death may result from ventricular fibrillation.

REACTION TIME: Immediate.

ANTIDOTES AND TREATMENTS: Gastric lavage and support for the cardiac system.

NOTES: Usually given orally, it can also be administered intravenously or intramuscu-larly. The latter two can be quite painful. A white, water-soluble alkaloid obtained from cinchona bark, it is used in the treatment of cardiac irregularities. Quinidine enhances the effects of muscle relaxants.

SODIUM THIOCYANATE / POTASSIUM THIOCYANATE

TOXICITY: 5

FORM: Tablet or liquid.

EFFECTS AND SYMPTOMS: Sodium thiocyanate depresses the metabolic activities of all cells, but acts most noticeably on brain and heart, just like regular sodium or potassium. Symptoms include disorientation, weakness, hypotension, confusion, psychotic behav-ior, muscular spasms, convulsions, and death.

REACTION TIME: Immediate.

ANTIDOTES AND TREATMENTS: Remove by cleansing the blood through dialysis.

NOTES: This drug was formerly used for treatment of hypertension, but now has been replaced with safer drugs. Sodium thiocyanate is still sometimes prescribed, especially by older doctors, and can still be found in many hospitals.

Psychotic behavior is commonly seen, and someone could be committed on the basis of that, or have a death that may look like suicide.

More than twenty fatalities have been reported from sodium and potassium thiocyanate.

If kidney disease is present, the drug is urinated out of the body more slowly than with a healthier patient; therefore, toxic symptoms are seen quicker.

The patient can show recovery when the medication has stopped, but even after several days of improvement, a relapse can occur, and death has been known to happen as long as two weeks after taking the drug.

Dopamine, Intropin, and dopastat are similar. They support blood pressure during shock due to a heart attack, during open heart surgery, and in congestive heart failure. They are short-lived drugs.

Nitroprusside, or Nipride, is given intravenously, not only for hypertensive crisis, but to control blood pressure and bleeding during an operation. It takes effect in two minutes and lasts about ten minutes. Other drugs should not be mixed with it at the same time. If a patient needs it for more than forty-eight hours, one nursing journal states, blood must be drawn to check for lab levels of metabolite thiocyanide, as the drug is potent and toxic.

APPETITE SUPPRESSANTS

Some of these drugs—Dexedrine, Benzadrine, Didrex (benzphetamine), Tenuate and Tenuate Dose Span (diethylpropion), Fastin or Ionamin (phentermine), and Preludin (phenmetrazine)—will not only reduce the appetite but elevate the blood pressure, disturb the heart rhythm, and cause hyperactivity, restlessness, insomnia, euphoria, tremor, headache, dryness of mouth, unpleasant tastes, diarrhea, upset stomach, changes in sex drive, and impotence, as well as depression and psychosis. They are very addictive and often used by students as stimulants to keep awake. Overdoses or prolonged use can cause hallucinations, aggressiveness, and panic, which might result in an accidental death.

Many of these drugs are time-released capsules or coated pills.

Meth is the street version of these drugs.

These drugs should not be taken by people suffering from heart disease or from high blood pressure or other blood vessel problems. These drugs may impair blood pressure reducers, so even the victim taking blood pressure medication may still suffer a fatal stroke. If MAO inhibitors are taken with this, the blood pressure can increase dramatically. Some alcoholic drinks, chocolate, and meat may cause the blood pressure to rise when taken with these drugs.

Withdrawal can cause depression and suicide.

PRELUDIN

SCIENTIFIC NAME: Phenmetrazine hydrochloride.

TOXICITY: 5

FORM: Tablets or injectable.

EFFECTS AND SYMPTOMS: Similar to amphetamines, these drugs stimulate the central nervous system stimulation and raise blood pressure. Tachycardia and addiction are common. The drug causes circulatory collapse and coma.

Tolerance develops within a few weeks of using this drug. The symptoms of overdoses are appetite suppression, impaired judgment, incoordination, palpitation, elevation of blood pressure, restlessness, dizziness, dry mouth, euphoria, insomnia, tremors, confusion, headache, hallucinations, panic states, fatigue, depression, and aggressiveness to the point of assaulting others. An unpleasant taste in the mouth is noticed, as well as diarrhea or constipation and other gastrointestinal disturbances like nausea and vomiting. Psychotic episodes can occur even at therapeutic doses. The psychosis can often be confused with schizophrenia.

Impotence and changes in libido occur as well. Circulatory collapse, coma, hyper- or hypotension, and death can result from an overdose. Abrupt cessation causes extreme fatigue, mental depression, irritability, hyperactivity, and personality changes.

REACTION TIME: Within an hour.

ANTIDOTES AND TREATMENTS: Sedation with a barbiturate.

NOTES: Preludin is a white, water-soluble crystalline powder used for diet control in obese people.

MISCELLANEOUS DRUGS

AIR EMBOLISM

TOXICITY: 5

FORM: Given by syringe.

EFFECTS AND SYMPTOMS: The presence of air can cause death by cutting off the blood supply to a vital part: Air in the heart would froth, blocking blood flow; air lodging in the brain would cause coma and death by cutting off the blood supply and oxygen. Symptoms depend on where the air embolism lodges.

A small amount of injected air into the vein can cause the victim to become very ill or frantic with pain, to lose control of bladder and bowels, and to want very much to die. But, in and of itself, this small amount does not usually kill. It would however cause all the machines attached to the patient to go haywire.

Air going into the heart contracts and compresses it, blocking the vascular system so that oxygen can't get through.

Air embolisms can be detected in the body after death.

REACTION TIME: A few minutes to a half-hour.

ANTIDOTES AND TREATMENTS: There is no practical treatment short of open heart surgery. The only treatment is opening the chest and getting the heart chamber refilled with blood or restarting the heart, not just CPR.

NOTES: Air, though not technically a drug, is related to medicine. Air usually enters the body during operations on the neck or during an attempt to inject air into the chest during a test. Sometimes the needle accidentally hits a vein and the air goes into the blood instead.

Usually we picture the villain sneaking into the hero's room to inject his IV with a syringe filled with air. This can be done with fatal results, but a small amount of air does not necessarily cause death. At least a 10cc syringe would be needed to kill a victim, and it is not easy to push that much air into an unwilling vein. The average syringe seen in the movies would not be sufficient.

Air emboli can also be confused with other types of emboli (clots) that accomplish the same thing—impeding the flow of blood to the heart and oxygen to the cells, causing death.

As we have said, anything in excessive dose can be a poison—even oxygen. One hundred percent oxygen is very corrosive and is poisonous to the system. When used for any length of time, it can cause serious damage to the body.

CASE HISTORY:

In Dorothy Sayers's *Unnatural Death*, a woman was suspected of killing a number of people. She was the only one with motive and opportunity, but all the deaths were attributed to heart failure. Lord Peter Wimsey discovered that she had injected air bubbles into the arteries and stopped the circulation with, as Lord Peter found out, quite a good-sized syringe.

BARIUM

TOXICITY: 5

FORM: Liquid, usually swallowed.

EFFECTS AND SYMPTOMS: The barium ion induces a change in permeability or polarization of the cell membrane that results in stimulation of all the muscle cells indiscriminately.

The symptoms include tightness of muscles in face or neck, nausea, vomiting, diarrhea, abdominal pain, anxiety, weakness, difficulty in breathing, cardiac irregularities, convulsions, and death from cardiac and respiratory failure.

REACTION TIME: One hour.

ANTIDOTES AND TREATMENTS: Magnesium or sodium sulfate.

NOTES: An absorbable salt, barium carbonate, hydroxide, or chloride is largely used in the paint industry and to kill pests. Barium sulfate is sometimes used for depilatories, and soluble barium sulfate salt is used as radiopaque contrast medium, especially for lower gastrointestinal X-rays, to help highlight the insides of the intestines and stomach. Poisoning often comes from using the soluble salts in place of the insoluble sulfate.

It's also used to color fireworks.

CAFFEINE

OTHER SIMILAR: Aminophylline, dyphylline, pentoxifylline, theophylline, Trental, No-Doz, Tirend, Cafergot, and in compound with numerous other drugs.

TOXICITY: 3

FORM: Tablets, in drinks, solids, injectable.

EFFECTS AND SYMPTOMS: The general public isn't aware just how dangerous caffeine can be. Mildly addictive caffeine works on the central nervous system to increase the stimulation to a point of hyperexcitability, possible convulsions, and death.

Overdose of caffeine taken orally causes gastric irritation, projectile vomiting, muscle twitching, alternating states of consciousness, agitation, irritability, sweating, insomnia, inability to walk, rapid heartbeat, palpitations, photophobia, and convulsions. There are also cases of caffeine-induced manic-depression, and caffeine-induced psychosis.

Oral theophylline causes vomiting, coma, hyperreflexia, and ventricular arrhythmias including fibrillation, hypotension, convulsions, and respiratory arrest. Tolerance does build up. A person accustomed to six cups of coffee a day would need quite a bit to cause a toxic reaction.

REACTION TIME: One to two minutes. Administration of intravenous aminophylline is sometimes followed by sudden collapse and death. Toxic symptoms begin after one gram, though much more is needed for a lethal dose.

ANTIDOTES AND TREATMENTS: The main effort is to control the convulsions and keep an airway open.

NOTES: Fifty percent of patients with theophylline convulsions die. Caffeine convulsions are less fatal, but combined with theophylline, or other convulsion-encouraging drugs, they could be fatal. We drink caffeine, and it is used for the treatment of shock, asthma, and heart disease. A vasodilator, it is used for migraines, but can have a rebound effect.

It is also a diuretic and can be administered intravenously, orally, or rectally as suppositories or an enema solution. In alternative health circles it is used as a colon cleanser and detoxifier.

Injection of aminophylline in hypersensitive subjects causes immediate vasomotor collapse and death. There are more people sensitive to caffeine than many of us know. As people get older they tend to be less tolerant of the drug, but there's always the odd case of the woman who at eighty can continue to consume fifteen to twenty cups of coffee a day, despite what her doctor warned. Rapid intravenous injection can shock the heart into stopping.

Historically, sources of caffeine include the coffee bean, tea (green and black), kola nut, chocolate, the ilex plant, and cassina (the Christmas berry tree), as well as other naturally occurring sources including the yaupon (the North American tea plant), which was used during the Civil War as a coffee substitute.

While an average cup of coffee contains only 60 to 150mg of caffeine, caffeine is hidden in a variety of foods and medications.

There have been numerous studies about caffeine. Some show it is good for you (in moderation, of course) and that it will improve concentration; others show it impairs health. None have been conclusive.

CAMPHOR

OTHER SIMILAR: Vicks VapoRub, Campho-phenique, numerous topical and inhalants.

TOXICITY: 5

FORM: Liquid, oil, crystal, gas, and topical.

EFFECTS AND SYMPTOMS: Early symptoms include headache, sensation of warmth, excitement, nausea, and vomiting. There is a camphor odor on the breath, the skin becomes clammy, and the face alternates between flushed and pale. Symptoms include burning in mouth and throat, epigastric pain, thirst, feelings of tension, dizziness, irrational behavior, unconsciousness, rigidity, rapid pulse, slow respiration, twitching of facial muscles, muscle spasms, generalized convulsions, and circulatory collapse. Convulsions occur from stimulation of the cerebral cortex cells.

REACTION TIME: Fifteen minutes to one hour. Absorption through the mucous membranes occurs rapidly. Toxic levels may be achieved after prolonged vapor inhalation or within a few minutes after ingestion.

ANTIDOTES AND TREATMENTS: Gastric lavage and activated charcoal. Vomiting is not induced since it might cause seizures. Valium is given for agitation or convulsions and dialysis is sometimes done to help with the elimination of the drug.

NOTES: There is a pungent smell. Still used in moth-damage preventives, camphor oil is a respiratory aid and stimulant. As a medication, it can be administered topically, orally, or intramuscularly by injection.

Autopsy findings include congestion, swelling in the intestinal tract, and destruction of the kidneys and the brain.

And yes, camphor is used by investigators when they have a decomposed body to examine since the odor overwhelms their senses and masks the other, more unpleasant smells.

CANTHARIDIN

SCIENTIFIC NAME: Cantharis vericatoria.

OTHER: Spanish fly.

TOXICITY: 6

FORM: Liquid.

EFFECTS AND SYMPTOMS: The principal manifestations are vomiting and collapse. Other symptoms are severe skin irritation, blister formation on the mucous membranes, abdominal pain, nausea, diarrhea, vomiting of blood, severe fall in blood pressure, hematuria, coma, and death due to respiratory failure.

REACTION TIME: Immediate.

ANTIDOTES AND TREATMENTS: None.

NOTES: A white powder with very little taste, cantharidin is used as a skin irritant or vesicant (blister inducer). A potent irritant to all cells and tissues, it has an undeserved reputation for being an aphrodisiac.

This myth originated in the Middle Ages, when Spanish fly was used as a painful stimulus to assist with cattle breeding. While it caused the cattle penis to be erect, the experience couldn't have been pleasant.

Autopsy findings are necrosis of esophageal and gastric mucous membranes, intense congestion of blood in the genital and urinary organs, damaged cells in the renal tubules, and hemorrhagic changes in the ovaries.

CASE HISTORY

One of the most sensational cases involving cantharidin was in London's Old Bailey in 1954, when a pharmacist, Arthur Ford, was tried on the charge of manslaughter of the two women who worked for him. Apparently happily married, he had heard while in the army of the aphrodisiac qualities of Spanish fly. One day, discovering that cantharidin was the technical term for Spanish fly and that supplies were available at his shop, he asked the senior pharmacist for some, saying one of his neighbors bred rabbits and that he thought the drug might be useful in the mating process. He was told the drug was a "number one" poison and that, if administered to a human in anything but a minute dose, it could be fatal. Ford bought a bag of pink-and-white coconut ice candy and, back at the office, pushed quantities of Spanish fly into the candy with a pair of scissors. He gave a piece to each of the women and then took one himself. Within an hour, all three were violently sick. The two women died shortly, though he survived somehow. The autopsies showed the internal organs had literally been corroded by the drug.

FLAGYL

SCIENTIFIC NAME: Metronidazole.

TOXICITY: 2

FORM: Vaginal suppositories.

EFFECTS AND SYMPTOMS: Used to combat yeast infections, the most frequent overdose symptoms are nausea, headache, and loss of appetite. Vomiting, diarrhea, abdominal cramping, constipation, a metallic taste in the mouth, sore throat, vertigo, changes in heartbeat, seizures, incoordination, irritability, depression, confusion, fever, dark-colored urine, and decreased sex drive may also be experienced. If taken with alcohol, it will make the victim quite ill.

REACTION TIME: Thirty minutes to several hours.

ANTIDOTES AND TREATMENTS: Symptomatic.

NOTES: This drug acts much like Antabuse, which is given to alcoholics to stop their drinking. Severe behavior and emotional problems may also result if taken with alcohol.

CASE HISTORY

One young woman who was taking Flagyl attended a friend's wedding party. Not normally a drinker, she was encouraged to imbibe to celebrate the occasion. Shortly, she began experiencing "odd sensations." These continued with nausea, vomiting, confusion, depression, and a full-blown seizure.

The woman was hospitalized, but the doctors were puzzled because the woman's lab tests showed no reason for her convulsions. She continued to become more critically ill. Only when her boyfriend told the physician that she was taking Flagyl and had drunk several glasses of wine did the answer come. The woman hadn't recalled hearing her doctor give any warnings about drinking alcohol while on the medication, "But even if he had," she added, "who really listens to those things?" Luckily, she recovered.

INSULIN

TOXICITY: 6

FORM: A clear liquid, administered by subcutaneous injection, used mainly for the treatment of diabetes mellitus; a new inhaler form of insulin is in clinical trials at the time of this writing.

EFFECTS AND SYMPTOMS: Insulin overdose, or insulin shock, causes hypoglycemia resulting in fatigue, reddening of the face, sensation of hunger, nervousness, rapid heartbeat, nausea, vomiting, chills, sweating, tachycardia, shallow breathing, low blood pressure, shock, coma, and death.

REACTION TIME: Ten minutes after injection.

ANTIDOTES AND TREATMENTS: Administration of glucose (sugar)—for example, orange juice or candy bars—to keep the insulin temporarily bound up and lessen the symptoms.

NOTES: Injectable insulin is measured in units rather than milliliters, and is available in several types: regular, NPH, Lente, Ultralente, Semi-Lente, humulin, or crystalline. The dose varies with each type. Many patients are on a sliding dosage scale, depending on their morning glucose test.

Insulin is the water-soluble hormone of the Langerhans islets of the pancreas. Diabetes mellitus, the most common version of diabetes, is controlled by diet and injected insulin.

Drugs in the beta-adrenergic class, such as propranolol, will greatly increase the effects of these diabetic drugs and lower the blood sugar, even to a lethal level. Other drugs, such as aspirin, adrenal hormones, epinephrine, oral contraceptives, and diuretics, can decrease effectiveness so that even though the victim is taking the insulin properly, she could still go into diabetic shock and coma.

Postmortem specimens of brain, liver, or kidney have not shown significant amounts of insulin either in normal subjects or victims of overdose, but in several instances tissue from the site of injection has been analyzed and the results used to prove administration of an overdose.

CASE HISTORY

In May 1957, Ken Barlow, a male nurse, asked a neighbor to call a doctor to his home, saying his wife, Elizabeth, had died in the bath. When the doctor arrived, Barlow said his wife had been ill all evening and had vomited in bed about 9:30 P.M. She had decided to have a bath, and he had gone to bed and dozed off after changing the sheets. When he woke at eleven o'clock, he found that his wife was not beside him and hurried to the bathroom. Finding his wife apparently drowned, he had pulled the plug and made frantic but unsuccessful attempts to pull her out and revive her with artificial respiration.

The doctor found the body lying in the empty bath, on her right side. She had apparently vomited, and there were no signs of violence on the body, but the eyes were dilated. The doctor called the police and Barlow repeated his story. The police noted that although Barlow claimed to have made "frantic efforts" to save his wife, his pajamas were still dry and there was no sign of splashing on the bathroom floor. Then a detective noticed water in the crooks of Mrs. Barlow's elbows. Since artificial respiration would have required her husband to turn her slightly, or at least move her arms, the water in the crooks of her elbows indicated that artificial respiration had probably not been done—that, in fact, the body had probably not been moved since her attack and death.

Two hypodermic syringes were found in the kitchen, which Barlow explained by saying he had been treating himself for a carbuncle with penicillin. The syringes did have some penicillin in the needles, and the coroners could find no trace of drugs in the woman's body. However, with the aid of a magnifying glass, they went over every inch of her skin, looking for marks of injection—with difficulty, as Mrs. Barlow had a great many freckles. Finally, they found two telltale puncture marks on the right buttock and another two in the fold of skin under the left buttock.

An incision showed characteristic redness and slight swelling, suggesting an injection had been given a short time before death. Some of her symptoms—dilation of the eyes and vomiting—described hypoglycemia, a deficiency of blood sugar (and characteristic of insulin shock); however, an exam of the heart showed an average sugar level. Biochemical research had shown increased sugar levels in the hearts of victims of violent death, due to the liver trying the assist survival by discharging a heavy dose of sugar into the bloodstream moments before death. Forensic experts felt that, since Mrs. Barlow's blood sugar level was normal, she could not have died violently. Since there were no prescribed tests for detecting insulin in the body tissues, the police were at a loss.

However, the experts found another way to catch Barlow. Until that time, it had been a common belief among doctors and nurses that insulin disappeared very quickly from the body. But new research came up to prove them wrong. The acidic conditions of the body preserved the insulin, and the formation of lactic acid in the muscles after death had prevented the insulin breakdown.

On July 29, 1957, Barlow was arrested and charged with murdering his wife. The defense stated that, with the fearful realization that she was slipping into the water, Mrs. Barlow's pancreas had released an incredible dose of insulin—fifteen thousand units. Barlow confessed to having given her a dose of ergonovine to induce an abortion, but not to the insulin. He was found guilty. It later came out his first wife had died in 1933—cause of death unknown.

LOMOTIL

SCIENTIFIC NAME: Diphenoxylate plus atropine.

TOXICITY: 4

FORM: Liquid or tablet.

EFFECTS AND SYMPTOMS: This drug contains both atropine and codeine, which contribute to its symptoms. There is a sudden high fever, a flushed appearance, and rapid breathing. The second phase of symptoms includes abdominal discomfort, severe constipation, swelling of gums, retention of fluid, lethargy, depression, tingling sensations, restlessness, and progressive central nervous system depression, with pinpoint pupils, cyanosis, severe respiratory depression, seizures, and coma. The drug may be excreted in the urine up to ninety-six hours later.

REACTION TIME: Thirty minutes.

ANTIDOTES AND TREATMENTS: Gastric lavage and naloxone administration.

NOTES: This anti-diarrheal agent is a narcotic (codeine is the active agent to slow the intestines) and it can be addictive. Numerous cases of poisoning and fatalities have been reported.

The drug has a small amount of atropine in it; at normal doses it is not addicting, but can be at higher doses. Sedation increases when it is taken with tranquilizers, alcohol, or narcotics. If taken with MAO inhibitors, excessive rise in blood pressure may result.

The tablet is so small as to be deceptive, and overdosing is very easy.

PHENERGAN

SCIENTIFIC NAME: Promethazine hydrochloride.

OTHER SIMILAR: Compazine (prochlorperazine), Sparine (promazine).

TOXICITY: 4

FORM: Injectable, pill, or suppository.

EFFECTS AND SYMPTOMS: Symptoms include drowsiness, confusion, tinnitus, diplopia, blurred vision, dilated pupils, insomnia, dizziness, headache, nightmares, hysteria, agitation, impaired mental and physical abilities, and extrapyramidal symptoms (EPS). Sometimes the administration of this drug can confuse doctors and mask other central nervous system problems, brain disease, or Reye's syndrome (a disease affecting the organs, especially the liver and brain).

REACTION TIME: Within ten minutes.

ANTIDOTES AND TREATMENTS: Symptoms are treated as they occur.

NOTES: Phenergan is used to relieve nausea and to sedate, as well as in pre- and post-operative situations and as an adjunct to painkillers. (Phenergen is often combined with Reglan and compazine and given intravenously to alleviate migraines.)

The drug reacts negatively to and increases the effects of other central nervous system depressants, such as alcohol, barbiturates, and narcotics. Patients with liver or heart disease are especially prone to problems when given this drug.

If given intra-arterially, there is likelihood of arteriospasm and possibly gangrene at the injection site, which would perhaps require an amputation. Taken with MAO inhibitors, extrapyramidal symptoms are increased.

If given by suppository, which melts, there are no marks on the body.

QUININE

OTHER SIMILAR: Quinacrine, chloroquine, Atabrine, Plaquenil.

TOXICITY: 5

FORM: Tablets and injection.

EFFECTS AND SYMPTOMS: Quinine depresses the functions in all the cells, especially the heart. The kidney, liver, and nervous system may also be affected.

Progressive tinnitus, blurring of vision, weakness, fall of blood pressure, hematuria, oliguria, and cardiac irregularities occur. Injection or ingestion of large doses causes sudden onset of cardiac depression. Convulsions and respiratory arrest can also occur.

REACTION TIME: Immediate.

ANTIDOTES AND TREATMENTS: Removal of swallowed drug by gastric lavage.

NOTES: Quinine is used to treat malaria and was used by the military for that purpose. It is also found in tonic water and other bitters. (See cinchona bark in chapter five, page 83.)

TAGAMET

SCIENTIFIC NAME: Cimetidine.

TOXICITY: 5

FORM: Tablets.

EFFECTS AND SYMPTOMS: Diarrhea, headache, fatigue, dizziness, muscle pain, rash, confusion, delirium, and low blood pressure. Also, liver and kidney damage can occur from overdose, resulting in renal failure.

REACTION TIME: Fifteen to thirty minutes.

ANTIDOTES AND TREATMENTS: Gastric lavage and activated charcoal. Respiration is maintained and atropine is sometimes used.

NOTES: Used to treat ulcers, Tagamet decreases the flow of stomach acid. The activity of anti-clotting drugs may be increased, causing someone to bleed to death. Sedatives and sleeping drugs also increase their action combined with Tagamet.

If the drug is stopped, ulcers may return and ultimately perforate.

THYROLAR

SCIENTIFIC NAME: Liotrix.

OTHER: Euthroid, Synthroid, Cytomel, Proloid, Levothroid, thyroxine, thyroglobulin, liothyronine, levothyroxine.

TOXICITY: 4

FORM: Pills.

EFFECTS AND SYMPTOMS: If the medication brings the thyroid up to normal range, then there are no side effects. If overdose occurs, nervousness, tremor in hands, weakness, sensitivity to heat, reduced sweating, overactivity, weight loss, pounding heartbeat, bulging eyeballs, headache, nausea, abdominal pain, diarrhea, high blood pressure, and heart failure are possible.

REACTION TIME: Twenty to thirty minutes.

ANTIDOTES AND TREATMENTS: Symptoms are treated as they occur.

NOTES: Given as replacement therapy for underactive thyroid, these drugs should be used carefully with people who have had previous heart problems. Anti-clotting drugs, digitalis preparations, and tricyclic antidepressants will have their effects increased. On the other hand, if the patient is taking barbiturates, the effect of the barbiturates will be decreased. Aspirin and phenytoin (Dilantin) also increase the effects of Thyrolar.

AUTHOR NOTE

There are just so many medications that can be used as poisons that we have not the space, nor is it practical, to mention them all. There are many that, although they will not kill on their own, may do so in combination—but there is an infinite number of combinations. And there are many drugs, such as Klonopin (the American version of Rohypnol), that can harm and be used against people, but do not cause death. And new drugs are being released every day.

In addition to the books listed in the bibliography, some everyday sources you can take advantage of are:

- Your own pharmacist or doctor.
- Caution labels on medication bottles and the throwaway inserts in the packages.
- The Internet: Medline, CDC, FDA, and individual pharmaceutical companies all have Web sites; there are also many other medically related Web sites, as well as numerous search engines.
- Your state's Department of Consumer Affairs: These organizations frequently issue cautions and recall notices.
- Local poison control centers and city, county, and state health departments
- American Drug and Chemical Index.
- Drug Guides like the *PDR* (*Physician's Desk Reference*) or the Nurses' Drug Guide books.

PESTICIDES

MR. PUGH: Here is your arsenic, dear.
And your weedkiller biscuit,
I've throttled your parakeet,
I've spat in the vases,
I've put cheese in the mouseholes. Here's your ... [door creaks
open] nice tea, dear.

—DYLAN THOMAS, UNDER MILK WOOD

Pesticides of all kinds remain a controversial topic. There is evidence that many of the human-made toxins that control unwanted insects, weeds, and rodents can cause considerable harm to humans and to our environment. Unfortunately, this harm is not usually the quick kind of harm that interests most mystery writers, but the slow deterioration of cancer, or the destruction of endangered plants and animals. The reason the damage is slow is simple, and goes back to the old truth that toxicity is a matter of dosage. Bugs are a lot smaller than humans, so even the tiniest micrograms of toxin will do bugs in rather quickly without causing immediate illness in humans. The same goes for most herbicides, some of which are included here.

During the twentieth century, as pesticides grew more powerful, they were hailed as a blessing by farmers who had long been at the mercy of whatever bugs developed a taste for their crops. Nowadays, the tide is turning back, as interest in sustainable and organic agriculture grows and pesticides are increasingly looked upon with suspicion by the general public.

Simple, though highly dangerous, chemicals such as arsenic and nicotine were used as pesticides for many years. They were replaced in the late 1970s by a large number of chemical compounds stemming from the discovery of DDT, which came into widespread use during World War II. From there, the cholinesterase inhibitors were developed, some because they were supposedly less toxic and easier on the environment.

As with any poison, children, the ill, and the aged are more susceptible to the pesticides effects.

An interesting case popped up on a May 2006 episode of the Discovery Channel show *Mythbusters*: In the 1930s, an herbicide in New Zealand was apparently responsible for a farmer's pants exploding. Mythbusters Kari Byron, Grant Imahara, and Tori Belleci, using chemicals that were common in New Zealand at the time (although they refused to name them), did find that the herbicide could, indeed, cause cotton pants to suddenly burst into flames. Imahara pointed out that it wasn't a true explosion; Byron, however, said it was close enough.

Insecticides generally fall into six major categories:

- **Minerals,** like sulfur and borax, while not technically insecticides, are among the earliest substances to be used that way. Borax and kerosene are covered in chapter four, Household Poisons.
- **Botanicals,** such as nicotine, pyrethrin, and rotenone.
- **Chlorinated hydrocarbons,** such as DDT, lindane, and chlordane.
- **Organophosphates,** such as malathion and diazinon.
- **Carbamates,** such as carbaryl and propoxur.
- **Fumigants,** such as the well-known materials naphthalene and hydrogen cyanide. Naphthalene is covered in chapter four, Household Poisons, and hydrogen cyanide is in chapter three, The Classics Poisons.

The sections covering chlorinated hydrocarbons, organophosphates, and carbamates will be organized a bit differently than the others. Each of these three close-knit families of pesticides comprises many different substances with similar effects, reaction times, and antidotes. The sections will include the family name, followed by each family's common attributes, with individual pesticide names listed from most to least toxic.

We'll also look at a couple herbicides and two rodenticides. The other well-known rodenticide, warfarin, has fallen out of use in that application, and is more commonly used as a medicine for its blood-thinning properties (see chapter eight, page 188).

Almost all the substances in this chapter can be absorbed by ingestion, inhalation, or skin contact. When it comes to pesticides, acute poisoning is very rare. Most poison cases involving pesticides are chronic poisonings suffered by the people who work in the fields or are responsible for applying them. Most acute or fatal poisonings happen only when large quantities are ingested either accidentally or intentionally (as a means of suicide).

However, emergency personnel and other rescuers do need to be careful when rescuing victims of pesticide exposure. Residue from sprayed or inhaled pesticides can contaminate the rescuers by secondary contact.

INSECTICIDES

CARBAMATES

TOXICITY: 5: Aldicarb, bendiocarb, carbofuran, isolan, mecarbam, methomyl, oxamyl
　3 to 4: Benfuracarb, carbosulfan, dioxacarb, promecarb, propoxur
　2 to 3: BPMC, carbaryl, MTMC, XMC

FORM: All are or have been available as liquids and powders, some are also available as pellets.

EFFECTS AND SYMPTOMS: Increased sweating and salivation, gastrointestinal cramping, diarrhea, vomiting, twitching, difficulty breathing, and loss of muscle strength, which can result in respiratory arrest in severe doses.

REACTION TIME: Less than an hour.

ANTIDOTES AND TREATMENTS: Emphasis is on keeping the respiratory system going, including with intubation. Atropine can also be given to work against the effects of the poison. Pralidoxime can also be given, but may not be necessary, as the anti-enzyme action does reverse itself.

NOTES: The average person (as opposed to a farmer) is most likely to find carbamates in household insecticides because they are generally of a lower toxicity than organophosphates and stay in the environment for a shorter time. They are included here because there are some high-toxicity versions. They work the same way as the organophosphates, and poisonings trigger the same symptoms, with one important difference: Enzyme inhibition caused by carbamates will reverse itself with time, making them much less dangerous in the long term.

CHLORINATED HYDROCARBONS

OTHER: Organochlorines, Organochlorides.

TOXICITY: 5: Aldrin, dieldrin, endrin, endosulfan
　3 to 4: Chlordane, DDT, heptachlor, kepone, lindane, mirex, toxaphene
　2 to 3: Benzene hexachloride, ethlyan, methoxychlor

FORM: All are or have been available as liquids and powders, some are also available as pellets.

EFFECTS AND SYMPTOMS: These are neurotoxins, depressing the central nervous system, particularly the brain. Kidney and liver damage are possible. Symptoms start soon after ingestion, with nausea and vomiting. Depending on the dose and the substance, symptoms will progress to seizures, coma, hematuria, and respiratory failure. Because chlorinated hydrocarbons stay in fatty tissues, seizures can sometimes be delayed for a matter of hours, or reoccur. Poisons stored in fatty tissues will be released into the bloodstream once the body starts to burn fat stores. Therefore, small, non-lethal doses over a long period of time can become deadly with rapid weight loss, for example during dieting.

REACTION TIME: Thirty minutes after ingestion.

ANTIDOTES AND TREATMENTS: Supportive care is given, based on symptoms. In the case of skin contact, contaminated clothing is removed and the patient thoroughly washed with soapy water. Since seizures can be delayed, patients should be monitored for up to eight hours.

NOTES: DDT, the first of the chlorinated hydrocarbons, came into widespread use during World War II. Chlorinated hydrocarbons were among the most heavily used insecticides from the 1940s until the 1960s, when people began to realize the serious damage they cause to the environment.

One reason they are so dangerous is that they are fat soluble: They get absorbed into fatty tissues and stay there. DDT, in particular, was banned in many countries when it was discovered that it was endangering eagles and other raptors. The raptors were eating rodents contaminated with the pesticide, which was then transmitted to the birds. The DDT caused the shells of the raptors' eggs to become so thin and fragile that many broke during incubation, before new little ones could be hatched.

There are numerous cases on record of people and animals poisoned, sometimes fatally, by eating vegetables or grains sprayed with these toxins, or by eating other animals that ate the sprayed vegetables or grains.

Lindane is the only chlorinated hydrocarbon that has a medical application (treating lice infestations and scabies, a rash caused by parasitic mites), although its sale has been banned in California since 2002.

CASE HISTORY

In one account, two men died following ingestion of a low dose of chlordane. Autopsies showed severe fatty degeneration of the liver caused by chronic alcoholism. In this case, the chlordane was not the direct cause of death, but sufficiently aggravated the existing liver condition to cause death.

A fifty-eight-year-old accidentally drank from a bottle of 5 percent DDT. Even though he noticed his mistake and drank one-quarter of a liter of milk and several glasses of beer, (which he thought would dilute the poison but did not), within an hour he had severe gastric pain and irritation and was vomiting every thirty to sixty minutes. Thirty-six hours after the ingestion of the poison, vomiting persisted, and spastic cramps in the arms and calves appeared. He was admitted to the hospital on the sixth day after poisoning. Despite transfusions, he died a few hours later.

NICOTINE

OTHER: Beta-pyridyl-alpha-N-methylpyrrolidine.

TOXICITY: 5

FORM: A pale yellow to dark brown liquid with a slightly fishy odor when warm, it poisons by inhalation, skin absorption, ingestion, or eye contact.

EFFECTS AND SYMPTOMS: Nicotine stimulates and then depresses the brain and spinal cord and paralyzes skeletal muscles, including the diaphragm.

A burning sensation in the mouth can occur, but the principal symptoms are nausea, vomiting, diarrhea, confusion, twitching, headache, dizziness, difficulty breathing, rapid heartbeat, confusion, convulsions, slowing respiration, cardiac irregularity, coma, and death, usually from respiratory failure.

REACTION TIME: Symptoms can start thirty to ninety minutes after exposure. Without treatment, death can occur at any time, usually within four hours.

ANTIDOTES AND TREATMENTS: Nicotine spilled on the skin must be thoroughly washed off. If ingested, activated charcoal is given. Atropine may also be used to control convulsions.

NOTES: Nicotine has the distinction of being the oldest insecticide in current use. It was first employed as concentrated tobacco juice. While nicotine is best known as the addicting ingredient in cigarettes, it was most widely available up until the 1970s as a pesticide. This is why it is listed here, even though people are far more likely to acquire it in the form of tobacco products or anti-smoking aids, including gums, patches, sprays, and inhalers.

CASE HISTORY

A woman living in England in 1940 mixed nicotine with her husband's aftershave lotion. He liberally applied it to his face and body and died quickly.

In 1968, another woman did in her wealthy elderly sister by mixing the residue of several cigarette butts into a jug of water, straining it, and placing the poisoned water at her sister's bedside. The sister died, but the killer was caught.

In *The Bilbao Looking Glass,* Charlotte MacLeod killed off her victim by putting nicotine in a martini, which the victim drank in one gulp without noticing the poison.

A dentist in Ed McBain's *Poison* used nicotine twice to murder his victims. He obtained the chemical from a lab, claiming that he was doing tests on cigarette-stained teeth. The dentist then put some in one victim's bottle of scotch and hid more in the temporary crown covering his second patient's root canal, making sure the crown had a thin spot that could be worn away by normal chewing or brushing.

ORGANOPHOSPHATES

TOXICITY: 5 to 6: Bomyl, Demton, dialifor, EPN, parathion, TEPP
  3 to 4: Acephate, chlorpyrifos, diazinon, Ethion, methyl trithion, phosmet, trichorfon
  2 to 3: Bromophos, etrimfos, malathion, phoxim, temephos

FORM: All are or have been available as liquids and powders, some are also available as pellets.

EFFECTS AND SYMPTOMS: Symptoms experienced are increased sweating and salivation, gastrointestinal cramping, diarrhea, vomiting, twitching, difficulty breathing, and loss of muscle strength, which can result in respiratory arrest. A generalized weakness can reoccur a few days after the original acute poisoning, even after treatment.

REACTION TIME: One to two hours, but can be even more delayed, especially after contact with the skin.

ANTIDOTES AND TREATMENTS: Emphasis is on keeping the respiratory system going, including with intubation. Atropine can also be given to counteract the effects of the poison, but pralidoxime is a more specific antidote and should be given as soon as possible.

NOTES: These insecticides are the first of the cholinesterase inhibitors introduced as a replacement for DDT, and include some of the most toxic there are. They work (as do the carbamates below) by inhibiting the enzyme acetylcholinesterase, which helps to regulate the amount of acetylcholine in the body. (Acetylcholine is needed to send messages from one nerve synapse to another and then to the brain.) With organophosphates, the inhibition of the enzyme can become permanent unless the antidote pralidoxime is given right away.

The majority of parathion poisonings seem to occur when spraying against the wind, cleaning airplanes used for the spraying, or gathering vegetables and fruit that have been sprayed. Poisoning has been observed in factory workers, who probably absorbed the material through their skin.

PYRETHRIN

OTHER: Pyrethrum (usually refers to the extract from the plant, which is refined into pyrethrin), pyrethrum flowers, dalmatian insect powder.

TOXICITY: 4

FORM: Pyrethrin is a neurotoxin. While inhalation causes the most toxic reaction, pyrethrin also reacts through skin absorption and, less effectively, through ingestion.

EFFECTS AND SYMPTOMS: Most of the symptoms are actually allergy symptoms, ranging from a stuffy or runny nose all the way to anaphylactic shock. Inhalation victims may also experience irritation in the mucous membranes and upper airway. Skin exposure will mostly cause itching and a rash. Massive ingestion can cause seizures, coma, or respiratory arrest.

REACTION TIME: About thirty minutes.

ANTIDOTES AND TREATMENTS: Removal from exposure and treat rest of symptoms.

NOTES: This extract of the chrysanthemum flower is one of the oldest pesticides known. While not terribly toxic to humans, it can cause some harm and is listed here mostly for its historical value and because it is a strong allergen, which can cause anaphylaxis or aggravate asthma.

If your fictional victim is highly sensitive to pollens, your villain might be able to use pyrethrin, perhaps intending to scare the victim, only to have the allergic reaction kill the person instead.

ROTENONE

OTHER: Derrin, derris, nicouline, tubatoxin.

TOXICITY: 4

FORM: A white or red odorless crystalline solid derived from the derris root.

EFFECTS AND SYMPTOMS: Rotenone affects the nervous system. Inhalation causes numbness of the mouth, nausea, vomiting, abdominal pain, muscle tremors, ataxia, convulsions, and stupor. Skin contact is mildly irritating. Chronic exposure leads to kidney and liver damage.

REACTION TIME: Skin irritation occurs immediately; other symptoms follow within a few hours.

ANTIDOTES AND TREATMENTS: Symptomatic.

NOTES: Rotenone used to be found in lotions for chiggers and as an emulsion for scabies. Ingestion can also cause problems, but will seldom lead to death; it is much more toxic when inhaled.

HERBICIDES

CHLOROPHENOXY HERBICIDE

OTHER: 2,4-dicholorphenoxyacetic acid; 2,4-D.

TOXICITY: 4

FORM: Varies with the specific product and formulation.

EFFECTS AND SYMPTOMS: Vomiting, abdominal pain, and diarrhea. Weakness and spasms in the muscles start soon after ingestion, and eventually progress to generalized weakness and coma. The blood pressure drops and does not normalize, and death comes within twenty-four hours. Exposure to the skin produces irritation.

REACTION TIME: Within thirty minutes.

ANTIDOTES AND TREATMENTS: Activated charcoal and supportive treatment. In the case of skin or eye exposure, decontamination by flushing and clothing removal is done.

NOTES: There are almost fifty different formulations of chlorophenoxy herbicides. Depending on the exposure time and environmental conditions, small doses can cause fatalities. But these herbicides do not work well in cold weather or high winds.

PARAQUAT

OTHER: Methylviologen; 1,1'-dimethyl-4,4'-bipyridinium dichloride or dimethosulfate; gramoxone; 1,1'-dimethyl-4,4'dipridrium dichloride; 1,1'-dimethyl-4,4'-bipyridylium chloride.

TOXICITY: 6

FORM: A solid, water-soluble, yellow herbicide, paraquat poisons mostly by ingestion, and occasionally by prolonged skin contact or by absorption through an abrasion.

EFFECTS AND SYMPTOMS: Initial symptoms include burning mouth and throat, vomiting, abdominal pain, diarrhea, ulceration of the tongue, and fever. After two or three days, liver and kidney toxicity develop, showing as jaundice and oliguria. This is followed by respiratory distress and fatal lung scarring, sometimes a week or two later.

REACTION TIME: Two to five days for first symptoms; five to eight days for final symptoms.

ANTIDOTES AND TREATMENTS: Care must be taken, as paraquat is often corrosive to the gastrointestinal system. Before transport to the hospital, patients are encouraged to eat, as food can bind with the paraquat in the stomach and perhaps lessen the effects. In the hospital, activated charcoal is given. Although fuller's earth and bentonite (two types of clay) have been recommended, there is no evidence that either of these work any better than the charcoal to bind the paraquat. The rest of the treatment is symptomatic.

NOTES: Diquat, paraquat's chemical brother, produces the same symptoms as paraquat, although without the lung scarring. It is slightly less toxic than paraquat but, as one source put it, the distinction may be of little comfort, as the toxicity of both is very high.

Interestingly enough, though paraquat (and its brother herbicide diquat) are extremely toxic and affect the lungs when swallowed, the drops of the spray are actually too large to be absorbed by lung tissues, so the toxin doesn't cause much damage when it's inhaled.

Paraquat first became infamous during the late 1960s and early 1970s, when the U.S. government decided to kill illegal marijuana fields by spraying them with the toxin. There was a certain amount of hysteria as marijuana smokers feared they were being poisoned when smoking pot from sprayed fields in both the U.S. and Mexico. A sudden explosion in the number of fields in eastern Kentucky during the early 1990s inspired the Drug Enforcement Administration (DEA) to try again, to considerable outcry.

However, there are no known cases of marijuana smokers dying from paraquat poisoning. The reason is simple. Once paraquat is sprayed, it binds quickly to plants and soil and, once bound, loses its toxic effects. When the plant is burned, the paraquat burns off with minimal harm. Trace amounts of the poison can presumably lodge in smokers' bodies, although the damage from the marijuana smoke itself, and what the smoker might do while under its influence, are far more likely to cause serious harm.

RODENTICIDES

FLUOROACETATE

OTHER: Compound 1080, fluoroacetic acid, sodium salt, fratol, sodium fluoroacetate, sodium monofluoroacetate.

TOXICITY: 6

FORM: A fine, water-soluble white powder; the dust can be inhaled and the powder or solution ingested. Fluoroacetate has no smell or taste.

EFFECTS AND SYMPTOMS: The chemical blocks cellular metabolism, affecting all body cells, especially those of the central nervous system.

Symptoms include vomiting, irregular breathing, auditory hallucinations, numbness and twitching of the face, anxiety, ventricular arrthymias (irregular heartbeats) convulsions, and coma. Death is from respiratory failure due to pulmonary edema or ventricular fibrillation.

REACTION TIME: Within minutes up to six hours.

ANTIDOTES AND TREATMENTS: Symptoms are treated as they appear.

NOTES: One of the most toxic substances known, fluoroacetate was generally used to kill rodents by professional exterminators, but it's been mostly off the market in the U.S. for years because it's so hazardous.

Fluoroacetate is not easily absorbed through intact skin, but can be introduced through an open wound.

In one case, a few drops of fluoroacetate landed in some water that was then drunk by a horse. The horse died, as did a dog that later ate some of the horse meat.

Fluoroacetate is still sometimes attached in packets to sheep, so that if any wolves or coyotes decide to chow down on lamb chops, they are poisoned—a possible way to move your plot along if your story has a pastoral setting.

VACOR

OTHER: PNU.

TOXICITY: 5

FORM: Yellow, resembling cornmeal in color and texture. Before it was removed from sale, it came in 38-gram packets.

EFFECTS AND SYMPTOMS: It works by inducing insulin-dependent diabetes and by affecting the autonomic nervous system, which runs the involuntary functions in the body, such as the heart's beating.

The first symptoms are nausea and vomiting. Confusion and stupor can occur several hours after ingestion, followed by coma. Between six and forty-eight hours after ingestion, as damage to the autonomic nerves begins, the victim suffers from drops in blood pressure when standing, which can cause dizziness and fainting. Vomiting can also continue, along with constipation. Assuming the above symptoms haven't already killed the victim, the diabetes sets in after a few days.

If the victim recovers, the diabetes is permanent.

REACTION TIME: The first symptoms can appear within thirty minutes.

ANTIDOTES AND TREATMENTS: Nicotinamide is injected immediately and may prevent the diabetes. Supportive care, including activated charcoal, is given. In cases of chronic poisoning, a high-salt diet is sometimes prescribed to combat the drop in blood pressure when the patient stands.

NOTES: This rodenticide was taken off the U.S. market in 1979, but some homes may still have it and it is still used by licensed exterminators.

Because of its cornmeal-like appearance, your fictional victim may be able to hide a packet or two of the stuff in food using cornmeal or corn bread. The food should be strongly flavored, however, to prevent alerting the proposed victim. Also, if the story is set after 1979, your villain is going to need a believable reason both to possess the packets and know what they are.

CHAPTER 10

INDUSTRIAL
POISONS

> *We certainly leave the handsomest paint and clapboards behind in the woods, when we strip off the bark and poison ourselves with white-lead in the towns. We get but half the spoils of the forest.*
>
> HENRY DAVID THOREAU (1817–1862)

Prior to 1950, industrial poisons were primarily limited to organic materials. But as industry expanded and more products were needed, newer by-products and poisons were created. Often the deadly nature of the chemicals took years to discover, as death came in the form of slow-acting cancer.

ACID

OTHER: Hydrochloric acid, osmic acid, ethyl chlorocarbonate, and chloroacetylchloride.

TOXICITY: 6

FORM: Both liquid and gaseous states. Acids can be swallowed, but skin absorption (usually total immersion) and breathing in vapors are the most likely methods to produce fatal results.

Highly corrosive to skin, eyes, and mucous membranes, acid produces burns, ulcerations, peeling, and scarring, destroying any tissue it comes into contact with.

Eye contact may result in reduced vision or blindness. The irritating effects of the vapors may produce an inflammation of the throat, tongue, and lungs. Inhalation of acid fumes results in coughing, a choking sensation, and sometimes drooling. Pulmonary edema can develop.

Severe, burning pain is the principal symptom when acid is swallowed. The back of the throat can swell and suffocate the victim.

Corrosion and irritation are the primary findings in an autopsy. Brown and black stains are found wherever the acid had contact. Thick, coffee-colored blood is often found in the stomach.

REACTION TIME: Immediate, but death may not occur until several days later, depending on the severity of the reaction and the dose.

ANTIDOTES AND TREATMENTS: Water or milk is given to dilute the acid. The physician will use an endoscope (a tube inserted into the throat that lets a physician see inside the esophagus and stomach) to find and assess injuries, which may then be surgically repaired. Supportive care for the burns is given.

NOTES: Acids are used in production of fertilizers, dyes, artificial silk, electroplating, tanning, soap refining, and metal cleaning. Some are produced as by-products of other chemical reactions. Most acids have a similar corrosive effect, and thus similar treatments. They vary in strength, depending on the concentration of the solution.

If the victim recovers, the flesh will be permanently scarred.

ACRYLAMIDE

OTHER: Propenamide, acrylic amide, acrylamide monomer.

TOXICITY: 5

FORM: A flakelike crystal, it dissolves easily in water and melts at a relatively low temperature (around 176 degrees Fahrenheit, or 80 degrees Celsius) and breaks down into nitrogen oxide gases, so should be kept in a dark, cool spot. It can be inhaled, swallowed, or absorbed through the skin.

EFFECTS AND SYMPTOMS: A neurotoxin, acrylamide affects the nervous system as well as the skin by attacking the sensory neurons in the body.

The most obvious sign of acrylamide poisoning is peeling and redness of skin on the victim's hands and sometimes feet after the poison has been ingested. The symptoms start with drowsiness and sleepiness. With more acute poisoning, hallucinations and disorientation are possible, along with increasing ataxia, tremors, sometimes seizures, and finally cardiovascular failure. Sensory symptoms, such as tingling and numbness, start in the fingers and toes and progress to the center of the body. In less serious cases, a tingling sensation from the nerve damage can present after a couple of weeks. Stumbling and weak or absent reflexes are also symptoms.

REACTION TIME: The effects are delayed after initial exposure—sometimes as long as a few days—which can be useful if time is needed to establish as alibi.

ANTIDOTES AND TREATMENTS: Supportive care is given, and pyridoxine (aka vitamin B6) may be used, as the vitamin helps the nerves to function properly.

NOTES: A fairly potent toxin, acrylamide is used to treat wastewater, and also as a strengthener in the papermaking process. It's also used in grout, gels, and adhesives.

ANILINE

TOXICITY: 5

FORM: While aniline is a viscous liquid and can be swallowed, it is very easily absorbed by inhalation of fumes and through the skin.

EFFECTS AND SYMPTOMS: Aniline changes the hemoglobin (the red blood cells that transport oxygen through the body) to methemoglobin, thus interfering with oxygen transportation in the central nervous system.

Symptoms progress from cyanosis, headaches, shallow respiration, dizziness, confusion, drop in blood pressure, and lethargy to convulsions, coma, another drop in blood pressure, and death. An autopsy will show chocolate-colored blood (methemoglobin); damage to the kidneys, liver, and spleen; and petechial spots on the organs due to a lack of oxygen. Sometimes the bladder shows small ulcers with necrotized (decayed) tissue in them.

REACTION TIME: The first symptoms appear within one to two hours. Aniline works fairly slowly, depending on the dose.

ANTIDOTES AND TREATMENTS: Methylene blue dye is sometimes given to reverse the effect on the red blood cells. A blood transfusion may be necessary; also dialysis, if the patient goes into kidney failure.

NOTES: When people think of aniline, they usually think of aniline dyes, but this toxin has a wide range of industrial uses as a chemical intermediary in the processing of resins, perfumes, and photographic chemicals, and in vulcanizing rubber. (Aniline is not necessarily in any of these things, but it is used in making them.) Most poisonings happen by inhalation of the vapor. Fortunately for most potential victims—but perhaps not for your villain—aniline vapor can be smelled and causes mild eye irritation long before it becomes concentrated enough to kill anyone.

Aniline dyes seem to be most popular with advanced woodworking enthusiasts (beginning woodworkers and casual hobbyists will probably not use them, as stains and other finishes are more readily available, and are a lot easier to use). One finish company noted that not all aniline dyes actually have aniline in them—because aniline was the first synthetic dye (developed in the 1850s), the word *aniline* has come to mean any synthetic dye, as opposed to natural dyes like indigo.

ANTIMONY

OTHER: Antimony regulus, tartar emetic, and stibine.

TOXICITY: 6

FORM: Antimony is a silvery-white, soft metal that does not dissolve in water. Tartar emetic, a white powder, has been hidden in food, but there is a slight bitter taste. Stibine is the colorless gas released when ore or slag (the residual waste from the mining process) containing antimony comes into contact with acids.

EFFECTS AND SYMPTOMS: The clinical picture is similar to arsenic poisoning. Poisonings in which antimony were suspected were historically diagnosed as "gastric fever" because the symptoms include nausea, frequent vomiting, dehydration, and severe diarrhea, sometimes with blood. It can sometimes cause liver and kidney damage. Inhalation of stibine can also cause weak pulse, jaundice, anemia from the destruction of the red blood cells, and generalized weakness.

Chronic antimony poisoning is very similar to chronic arsenic poisoning, and presents the additional symptoms of headache, loss of appetite, and dermatitis.

The autopsy may show damage to the liver and other organs.

REACTION TIME: Thirty minutes to several hours.

ANTIDOTES AND TREATMENTS: Treatment is supportive care, including giving fluids to replace those lost by the vomiting and diarrhea.

NOTES: Many chemicals and commonly used items once contained antimony. In Victorian times, it was commonly found in ant paste. Nowadays it's mostly found as a hardening agent in metals, such as lead. It's also used in typesetting metals, batteries, and glazes, and found in pewter.

Tartar emetic (antimony potassium tartrate) has historically rivaled arsenic as a poisoner's favorite. In fact, several well-known Victorian murderers (one of whom was Dr. Pritchard) combined the two drugs. Catherine de Medici used it in France, as did the Borgias in Italy (see chapter one, A Short History of the Dreaded Art).

BENZENE

OTHER: Benzol, phenyl hydride, coal naphtha, phene, cyclohexatriene.

TOXICITY: 4

FORM: A very volatile, colorless liquid. Its odor is distinct, although it has been described as both pleasant and acrid.

Acute poisoning is most commonly from inhalation of the vapor or from ingestion. Absorption through the skin is limited.

EFFECTS AND SYMPTOMS: The chemical affects the central nervous system first; headache, nausea, and vomiting are the primary symptoms, along with convulsions and coma. Inhalation can also cause euphoria, nervousness, and eventually ataxia. Occasionally, sudden death from cardiac problems can happen.

In chronic poisoning, benzene attacks the bone marrow. Symptoms start with fatigue, headache, loss of appetite, and nausea. Blood studies will show anemia. Lab tests find it difficult to distinguish between aplastic anemia (a condition in which bone marrow stops producing new blood cells) and bone-marrow failure due to benzene poisoning.

Skin contact will reveal redness, scaling, and cracking.

REACTION TIME: Immediate upon inhalation, about thirty minutes for ingestion.

ANTIDOTES AND TREATMENTS: As in the case with all poisonous vapors, the victim should be removed from contaminated air immediately and given artificial respiration. Convulsions or spasms can be treated with diazepam. Epinephrine or ephedrine can trigger heart attacks.

NOTES: Benzene is one of the most commonly found industrial chemicals. A by-product of gasoline, it's used as a solvent in paints and thinners and in the manufacture of hundreds of other products and substances. Kids into huffing (spraying a substance into a bag and inhaling it to get high) are frequently exposed because benzene is in so many products, like spray paint and glues. Cigarette smokers typically breathe in between one and two milligrams a day.

Benzene is highly carcinogenic, and is known to cause leukemia.

A pattern of apparent drunken behavior due to benzene—called the benzol jag—consists of unsteady gait, euphoria, and confusion. This occurs after a small amount of inhalation.

CASE HISTORY

In May 2006, lawsuits were filed against several beverage companies after it was found that some of their drinks had developed trace amounts of benzene, because of a reaction between some of the otherwise harmless chemicals among the ingredients. The reaction was thought to be triggered by light. Because of benzene's highly carcinogenic nature, water is considered unsafe if it contains more than 5 parts per billion (ppb) of benzene. The sodas reportedly had just under 80 ppb, which is a source of concern. However, as one official noted, you're likely to take in more than that every day just breathing.

CADMIUM

TOXICITY: 4

FORM: A bluish-white metal, cadmium can be ingested or the fumes inhaled. The fumes are by far more deadly.

EFFECTS AND SYMPTOMS: Cadmium damages all cells of the body, but especially the kidneys. Kidney and liver damage can happen whether cadmium is ingested or inhaled.

The earliest symptoms from inhaled fumes, occurring several hours after exposure, include a slight irritation of the upper respiratory tract, which can be followed over the next few hours with coughing, chest pain, and pneumonia. Pulmonary edema will also set in.

Ingesting the poison causes immediate nausea, vomiting, diarrhea, headache, and stomach pain, shock, and renal failure. Although ingestion can be fatal, because of the strong irritation to the gastrointestinal tract, it can be hard to get enough absorbed into the system to cause death.

Chronic poisoning includes weight loss, anemia, irritability, yellow-stained teeth, and sometimes pain in the bones.

If the patient survives, liver and kidney damage will take the longest to recover from, and may be permanent.

Autopsy reveals severe liver and kidney damage. Lung tissue is scarred; fluid might be present from edema.

REACTION TIME: With inhalation, there is a latent period of several hours before symptoms begin. Ingestion causes an immediate reaction.

ANTIDOTES AND TREATMENTS: Treatment is supportive. Even though cadmium is a metal, using a binding drug like dimercaprol is not usually done because it can aggravate the kidney damage.

NOTES: Cadmium is used for plating metals and in the manufacture of alloys. Various compounds are also found in glazes, paints, insecticides, and in wide use in the photographic industry. It's also found in a variety of ores, and exposures during the mining and smelting of zinc, copper, and lead are common. And, of course, it's a primary element of NiCad or nickel cadmium batteries.

Once absorbed, the cadmium has a long half-life and stays in the body for a number of years.

Early chest X-rays may reveal what looks like bronchial pneumonia, so victims may not necessarily realize they are being poisoned.

Cadmium is an element of cigarette smoke, and heavy smoking appears to increase the toxic effects of the poison.

In Japan, environmental exposure resulted in *itai-itai* ("ouch-ouch") disease, so named for the bone pain connected to chronic cadmium poisoning.

CARBON TETRACHLORIDE

OTHER: Carbon tet.

TOXICITY: 6

FORM: Carbon tetrachloride is a colorless, nonflammable liquid with a distinctive odor. It can be inhaled, absorbed through the skin, or swallowed.

Carbon tetrachloride attacks the central nervous system, liver, and kidneys.

Whether the exposure is through inhalation, ingestion, or skin contact, the first symptoms are abdominal pain, nausea, vomiting, dizziness, and confusion. The mucous membranes are irritated when the chemical is ingested or inhaled. Respiratory arrest, irregular heartbeat, and coma may occur with more serious exposures. Further symptoms might be seen between one day and two weeks. This is when liver or kidney damage becomes obvious. Liver damage may cause jaundice. Kidney damage shows up as a decrease in urine output, swelling, and uremia. Death often results from kidney failure if immediate steps are not taken to start dialysis. Coma and liver or kidney damage can all appear independently or can all occur at the same time.

REACTION TIME: Almost immediate.

ANTIDOTES AND TREATMENTS: When the substance is inhaled, the first step is to administer artificial respiration until the victim regains consciousness. Any clothing contaminated with the chemical should be removed. Treatment is symptomatic. Stimulants are not given, as they can induce a heart attack.

Acetylcysteine is sometimes given to minimize the liver and kidney damage.

NOTES: This industrial solvent is an extremely dangerous chemical. Used in the manufacture of fluorocarbons, it was also employed as a dry-cleaning agent and occasionally in fire extinguishers. It's falling out of use because it is so toxic; however, some households may still have it around as a spot remover. It is the chemical cousin of that well-known knock-out agent, chloroform.

Workers are warned not to drink alcohol around carbon tet since that intensifies the effect of the poison. If the victim has drunk alcohol at the same time as exposure, damage to all of the organs is increased.

In the 1950s, it was used as a solvent for cleaning airplane motors.

CHROMIUM

TOXICITY: Varies, but 5 to 6 for the most toxic varieties

FORM: Chromium is a metal, but also shows up as an acid and as various salts. Exposure comes from inhalation of the dust, ingestion, or skin contact.

EFFECTS AND SYMPTOMS: A systemic poison, it is also corrosive. Inhalation causes irritation in the upper respiratory tract, wheezing, and pulmonary edema (lungs filling with fluids). Skin contact usually involves burns and sometimes ulcers. Ingestion causes stomach pain, bloody vomiting, and diarrhea. Shock and kidney failure from the massive fluid loss are also possible.

REACTION TIME: Quick, although the pulmonary edema may be delayed for several hours—one source notes a case in which the edema did not show up for seventy-two hours.

ANTIDOTES AND TREATMENTS: Treatment is supportive. In the case of ingestion, water is given immediately to dilute the chromium, then aggressive fluid and blood replacement is done. Ascorbic acid is sometimes given after ingestion of one of the hexavalent forms, and while its value is unproven, the treatment is benign.

NOTES: The bright mirror-like shine of chromium made it quite popular for the bumpers on cars for many years. But chromium has a wide variety of uses and comes in several different forms. These include chromic acid, potassium chromate, potassium dichromate, and sodium dichromate. Even the less toxic versions can be problematic because chromium is a carcinogen.

Chromium is also an allergen. There are reports of people going into anaphylactic shock after breathing chromium dust. But it mostly shows up as a contact allergy, causing a rash that is sometimes yellow to orange colored.

CASE HISTORY

The film *Erin Brockovich* is based on a real story in which a company had allowed chromium to leak into a community's water supply. The lawsuit featured in the film did not involve any acute poisonings, however. The victims were all getting cancer from the chromium in the water supply.

COPPER

TOXICITY: Varies with the form, but the most toxic form is copper sulfate, which is a 5.

FORM: A reddish-brown metal, copper is in a wide variety of substances, including copper sulfate, a salt. It can be inhaled as a fume or dust. Copper sulfate and other copper salts are generally ingested.

EFFECTS AND SYMPTOMS: When inhaled as fumes or dust, copper causes muscle aches and fever, along with sneezing and nausea. Kidney damage can also occur. When ingested as a salt, nausea with blue-green vomit comes on quickly. Diarrhea and bleeding in the gastrointestinal system can also happen. Shock from loss of fluids and eventual liver and kidney damage can lead to death.

REACTION TIME: Within five minutes.

ANTIDOTES AND TREATMENTS: Supportive therapy is given, and in serious ingestions, dimercaprol or penicillamine is given to chelate (bind) the copper.

Most people think of pennies and wiring when they think of copper. But this elemental metal appears in a wide variety of forms and is used in the manufacture of batteries and in electroplating, plumbing, welding, ceramics, petroleum distillation, and pharmaceuticals. Everyone has trace amounts of copper in their systems, and as a simple metal, it's not seriously toxic—a coin is likely to pass through your system before causing any serious trouble. Not that you don't want to take your toddler to the doctor if she swallows a penny, especially one from after 1982. Not only are coins a serious potential choking hazard, gastric acids can interact with the zinc in the penny and cause systemic poisoning that way.

Wilson's disease happens when the liver cannot remove the copper that is naturally in our systems. The damage from the disease can lead to a liver transplant.

DIMETHYL SULFATE

OTHER: Sulfuric acid, dimethyl ester, methyl sulfate, DMS.

TOXICITY: 6

FORM: A colorless, odorless, oily liquid, dimethyl sulfate is only slightly soluble in water but readily dissolves in organic solvents and becomes sulfuric acid. It can be ingested, inhaled, or absorbed by skin or eye contact.

EFFECTS AND SYMPTOMS: Dimethyl sulfate is strongly corrosive to the skin, but the effects don't start until four to five hours after contact. Exposure to the vapor immediately produces tearing; runny nose; swelling of mouth, lips, and throat tissues; sore throat; hoarseness; difficulty breathing; cyanosis; and death. Eye irritation causes conjunctivitis (pinkeye), perforation of the nasal septum through the sinuses (much like one might see in a cocaine addict), and permanent vision problems. Liver and kidney damage may also occur.

Ingestion causes respiratory distress and bronchitis within six to twelve hours. Swelling in the brain and other central nervous system effects, such as drowsiness, temporary blindness, heart irregularities, and nerve irritation, occur before possible convulsions and death. Pulmonary edema also occurs and is generally the cause of death.

REACTION TIME: Exposure produces no immediate effects except for nasal and eye irritation. There is a latent period of up to ten hours before the onset of symptoms. Death may occur in three to four days or be delayed for several weeks.

ANTIDOTES AND TREATMENTS: Oxygen is given for pulmonary problems, and hydrocortisone is used to reduce injury. Other symptoms are treated as they appear.

NOTES: Used in manufacturing dyes, drugs, perfumes, and pesticides; most poisonings from dimethyl sulfate come from leakage of liquid and vapors from the apparatus holding the toxin. If the victim is drinking alcohol, the poisoning can be worse—something that might be useful for your potential villain.

ETHYLENE CHLOROHYDRIN

OTHER: Glycol chlorohydrin, 2-chloroethanol, beta-chloroethyl alcohol.

TOXICITY: 6

FORM: Ethylene chlorohydrin is a colorless liquid that smells like ether. The highly toxic chemical can be inhaled, absorbed, or ingested. Ethylene chlorohydrin will react with water or steam to produce toxic and corrosive fumes.

EFFECTS AND SYMPTOMS: A narcotic poison, the chemical affects the liver, spleen, and lungs. Initial symptoms may be slight. After several hours, symptoms include nausea, vomiting, headache, abdominal pain, excitability, dizziness, delirium, slowed breathing, a drop in blood pressure, muscle twitching, cyanosis, and coma.

The autopsy shows infiltration of the chemical into the fatty part of the liver, swelling of the brain, and congestion and swelling in the lungs.

REACTION TIME: Symptoms will usually begin within one to four hours.

ANTIDOTES AND TREATMENTS: Removal from further exposure; CPR and oxygen are administered; shock and pulmonary edema are treated.

NOTES: This highly dangerous chemical is used in both industry and agriculture. Used to make indigo dye and novocaine, the chemical is also found as a solvent to clean machines and remove tar from clothing, and is used to speed up the germination of potatoes and other seeds.

The chemical readily penetrates the skin and most rubber gloves. Frostbite can occur from handling the chemical's container.

FORMALDEHYDE

OTHER: Formalin, methanol, formic aldehyde, oxomethane, oxymethylene, methylene oxide, methyl aldehyde.

TOXICITY: 6

FORM: Formaldehyde is a colorless gas with a strong and unpleasant odor. The chemical is more commonly found as formalin, a solution made of 40 percent formaldehyde, water, and sometimes methanol. Formaldehyde is most dangerous when inhaled or ingested in solution. Absorption through the skin is less severe.

EFFECTS AND SYMPTOMS: Formaldehyde attacks the respiratory system. Upon ingestion, tearing and severe abdominal pain is immediate, followed by collapse, loss of consciousness, shutdown of the liver, and circulatory failure. Vomiting and diarrhea can also occur. Breathing formaldehyde irritates the respiratory tract and the eyes. Inhalation for prolonged periods of time causes pulmonary edema and death. Contact with the skin is irritating and may cause lesions.

The principal findings of an autopsy are decayed and shrunken mucous membranes, along with possible liver, kidney, heart, and brain damage.

REACTION TIME: Ingesting formaldehyde causes an immediate reaction. Within thirty minutes of exposure to the gas, symptoms become pronounced.

ANTIDOTES AND TREATMENTS: Milk, activated charcoal, or tap water are given to dilute the poison. Afterward, the victim is treated for shock and liver shutdown.

NOTES: Formaldehyde, which most of us associate with the solution that keeps dead frogs and other biology specimens from decomposing, is more common than most people realize. It's been used as a disinfectant, as an antiseptic, as the adhesive in plywood and particle board (although this use is declining), as sizing on new fabrics, and is even in some explosives.

Paper and cloth containing formaldehyde have caused allergic skin reactions in some people. It is also a potential explosion hazard. The higher the concentration of formaldehyde, the lower the flash point. It will easily catch fire.

GOLD

TOXICITY: Varies widely, depending on the compound involved.

FORM: The familiar yellow metal; as a medicine, it's available as a capsule, Auranofin (Ridaura), or an injectable, gold sodium thiomalate (Myochrisine).

EFFECTS AND SYMPTOMS: Gold inhibits enzymatic activity in the body and can also suppress bone marrow function.

Symptoms include a racing heart, wheezing, diarrhea, and colitis. Small sores in the mouth are common. There is damage to the blood cells and the brain, sometimes leading to paralysis, starting with the legs and moving upwards through the body. Stroke is also possible.

REACTION TIME: Slow and cumulative.

ANTIDOTES AND TREATMENTS: Supportive care along with activated charcoal and chelation therapy with dimercaprol or penicillamine. Note that penicillamine cannot be used in patients allergic to penicillin.

NOTES: Poisoning someone with jewelry may be a little crazy, but gold can be used as a toxin. Gold is used in dentistry as fillings and crowns. Compounds with gold are also in a variety of medications for rheumatoid arthritis, which your villain could disguise as a vitamin for the victim, assuming you've got a villain who can believably get these medications.

CASE HISTORY

One episode of *House* had Dr. Gregory House's team testing for possible heavy metal poison. The tests, which looked for lead and other common metals, kept coming back negative until House found a way to catch the victim's wife, literally, gold-handed. The tests weren't programmed to find gold, maybe because, as Daniel Anderson of the Los Angeles County Coroner's Office, put it, "That's an expensive way to poison someone."

HYDROGEN SULFIDE

OTHER: Hydrosulfuric acid, sulfureted hydrogen.

TOXICITY: 6

FORM: A gas, hydrogen sulfide is inhaled. In lower concentrations it is an irritant.

EFFECTS AND SYMPTOMS: Hydrogen sulfide has anoxic effects (reduces the body's oxygen supply). It directly damages the cells of the nervous system and paralyzes the respiratory system.

When breathed in lower concentrations it causes eye and nasal irritation, and the victim loses the ability to smell as the olfactory nerves are paralyzed. Pulmonary edema can also occur. As the concentrations get stronger, headache, nausea, dizziness, seizures, and coma can occur. Very high concentrations cause immediate coma, with death quickly following.

If death is delayed twenty-four to forty-eight hours, pulmonary edema (congestion of the lungs) is found. A rotten-egg odor is noticeable at autopsy.

REACTION TIME: Immediate. Death usually occurs in thirty to sixty minutes.

Removal from exposure and giving oxygen are the only known treatments. Amyl or sodium nitrite can sometimes be used to bind up the sulfide in the tissues and remove it.

If the patient can be revived right away, then chances are good for a full recovery. However, because the gas suffocates its victims, if the brain has been without oxygen too long, permanent brain damage may be the result.

NOTES: Hydrogen sulfide occurs whenever organic matter of any kind decays. It's easily identified by its characteristic rotten-egg smell, which is quite pronounced even when at its lowest concentrations. Heavier than air, the gas can be found in manure pits, sewers, and other closed-in places, where it can easily reach fatal concentrations. Poisoning also occurs in coal mines. Hydrogen sulfide is found too as a by-product in numerous chemical processes at places such as blast furnaces and petroleum refineries. Finally, hydrogen sulfide is one of two volcanic gases; the other is carbon dioxide. Sometimes called a one-whiff or knockdown gas, in higher concentrations, hydrogen sulfide is very deadly.

CASE HISTORY

In one case, a man entered a manure pit and was knocked unconscious by the hydrogen sulfide gas present. His wife and a neighbor both entered the pit to rescue him and were knocked out, thus illustrating the need for rescuers to be sure they have protective breathing gear on before attempting a rescue.

Hydrogen sulfide was one of the two gases (the other was carbon dioxide) that killed a ski patrol officer in the early spring of 2006. A volcanic fumarole, or vent, had opened up, creating a soft spot in the snow on California's Mammoth mountain. The officer was looking for skiers when the snow broke and he fell in, suffocating almost immediately in the resulting hole.

Home winemakers are familiar with hydrogen sulfide. The gas causes "the stinkies," a foul odor that is a common flaw in homemade wines. It can sometimes blow off, fortunately in very, very low concentrations, and as such is harmless.

LEAD AND LEAD COMPOUNDS

OTHER: Plumbum.

TOXICITY: 5

FORM: There are many compounds containing lead; the metal itself is blue-gray, very malleable, and heavy.

Lead and lead compounds are common air contaminants in the form of dust, fumes, mists, or vapors, often coming into contact with the skin. While it is not absorbed through intact skin, it is often ingested after inhalation—inhaled residue from the upper respiratory tract may be swallowed. Lead dust can also be introduced into the body on food, tobacco, fingers, or anything going into the mouth.

EFFECTS AND SYMPTOMS: Lead works on the brain and the peripheral nervous system.

Chronic poisoning causes a number of symptoms, including a blue lead line on the gums, vomiting, wasting away, and other nervous system symptoms. Acute poisoning causes a metallic taste in the mouth, abdominal pain, vomiting, diarrhea, black stools, oliguria, collapse, and coma.

When large amounts are taken in, the central nervous system is affected, leading to severe headache, convulsions, coma, delirium, and possibly death.

An autopsy of an acute poisoning will reveal inflamed mucous membranes in the gastrointestinal tract, and damage in the liver area. Chronic poisoning shows cerebral edema and damage to the nerve and muscle cells.

Chronic lead poisoning can be useful to the writer in that lead is not eliminated from the body very quickly, and can stay in one's system, particularly the bones, for years, sometimes causing relapses.

REACTION TIME: Death usually occurs only after repeated high-dose exposure.

ANTIDOTES AND TREATMENTS: Care for seizures and coma is supportive. Dimercaprol and calcium disodium EDTA are given as antidotes, followed by penicillamine.

NOTES: Most people connect lead with peeling house paint and the poisoning of children. Lead and lead compounds are used in enameling, pottery glazes, alloys, solders, rubber, some gasoline, ammunition, ink, leaded glass, battery plates, and piping. Lead dust is found in shooting galleries and in the occasional bad batch of moonshine when the still's lead lining is improperly constructed.

Lead is no longer found in gasoline, except in some countries. U.S. gasoline producers began phasing out leaded gasoline in the 1970s, and by 1996, it was officially banned.

Pottery glazes have been known to leak some lead into food, and consumers have been warned not to cook or store food in ceramic containers that have not been clearly labeled as lead-free or food safe.

Lead has been banned in house paints for a long time. However, home buyers who purchase houses built before the late 1970s are often cautioned about the potential for lead paint on their new property.

Lead poisoning is one of the most common occupational diseases. Inhalation is the quickest way for the poison to reach the body.

The severe brain damage caused by lead poisoning might be just the thing needed in a story when the villain wants to take control of a relative's estate without killing him.

CASE HISTORY

Some years back, the Los Angeles water system was found to have a substantial quantity of lead form the old lead pipes, and pregnant women were urged to drink bottled water.

For centuries, fine ladies—and some men—used face and wig powders containing lead oxide, unknowingly putting themselves in harm's way in the name of vanity. These cosmetics caused numerous physical problems and even deaths up until the nineteenth century, when lead was replaced by zinc oxide as a whitening agent.

MERCURY

OTHER: Quicksilver, mercury vapor, mercury liquid, and mercury salts.

TOXICITY: 5

FORM: Elemental mercury is a silvery, mobile liquid that beads up easily. Elemental mercury vaporizes very easily, and because 80 percent of the fumes will be absorbed, it is very toxic when inhaled.

Mercury salts are solids, with mercuric salts being more toxic than mercurous salts. Both are generally ingested.

Methyl mercury can be swallowed, or, less commonly, inhaled as fumes.

EFFECTS AND SYMPTOMS: Because of mercury's effects on the central nervous system and brain, it is one of the few toxins for which chronic poisoning is useful to the writer.

Acute inhalation of elemental mercury can cause difficulty breathing, cough, and eventually bronchitis, pneumonia, and pulmonary edema. Chronic inhalation leads to problems with the central nervous system, including tremors, insomnia, and personality changes such as withdrawal, depression, and explosive irritability. Mouth sores and loosening of the teeth are also characteristic.

Mercuric salts are corrosives, and swallowing them will cause nausea, vomiting, abdominal pain, hemorrhaging, shock, and death. If the patient survives, then acute kidney failure can happen within the next twenty-four hours to several days. Chronic exposure leads to the same central nervous system ailments as those caused by elemental mercury.

Methyl mercury goes after the brain and kidneys. Symptoms of poisoning are often delayed for weeks, even months. They include incoordination, difficulty speaking, hearing impairment, and constriction of the visual field. Over time, as the central nervous system effects worsen, the patient may eventually start suffering the same mental state changes as with elemental mercury, or fall into a coma and die.

REACTION TIME: Initial symptoms of inhaling a strong dose of elemental mercury vapor can be immediate; however chronic poisoning is more likely. Chronic poisoning may take several weeks to years.

ANTIDOTES AND TREATMENTS: Dimercaprol (BAL), succimer, or penicillamine is administered in addition to symptomatic treatment.

NOTES: Mercury is best known as the silvery, mobile liquid that comes out of thermometers. It has numerous uses in all of its three main forms; however, it is getting a bad name as an environmental hazard, especially for showing up in fish.

Elemental mercury is the quicksilver mentioned above, and it's used in thermometers, barometers and other instruments, dental fillings, fluorescent light bulbs, and to extract gold and silver ore.

Inorganic mercury is usually found in a large number of compounds as a salt, and is mostly used in industrial applications.

Organic mercury shows up in a variety of industrial uses, including germicides and timber preservative. In fact, some adults may remember mercurochrome—a topical germ killer that used to be applied to cuts. While large ingestions can lead to nerve and kidney damage, organic mercury is not nearly as toxic as methyl mercury.

CASE HISTORY

The Mad Hatter of *Alice in Wonderland* fame was not entirely fictional. In the 1800s, the hatting industry was well known for its use of mercury in shaping felt hats. Many hatters went insane from breathing mercury fumes.

Most mercury poisonings occur as industrial accidents. In one reported case, a middle-aged woman who had worked for twenty years as a dental assistant died of mercury poisoning from the amalgams she regularly handled, which contained 40 percent mercury compound.

METHANOL

OTHER: Methyl alcohol, wood alcohol.

TOXICITY: 5 (The toxic dose varies by individual metabolism of alcohols.)

FORM: Like other alcohols, methanol is a liquid at room temperature and evaporates quickly. Methanol is almost always swallowed.

EFFECTS AND SYMPTOMS: Methanol, after it has metabolized, basically creates acidosis—an imbalance of acid in the body that can lead to shock and death. Initial symptoms are of inebriation with possible upset stomach. After the characteristic latency period, visual disturbances (according to one source, haziness, like standing in a snowfield), blindness, seizures, coma, and death may occur. If the patient recovers, the blindness is usually permanent.

REACTION TIME: A prominent feature of methanol poisoning is the latent period of eight to thirty hours before the critical symptoms appear. This is due to the slow metabolism of methanol into its toxic metabolites.

ANTIDOTES AND TREATMENTS: Ethanol or fomepizole is given to slow the metabolizing of the methanol. Kidney dialysis is used to remove methanol from the blood.

NOTES: Ethyl alcohol's country cousin, methanol or methyl alcohol, has a myriad of industrial uses and is found in perfumes, antifreeze, paint removers, and as a solvent in shellac and varnish. Windshield wiper fluid is among its most common uses. It is considerably more toxic than booze, probably because it metabolizes into formaldehyde in the body, rendering a victim truly pickled.

While it is technically illegal, distilling your own alcohol is still done in some parts of the United States. Methanol is made the same way as ethanol, only its source is wood, which accounts for its more deadly effects. So a clever villain could arrange to "accidentally" change out Grandpa's fermented grain mash with one made from wood chips, thus creating a deadly white lightening. Blindness from a bad mash was not an unheard of complaint among bootleggers in the South.

OXALIC ACID

TOXICITY: 5

FORM: Oxalic acid is usually found in solution, although the vapor is dangerous in high concentrations as well.

EFFECTS AND SYMPTOMS: Skin contact is painful and if not treated, can cause gangrene. Ingestion, however, causes the deadliest effects. Skin or eye contact causes irritation and burning, with severe damage from the corrosive effects at high concentrations. Inhalation can cause sore throat, cough, and wheezing, with pneumonia and pulmonary edema possible with concentrated or ongoing exposures.

Ingestion of the acid will cause the same effects as swallowing any other strong acid. However, swallowing one of the soluble oxalates can cause weakness, muscle spasms, convulsions, and cardiac arrest. If the patient recovers from swallowing the acid or smaller doses of the oxalate, symptoms can progress to kidney failure.

REACTION TIME: Immediate in the case of the acid. Soluble oxalates take time to infiltrate the system.

ANTIDOTES AND TREATMENTS: Supportive care is given as symptoms appear.

NOTES: Used in bleaches, metal cleaners, and rust removers, oxalic acid reacts like other acids, but is included here because it can cause kidney damage. Oxalate salts are found in many plants, as well, particularly in the leaves of rhubarb.

PHOSGENE

OTHER: Carbon oxychloride, carbonyl chloride.

TOXICITY: 5

FORM: Phosgene is a gas and is usually inhaled.

EFFECTS AND SYMPTOMS: Phosgene is an irritant. But it is not very water soluble, so at low concentrations, it doesn't always cause irritation to the nose and throat right away, thus allowing a victim to breathe more of it longer. After a while, the phosgene reacts with the body's internal moisture to become hydrochloric acid, causing necrosis in the lungs.

Symptoms start as a burning sensation in the throat, and a mild cough. After an interval of difficult breathing, severe pulmonary edema can develop, and death can occur from respiratory and circulatory failure. If the patient survives, any lung impairment may be permanent.

The autopsy shows extended damage to the trachea and bronchial tubes, and pneumonia with hemorrhages and petechiae.

REACTION TIME: The interval without symptoms can be as short as thirty minutes or be delayed up to eight hours or longer, with symptoms caused by more concentrated exposure coming on sooner. The latency period has been known to last as long as three days after exposure.

ANTIDOTES AND TREATMENTS: The victim is removed from further exposure, and oxygen is given as soon as possible. The patient should probably be observed for at least forty-eight hours because of the problems with the late appearance of symptoms.

NOTES: Phosgene was developed during World War I as a war gas. Today it's used in making dyes and other chemicals. However, it's better known for its involvement in accidents. When various chlorinated compounds are burned, phosgene is the product. Some solvents, paint removers, and nonflammable dry-cleaning fluids become extremely dangerous in the presence of fire or heat for this reason.

There may be no immediate warning that a dangerous level of the gas is being breathed, which may prove useful to a fictional villain interested in causing maximum harm.

PHOSPHINE

TOXICITY: 5

FORM: It is a gas and is inhaled.

EFFECTS AND SYMPTOMS: Phosphine attacks the lungs, brain, kidneys, heart, and liver.

Initial symptoms are cough, difficulty breathing, headache, dizziness, and vomiting. Sudden kidney failure, hepatitis (liver damage) and seizures can occur, as well as cardiac trouble and pulmonary edema.

REACTION TIME: The onset is usually rapid, although the hepatitis and pulmonary edema can be delayed.

ANTIDOTES AND TREATMENTS: Oxygen is given, as well as care for other symptoms as they develop. Cardiac problems that do not respond to normal treatment may indicate the use of magnesium, given intravenously.

NOTES: A colorless, heavier-than-air gas, phosphine in its pure form is odorless. But impurities usually give it a garlicky or fishy odor. It does have some industrial uses, including the treatment of silicon crystals in the semiconductor industry, but it is mostly released accidentally during the metal refining process.

PHOSPHORUS (WHITE OR YELLOW)

TOXICITY: 6

FORM: A translucent, waxy crystal, it can be colorless or yellow and is soluble in fat or oil. It is not soluble in water.

EFFECTS AND SYMPTOMS: Contact with the chemical causes tissue destruction; it attacks the liver, lungs, and eyes. It is also toxic on the cellular level. Chronic inhalation destroys the jawbone, a condition called phossy-jaw, and can also cause a general wasting away.

Acute inhalation brings on upper airway irritation, cough, wheezing, pneumonia, and delayed pulmonary edema.

Ingestion of yellow phosphorus is followed by burning in the gastrointestinal tract, abdominal pain, severe vomiting, and diarrhea. The vomit and feces may smoke as the phosphorous in them is exposed to the air, and may also be luminescent. Headache, delirium, seizures, coma, and cardiac irregularities can occur.

The victim may appear to improve for one or two days; then the symptoms of liver and kidney failure may appear, with liver tenderness and enlargement, jaundice, muscle spasms, and scanty urine. Death may occur as late as three weeks after poisoning. Autopsy findings include jaundice; necrosis of liver, kidney, and heart; and hemorrhages in the intestinal tract.

If yellow phosphorus dries on the skin, it will cause second- and third-degree burns.

In chronic poisoning, the first sign is often a toothache, followed by swelling of the jaw, and then necrosis of the jawbone.

REACTION TIME: Symptoms begin within two hours and may continue for one to three weeks before death. Cardiac arrest or coma may occur in the first twenty-four to forty-eight hours, or symptoms may improve for one to two days and then return.

ANTIDOTES AND TREATMENTS: Removal from exposure. Copious amounts of water are used to remove the chemical from skin or eyes. Treatment of pulmonary edema, shock, and liver failure. Treatment of jaw necrosis by surgical excision of infected bone.

NOTES: Yellow and white phosphorous are unstable, highly toxic, and combust at room temperature. The red form is pretty much nontoxic, although prolonged exposure has reportedly caused illness. Yellow or white phosphorous is useful in the manufacture of fireworks, fertilizers, and rodenticide.

CASE HISTORY

In the 1950s, Louisa May Merrifield and her husband, Alfred, worked as housekeepers for the elderly Mrs. Sarah Ann Ricketts in Blackpool, England. Louisa was heard to boast that her employer had left the Merrifields an inheritance. "She's not dead yet," Louisa reportedly said, "but she will soon be." Mrs. Ricketts died on April 14, 1953. An autopsy showed Mrs. Ricketts had died of phosphorus poisoning, in the form of rat poison. Although no poison was found during a search of the grounds, Louisa was found guilty and hanged on September 18, 1953. Her husband was acquitted and received a half-share of Mrs. Ricketts's estate.

SODIUM AZIDE

TOXICITY: 5

FORM: A white, crystalline solid. It easily acidifies into hydrazoic acid, which easily vaporizes and is explosive at high concentrations. Ingestion and inhalation cause most of the toxic effects, although there are reports that skin contact can also be toxic.

EFFECTS AND SYMPTOMS: Exposure to the gas or dust will cause pinkeye, and irritation in the nose and throat can progress to pulmonary edema.

Symptoms for inhalation and ingestion are similar: low blood pressure, then a progression of various cardiac irregularities until the heart fails. Nausea, vomiting, diarrhea, and profuse sweating are also symptoms, as are headache, agitation, weakness, reduced reflexes, seizures, coma, and respiratory failure.

REACTION TIME: Varies widely depending on the situation. Some symptoms of inhalation are immediate. Death can happen in as little as one to two hours, or as long as seventy-two.

ANTIDOTES AND TREATMENTS: Because sodium azide becomes hydrazoic acid in the stomach, rescuers and health care providers can be intoxicated by vapors from the vomit or any other stomach contents. The patient must be kept in a well-ventilated area, and protective clothing and breathing gear should be used by rescuers. Also, the azide must be disposed of carefully, as contact with heavy metals, such as the lead and copper in water pipes, can form highly explosive metal azides.

Other than those precautions, treatment is supportive.

NOTES: While it once was used in minute amounts as a laboratory preservative, sodium azide is now used as the bang that inflates air bags in automobiles. It is highly toxic, but explosively decomposes to relatively harmless nitrogen gas, which is actually what inflates the bag.

CASE HISTORY

One of our sources mentioned a case in which a scientist intentionally sniffed the vapor of a 1 percent hydrazoic acid solution. It doesn't say why he did it, but his blood pressure immediately dropped and he collapsed, but recovered fifteen minutes later with nothing more than a headache.

TETRACHLOROETHANE AND TETRACHLOROETHYLENE

TOXICITY: 5

FORM: They are both heavy, clear liquids, although tetrachloroethane can be light yellow. Their sweetish, chloroform-like odor is detectable in only small amounts because both oxidize into a vapor easily. Although they most frequently poison by inhalation, swallowing also causes serious toxicity. Tetrachloroethane can be absorbed by the skin; tetrachloroethylene does not absorb as well.

EFFECTS AND SYMPTOMS: The vapors of both toxins will irritate the eyes and respiratory tract at higher concentrations, although it takes a lower concentration of tetrachloroethane to cause irritation.

Eyes, nose, and throat irritation are the first signs. Other symptoms of tetrachloroethane poisoning include nausea, vomiting, diarrhea, confusion, delirium, and coma. Tetrachloroethylene causes headache, irritability, rash, short-term memory loss, personality changes, euphoria, stumbling, nausea, cough, and sweating.

Both can cause liver and kidney damage.

REACTION TIME: The first symptoms can be immediate. Mild symptoms of liver and kidney damage can continue up to three months, then suddenly become serious and cause death.

ANTIDOTES AND TREATMENTS: Supportive care is given.

NOTES: These are industrial solvents. Tetrachloroethane is used in metal cleaning, paint removers, varnishes, and photographic films. Tetracholorethylene is also known as Perc or percholoroethylene, the stuff dry cleaners use to get your clothes clean. While tetrachloroethylene is less toxic, both are central nervous system depressants. Both, when heated up, can release hydrogen chloride and phosgene gases, which are highly toxic and corrosive.

THALLIUM

TOXICITY: 5

FORM: A soft metal in pure form, it is usually found in nature in several different compounds, or salts, all of which are highly toxic.

EFFECTS AND SYMPTOMS: Thallium attacks the cells of the body. Acute poisoning will initially cause abdominal pain, nausea and vomiting, and diarrhea. If the victim survives the shock from loss of fluids, then over the next ten to fourteen days the hair will start to fall out, the fingernails will show Mees' lines (horizontal lines of discoloration found after episodes of arsenic or thallium poisoning), and the victim will feel pain in the feet and hands. Delirium, seizures, twitches, coma, and cardiac disturbances are all possible as well.

REACTION TIME: Symptoms occur twelve to fourteen hours after ingestion.

ANTIDOTES AND TREATMENTS: Supportive care; also Prussian Blue, a medicine used to rid the body of thallium (this is used in Europe, but not for medicinal purposes in the U.S.). Activated charcoal binds well with thallium, and the patient may be put on a dialysis machine to remove any remaining thallium in the system.

NOTES: Thallium is used in the manufacture of jewelry and semiconductors. It used to be available as a rodenticide, but was banned by the EPA in 1972. One source noted its former role as a depilatory (substance for removing hair), which makes sense since one of the most distinctive signs of thallium poisoning is alopecia (loss of hair). But because of its high toxicity, it is no longer used this way. One source notes that thallium is tasteless.

TRICHLOROETHANE

OTHER: Methyl chloroform, l,l,l-trichloroethane.

TOXICITY: 5

FORM: Trichloroethane is a colorless liquid that smells like chloroform and evaporates readily. It can be swallowed or its fumes can be inhaled.

EFFECTS AND SYMPTOMS: Trichloroethane depresses the central nervous system.

Symptoms include headache, dizziness, nausea, fainting, unconsciousness, slow breathing rate, skipped heartbeats, and a drop in blood pressure.

An autopsy reveals nothing particularly significant, except some petechiae (small hemorrhages) in the lungs and brain in severe inhalation cases.

REACTION TIME: Five minutes when inhaled; twenty to thirty minutes when ingested.

ANTIDOTES AND TREATMENTS: Supportive care is given.

NOTES: This is another industrial solvent, but this one used to be a part of typewriter correction fluid, such as Wite-Out or Liquid Paper. Like tetrachloroethane and tetrachloroethylene, it has the distinctive smell of chloroform, but is considerably more toxic.

TRINITROTOLUENE

OTHER: TNT, a-trinitrotoluol, sym-trinitrotoluol, 2,4,6-trinitroltolune, 1-methyl-2,4,6-trinitrolune, sym-trinitrotoluene, triton.

TOXICITY: 5

FORM: TNT is a solid, colorless, or pale yellow crystal. It explodes when exposed to heat or electric current. Inhalation, ingestion, and skin absorption are all toxic.

EFFECTS AND SYMPTOMS: TNT is primarily a central nervous system depressant, although one source suggests that it can destroy red blood cells.

Sneezing, coughing, and sore throat start the symptoms after dust or vapor inhalation. Skin, hair, and nails of exposed workers, or your fictional villain, may be stained yellow. Other symptoms include rash, pallor, stumbling, fever, insomnia, dizziness, seizures, low blood pressure, and headache. Severe cases show delirium, convulsions, and coma. Cardiac disturbances are also common.

REACTION TIME: First symptoms begin within several hours, and death can occur within two to four days.

ANTIDOTES AND TREATMENTS: Supportive care is given. The drug methylene blue may be given to counteract the destruction of the red blood cells.

NOTES: This is dynamite. While it is mostly used for blasting purposes, it is also used to make dyes and photographic chemicals.

Many are surprised to learn that the inventor of dynamite was Alfred Nobel, who believed it would both help industry and end war. When he realized that his legacy would be one of destruction and death, he secretly rewrote his will to establish prizes in five areas (physics, chemistry, medicine, literature, and peace) to "those who, during the preceding year, shall have conferred the greatest benefit on mankind." The first Nobel Prize was awarded in 1901.

TNT is relatively stable for an explosive, meaning that it does not blow up easily if it is jostled, knocked around, or rubs up against something.

CASE HISTORY

In the 1960s, a young radical making a bomb carelessly forgot to use gloves and absorbed a little too much TNT. He was brought into the emergency room, where he died of kidney failure.

STREET
DRUGS

[Holding up an egg] This is your brain.

[Picking up a hot, sizzling frying pan] This is drugs.

[Cracking the egg, frying the contents] This is your brain on drugs.

Any questions?

—1987 PUBLIC SERVICE ANNOUNCEMENT FOR THE
PARTNERSHIP FOR A DRUG-FREE AMERICA

There are two definitions of street drugs: 1) illicit drugs, such as cocaine, heroin, and ecstasy; and 2) prescription drugs that are sold on the black market. For the purposes of this book, we'll concentrate on the illicit drugs. Most of the drugs in this chapter are the ones emergency physicians and pathologists are looking for when they order a tox screen.

But emergency physicians and pathologists need to stay on their toes, as the world of drug abuse is constantly changing. New drugs appear on the market; the popularity of the traditional drugs of abuse grows and fades; old drugs take on new forms. Drug trends are also regional—cocaine use may be on the rise in New York City, while in Los Angeles, heroin is getting popular. Or vice versa.

Prescription drugs such as barbiturates and oxycodone (for example, Percocet) still remain very popular, but are covered in chapter eight, Medical Poisons, as is Ritalin, an amphetamine used to control narcolepsy and attention deficit disorder, which is emerging as a drug of abuse.

Another practice that continues is that of cutting (diluting) highly expensive and toxic drugs, such as heroine and cocaine, with various fillers. Most fillers, such as cornstarch are harmless, but strychnine has recently become a popular filler for heroin. The presence of unexpectedly pure drugs is also responsible for a good many fatalities.

The interesting thing is that while heroin, cocaine, and PCP are highly toxic, many street drugs are not. In fact, some are generally considered nontoxic, but are still highly dangerous because of what the victim can do while under the influence. Others are only moderately toxic, but because of routine abuse, the potential for deadly overdose becomes quite high.

Also, new drugs are always coming down the pike. An article in the *Medical Clinics of North America* in November 2005 cited three new ecstasy substitutes, as well as two herbals that have been around awhile but that are now becoming popular in North America. Unfortunately, there wasn't enough information on them at the time of this writing to include them here. So it doesn't hurt to check in with your local law enforcement or drug rehabilitation expert before writing about these drugs, to make sure you've got the current slang names, regional preferences, filler substances, or the latest new problem drug.

One of those old-time Hollywood plot devices often had a police officer dipping a finger into a mysterious white powder, then tasting it and proclaiming it was heroin or cocaine or whatever. This, of course, is pure nonsense. Any real cop knows there is no way to tell drugs apart by taste; not to mention that, if the substance happened to be something highly toxic, that little taste could be the cop's last.

Finally, a word on huffing. This practice of sniffing any of a wide variety of products is growing among teenagers, with up to 1.8 million teens engaging in the practice, according to an article in the April 2006 issue of *Pediatric News*. The practice is deadly, and involves toxins, but is difficult to class by specific toxin since the range of products used is so wide. Shoe polish, glues, gasoline, whipped cream from aerosol cans, even compressed air from cans of computer keyboard cleaners, can be sprayed into a bag, which is then held up to the face and the contents inhaled.

While most inhalers just get a nice buzz or high, inhaling can cause sudden extreme excitability, cardiac instability and arrest, and death. Hallucinations can also occur. It's a little too uncertain to use as a potential weapon for a fictional villain. However, it may be useful to the writer to set up a revenge motive or as an unintentional murder that sets one or more others into action.

AMPHETAMINE

OTHER: Methamphetamine, crystal meth.

FORM: Amphetamine is a white powder or a colorless liquid. Frequently taken orally in pill or capsule form, it can also be injected when in solution.

Methamphetamine is often injected and, as crystal meth, can also be smoked.

EFFECTS AND SYMPTOMS: Amphetamines stimulate the central nervous system and, with it, the sympathetic nervous system. Symptoms include insomnia, restlessness, tremors, palpitations, nausea, vomiting, diarrhea, anorexia, delirium, hallucinations, euphoria, nervousness, confusion, irritability, short temper, and depression. More severe reactions include cyanosis, sweating, convulsions, coma, and cerebral hemorrhage.

Chronic users often become paranoid and can develop hyperpyrexia (a sudden high fever). In addition, because their tolerance of the drug gets stronger with repeated use, they will require larger and larger doses to get high, which can lead to a fatal overdose.

REACTION TIME: An oral dose will start to take effect in thirty to sixty minutes, and will last four to twenty-four hours. An injected dose takes effect in only minutes.

ANTIDOTES AND TREATMENTS: Supportive care is given, with emphasis on slowing the racing heartbeat with diazepam or other drugs.

NOTES: This is a whole class of drugs, many of them available by prescription for a variety of therapeutic uses, including the treatment of narcolepsy and attention deficit disorder. And almost all of them are abused. Before laws limiting the amount of time truck drivers could be on the road, it was not an uncommon practice to take "go-fast" to stay awake and thus drive for longer periods of time.

Once popular for weight loss, amphetamines are seldom prescribed for it today, especially since the fen-phen debacle in the late 1990s, in which fenfluramine and dexfenfluramine were found to cause irreparable heart damage in some patients.

Methamphetamine is probably the best known amphetamine today. Thanks to the Internet, recipes for this substance abound. In fact, late in the winter of 2006, an alternative weekly newspaper in San Luis Obispo, California, created quite a ruckus by printing just such a recipe to show how easily one could be obtained. Unfortunately for people with nasal allergies, one of the principle ingredients is pseudoephedrine, an over-the-counter decongestant that has now gone back *behind* the counter to make it harder for people making meth to obtain the large quantities needed.

Addicts frequently become anorexic, and the appetite can remain suppressed for up to eight weeks after the drugs have been terminated. Amphetamines can be emotionally and physically addicting. If someone has hypertension, an overdose might cause a stroke and coma, leading to death.

Ecstasy, or MDMA, is an amphetamine derivative as well as a hallucinogen, and appears below.

Methamphetamine has become a major concern for bomb squads all over the country. Meth labs, the number of which is growing almost exponentially, pose a serious explosion threat, as many of the solvents used in the process are extremely volatile. Exposure to these toxins, as well as to heavy metals, is also a problem for meth makers and their family members.

COCAINE

OTHER: Methyl benzoylecgonine, benzoylmethylecgonine.

TOXICITY: 5

FORM: A colorless to white crystal, or a white or off-white powder, cocaine is a habit-forming alkaloid. Mixed with baking soda to make a paste, then dried, it becomes rock cocaine or crack, as it is known on the street. Crack resembles chunks of dirty rock candy.

Cocaine can be absorbed through the mucous membranes or skin abrasions, or be inhaled, ingested, injected, or smoked in the form of crack. Smoking cocaine through a liquid or mixed with ether is called freebasing, and this practice often causes fires when the mixture explodes from the heat.

EFFECTS AND SYMPTOMS: Cocaine first stimulates, then depresses the central nervous system.

Crack, injection, and freebasing produce the fastest, most intense highs.

The symptoms in an acute poisoning are hyperactivity, dilated pupils, hallucinations, fast heartbeat, abdominal pain, vomiting, numbness, and muscular spasms; in some cases, irregular respiration, convulsions, coma, and heart failure occur. Cocaine affects people differently. Addicts can be hyperactive or lethargic. They are prone to paranoia, weight loss, sniffles, and reddened noses.

Chronic symptoms include mental deterioration, confusion, hallucinations, psychotic and paranoid behavior, weight loss, severe character changes, and possible perforation of the nasal septum.

REACTION TIME: Smoking and injection cause a reaction within minutes, while ingestion can take longer. Coke snorted through the nose can also act quickly. Death from cardiac disturbances can happen within minutes, as can respiratory arrest.

ANTIDOTES AND TREATMENTS: Treatment focuses on controlling symptoms as they occur, particularly the agitation and cardiac problems. The drug Narcan, if given in time, can neutralize the cocaine.

NOTES: Once known as God's way of saying you have too much money, because it was so expensive, cocaine use has grown and spread throughout much of the economic spectrum. After alcohol, it is currently the most commonly abused drug in the U.S. It does have a medical use as a topical anesthetic, usually used in nasal surgeries. However, much of the coke out there today is in the form of crack. Cocaine is a derivative of the coca plant, native to South America, where huge drug cartels have wreaked havoc on the local populace.

No matter what its form, cocaine is extremely addictive.

For centuries, natives of the Andes Mountains in South American have chewed the leaves of the coca plant and used them to tell fortunes. Mixed with lime and chewed by the Peruvian Indians as early as the sixth century, it was an essential part of the Inca religion. Cocaine was thought to be a gift of Manco Capac, the royal son of the Sun God of Incan mythology.

Until 1903, cocaine was part of the "up" in Coca-Cola. Once the company became aware of the dangers of the drug, it substituted caffeine.

CASE HISTORY

Cocaine was the designer drug of the 1980s, and most of the best known cases are from then. The late comedian Richard Pryor set himself on fire while freebasing and was fortunate enough to survive the experience.

Body packers, or mules, put themselves at serious risk by swallowing rubber or plastic packets of cocaine to smuggle them into the U.S. The 2004 film *Maria, Full of Grace* tells the story of one such woman. Packets have been known to burst, thus seriously poisoning the person carrying them.

The small children of cocaine addicts are at serious risk of being poisoned as well, and cases of children who ate their addict parents' crack abound, including many fatalities.

In Janet Dailey's 1985 novel *The Glory Game,* about the fast-paced world of polo, the heroine's brother dies in an explosion caused while freebasing.

ECSTASY

OTHER: MDMA, the acronym for 3,4-methylenedioxymethamphetamine.

TOXICITY: Variable.

FORM: Although it is soluble in water and can be injected, it is almost always ingested as a tablet.

EFFECTS AND SYMPTOMS: Since ecstasy is an amphetamine, the symptoms are the same as for other amphetamines (listed above), but also include hallucinations and feelings of sexual arousal.

REACTION TIME: Fifteen to twenty minutes.

Supportive care is given, particularly for agitation and psychological effects.

NOTES: Ecstasy, or MDMA, is the drug associated with raves—extended, very large parties featuring loud music and exotic lighting. A derivative of methamphetamine, it has become popular not only because it can help ravers party all night, basically by keeping them awake, but because of its hallucinogenic effects, which supposedly enhance the experience. The exotic lighting at raves stimulates the nerves, causing them to go off rapidly and repeatedly. It is also sometimes considered a date rape drug, not so much because it knocks out the potential victim, but because it supposedly enhances sexual arousal, and females under the influence of ecstasy have been known to engage in sexual acts they otherwise would not have.

While the drug got its reputation as being a "safe" drug (that is, not likely to kill), numerous fatalities have dispelled that notion. The problem is in establishing a fatal dose, since it can kill at very low doses depending on a variety of very unpredictable factors. Ecstasy users are frequently tripping on other drugs at the same time, complicating matters in the emergency room.

Because ecstasy is usually homemade, as opposed to commercially available, the quality of the tablets is never guaranteed, and they are sometimes contaminated—another reason they can be so deadly.

ETHANOL

OTHER: Ethyl alcohol, grain alcohol, methyl carbinol.

TOXICITY: 3

FORM: Ethyl alcohol is found in a liquid or gaseous state and is used as a solvent, an antiseptic, a chemical intermediate—meaning it's not in certain products, but is used to help make them—and, most popularly, a beverage. It is also found in mouthwashes, perfumes, and flavoring extracts such as vanilla. In its pure state, ethanol is a clear, colorless, fragrant liquid with a burning taste. It is almost always ingested, but industrial vapors can intoxicate by inhalation.

EFFECTS AND SYMPTOMS: Alcohol depresses the central nervous system and can be used as an anesthetic, but the amount needed is perilously close to a fatal dose. Symptoms vary with the drinker and the amount consumed.

Someone mildly inebriated—or tipsy—may stumble slightly and experience a relaxation of inhibitions and slower-than-normal reaction times. Other symptoms are talkativeness, impaired judgment, and slight drowsiness.

Someone moderately inebriated shows increased symptoms and slightly slurred speech.

Large amounts of consumed alcohol will cause nausea, vomiting, dizziness, excessive sweating, difficulty breathing, ataxia, blurred or double vision, convulsions, unconsciousness, and coma. Death occurs when the drinker has consumed too much too fast. A quart of bourbon ingested over a twenty-four-hour period would metabolize and be eliminated by the body; the same amount consumed in less than two hours could induce coma and death.

Because ethanol can cause considerable nausea and vomiting, there is some risk of dehydration, which can lead to shock.

In industrial situations, where alcohol vapors are inhaled, irritation of the eyes and mucuous membranes is present, along with drowsiness and headache.

REACTION TIME: Fatalities occur when large amounts of alcohol are consumed within an hour or less. Otherwise, reaction times vary widely, even with experienced drinkers depending on whether there is food in the stomach, and how fast the alcohol is being consumed; even the weather can play a role. Neophytes are going to react much more quickly.

ANTIDOTES AND TREATMENTS: Treatment is for the symptoms as they occur. Glucose can be given to stop the shakes, and thiamine may be given to counteract dehydration.

NOTES: Ethanol is the fancy word for the type of alcohol that gives wine, beer, and spirits their kick. It results when yeasts consume the sugars in juice or grains and excrete them as alcohol, a process called fermenting. Spirits, such as whiskies, vodkas, and some brandies, are processed by the additional step of distilling. Though legal, ethanol is well known as a drug of abuse.

When we talk about wine or beer being deadly, it is usually as the result of alcoholism or someone getting behind the wheel of a car after drinking. However, as far too many fraternity parties have proven, drinking too much alcohol too quickly can bring on hallucinations, psychosis, coma, and death.

The tastes of various alcoholic beverages differ, from the harsh, burning taste of the cheapest rotgut to the delicate balance of a well-aged Bordeaux. It can be strong and almost syrupy-sweet, as are some cordials, or almost tasteless—premium vodkas are supposedly in this category. Colors vary as well, from the electric blues and greens of some liqueurs (a potential hazard for young children, who are attracted to the bright colors) to clear, to the deep, dark brown of a porter or other ale.

You may have seen the graphic showing that a twelve-ounce serving of beer, a six-ounce serving of wine, and a one-ounce shot of whisky all contain the same amount of alcohol. This is because the percentage of ethanol in beer, wine, and spirits is different. The alcohol content in beer and wine is measured by percentage, with most wines containing between 12 and 14 percent. (Some "hot" zinfandels will have as much as 15 percent alcohol.) The alcohol content of spirits is measured as a proof, which equates to approximately twice the percentage of the alcohol content. A 100-proof scotch contains 50 percent alcohol, while

200-proof indicates 100 percent alcohol. Everclear, a brand of almost pure grain alcohol, is 190 proof, or 95 percent alcohol. This potent brew is illegal to sell in many states.

Liquors can be mixed to disguise the potency and taste of the alcohol in a given cocktail, possibly misleading someone into thinking he is drinking something far less intoxicating, as anyone knows who has ever had trouble standing up after knocking back a Long Island iced tea. Putting a drug into mixed drinks (like a Long Island ice tea) is also one of the few ways drugs might be believably hidden in the alcohol. Some drinks contain drops of bitters, making them even more appropriate.

Alcohol is well known for increasing the effects of many drugs, particularly those with depressant side effects. Some of these chemical substances, such as barbiturates and carbon monoxide, produce the same drunken reaction as alcohol.

GHB

OTHER: Gamma hydroxybutyrate.

TOXICITY: 4

FORM: A white powder or clear liquid, it is ingested.

EFFECTS AND SYMPTOMS: GHB is a central nervous system depressant. Abrupt onset of sleep is the primary symptom, although respiratory distress, low blood pressure, slow heartbeat, coma, hallucinations, and seizures are also sometimes possible. All of these effects can be amplified when GHB is taken with alcohol or other depressants, or on an empty stomach. However, effects usually wear off within six hours at the longest.

REACTION TIME: Fifteen to twenty minutes.

ANTIDOTES AND TREATMENTS: Supportive care is given, with emphasis on maintaining the patient's airway and controlling any seizures.

NOTES: GHB, another popular rave drug, is mostly known as a date rape drug, because it quickly causes unconsciousness.

GHB is also used by body builders, because it supposedly releases growth hormones.

It is made in home labs, so purity cannot be guaranteed, and recipes can be found on the Internet.

HEROIN

OTHER: Diacetyl morphine, diamorphine.

TOXICITY: 6

FORM: Heroin is usually a white, odorless, bitter crystal or crystalline powder; however, the substance varies in color from brown to white, depending on where it has been processed. Mexican heroin tends to be brown, whereas Middle Eastern is white. It is sniffed, smoked, or injected.

EFFECTS AND SYMPTOMS: Heroin depresses the central nervous system, creating a feeling of euphoria.

If conscious, the victim of an overdose exhibits such symptoms as pinpoint pupils; slow, shallow respiration; disturbed vision restlessness; cramps in extremities; cyanosis; weak pulse; very low blood pressure; coma; and death from respiratory paralysis.

Heroin acts more on the respiratory system than morphine and codeine, making it more toxic. Though it would be recognizable in a blood analysis, heroin leaves no distinctive signs in the autopsy aside from possible scars—called tracks—left from frequent injection.

REACTION TIME: The victim will feel an immediate rush upon intravenous injection. In the case of an overdose from an intravenous injection, death occurs within minutes. If the drug is sniffed or injected subcutaneously, however, death may take anywhere from two to four hours.

ANTIDOTES AND TREATMENTS: Naloxone, a drug that binds up addictive drugs, is often given. Other treatment is symptomatic.

NOTES: This derivative of opium is highly addictive and highly toxic. One source suggests that heroin is responsible for up to 10,000 deaths per year; another counts just over 76,000 mentions of it in emergency department reports, nationwide, in 1995. The only street drug more common is cocaine, which is sometimes combined with heroin to make speedballs. Amphetamines are also used for this purpose.

There is no accepted medical use for heroin in the United States. Heroin, like cocaine, is frequently cut with other substances to make it go farther. Estimates vary, but a street dose may have anywhere from 20 to 60 percent heroin, the higher estimate reflecting concerns that street heroin is getting purer.

As with cocaine, heroin can be smuggled into the United States by body packers or mules. The packets are excreted once the mule has arrived in the U.S., but sometimes the packaging fails and the mule is subject to severe poisoning and often dies.

CASE HISTORY

Comic actor John Belushi died of a heroin overdose, as did rock singer Janis Joplin. Thomas Noguchi, M.D., chief medical examiner/coroner for the County of Los Angeles from 1967 to 1982, stated in his memoir that he believes these and many other heroin deaths resulted from unexpectedly pure heroin.

LSD

OTHER: Lysergic acid diethylamide, lysergide.

TOXICITY: 2

FORM: LSD is usually found as a clear liquid and can be injected or ingested. A common method of ingestion was LSD-soaked sugar cubes.

EFFECTS AND SYMPTOMS: LSD works on the brain, producing hallucinations. Scientists are not clear on how the drug works.

Besides hallucinations, symptoms may include extreme excitability, tremors, prolonged mental dissociation, exaggerated reflexes, psychopathic personality disorders, convulsions, and coma. There is an increased homicidal or suicidal risk.

Sometimes, high fever occurs that can cause complications resulting in death.

Habitual users report occurrences of flashback reactions, years after the last dose has been taken.

REACTION TIME: Within twenty minutes after ingestion.

ANTIDOTES AND TREATMENTS: Diazepam (Valium) usually controls the hyperactivity or convulsions. The coma is treated similar to a barbiturate coma.

NOTES: If any drug defines an era, LSD certainly defines the 1960s. Though it is still around, its use has greatly declined: Los Angeles County Coroner's toxicologist Daniel Anderson said he doesn't even test for it anymore. A synthetic derivative of ergot, it is considered a psychosis-inducing or hallucinogenic drug.

There are several other hallucinogens that react with similar symptoms and are treated the same way. They include marigold seeds; kava-kava; peyote and its derivative, mescaline; and nutmeg. Please note that the amount of nutmeg needed to cause these effects, while not huge, is going to make the baking taste extremely unpleasant.

CASE HISTORY

LSD flowed like water in Jacqueline Susann's *Once Is Not Enough*. The Beatles' song "Lucy in the Sky with Diamonds" is said to be about LSD, though the Beatles claim the inspiration was a drawing done by Julian Lennon of his classmate Lucy Richardson.

MARIJUANA

SCIENTIFIC NAME: *Cannibis sativa.*

OTHER: Cannabin resin, Indian hemp, Indian cannabis, hashish, guaza, marihuana.

TOXICITY: 3

FORM: Dried marijuana leaves can be mistaken for oregano. Marijuana is mostly smoked, but can also be baked into brownies or cookies for ingestion. It's possible to see the leaves and stems in the finished baked goods, although unsuspecting victims have been known to eat the goodies anyway.

Hashish, often called hash, is a concentrated resin from the plant's flower that is fried into a brownish black cake, or is sometimes found as an oil.

Both marijuana and hashish are smoked. Bongs (water pipes), bowls, and pipes are popular variations on the hand-rolled cigarettes, and used to be sold in a variety of "head shops." Nowadays, you can find them on eBay.

EFFECTS AND SYMPTOMS: Marijuana reacts in much the same way as LSD, often producing mild to severe hallucinations.

Symptoms also include widely dilated pupils, reddened eyes, euphoria, increased sensory awareness, hunger, lethargy, distorted depth perception, memory loss, slowness in thinking, uncontrolled laughter, drowsiness, weakness, stiffness, and loss of consciousness. While marijuana is not usually deadly, deaths can result from ingested overdoses or accidents occurring while the victim is under its influence. Heavy, chronic use usually takes its toll in psychological effects as increased anxiety, paranoia, and phobias. Users can also experience lung and other cancers and emphysema. It can also cause birth defects in a user's offspring.

REACTION TIME: Marijuana's effects start shortly after smoke is inhaled and last from ninety minutes to four hours. Ingested effects start within two hours, but last longer.

ANTIDOTES AND TREATMENTS: Treated symptomatically.

NOTES: Marijuana is considered psychologically addicting, with all of the problems associated with that. However, unlike a lot of street drugs, marijuana is getting some respect: Its active ingredient, THC, can help stop the eye pressure that comes with glaucoma, as well as ease the nausea of chemotherapy. It can also stimulate the appetite, and has been helpful combating the wasting-away syndrome caused by AIDS. Early American settlers called the plant loco weed, because animals that ate it reacted strangely.

CASE HISTORY

In May 2006, a prankster left a box of baked goods in a teacher's lounge at Lake Highlands High School in Richardson, Texas. The muffins, which were consumed by several staff members and teachers, had been laced with marijuana and possibly also an antihistamine. One staff member, who was over eighty years old, was hospitalized when she couldn't stop giggling.

California and nine other states legalized medical marijuana in 2000, but the laws were struck down in 2001 by the U.S. Supreme Court, which ruled that federal laws against giving marijuana to sick people trumped the states' laws.

OPIUM

SCIENTIFIC NAME: Papaver somniferum.

OTHER: Gum opium, poppy seed.

TOXICITY: 5

FORM: Opium is a gummy substance found in the fruit and juices of the opium poppy. Smoked or chewed, it can also be drunk. In liquid form, the syrup is usually thick and very sweet. Combined with other drugs, it becomes paregoric, laudanum, or other such medications.

EFFECTS AND SYMPTOMS: Opium depresses the central nervous system and causes symptoms similar to those of heroin and morphine, including euphoria; pinpoint pupils; slow, shallow respiration; very low blood pressure; cardiovascular irregularities; general unresponsiveness; deep coma; respiratory failure; and death.

REACTION TIME: Fatal reaction occurs two to four hours after ingestion or inhalation.

ANTIDOTES AND TREATMENTS: Similar to the treatment of any central nervous system depressant; vital signs must be maintained and monitored. Other treatment is symptomatic and naloxone is sometimes given.

NOTES: Opium is included here more for its popularity in the past—particularly in the nineteenth century—than for any prevalence on today's streets. Cultivated for centuries in China and other parts of Asia for its pain-killing and sleep-inducing effects, in modern times it became the source of all kinds of opiate or narcotic painkillers, including morphine, heroin, codeine, and hydrocodone.

Victorian-era use of the drug was especially heavy. Opium dens, smoky places where addicts lay about in a stupor, were romanticized or sensationalized in many novels of the time. Laudanum was used by Victorian- and Edwardian-era physicians in treating feminine "hysteria" and "the vapors."

Popular reforms in the early twentieth century resulted in the abolition of many patent medicines that contained opium. One of these, called Mother's Helper, turned countless children into opium addicts.

CASE HISTORY

Some critics speculate that *The Rime of the Ancient Mariner* and other works by Samuel Taylor Coleridge, a known user of opium, were the products of "poppy dreams." In any case, it is fairly certain that the drug contributed to the poet's death.

Lewis Carroll was said to be high on opium while creating his stories of Alice; the hookah, as smoked by the caterpillar, was traditionally used to smoke opium.

In Agatha Christie's *By the Pricking of My Thumbs*, one of the characters was drugged by morphine so she wouldn't tell what she knew.

Amelia Peabody Emerson makes a trip to an opium den in *The Deeds of the Disturber* by Elizabeth Peters.

In the film *The Last Emperor*, Emperor Pu Yi's wife became an opium addict.

In the book and film *The Joy Luck Club,* by Amy Tan, Auntie An-Mei's unnamed mother killed herself with poison-filled sweet dumplings, "the kind used to celebrate," as the book describes them. An-Mei tells the story in the book, and she claims that the dumplings contained a bitter poison and not the opium the adults around her were saying was in the dumplings. But in the film, An-Mei says it was opium in the dumplings.

PHENCYCLIDINE (PCP)

OTHER: Ketamine, sernyl.

TOXICITY: 5

FORM: PCP is most frequently found as crystals or granules. PCP can be ingested, smoked, or snorted, and occasionally is injected intravenously. The powder form is usually the purest.

EFFECTS AND SYMPTOMS: PCP and ketamine are dissociative anesthetics, which means they inhibit the sensation of pain without affecting the victim's ability to breathe.

Both drugs cause lethargy, euphoria, hypertension, racing heartbeat, hallucinations, and swings between quiet spaciness and loudly violent behavior. The eyes spasm vertically and horizontally, and the victim feels little to no pain. Excessive salivation and tearing can happen. With higher doses, psychosis, respiratory failure, rigidity, pulmonary edema, convulsions, and coma are possible.

REACTION TIME: Fairly rapid, especially if smoked.

ANTIDOTES AND TREATMENTS: Symptoms are treated as they occur.

NOTES: These two hallucinogenic drugs are listed here together because they are chemically very similar, and react and are treated in much the same way. Even though PCP is highly toxic, it is seldom consumed in fatal doses. If anything, people are far more likely to die from what they do while under the influence of PCP and ketamine than they are from the drugs themselves.

As an analgesic and a short-acting intravenous anesthetic agent, PCP was first developed in the 1950s. The side effects were found to be so toxic in humans that the drug was switched over to veterinary purposes under the trade name of Sernyl or Sernylan.

PCP became popular as a street drug in the late 1960s and soon was mixed with LSD, psilocybin, or mescaline. PCP is sprinkled onto parsley or marijuana for recreational smoking. Mixing these drugs with amphetamines and other substances can not only produce deadly effects, it can seriously complicate diagnosis and treatment.

Ketamine is found on veterinary shelves and is easily obtainable. It is one of the many date rape drugs that disappear quickly from the body. Symptoms can persist over several days, as the drug excretes itself into the stomach and is reabsorbed through the intestines.

PCP gives the user a sense of being bigger and stronger, and those under its influence have done things ranging from bizarre to horrific.

ROHYPNOL

OTHER: Flunitrazepam

TOXICITY: 4to 5, depending on the tolerance of the victim.

FORM: While it is available as a liquid for injecting, it is most commonly found as a white tablet.

EFFECTS AND SYMPTOMS: A central nervous system depressant; the basic symptoms are drowsiness, slurred speech, and unconsciousness.

Other possible symptoms are difficulty breathing, stumbling, headache, coma, amnesia, and sometimes hallucinations. Collapse from cardiac disturbances is possible with extreme overdose.

REACTION TIME: Onset happens in twenty minutes, with the sedation lasting about eight to twelve hours.

ANTIDOTES AND TREATMENTS: Activated charcoal can be given.

NOTES: Rohypnol is an ultra-fast-acting sedative, one of the reasons it has become popular as a date rape drug. But abusers also reportedly use it to increase the euphoric effects of heroin and to counteract the hard crash following a cocaine binge. Users can also develop a tolerance to the drug, meaning that it takes more to get high, thus creating the possibility of a life-threatening overdose.

CHAPTER 12

BIOLOGICAL, CHEMICAL, AND
RADIOLOGICAL WEAPONS

"What is the potential casualty of this?"

"Sixty or seventy."

"That's not so bad."

"Thousand. Sixty or seventy thousand. One small drop of this on the ground is lethal up to a hundred feet. One teaspoon of this shit in the air will kill every living thing in an eight-block radius."

The Rock, 1996

This chapter deals with two very different types of poisonous weapons that have potential for mass destruction: biological and chemical weapons. It also touches on a third type of poisonous weapon: radiological.

Biological weapons use toxins from microorganisms, such as viruses or bacteria, to injure or incapacitate people.

Chemical weapons, such as the poison gases used in World War I, use noxious chemical properties to poison victims.

A radiological, or nuclear, weapon is defined as any weapon using a radioactive or radiation-emitting source as the primary source of destruction. The other way a radiological weapon may be used is by exposing a person to radiation or contaminating an object or area, rendering it useless or dangerous.

The most effective dosing, delivery, release characteristics, and environmental conditions for these weapons have been perfected by the military, even if they are not frequently used. In fact, the Geneva Conventions forbid this type of warfare, but that doesn't mean the weapons and technology don't exist, since you must be a signer of the Geneva agreements to be held accountable.

BIOLOGICAL AGENTS

These include some things we have already mentioned, such as poison darts and arrows, but this category includes more than just poison.

Biological agents are weaponized diseases and toxins created by living organisms. Surprisingly, they've been used since ancient times.

Odorless, tasteless, and invisible to the naked eye, they can be disseminated easily. There is also potential for a greater toxicity than with chemical weapons.

With very few exceptions, there is a time delay between exposure to the bio-agent and the onset of symptoms: usually days or weeks, but never less than several hours. If the chosen attack takes place during flu season, it might be some time before the authorities realize the problem is more than just a bad flu.

It is important to note that diseases are treated: biological toxins have antidotes.

ANTHRAX

SCIENTIFIC NAME: *Bacillus anthracis* (from *anthrakos*—the Greek word meaning "coal"—which describes the color of the skin lesions).

TOXICITY: 6

FORM: Anthrax can manifest itself in two distinct forms. It can be inhaled and cause lung problems, or it can appear on the skin. Both manifestations are caused by the same bacteria.

Anthrax is spread by spores of the bacteria, which are resistant to environmental stressors. These activate once they come in contact with the right environmental surface of the body (e.g., the lungs). They then reproduce in the body, causing the disease. Once anthrax spores are inhaled, are ingested, or settle on the skin, they germinate in the lymph nodes (between the heart and the lungs) and from there cause hemorrhages and infection in the lung cavity. Airborne deployment will cause the most casualties, through inhalation.

Spores can be freeze dried, purified, and made into a powder.

Found in the soil worldwide, anthrax orginates where animals graze but is rare in the United States as a disease. The affliction was first called woolsorters' disease because it was found primarily as an occupational disease for those working with sheep, cattle, and other animals.

The most effective method of dispersion is through aerosolized spores spread through contact with individuals.

The other form of the disease is cutaneous; anthrax spores enter through any break or lesion in the skin. It may progress slightly differently but has the same end result.

EFFECTS AND SYMPTOMS: The symptoms of anthrax inhalation are a two- to six-day incubation period, followed by fever, muscular pain, abdominal or chest pain, cough, fatigue, and flu-like symptoms. The victim may then improve, only to have a rapid onset of respiratory distress, shock, cyanosis, and stridor (the sound made by air flow that is restricted in the respiratory tract). There is a 90 percent mortality rate at this point, even with treatment.

Chest X-ray will show ill-defined nodules and shadows (infiltrates) and increased liquid in the lung cavity (pulmonary effusion), which causes extreme shortness of breath. Fifty percent of victims develop bleeding into the brain.

Inhaled anthrax is not considered contagious, as no transmission of inhalation anthrax has ever been documented. Spores are inhaled, but the bacteria cause the disease. Patients are kept in reverse isolation to protect them as they are more susceptible to other infections, like pneumonia.

Cutaneous anthrax, on the other hand, can be transmitted through open wounds, so gloves and masks are necessary.

Bacteria produce more spores once they hit the body. Spores must be active before antibiotics can work on them. The infection is persistent and treatment is often prolonged.

REACTION TIME: Symptoms start within twenty-four hours but usually take several days to become full-blown.

Spores can remain dormant for years, but once they hit a favorable environment they start to produce symptoms. (If the spores are sprayed over a wide area and hit water, someone who bathes in the water may become infected.)

ANTIDOTES AND TREATMENTS: The victim of anthrax should be isolated (masks, gowns, washing hands to keep the infection from getting out) until decontamination. Inhalation anthrax patients should be in reverse isolation (even after decontamination to keep the victim from catching anything else), since secondary infections, like pneumonia, are a risk.

In the case of the direct aerosol attack, simple removal of clothing eliminates much surface contamination. Showering with soap and water removes 99.9 percent of the few organisms left on the skin after disrobing. Most biological agents do not penetrate *unbroken* skin, but a few usually adhere to skin or clothing. Clothing should be placed in triple plastic bags. A 1:10 dilution of household bleach may be used on surfaces not cleaned with soap and water. Nevertheless, spores do find places to hide.

Inhalation anthrax is difficult to treat once symptoms begin. Immediate antibiotics are the principal strategy (ciprofloxacin is the most common choice, but recently approved are doxycyline and penicillin). Often there is a period of improvement at thirty-six to forty-eight hours, but it does not necessarily mean the patient is getting better. Treatment is continued for sixty days, because many times the spores, which might cling to unknown pockets of the skin, can remain dormant outside the body, only to become active again months after exposure, once they are inhaled or find a break in the skin (in which it becomes cutaneous anthrax).

In case of cutaneous anthrax, a thorough cleaning of the body and clothes (above) as is recommended above. The spores can hide and go dormant.

Progressive respiratory insufficiency (breathing problems) will require ventilation. Patients are often placed in the ICU for monitoring and management of septic and hemorrhagic shock, which is characteristic of the terminal stage of anthrax infection.

NOTES: Anthrax is classified by the CDC as Category A, a potential bioterrorism agent that poses the greatest possible threat for public health, may spread across a large area or need public awareness, and needs a great deal of planning to protect the public's health. (Also in this category are smallpox, plague, botulism, tularemia, filoviruses as Ebola.)

A cluster of cases would indicate a mass release of the anthrax spores rather than an isolated incident.

CASE HISTORY

Known for centuries, anthrax was not really used as a weapon until World War I, when the Germans used it and glanders (an infectious disease for livestock that does not affect humans) among allied livestock and draft animals.

British tested anthrax on Gruinard Island in 1942, and the Japanese used it in Manchuria.

In 1979, in Sverdlovsk (the Soviet city roughly 850 miles east of Moscow, now called Ekaterinburg), anthrax was accidentally released into the air from a Soviet biological warfare research facility.

Before the Persian Gulf War, Iraq admitted to having 125,000 gallons of a biological agent that included anthrax, aflatoxin B, and botulinum toxin in over two hundred missiles and bombs.

The late 1990s saw the anthrax letter scare (letters mailed that contained anthrax spores and powders) spread throughout the country. In reality, only a few people were exposed.

The 1991 Gulf War marked Iraq's active biological weapons program.

In 2001, terrorists threatened more mass anthrax exposures.

BOTULISM TOXIN

SCIENTIFIC NAME: Clostridium botulinum.

TOXICITY: 6

FORM: The culprit is the toxin and not the bacteria itself (the spore turns into the bacteria, and the bacteria releases the toxin).There are several forms of botulism, the most common of which is food poisoning, followed by wound poisoning, infantile, and, lastly, overdose of Botox injections.

A neurotoxin, it is fifteen thousand times more potent than the nerve agent VX. It takes very little to kill—.7mmg (micromilligrams μ) of toxin to 10mg of nerve agent VX.

EFFECTS AND SYMPTOMS: All forms have the same clinical features, including cranial nerve palsies (diplopia, ptosis, dysphonia, dysphagia), dry mouth, and blurred vision. Symmetric, descending paralysis ends with death from respiratory failure (suffocation). It is the paralysis, in minute amounts, that creates Botox's popularity as a wrinkle remover.

Patients with cranial nerve palsies and sore, dry throats may have a mild version of the toxin. Even minor paralysis needs to be noted. Preexisting breathing problems could become worse.

REACTION TIME: Dependent on whether the toxin is ingested or injected. If the toxin is injected, reaction time is almost immediate. If it is ingested, symptoms will occur within an hour.

ANTIDOTES AND TREATMENT: If foods are heated to 212 degrees Fahrenheit and boiled for at least ten minutes, the toxin will be destroyed, as it is sensitive to heat and breaks down. Antibiotics do not work, because it is a toxin. Horse serum made from infected horses may halt progression, but does not reverse the disease. (This is not recommended in infants.)

Antitoxin ABE blocks the action of the toxin in the blood stream. This will only work if diagnosed early—seventy-two hours after exposure, it might not work. Since breathing and respiratory reflexes are impaired, supportive treatment may require intubation.

Other than antitoxin, treatment is supportive care, along with nasogastric tube feeding to stimulate peristalsis (movement of the digestive tract) and cathartic agents, both of which remove the toxin from the gastrointestinal tract.

Recovery takes many weeks, even with antitoxin.

NOTES: It is unlikely that botulism would be a biological weapon of choice because it would be difficult to actually contaminate the food, and the source would likely be discovered before too many people were affected. (also chapter four, page 37.)

PLAGUE

SCIENTIFIC NAME: *Yersinia pestis.*

OTHER: Black death.

TOXICITY: 6

FORM: Spread by fleas riding on rodents, especially rats, the bacteria comes in three major types: bubonic (affecting the lymph nodes, and the most common), pneumonic (affecting the lungs), and septicemic (affecting the blood).

EFFECTS AND SYMPTOMS: Bubonic plague is carried exclusively by fleas, and even a single flea bite can be deadly. Swelling of a lymph gland called the buboe is the classic sign, in addition to a high fever with chills, muscle aches, severe headaches, seizures, and general malaise, which occur two to five days after exposure. Most of the swellings appear first in the groin but then move to the armpits or neck. The area is painful before the swelling occurs.

Neither this version nor the septicemia plague is communicable.

If left untreated, the bacteria become systemic and invade the blood stream. Septic shock will be present in most cases. Fourteen percent of all plague cases in the U.S. are fatal.

Native Americans, hunters, miners, or tourists are the ones usually infected. Whole households become ill when domestic animals (especially cats) bring in fleas. Houses with guinea pigs or pet rats are especially at risk.

Pestis pneumonica, or pneumonic plague, occurs when the lungs are infected and is easily spread by coughing. Often it comes as a secondary infection to the bubonic version. With this variety, symptoms start quickly—within hours after exposure—and include frothy bloody sputum and severe cough with difficulty breathing. Hospitalized patients require forty-eight hours of strict isolation or until the pus is gone. A victim who survives these forty-eight hours, will likely get well.

The last variety, septicemic plague (pestis septichaemica) can combine with either of the two since it is a systemic infection caused when the bacteria *yersinia pestis* multiplies in the blood. Those who come down with it are often hunters. Symptoms include extreme fatigue, low blood pressure, nausea, vomiting, and abdominal pain. Many (sometimes all) of the organ systems fail, and it can kill in a matter of hours.

REACTION TIME: Variable, depending on the type of plague. Symptoms from bubonic plague take two to five days; symptoms from pneumonic plague begin within hours; and septicemic plague can cause death within hours.

ANTIDOTES AND TREATMENTS: Immediate treatment is essential. If massive antibiotics are not given within twenty-four hours, death will be unavoidable. Since kidney failure is one of the crucial signs, the amount of fluid that a victim takes in and gives out is closely observed, as is the cardiac status.

Anyone who has been in contact with the victim needs preventive antibiotics, as well. All clothing needs to be incinerated.

NOTES: Plague is a potential biohazard to lab personnel when attempting to culture the organism. The specimen must be handled in a biosafety cabinet.

CASE HISTORY

History records three pandemics of the Black Death, the most deadly in the 1300s in Eurasia. From 1344 to 1346, the Tartars catapulted plague-ridden corpses over the city walls of Kaffa (Crimea, Russia) to infect the opponent. In 1710, Russians did the same to Swedish-held Estonia.

In the late 1930s, the Japanese learned to infect fleas with plague, and created five hundred plague deaths in their Chinese victims. In World War II, Unit 731 (a secret military medical unit of the Imperial Japanese Army) performed numerous experiments on prisoners, using plague and other biological weapons.

From 1995 to 1998 there were annual outbreaks of bubonic plague in Mahajanga, Madagascar, and it remains a severe problem today, with outbreaks continuing to come at regular intervals.

RICIN

A poison made from the byproducts of castor beans. Accidental exposure is unlikely. (See chapter five, page 69.)

SMALLPOX

SCIENTIFIC NAME: *Variola* virus.

OTHER: Fulminating smallpox, variola hemorrhagica.

TOXICITY: 6

FORM: Virus; hemorrhagic small pox is a severe and frequently fatal form of smallpox.

EFFECTS AND SYMPTOMS: While the flu-like symptoms might initially cause victims to use OTC drugs, the severity of the illness will often drive them to seek treatment immediately.

The disease is accompanied by extravasation of blood as the capillaries break and blood flows into the tissues of the skin. This causes the small swellings early on, or the pustules at a later stage. Often these are accompanied by nosebleed and hemorrhage from other orifices of the body, like the eyes, mouth, anus, etc.

Easily weaponized, it is effective in causing disease in a minimum of 30 percent of the population hit. It is also highly transmittable. Secondary and tertiary infections like pneumonia are likely. There is a 75 percent fatality rate, depending on when it is diagnosed.

REACTION TIME: There is a ten- to fourteen-day gestation period from the time of exposure.

ANTIDOTES AND TREATMENTS: Once the disease is manifested fully, only supportive treatment is available. Sometimes doctors will attempt to treat with an experimental drug, cidofovir, which at this writing is only approved in cases of lethal epidemics.

Vaccination is the mainstay of prevention and can be given within three days of exposure to prevent or significantly modify the appearance of the disease. If not done until the fourth day, there might be some modification of the disease process, but it will still occur. Supportive care is the primary treatment: hydration therapy for fluid loss through the fever and skin breakdowns.

Patients with smallpox must be isolated immediately: One infected patient can create twenty or more cases during the infectious stage. If a person has been exposed but no infection or symptoms are seen, then a strict, seventeen-day quarantine period is required. Those with whom the patient has been in contact during the past seventeen days also must be monitored. This means strict body fluid, blood, and droplet protection.

The major toxicity with treatment is renal impairment.

NOTES: There are only two known smallpox repositories—the CDC in Atlanta and Vector lab in Russia. Both scheduled the virus for destruction in 1999, but retained their supply because of the risk of bioterrorism.

Smallpox is the only disease to have been totally eliminated from the face of the earth. There have been no reported cases since 1976, which is why the vaccine is no longer routinely required for travel even to third world countries. Only two sources of infection are possible: a military or bioterrorist attack, or accidental exposure at one of the two repository sites.

Individuals who were inoculated against smallpox were thought to be protected for life; however, it is now believed that the protection drops off sharply after twenty years.

Children and the elderly, because of their weaker immune systems, are the most susceptible, but anyone with compromised immunity, such as HIV or chemotherapy patients or pregnant women, will have high mortality rates.

The CDC has contracted with several pharmaceutical laboratories to produce more vaccine from cell line cultures, estimated to be available sometime in 2008.

CASE HISTORY

During the British rule of America, English soldiers gave smallpox-infected blankets to the Native Americans during Pontiac's Rebellion. Half the tribal population, which had had no previous exposure to the disease, soon died.

TULAREMIA

SCIENTIFIC NAME: *Francisella tularensis.*

TOXICITY: 6

FORM: A rare disease shared by animals and humans, it is a serious bacterial pathogen and highly contagious between animals and humans, but not between humans and other humans. It is transmitted by flea and tick bites. Most cases occur in the south central and western United States. Nearly all cases occur in rural areas from handling infected rodents (rabbits) or from inhaling airborne bacteria. As few as ten organisms can cause the disease.

There are two types of the disease: ulceroglandular, naturally occurring and often found when skinning rabbits; and typhoidal, a pulmonary syndrome spread through the air.

EFFECTS AND SYMPTOMS: Signs depend on how the victim is exposed. Possible signs include skin ulcers, swollen and painful lymph glands, inflamed eyes, sore thoat, mouth sores, diarrhea, or pneumonia. If the bacteria are inhaled, symptoms can include abrupt onset of fever and chills, headache, muscle ache, joint pain, dry cough, and progressive weakness. People with pneumonia develop chest pain, difficulty breathing, bloody sputum, and respiratory failure. The often life-threatening complications include acute respiratory distress, meningitis, and peritonitis.

It takes from three to five days for symptoms to appear but can take as long as fourteen.

Persons with the typhoidal form are at particular risk and have a poorer prognosis.

REACTION TIME: Anywhere from four to fourteen days from exposure.

ANTIDOTES AND TREATMENTS: Treatment with doxycycline and ciprofloxacin should be started even before the lab results of the blood come back. The lab must be informed of a possibility of disease so that they can take precautions in handling the blood.

The patient is often placed in respiratory isolation until the possibility of pneumonic plague, which is transmittable and has similar symptoms, is ruled out.

NOTES: Multiple cases of tularemia over a short period of time should immediately make authorities consider bioterrorism, as this is rare. There are about two hundred cases each year in the U.S.

A history of antibiotic failure is important in the differential diagnosis of tularemia; e.g., a presumed strep throat that fails to improve with penicillin within a short time might be oropharyngeal tularemia. For this reason an antibiotic sensitivity test should be made.

If used as a blowweapon, the bacteria would be airborne so that it could be inhaled, which can cause pneumonia.

The bacteria can remain alive for weeks in the soil and water and thus infect anyone in the immediate area.

A vaccine was used in the past to protect lab workers, but it is not currently available.

CASE HISTORY

In 2001, the threat of bioterrorism and a naturally occurring outbreak of tularemia in New England was caused by the death of a housepainter. It heightened the public awareness of this disease in areas where it was not usually found.

VIRAL HEMORRHAGIC FEVER (VHF)

OTHER: Yellow fever, dengue HF, Rift Valley fever, Crimean-Congo HF, Kyasanur Forest disease, Omsk HF, Hantaan virus/hantavirus, Junin virus, Muchupo virus, Lassa fever, Marburg virus, and Ebola virus.

TOXICTY: 6

FORM: Virus; an acute condition with multiple organ involvement, VHF is spread primarily through direct or indirect contact with blood and body fluids from infected individuals, or in some cases by insect bite. Airborne infections have been observed in animal experiments, but not from human to human.

EFFECTS AND SYMPTOMS: Early symptoms include a prominent cough, vomiting, diarrhea, and hemorrhaging from body orifices. Precautions must be taken to avoid the airborne particles of the virus.

Acute blood abnormalities consistent with VHF are leukopenia, neutropenia, thrombocytopenia, decreased clotting factors, and albuminuria.

REACTION TIME: Forty-eight to seventy-two hours.

ANTIDOTES AND TREATMENTS: Anyone with suspected VHF should be isolated immediately and given supportive care (often those suspecting an illness will first try OTC treatment before admitting their disease is serious). Those entering the isolation room should wear personal protective respirators; all environmental surfaces or inanimate objects should be disinfected using a bleach/water solution. Medical waste such as contaminated needles, syringes, and tubing must be incinerated or immersed in chemical germicides.

Supportive care includes maintaining oxygen status, blood pressure, and fluid and electrolyte balance, and treating any complicating infections.

Ribavirin is one of the first choices for suspected cases of VHF. It has been found to be effective against most of the variations, including Lassa virus and Congo-Crimean,

Argentine, and Bolivian hemorrhagic fever, but does not seem to touch the filoviruses such as Ebola, Marburg, yellow fever, or West Nile virus.

Persons with any exposure, even with unbroken skin, must wash with soap and water very carefully. Mucous membranes (such as the conjunctiva of the eye) should be washed out with copious amounts of water or eyewash solution. These diseases are often fatal, and anyone with exposure must be watched carefully for the spreading of the illness.

A Lassa virus vaccine is being developed at the time of this writing. Yellow fever vaccine is readily available and effective; it is recommended for travelers in areas where the disease is found, but is not recommended for individuals allergic to eggs, since it is grown in eggs. RVF and Hantaan (HFRS) vaccine is also available.

CASE STUDIES

A vaccine for Ebola was recently tested on primates, but not yet on humans. In 1995, eight Ebola patients in Zaire received blood transfusions from Ebola survivors, and seven survived. However, there is no clear evidence linking their survival to this therapy.

CHEMICAL AGENTS

Toxic chemical agents are chemicals deployed by those desiring to produce mass casualty and terror. Many of them (sarin, VX, mustard gas) were designed specifically by the military for just this purpose. Others (chlorine, phosgene, cyanide, ammonia) are routinely used in industrial processes. There are five classes of modern chemical weapons recognized by the U.S. Army: nerve agents, blistering agents (vesicants), cyanide, pulmonary agents, and riot control agents.

Early history shows chemicals being used defensively as smoke clouds. The Chinese created noxious arsenic smoke as early as 1000 BCE as they fought the Japanese. In 423 BCE, the Spartans created sulfur dioxide by burning coal, sulfur, and pitch, and directed the clouds into the Athenian forces during the Peloponnesian Wars.

In the late fifteenth century, Leonardo da Vinci suggested the dispersal of sulfide of arsenic and verdigris (copper acetates) against invading ships.

It was not until April 1915 that the Germans launched the first large-scale use of a chemical agent in war by releasing 150 tons of chlorine gas against French and Canadian troops. That sparked further chemical attacks, and by the end of the war, 25 percent of all artillery shells contained chemical agents of some kind.

During World War I, Great Britain preferred chlorine gas, France used cyanide and cyanogen chloride, and Germany topped the list with chlorine, phosgene, diphosgene, mustard, and chloropicrin. The Geneva Protocol of 1925 condemned the use of chemical agents; nevertheless many countries continued to research and stockpile them.

No toxic chemical agents were confirmed to have been used in World War II against military combatants; however, Germany used poison gases, such as Zyklon B, against its civilian population. Several chemical agents were developed before World War II, including sarin, soman mustard, tabun, Lewisite, phosgene, hydrogen cyanide, and cytogen cyanide.

VX was synthesized in the 1950s during the Cold War.

In 1967, during the Yemen Civil War (1963–1967) Egypt dropped mustard gas and nerve agent bombs on the villages of North Yemen, killing five hundred people. Chemical agents were used again in the Iran-Iraq war (1980–1988): Iraq tested its chemical weapons by dropping sarin gas on its Kurdish nationals. At the end of the 1991 Gulf War, Iraq reportedly had stockpiles of mustard, sarin, and tabun. Around this time, the United States and Russia began destroying their chemical agents.

In 2002, the Russians used an unnamed gas on a group of Chechen terrorists holding schoolchildren in a school auditorium to effect their rescue.

Chemical weapons can be delivered by skin contact, ingestion, or inhalation (aerosol or vapor). The use of aerosols or vapors is dependent on weather conditions and a closed space is preferred for their deployment.

If the attack is to be outside, chemical agents that are heavier than air must be used; wind must be light and its direction closely monitored.

Aerosols work best, as they are heaver than air, can be inhaled while airborne, and can contaminate the ground, foodstuffs, and any other items they come in contact with (bodies, clothes). They can vaporize at specific temperatures and cause injury and death miles from the original attack site. Most mass casualty created by chemical weapon exposure will come from inhalation. Even those deploying the agent can be at risk, however, if there is a change in wind direction, or the chemical agent is handled by untrained personnel.

When a chemical agent is suspected, the following immediate action is required.

1. Use protective equipment, such as a gas mask, if available. If the victim has any warning and has good personal protective equipment (PPE), their chances of exposure are far less.
2. Leave the area immediately in an upwind direction.
3. Go to high ground—remember, most agents are heaver than air and will sink.
4. Seek immediate medical treatment.

Not all exposure to chemical agents are military- or terrorist-related; in fact, most are caused by industrial accidents, such as train derailments, chemical spills, oil refinery fires, or the improper mixing of household cleaners.

Most chemical weapons do not degrade by sunlight, heat, or moisture as rapidly as can biological weapons.

Vesicants

These agents produce skin and mucous membrane irritation, blistering, and then necrosis.

LEWISITE

An arsenic-based vesicant with an odor of geranium, it was developed at the end of World War I but never used as a weapon. Difficult to make and very unstable, it is no longer being produced as a weapon, though is still is used as a heavy metal chelator. It is immediately painful on contact. The British developed an antidote called BAL (British Anti-Lewisite) .

SULFUR MUSTARD

A colorless to pale yellow oily liquid, this potent alkylating agent has a mustardy or garlicky odor. Decontamination (usually with a household bleach/water solution) must be immediate to avoid irreversible damage.

There is no real antidote, and the care is supportive and symptomatic to avoid secondary infection, since the skin breaks open when the blisters burst. Antibiotics have no effect; their only use would be to help prevent secondary infections.

Cyanides

Relatively ineffective in warfare, cyanide is an all-or-nothing weapon—you either recover quickly or die. In a gaseous form, hydrogen cyanide is used for executions in some states. Prussic acid is also used for assassinations, as it mimics heart attacks when inhaled.

It works better in enclosed spaces, since it is difficult to achieve an air concentration high enough to make it deadly. It works by depriving the cells of oxygen, even in a normally oxygenated room. (See chapter three, Classic Poisons.)

Pulmonary Agents

CHLORINE

Chlorine (Cl). a greenish gas with a pungent odor, was the first mass-casualty chemical agent used in World War I. The gas can be made easily by mixing household cleaning products—as any housewife knows, if she makes the mistake of mixing chlorine bleach with tile cleaner.

In high concentrations, inhalation immediately causes mucous membrane irritation, burning eyes, cough, and difficulty breathing; pulmonary edema can take hours to days to develop depending on exposure time and concentration. If the concentration is high, pulmonary edema will develop in a few hours. The individual dies by drowning in his own body fluids.

It can be deployed using rockets, artillery shells, and aerial bombardment.

PHOSGENE

Phosgene is used extensively in industry. Alone, it was responsible for 80 percent of the chemical weapon deaths in World War I, where it was deployed in artillery shells.

The gas has an odor of musty hay or newly cut corn or grass. It is not immediately irritating, but the victim needs to be evaluated for delayed pulmonary edema.

Phosgene gas is also used in small amounts as a ripening agent for fruit; it turns tomatoes and strawberries red. By the time you get the fruit, however, the poison has dissipated and is not harmful to you.

(See also chapter ten, Industrial Poisons.)

Nerve Agents

Nerve agents act similarly, so the general information below applies to all of them. Information specific to each agent is listed with the agent.

Most nerve agents are initially liquid that subsequently evaporates and becomes gases and vapors. They can be inhaled, ingested, or placed on skin. The LD_{50} (median lethal dose, or dose of a poison that will kill 50 percent of those exposed) is given in milligrams (mg) for a person weighing one hundred forty pounds.

G-type nerve agents (GA, GB, and GD) are clear, colorless liquids that are volatile at ambient temperature. They mix in water and most organic solvents, and evaporate at the same rate as water.

The odor, when there is one, does not provide adequate warning time.

Vapors of all four known nerve agents, which the military calls G type agents, are heavier than air, which means that those who fall to the ground—for example, with seizures—will have greater exposure than those who remain upright. Vapors are not absorbed through the skin except at very high concentration.

First synthesized by Gerhard Schrader in pre-WWII Germany, potent organophosphates work in the same way as pesticides: by interfering with normal neurotransmission and inhibiting acetylcholinesterase. That is, they prevent the proper operation of the chemical that acts as the off switch for the muscles and nerve cells. Without this off switch, the muscles are constantly being stimulated, causing convulsions. When they tire, they are no longer able to sustain breathing.

For the purposes of this book, the nerve agents are the ones to concentrate on. All the nerve agents are for military or paramilitary use only. There is no use for them in ordinary life. So, to access them, someone has to have military connections or clearance.

Since the nerve agents are water soluble, they are likely to require fewer days in ICU with respiratory support, as they are eliminated from the body faster than insecticides, which are lipid soluble.

Effects and symptoms are much the same for all the agents. The severity depends on which gas was used, density of the vapor or liquid, and length of exposure. Muscle spasms, followed by flaccid muscle paralysis, are classic symptoms.

Nerve agents are readily absorbed by eye contact and inhalation, and produce rapid, systemic effects. The liquid is absorbed through the skin, but it may take several minutes for effects to appear.

In severe attacks, the central nervous system collapses, causing violent seizures, confusion, and coma. Airway ventilation is compromised; therefore nerve agent casualties are most likely to die of convulsions (it is possible to convulse so violently that you bite through your tongue and break your back and neck) and respiratory distress. Rhinorrhea (runny nose) and tightness in the throat begin within seconds to minutes after exposure.

Nerve agent-induced status epilepticus (constant seizures without stop) does not resemble other forms of status epilepticus in its response—or lack of response—to anticonvulsant medications. Since the nerve-agent poison is considered multicentric, meaning it works in more than one arena, the drugs that work by dampening the spread of seizure discharges are not effective.

Only benzodiazepines such as Valium are effective with nerve agent seizures; therefore, 10mg autoinjectors of diazepam (Valium), called Convulsive Antidote for Nerve Agent (CANA), are given to any soldiers who may come in contact with this weapon. Also, atropine, if given *immediately,* can sometimes help. The initial dose, if severely poisoned, is 6mg. Many people have been saved with the use of atropine alone and have used as much as 50 to 100mg at once for a severe exposure. Another medication that has been used is 2-PAMCl (also known as pralidoxime chloride).

First responders must be appropriately attired before entering a contaminated area. Chemical protective clothing and butyl rubber gloves are required when skin contact is possible; pressure-demand self-contained breathing apparatus (SCBA gear) is recommended. If the responders have not been trained in special techniques for rescue of nerve agent victims, they may become victims themselves if they go in. Emergency guidelines are found with local HAZMAT teams and mutual aid partners and the closest metropolitan strike system (MMRS).

Removing the victim from the source of exposure is critical. Persons whose skin or clothing is contaminated with nerve agent can expose rescuers by direct contact or through vapors. Skin exposed to only nerve agent vapor poses no risk for secondary contamination. Clothing, however, can trap vapor, and all clothing must be removed and isolated. Before being transferred, all casualties must be decontaminated.

Survivors of nerve agent poisoning, unlike those of other chemical or biological poisoning, can return to healthy lives.

Research is still underway in the defense community to develop an antidote for nerve agent toxins.

Disease or problems that might mimic nerve agent poisoning include gastroenteritis; ingestion of muscarinic mushrooms (amanita, clytocybe, and inocybe; see chapter six, Fragile Fungi); pesticide poisoning (see chapter nine, Pesticides); carbamate overdose (medication used for myasthenia gravis); metal ingestion; and certain snakebites (see chapter seven, Snakes, Spiders, and Other Living Things).

During the 1980s, the U.S. military became concerned about nerve agents that deteriorate in long-term storage, such as soman. It was known that Iraq was interested in obtaining the starting materials for synthesis of soman. (They, however, did not use it during the Iran-Iraq 1980–1988 war.)

To deal with their concerns, the military turned to carbamate pyridostigmine, a reversible cholineserate inhibitor, used in medicine for myasthenia gravis patients. They reasoned that pretreatment with a large dose of pyridostigmine would keep the nerve cells viable long enough for the solider to survive the lethal exposure. The result of this study was the issuance of the medication to the coalition forces of the Gulf War.

SARIN

OTHER: GB is the U.S. military code.

TOXICITY: 5

FORM: Odorless sarin is the most volatile of all the nerve agents. It also spreads easier and achieves the highest concentration in closed spaces. It evaporates before it is absorbed by the skin, so most absorption is pulmonary, and the victim becomes quickly symptomatic.

EFFECTS AND SYMPTOMS: Eye problems and seizures are known to occur with moderate exposure. There are no delayed symptoms.

A drop of liquid sarin on the skin is often not irritating and thus is unsuspected until physical symptoms occur. Passage through the skin causes localized sweating. Transmittal times to other parts of the body depend on where the outer skin was affected: behind-the-ear applications will take less time to get into the body than if sarin contacts the soles of the feet.

Beneath the skin, the agent encounters neuromuscular junctions, producing localized lesions in the muscles. These may go unnoticed for a time as the nerve agent enters the bloodstream. Systemic involvement is usually first in the gastrointestinal area, then in the brain, stomach, skeletal muscles, heart, and respiratory system. At the end of its journey is the aqueous humors of the eyes, and the papillary muscle, which causes the visible symptom of miosis. Seizures are common with those affected by nerve gases and they usually have to be endotracheally intubated and receive specific anti-convulsants, such as Valium.

Those exposed to a small amount of sarin reported difficulty concentrating, mental confusion, giddiness, and insomnia. This did not seem to be dose-related, and some of the symptoms might have overlapped with post-traumatic stress disorder (PTSD).

REACTION TIME: A lethal drop of liquid on skin may take thirty minutes to react clinically so that symptoms are visible, whereas a vapor can take effect in seconds. From a small, nonlethal drop, symptoms may take as long as eighteen hours to develop.

ANTIDOTES AND TREATMENTS: Rapid removal from the source of exposure and decontamination is the first rule of order.

Depending on the amount of sarin and length of exposure, casualities of nerve agent vapor, if removed from the source, either die immediately or improve drastically if given antidote and treated symptomatically.

Decontamination of the skin, if delayed more than a few minutes, will not catch the entire agent and symptoms can be expected for several hours after exposure.

CASE HISTORY

In the 1995 sarin gas attack on a Tokyo subway, secondary contamination occurred when the victims were treated in a poorly ventilated hospital room. Health care workers then began to develop similar symptoms. There was also recondensation of the liquid droplets on the clothes and hair of the patients.

The majority of the people who were exposed to the sarin gas suffered only from anxiety, agitation, and post traumatic stress, but many complained of double and blurry vision and eye pain. There were two reported deaths, and a handful of patients had severe symptoms. The duration of hypoxia (lack of oxygen) seemed to have the most influence on the patients' symptoms and prognosis following the attack. Psychological trauma lasted even longer and included flashbacks, fear of entering the subway, and periodic anxiety attacks.

SOMAN

OTHER: Military code is GD.

TOXICITY: 5

FORM: A liquid and a gas, it has a slight camphor odor. It can be inhaled, ingested, or absorbed through the skin.

EFFECTS AND SYMPTOMS: Within ten minutes of exposure the victim's nerve cells are irreversibly blocked. The victim will need longer supportive care including mechanical ventilation because the window of treatment is very small. Immediate symptoms are almost identical to tabun's symptoms (see below).

REACTION TIME: Within seconds for the vapor form and within a few minutes to eighteen hours for the liquid form.

ANTIDOTES AND TREATMENTS: The use of the antidote oxime is useless. Atropine used quickly enough, however, will inhibit the agent's effectiveness.

NOTES: Because soman is short-lived in the environment, it allows rapid deployment of personnel into a recently exposed area with little danger.

TABUN

OTHER: Military code is GA.

TOXICITY: 4 to 5; LD_{50} is 1g liquid; for vapor, $400mg/m^3$

FORM: It is a liquid and a vapor. Tabun has slightly fruity odor. It mixes easily with water and can be used to poison water or food. It is not found naturally in the environment. Negative effects can be caused by contaminated water on the skin and by vapor trapped in a person's clothing for thirty minutes or more.

EFFECTS AND SYMPTOMS: Immediate symptoms include runny nose, watery eyes, blurred vision, drooling, excessive sweating, chest tightness, rapid breathing, diarrhea, increased urination, confusion, drowsiness, weakness, headache, nausea, vomiting, abdominal pain, abnormal heart rate, abnormal blood pressure, and muscle twitching. If a person is exposed to a high amount of soman, it can lead to loss of consciousness, convulsions, paralysis, respiratory failure, and death.

Central nervous system effects ranging from sleep disturbances to mood changes and easy fatiguability are reported in 51 percent of patients exposed to small doses.

REACTION TIME: Seconds for the vapor form and within minutes to eighteen hours for the liquid form.

ANTIDOTES AND TREATMENTS: Recovery is possible, but treatment (symptomatic and with atropine) must be given immediately. Seeking fresh air and getting out of the environment is the first thing, and then moving toward higher ground.

NOTES: The agent was developed in Germany in 1936. After forty hours the toxicity is dissipated.

It breaks down slowly in the body and so repeated exposures can have a cumulative effect.

VX

TOXICITY: 6

FORM: VX is an amber-colored, odorless, tasteless, oily liquid with low volatility unless temperatures are high. It evaporates very slowly, almost like motor oil. It is not found naturally.

Following its release in the air, people can be exposed through skin contact (the most toxic way), eye contact, or inhalation. Though it does not mix well with water, it can be released into water and people can be exposed by drinking contaminated water or getting contaminated water on their skin.

Clothing will hold the gas for thirty minutes after contact and can expose others.

Since VX breaks down slowly in the body, repeated exposures can have a cumulative effect.

EFFECTS AND SYMPTOMS: Immediate signs and symptoms include runny nose, watery eyes, small pinpoint pupils, eye pain, blurred vision, drooling and excessive sweating, cough, chest tightness, rapid breathing, diarrhea, increased urination, confusion, drowsiness, heartbeat that is too slow or too fast, abnormally high or low blood pressure, weakness, headache, nausea or vomiting, and abdominal pain. Exposure to a large dose will lead to loss of consciousness, convulsions, paralysis, and respiratory failure.

History of the victim's last twenty-four hours is crucial in making a correct diagnosis, as many other conditions have the same symptoms.

Even a tiny drop of VX on the skin can cause sweating and muscle twitching.

REACTION TIME: Symptoms will appear a few minutes after vapor exposure, and within a few minutes up to eighteen hours for the liquid, depending on the amount of exposure. Onset of symptoms may be delayed for as long as eighteen hours for mild to moderate exposure.

ANTIDOTES AND TREATMENTS: Antidotes are available for VX; symptomatic treatment is also given.

NOTES: After forty hours, the poisonous effect has dissipated.

Developed by Britain in the 1950s, it was given to the U.S. for military use.

After exposure, victims should undergo a complete decontamination with water and alkaline solutions.

Riot Control Agents

These agents also come under the heading of chemical warfare and include several types of tear gas; Adamsite, which causes vomiting; and capsaicin, better known as pepper spray.

While not usually fatal, they can have nasty effects and can kill the elderly, children, and those with respiratory and heart conditions.

RADIOLOGICAL WEAPONS

Everyone is exposed to daily radiation without harmful side effects. It can be breathed in or ingested with food and water or one's skin can be exposed to intense beams. Sometimes those who live near nuclear power plants or who undergo medical tests or therapy involving radiation might experience more symptoms, but in general the amount is too small to be damaging and healthy cells can usually repair damage done by small doses.

Radiation exposure can be accidental (as in a nuclear power plant blowing up) or intentional (as in a nuclear bomb being set off). Writers will most likely encounter terrorists setting off a dirty bomb, which is a device using conventional explosives to spread radioactive materials such as waste from a power plant or radiation sources from a medical facility.

TOXICITY: 5

EFFECTS AND SYMPTOMS: Symptoms depend on how much radiation received, for how long, which organs were exposed, and how one is exposed. Symptoms include nausea and vomiting; diarrhea; skin burns (radiodermatitis); extreme weakness and fatigue; loss of appetite; fainting; dehydration; inflammation (swelling, redness, or tenderness) of tissues; bleeding from the nose, mouth, gums or rectum; low red blood cell count (anemia); and hair loss. Large doses of radiation can cause extensive damage to the cells and result in cell death as in cancer therapy.

Complications of radiation sickness depend on the type and amount of exposure. An acute exposure in a single large dose would have both immediate and delayed effects. Acute exposure, if severe enough, can cause rapid development of radiation sickness that may include bone marrow damage, gastrointestinal disorders, bacterial infections, hemorrhaging, anemia, and loss of body fluids. Delayed effects can include cataracts, temporary infertility, and cancer. Extremely high levels of acute radiation exposure can result in death within a few hours, days, or weeks, depending on the dose.

Chronic radiation exposure often produces effects that can be observed within weeks after the initial exposure. However, signs and symptoms of chronic radiation exposure may not show up until years later, or they may not develop at all.

Within a few hours to years.

No treatment can reverse the effects of radiation exposure. Treatment for radiation sickness is designed to help relieve its signs and symptoms. Doctors may use anti-nausea drugs and painkillers to relieve some symptoms, and use antibiotics to fight off secondary infection, as well as blood transfusions if anemia develops.

Drugs approved by the Food and Drug Administration (FDA) for treatment of radiation contamination from an industrial accident or a dirty bomb include Radiogardase, pentetate calcium trisodium (Ca-DTPA) and pentetate zinc trisodium (Zn-DTPA). These drugs are included in the national stockpile of products for use in the event of an emergency. Radiogardase, also known as Prussian Blue, may be used to treat people exposed to radiation containing harmful amounts of cesium-137 or thallium. Ca-DTPA and Zn-DTPA may be used for contamination by radioactive forms of plutonium, americium, and curium. All three drugs work to eliminate the radioactive substances from the body.

Another drug that may be helpful in cases of exposure to high doses of radiation is filgrastim (Neupogen), a drug currently used in people who've received chemotherapy or radiation therapy. The drug stimulates the growth of white blood cells and can help repair bone marrow damage.

If the cause of radiation exposure or contamination is unknown or consists of more than one source, multiple drugs can be used together to prevent or treat radiation sickness.

CHAPTER 13

IT'S NOT REALLY POISONING,
BUT ...

We are able to find everything in our memory, which is like a dispensary or chemical laboratory in which chance steers our hand sometimes to a soothing drug and sometimes to a dangerous poison.

—MARCEL PROUST (1871–1922)

In this section we deal with two areas related to poisoning. The first section of this chapter will deal with allergic reactions, which can be deadly. The second section will cover some fairly new information about the fairly old phenomenon of mass hysteria or mass sociogenic illness: What happens when a large number of people believe they are being poisoned when, in fact, they are not.

ALLERGIES

In recent years, there has been a growing awareness of the dramatic side of allergies—anaphylactic shock—especially in things like peanut allergies. Some elementary schools have banned peanut butter sandwiches because some students were so sensitive to peanuts that just being in the same room as peanut butter could trigger a potentially deadly reaction.

Allergic reactions are so variable and even idiosyncratic that there is a whole range of physical effects that can result—and all of them from the same basic mechanism: the body's immune system running amok.

The immune system is the body's way of fighting off disease or foreign bodies. When germs or other unfriendly microbes enter your body, your immune system goes into defensive action: Your nose runs, and you cough and sneeze to get rid of viruses that attack your nose and throat; you vomit or get diarrhea to rid your stomach or intestines of the organism attacking them. White blood cells multiply and go after unfriendly bacteria let in through a cut or caused by germs were ingested.

However, every now and then, your body classes something as a threat that it shouldn't. It could be a certain soap or food. It could be a type of medicine, or an insect bite or sting. It could be a pollen or dander from an animal. It could be just about anything that you consume, breathe, or touch.

So the immune system ramps up and starts fighting this new threat. Your skin itches and breaks out in a rash from a certain soap, or whenever you eat shellfish. You take penicillin for a bad case of bronchitis and you break out in hives and get a tight, constricted throat. A bee sting swells up more than it should. Hanging around your cat, or maybe just bringing in fresh flowers, starts you sneezing and sniffling.

There is a whole host of substances more likely to cause allergies than others. Milk, eggs, peanuts, tree nuts, and shellfish are among the most common food allergens. Pollen is the big bad guy behind most cases of hay fever, although grasses can be a significant problem as well. Molds are also a common allergen, as is cat dander (not the fur, as is commonly believed).

However, one can be allergic to anything, and the symptoms can be almost anything because reactions can vary wildly. One person may get a mild itchy feeling after eating shrimp, while another breaks out in bright red hives all over. And while children will sometimes outgrow food allergies, those who are sensitized (that is, become reactive to an antigen, such as pollen, especially by repeated exposure) to something as adults will probably carry that allergy for life.

Even more interesting, triggering one allergy can either trigger others, or make existing ones worse. For example, if a person who is allergic to a specific pollen that tends to crop up every spring also has a mild allergy to cat dander, when spring comes, and the pollen allergy is triggered, the cat allergy can get worse. Or a person with an allergy to a type of grass that grows in one part of the country moves to another part of the country and is temporarily allergy-free—until a pollen allergy crops up and triggers the full range of sensitivities to the grasses in the *new* area.

Most of the milder allergic reactions, including hay fever and rashes, are nuisances of varying degrees, depending on how badly one is sneezing or itching. But they are seldom life-threatening. Hay fever or other allergic reactions to things that are breathed in, such as dust mites and pet dander, can trigger asthma, which can be sometimes be deadly, but usually isn't.

The vast majority of allergic reactions fall into the nuisance group, but some can cause anaphylactic shock.

Anaphylactic shock—or anaphylaxis, the more medically appropriate term—is a severe, life-threatening allergic reaction affecting the entire body. Histamines are released into the whole body, constricting airways, which causes wheezing and difficulty breathing. Gastrointestinal symptoms, including nausea, vomiting, and diarrhea occur, as well as hives, particularly on the lips and throat, which can further constrict breathing. The reaction is sudden and dramatic, and can cause death within minutes.

Breathed allergens rarely cause anaphylactic shock (though they can), but drug and food allergies and insect bites or stings can easily cause anaphylactic shock.

When the body first sensitizes to an allergen, the first reaction is usually very mild. But often allergic reactions to many drugs and insects, and some foods, worsen with each exposure, so any exposure is treated as potentially life-threatening. For example, if a patient taking penicillin for a bout with bronchitis gets a mild reaction, such as a slight tightening of the throat and a mild rash, the chances of that person going into anaphylactic shock the next time they take penicillin increase dramatically. This is why, once an allergy to penicillin is established, it is unlikely that person will ever take it, or chemically similar drugs, again. (Unless your villain has arranged to substitute penicillin for your victim's substitute, as Harry Kemelman did in *Wednesday the Rabbi Got Wet*.)

People with severe food allergies have a particular problem: Foods that appear to be safe may, in fact, have a dangerous allergen hidden among the ingredients. People with these kinds of severe allergies usually carry an epi-pen (a pre-loaded syringe filled with epinephrine), which they can inject into their thigh to stop the anaphylaxis, or at least slow it down enough to allow them to get to the hospital.

Anaphylaxis is also treated by opening an airway, often by paramedics in the field, either by putting a tube down the victim's throat (if possible) or by doing an emergency tracheotomy and putting the tube directly into the victim's trachea. The victim is then treated with intravenous fluids for the shock, and with other medications for whatever symptoms present themselves. Prednisone and antihistamines may later be given to further combat the reaction.

MASS SOCIOGENIC ILLNESS

Mass sociogenic illness is also known as mass psychogenic illness, or epidemic hysteria, or mass hysteria. The reason there are so many names for the phenomenon is that it has not been studied with any depth until very recently, even though there are descriptions of it occurring all the way back to the Middle Ages, if not before.

The simplest way to describe it is the belief of a group of people that they have been exposed to a toxin and are suffering from its ill effects, when they either have not been exposed, or the symptoms they are experiencing were not caused by a toxin. There was just such a case in 2000 at a high school in Tennessee. A teacher, who thought she smelled gas, started experiencing the typical symptoms of a toxic exposure: headache, nausea, dizziness, vomiting, and difficulty breathing (in this case, because of hyperventilation). Her students started experiencing similar symptoms. Meanwhile, the paramedics and other emergency personnel rushed to the school, where more and more students and teachers became symptomatic, and in all the rushing around and the evacuation, more and more people became sick (victims really are sick, just not from poisoning).

Even so, no one could find evidence of any gas leak. The symptoms resolved themselves very quickly with no evidence that anyone had been exposed to anything.

So why were so many people experiencing symptoms? No one really knows why it happens, just that it does. One expert suggested that it's part of a natural empathy people have—if you see someone throwing up, you get nauseated yourself.

It is not terribly common, but it does happen more often than people think. Dr. Jawaid Akhtar, a medical toxicologist at the Pittsburgh Poison Center in Pennsylvania, said he hears about similar cases once or twice a year. Dr. Timothy Jones, a former epidemic intelligence officer for the CDC and currently deputy state epidemiologist for the state of Tennessee, said he's heard of multiple outbreaks since the 2000 high school case mentioned above. He also said that everyone he knows in the public health field is familiar with the phenomenon.

It happens most often during tense social times and in schools and workplaces, particularly factories. During the anthrax scares following the terrorist attacks of September 11, 2001, several post offices closed down when employees believed they smelled something and became ill, even though no trace of anthrax or other toxins was found in the buildings.

The victims experience real symptoms; they really *are* nauseated and having trouble breathing. But the cause of the symptoms is seeing others get sick, along with anxiety and fear of exposure rather than the toxin itself.

In fact, that is one of the hurdles emergency personnel face in dealing with such a situation. They can't afford to assume there is nothing present—there may be a gas leak or other hazardous substance floating around; there frequently is.

Most experts believe that helping emergency personnel recognize the phenomenon is the first step in developing protocols for dealing with it. It is also suggested that emergency responders separate the patients, treat their symptoms, and do as much as possible to soothe their fears without implying that their problems are imaginary, or that they're crazy.

Mass sociogenic illness is an increasingly studied phenomenon, so you may want to do a quick search on a Web site such as www.pubmed.gov to find out the latest about research.

CHAPTER 14

CREATE YOUR OWN
POISON

Nothing has really happened until it has been described.

— *Virginia Woolf (1882–1941)*

In an attempt to preserve a viral weapon for military use, the general had secreted away an antibody. Little did he know at the time that the virus, which first spread by physical contact— monkey to monkey and then monkey to human—was about to mutate to an airborne contagion. Now he had no control over the viral effects. Now the whole world would be affected, just like the common cold.

— *Robin Cook, Outbreak (Robin Cook)*

Hollywood's slogan has always been: Don't just steal it; steal it and make it one step better. In the above example, the author took a version of a hemorrhagic virus (one that caused high fevers and bleeding from every orifice) and made it fit his own purposes, forming one more deadly than ever imagined.

There are so many poisons and diseases out there, one wonders why someone would want to create a fictional means of death—but for authors who need a specific event to happen, or a certain effect, it can be helpful. There are many reasons an author might want to make up a poison. A novel set in the future may need something unheard-of to maintain believability. Perhaps an exceptionally fast-acting poison is needed to move the plot, and the antagonist has no acceptable access to those that truly exist. Often an obscure but distinctive poison can highlight the exceptional knowledge of a superior detective. And sometimes, a fictional poison can simply be more fun. (Or it can serve a practical purpose. If you want to talk about a certain drug or household product negatively, it might be safer to make one up than risk upsetting a pharmaceutical company or manufacturer.)

Take, for example, a *Star Trek* episode in which they used a generic aging disease—but instead of showing its progression over the course of years, they made the aging happen overnight.

As part of the research for this book, an attempt was made to identify the poison used by Umberto Eco in his masterpiece, *The Name of the Rose*. After exhaustive checking, it was concluded that Eco had devised a poison to suit his own purposes, since none could be found historically that would have matched all the characteristics of his poison.

The point of this chapter is not to tell you how to formulate a real poison or disease, but to create a fictional one. Whatever your reason for doing so, if you are going to create a fictional poison, several factors should be kept in mind at all times:

1. Do the research. Then you can write with authority and credibility.
2. Make it different. Expand on something. It can be interesting to have an agent mimic something else, but there should be something that distinguishes it from what it imitates. This can be a minor detail, providing an opportunity for your detective to show off. Like the poison Bloat in Terry Pratchett's *Pyramids*, a blowfish poison that causes human cells to expand by 2,000 times—a process used by the Assassins' Guild that is both fatal and explosive.
3. Be consistent. Even if the poison is an extremely bizarre toxin from the yellow weed of Mars (as Akpaloli from Clark Ashton Smith's *The Plutonian Drug*) that kills immediately with symptoms of a heart attack but that can also be used as a stimulant, and reacts differently in each person it contaminates, it should be consistent in its inconsistency.

The toxicity of the poison depends entirely on what sort of mayhem you have in mind. If you are creating a romantic suspense and want the heroine to slowly waste away until the antidote is discovered, then something moderately toxic will do. If the villain is just trying to scare off the hero, then something that will injure sooner than kill is appropriate. Most poison-oriented mystery stories depend on exposing something deadly to an unwitting victim by air, food, or touch.

FORMS

There are many means of administering the poison to a victim. Perhaps a rough pinprick from a photographer's tripod can open the way for a potent toxin to enter the bloodstream. And there is always the mysterious poisoned blowgun dart, as used in the movie *Young Sherlock Holmes*, and in spy and jungle stories.

The old interior design maxim that form follows function definitely applies when determining what form the poison should take. (In the case of the aforementioned photographer's tripod, a liquid, or perhaps grease, would be most effective.)

Decide how the poison or disease will be administered or spread, then make everything else reflect that. Again, it all depends what you want the poison to accomplish. If the poison is to be dropped into the victim's scotch and soda, it had better be a tasteless liquid or powder that dissolves easily. Or the drink has to be so sweet (like Long Island iced tea) that it will mask the bitterness. (This is how GHB and other date rape drugs are often slipped to the victim.)

Do you want to kill a whole family and make it look like an accident? If so, then you need an odorless, colorless gas that would be easily administered without causing suspicion. A barbeque is the simple answer here. Charcoal, when burned, creates carbon monoxide, a poisonous gas that will be toxic in an unvented room or house. Gas heaters, stoves, and other appliances can also kill in the same way if not properly vented. (In this case, the symptom of cherry red lips and fingertips will reveal what they died from.) The heater would be blamed and it would look like an accident—but was it?

SYMPTOMS

You can be truly creative when it comes to symptoms. When deciding what symptoms your victims should have, however, it is important to remember how the human body works. Knowing how a poison affects the human body, though it is rarely something that will be discussed in the story itself, can make it easier to tell how it will react in any given circumstance, and your knowledge will add to your credibility. Substances that affect smooth muscle operation can affect the breathing and cause respiratory distress and death. Cyanide that is ingested affects the absorption of oxygen into the lungs.

Most ingested or inhaled poisons will cause nausea and vomiting, and perhaps constipation or, more commonly, diarrhea.

Unusual reactions are better avoided when using a fictional poison, unless it has been set up that such things are a possibility, or the reaction is a red herring. Perhaps the detective mentions that someone taking aspirin daily will be immune to the substance.

Or, for more fun, perhaps the substance is deadly to most people but can help those with a given affliction, much as digitalis is good for heart patients. One story had a victim who had been ill for some time, but her family couldn't wait for her to pass on, and decided to help her by slipping arsenic in her food. To their amazement, she began getting stronger. In frustration, they finally shot her. They discovered later that she was one of those rare people who needed arsenic to live and that she had resisted the physician's efforts to give her the necessary medication. They had been making her healthier, not sicker.

SECONDARY SYMPTOMS

Poisons generally have certain primary effects and secondary symptoms.

Corrosion, or caustic action, is chemical destruction of the human tissue, usually by mere contact, as with an acid such as hydrochloric acid, or alkalis such as lye. The action leaves slow-healing burns that often become permanent scar tissue unless the victim dies. Burning pain is usually the initial symptom after swallowing, followed by vomiting, uncontrollable diarrhea, and bloodstained feces. A secondary effect here could be bleeding and systemic infection, which could be the end factor in the death.

Cytotoxicity means cell poisoning. Translated into symptoms, this means destruction and death of the cells. These can be any cells in the body. As previously mentioned, red blood cells are affected by carbon monoxide, which binds and doesn't let go, and prevents the absorption of oxygen. The body then becomes flushed (red-tinged), with cherry red lips and fingertips, since it's not getting the oxygen it needs. This mimics oxygen, so that the blood is brighter red than with oxygenated blood, whereas cyanide, which deprives oxygen, results in blue-tinged blood. Everything then shuts down.

Aniline is another example, since the red blood cells are changed into methemoglobin. Kidney cells are affected by salts of mercury, and kidney failure results. Nerve cells are affected by the neurotoxin curare, causes total paralysis and renders the person unable to breathe, thus causing suffocation and death. Skin lesions are also caused by gases, corrosives, or acids.

Some poisons affect the central nervous system. Depressants, such as barbiturates and alcohol, work in this way, interfering with the communications between the brain, heart, lungs, and muscles, slowing them down, leading to coma and paralysis. In severe alcohol poisoning (drinking a bottle of Scotch in five minutes), a person might appear to recover only to die two or three days later from the cerebral edema.

Arsenic, lead, and mercury (and other heavy metals) work by blocking the productions of vital enzymes, which in turn prevent the body from functioning.

These primary effects are specific to the poisons that cause them. Secondary effects can be caused by all or any of the primary effects and vary from individual to individual. These are symptoms relating directly to the vital body functions: respiration, circulation, and excretion. When breathing stops for a period of five minutes or more, the heart usually quits and the brain cells die. When the kidney or liver fails, then the body can't excrete its wastes—including the poison—and death occurs within a few days, unless extraordinary measures are taken to keep the victim alive. This might include kidney dialysis or transplants.

When creating your own agent, you can make the poison behave in any reasonable way you want. For example, a myth associated with radiation is that once exposed to radiation, you become radioactive, glow in the dark, and contaminate others. Not true. You can be exposed but not be contaminated. You are contaminated only if the agent is left on or in your being. You are not radioactive, just the material on or in your body is. That is why you strip your clothing off and even abrade your skin with stiff brushes when contaminated. But, in your story, if you give a plausible explanation, you can create a type of radiation that does make a person glow.

ANTIDOTES

Any antidotes and treatments used should be consistent with the symptoms and effects of the poison. Keep in mind that very few poisons actually have specific antidotes. Much of the treatment of poisoning revolves around removing the poison from the victim and treating the symptoms. Only a few can be neutralized with an antidote.

Some treatments or antidotes may consist of using antibiotics to kill bacteria, or antitoxins to block the specific effects of botulism, tetanus, and other biotoxins. Everything is treated symptomatically to prolong life. Many antidotes and treatments in of themselves can be deadly when not administered correctly.

Reaction times are also important and create conflict, such as in the 1988 movie *DOA*, in which the victim had twenty-four hours (one week in the 1950 version) to find out who had poisoned him. Some poisons, like the super-deadly gas VX, destroy the nervous system and cause a complete body breakdown in minutes unless the antidote (in this case, atropine) is *immediately* injected. (This is why the military issues atropine injectors with gas masks.) In *The Rock,* they used VX-2, which was a green liquid that caused the skin of its victims to bubble and melt. The only antidote here had to be administered immediately into the victim's heart. (There is now a weapon called Binary VX which, when mixed, produces the deadly VX nerve agent.)

Other agents, such as mushroom alkaloids, may take days or weeks to accomplish death with no antidote available.

If you need time to get to the hospital, or for the killer to accomplish his alibi, or the victim to leave a clue of sorts before his death, timing is important. Except in the case of something highly corrosive, it takes several minutes for substances that are swallowed to get into the stomach, and from there to the bloodstream where they create the damage. Even cyanide, which is extremely fast acting, takes up to fifteen minutes to react after swallowing. Poisons that act immediately are generally inhaled or injected. Skin absorption usually, but not always, has the slowest reaction time; but again, in the case of VX and other nerve agents, which are both liquid and a gas, you will have an immediate reaction.

Generally speaking, the more volatile and unstable the poison, the harder it is to handle, and more dangerous to those who are handling it as well.

NAME YOUR POISON

Once the symptoms and form are determined, you can find a known agent that meets your needs, or a combination of agents. Creating a fictional poison's name can be a tricky issue. Knowledge of chemistry helps. So does a basic knowledge of anatomy. Simple names are more suitable for natural poisons intended for period stories. Multisyllabic chemical names should not appear in stories set in the 1930s or earlier. Even now, people are more likely to use familiar names such as TNT instead of trinitrotoluene.

If you are working with a virus or bacteria, different naming rules apply. A virus is generally named based on:

1. Where it first originates (Hong Kong flu).
2. The animal that carries it (bird flu).
3. How it affects the human body (like HIV, which affects the immune system, or hepatitis, which affects the liver).

Mutations and variations are indicated by a letter or number after the name (hepatitis A, B, and C). Long names may be abbreviated (like HIV for human immunodeficiency virus). Bacteria, on the other hand, are named by the individual who discovered them, and there are no real rules. They can be named after themselves, friends, children, or foes. Often they will have a Latin name, but it is not necessary.

Reading a chemical list can help. Study how the names are put together, then try breaking them apart and putting different syllables together. If it sounds good, use it. Just remember that a long name can be a real nuisance to type over and over again.

If poisons are supposed to be combination of real chemicals, then it's important to know how those elements work, since the poison will be an offshoot of them. The movie *DOA* is an example in which this did not work. The poison used, radium chloride, would make it part radium and part chloride. Any form of radium will most likely cause radiation sickness, which usually includes nausea, vomiting, hair loss, dry skin, diarrhea, internal bleeding, infections, incontinence, dehydration, high fevers, wasting away, and coma before death. These can occur within twenty-four hours to several weeks, depending on the exposure. Chloride as a solid or chlorine as a gas would probably cause internal burning, strictures in the throat, inability to swallow, and other problems. Nowhere in the movie did the victim exhibit any of these symptoms, or indicate that radiation sickness was part of his disease.

To sum it up—use what you can from life and make up the rest!

A few examples of fictional poisons include:

- Meta-cyanide, from *Dune*: a fatal toxin delivered by the small needle Gom Jabbar.
- Brainwash gas, from *Dune 2*: a nerve gas that temporarily causes units to become loyal to House Ordos.
- Iocaine, from William Goldman's *The Princess Bride*: a deadly Australian poison that is odorless and tasteless and highly soluble; it is available in powder form, and one can build an immunity to it. It is used by the hero, Westley.
- Smilex, from *Batman*: used by the Joker to kill within minutes, leaving the victim with a frozen grin on his face.
- FEX-M3, from *Star Wars*: a deadly nerve toxin that kills in under ten seconds and is delivered through a dart.
- Sennari, from *Star Wars*: a fast-acting toxin delivered by a Kamino saberdart to eliminate Zam Wesell in *Episode II*.
- Sandbat venom, from *Star Wars*: the natural venom of a Tatooinan sandbat; used by Tusken Raiders.
- Krayt dragon poison, from *Star Wars*: a deadly toxin from Krayt dragons.
- Malkite themfar, from *Star Wars*: a signature poison used by the Malkite Poisoners, a group of assassins in the *Star Wars Expanded Universe*.
- Silent Night, from *XXX*: a gaseous nerve agent that can kill millions of people, and only breaks down in deep water.
- 2,4,5 trioxin, from the *Return of the Living Dead* series: a gas that brings the dead back to life as zombies; originally created by the military as an herbicide to use on cannabis plants.

POISONS BY METHOD OF
ADMINISTRATION

Administration is how the poison gets into your character's system. If your fictional villain has a wonderful way to trap an unsuspecting hero in a closed room, all the poisons under "Breathed" might be of use. Membrane absorption is different from skin absorption. Vaginal, rectal, and nasal passages are all membranes, as is the area under the tongue. These areas absorb medications and other toxins much more rapidly than skin.

BREATHED

Acid	Boric acid	Dimethyl sulfate
Acrylamide	Cadmium	Epinephrine
Ammonia	Camphor	Ether
Aniline	Carbon monoxide	Ethylene chlorohydrin
Anthrax	Carbon tetrachloride	Flouroacetate
Antimony	Chloramine-T	Formaldehyde
Arsenic	Chlorine	Heroin
Atropine	Chromium	Hydrogen sulfide
Barium	Cocaine	Isopropanol
Benzene	Copper	Ketamine
	Cyanide	Lead

Mercury

Nicotine

Nitroglycerin

Nitrous oxide

Oxalic acid

Petroleum distillates

Phencyclidine

Phenol

Phosgene

Phosphine

Phosphorus

Pyrethrin

Rotenone

Sarin

Smallpox

Sodium Azide

Soman

Strychnine

Tabun

Tetrachloroethylene

Tetrachloroethane

Trichloroethane

Trinitrotoluene

Tularemia

Turbantop

Turpentine

Ventolin

Veronol

VX

INJECTED

Adder

Air embolism

Amphetamine

Anectine

Atropine

Barium

Beaked sea snake

Benzodiazepene drugs

Black widow

Blue-ringed octopus

Botulism

Brown recluse

Caffeine

Catapres

Cinchona bark

Cinchophen

Cobra

Cocaine

Codeine

Common striped
    scorpion

Cone shells

Cottonmouth

Coumadin

Curare

Depakene

Ecstacy

Elavil

Epinephrine

Gila monster

Gold

Haldol

Heroin

Ipecac

Jellyfish

Ketamine

Lasix

Librax

Lithium

LSD

MAO inhibitor

Methamphetamine

Norflex

Norpramine

Nutmeg

Paral

Pavulon

Percodan

Petroleum distillates

Phencyclidine

Phenergan

Physostigmine

Plague

Portuguese man-of-war

Preludin

Procainamide

Procaine

Quaalude

Quinidine

Quinine

Rattlesnake

Rohypnol

Scorpionfish

Sodium pentathol

Stelazine

Stingray

Thorazine

Tularemia

Tubarine

Valium

Veronol

MEMBRANE ABSORPTION

Atropine

Benzodiazepene drugs

Boric acid

Chloral hydrate

Dimethyl sulfate

Flagyl

Haldol

Lithium

Nitroglycerin

Phenergan

Physostigmine

Potassium
    permanganate

Soman

Stelazine

Tabun

Thorazine

VX

SKIN ABSORPTION

Acid

Acrylamide

Alkalis

Aniline

Anthrax

Boric acid

Camphor

Cantharidin

Carbon tetrachloride

Cationic detergents

Chloramine-T

Chlorine

Chromium

Cyanide

Dimethyl sulfate

Diquat

Epinephrine

Ethylene chlorohydrin

Isopropanol

Monkshood

Nicotine

Nitroglycerin

Oxalic acid

Paraquat

Phenol

Poison dart frogs

Procaine

Pyrethrin

Radiation

Savin

Silver nitrate

Soman

Strychnine

Tabun

Tetrachloroethane

Trinitrotoluene

Viral hemorrhagic fever

VX

SMOKED

Cocaine

Heroin

Ketamine

Marijuana

Methamphetamine

Opium

Phencyclidine

SWALLOWED

Acid

Acrylamide

African milk plant

Akee

Albizia anthelmintica

Aldomet

Alkalis

Ambien

Ammonia

Amphetamine

Aniline

Anthrax

Antimony

Arsenic

Aspirin

Atophan

Atropine

Bacterial food poisoning

Baneberry

Barbados nut

Belladonna

Benzene

Benzodiazepene drugs

Betel nut seed

Bivalve shellfish

Black hellebore

Black locust

Bloodroot

Boric acid

Botulism

Bromates

Byrony

Cadmium

Caffeine

Cantharidin

Carbamates

Carbon tetrachloride

Cassava

Castor bean

Catapres

Cationic detergents

Celandine

Chloral hydrate

Chloramine-T

Chlorinated
    hydrocarbons

Chlorophenoxy
    herbicides

Chromium

Cinchona bark

Cinchophen

Cocaine

Codeine

Colocynth

Copper

Corn cockle

Coumadin

Croton oil

Cuckoopint

Cyanide

Daphne

Deadly webcap

Death camas

Death cap

Depakene

Digitoxin

Dimethyl sulfate

Diquat

Dog mercury

Dyphylline

Ecstacy

Elavil

Elderberry

Epinephrine

Ergot

Ethanol

Ethylene chlorohydrin

Ethylene glycol

False hellebore

Flouroacetate

Fool's parsley

Formaldehyde

Foxglove

Galerinas

GHB

Gold

Haldol

Hemlock

Henbane

Horse chestnut

Hydrangea

Inderal

Indian tobacco

Inocybe

Iodine

Ipecac

Iron

Isopropanol

Jimsonweed

Ketamine

Larkspur

Lasix

Lead

Lepiota

Librax

Lily of the valley

Lithium

Lomotil

LSD

Magic mushroom

Mandrake

MAO inhibitor

Marijuana

Meadow saffron

Mercury

Methamphetamine

Methanol

Monkshood

Moonseed

Mountain laurel

Naphthalene

Narcissus

Nicotine

Nitroglycerin

Norflex

Norpramine

Nutmeg

Oleander

Opium

Organophosphates

Oxalic acid

Panther mushroom

Paral

Paraquat

Passion flower

Paternoster pea

Peacock flower

Percodan

Persantine

Petroleum distillates

Phencyclidine

Phenergan

Phenol

Phosphorus

Physostigmine

Poinsettia

Poison dart frogs

Pokeweed

Potassium
    permanganate

Preludin

Privet

Prolixin

Prozac

Pufferfish

Pyrethrin

Quaalude

Quinidine

Quinine

Rhododendron

Rhubarb

Rohypnol

Rotenone

Savin

Silver nitrate

Sinequan

Smooth cap mushroom

Sodium azide

Sodium thiocyanate

Soman

Spindle tree

Star of Bethelehem

Stelazine

Strychnine

Tabun

Tagamet

Tanghin

Tansy

Tetrachloroethylene

Tetrachloroethane

Thallium

Thorazine

Thyrolar

Trichloroethane

Trinitrotoluene

Turbantop

Turpentine

Tylenol

Vacor

Valium

Veronol

VX

Water hemlock

White snakeroot

Yellow jasmine

Yew

POISONS BY

FORM

A poison can be found in almost as many different forms as there are poisons. And one substance can show up in more than one form. Nicotine, for example, can be either a brown or a yellow liquid. Chlorine shows up in liquids and as a gas.

AEROSOL SPRAY

Nitroglycerine

BACTERIA

Anthrax

Bacterial food poisoning

Botulism (actually the
    spore of a bacteria)

Plague

Tularemia

BLUISH-BLACK POWDER

Iodine

BLUISH-WHITE METAL

Cadmium

BRIGHT GREEN LIQUID

Ethylene glycol

BROWN LIQUID

Nicotine

CLEAR LIQUID

Chloral hydrate

GHB

Isopropanol

LSD

Procainamide

Tetrachloroethylene

Tetrachloroethane

CLEAR YELLOW LIQUID

Chlorine

COLORLESS CRYSTAL POWDER

Strychnine

Trinitrotoluene

COLORLESS LIQUID

Amphetamine

Benzene

Carbon tetrachloride
Depakene
Dilantin
Dimethyl sulfate
Ethylene chlorohydrin
Methamphetamine
Procaine
Soman
Trichloroethane
Veronol

CRYSTAL

Camphor
Cocaine
Heroin
Ketamine
Methamphetamine
Phencyclidine

DRIED LEAVES

Marijuana

FISH

Jellyfish
Portuguese man-of-war
Pufferfish
Scorpionfish
Stingray

FLAKELIKE CRYSTAL

Acrylamide

FROG

Poison dart frog

GAS

Acid
Air embolism
Ammonia
Antimony
Arsenic
Camphor
Carbon monoxide
Cyanide
Ether
Formaldehyde
Hydrogen sulfide
Isopropanol
Nitrous oxide
Phosgene
Phosphine
Veronol

GEL

Procaine

GRANULES

Ketamine
Phencyclidine

GRAY METAL

Arsenic
Lead

GUM

Opium

INSECT

Common striped scorpion

LIQUID

Acid
Aldomet
Alkalis
Ammonia
Anectine
Aniline
Atropine
Barium
Bromates
Caffeine
Camphor
Cantharidin
Carbamates
Catapres
Chlorinated hydrocarbons
Codeine
Coumadin
Dalmane
Digitoxin
Elavil
Ethanol
Ether
Formaldehyde
Gold
Haldol
Lasix
Librax
Lithium
Lomotil
MAO inhibitor
Methanol

Norpramine

Organophosphates

Oxalic acid

Paral

Pavulon

Petroleum distillates

Phenergan

Preludin

Prolixin

Quaalude

Quinidine

Quinine

Sarin

Silver nitrate

Sinequan

Sodium pentathol

Sodium thiocynate

Stelazine

Tabun

Tubarine

Turpentine

Tylenol

Ventolin

VX

LIZARD

Gila monster

METAL

Chromium

Thallium

MOLLUSK

Bivalve shellfish

Blue-ringed octopus

Cone shells

MUSHROOM

Deadly webcap

Death cap

Galerinas

Inocybe

Lepiota

Magic mushroom

Panther mushroom

Smooth cap mushroom

Turbantop

PILL (TABLET OR CAPSULE)

Aldomet

Ambien

Atropine

Caffeine

Carbamates

Catapres

Chloral hydrate

Chlorinated
   hydrocarbons

Codeine

Depakene

Digitoxin

Dilantin

Dyphylline

Ecstacy

Elavil

Gold

Haldol

Inderal

Iron

Lasix

Librax

Lithium

Lomotil

Nitroglycerin

Norpramine

Organophosphates

Paral

Phenergan

Preludin

Prolixin

Prozac

Quaalude

Quinidine

Quinine

Rohypnol

Sinequan

Stelazine

Sodium thiocynate

Tagamet

Thorazine

Thyrolar

Tylenol

Valium

Veronol

PLANT

African milk plant

Akee

Albizia anthelmintica

Baneberry

Barbados nut

Belladonna

Betel nut seed

Black hellebore

Black locust

Bloodroot

Byrony

Cassava

Castor bean

Celandine

Cinchona bark

Colocynth

Corn cockle

Croton oil

Cuckoopint

Curare

Daphne

Death camas

Dog mercury

Elderberry

Ergot

False hellebore

Fool's parsley

Foxglove

Hemlock

Henbane

Horse chestnut tree

Hydrangea

Indian tobacco

Ipecac

Jimsonweed

Larkspur

Lily of the valley

Mandrake

Meadow saffron

Monkshood

Moonseed

Mountain laurel

Narcissus

Nutmeg

Oleander

Passion flower

Paternoster pea

Peacock flower

Poinsettia

Pokeweed

Privet

Rhododendron

Rhubarb

Savin

Spindle tree

Star of Bethelehem

Tanghin

Tansy

Water hemlock

White snakeroot

Yellow jasmine

Yew

POWDER

Carbamates

Chloral hydrate

Chlorinated hydrocar-
bons

Codeine

Dalmane

Heroin

Ketamine

Organophosphates

Phencyclidine

Pyrethrin

RED CRYSTAL

Rotenone

REDDISH BROWN METAL

Copper

SALTS

Silver nitrate

Tubarine

SILVERY LIQUID

Mercury

SILVERY METAL

Antimony

Chromium

SNAKE

Adder

Beaked sea snake

Cobra

Cottonmouth

Rattlesnake

SOLID STICK

Silver nitrate

SPIDER

Black widow

Brown recluse

STRIPS

Tylenol

SYRUP

Dyphylline
Haldol
Norpramine
Opium
Stelazine
Thorazine

VAGINAL SUPPOSITORY

Flagyl

VAPOR

Atropine
Sarin
Soman
Tabun
Ventolin

VIRUS

Smallpox
Viral hemorrhagic fever

WAXY CRYSTAL

Phosphorus

WHITE CRYSTAL

Alkalis
Cocaine
Iodine
Naphthalene
Phenol
Rotenone
Sodium Azide

WHITE POWDER

Amphetamine
Antimony
Arsenic
Aspirin
Boric acid
Cocaine
Cyanide
Flouroacetate
GHB
Lead
Methamphetamine
Norflex

YELLOW CRYSTAL

Trinitrotoluene

YELLOW GAS

Chlorine

YELLOW GRANULES

Vacor

YELLOW LIQUID

Nicotine

YELLOW METAL

Gold

YELLOW POWDER

Iodine
Persantine

YELLOW SOLID

Paraquat

POISONS BY THE SYMPTOMS
THEY CAUSE

The vast majority of poisons cause several symptoms in varying degrees of sever-ity. Some poisons will generate some twitching; quite a few cause full convulsions. Some poisons will cause violent vomiting as opposed to just vomiting. The sever-ity of the symptom is not listed here, so be sure to read the full information in the main text. Also, there are those symptoms that are either very similar—twitching is a milder spasm—or have different names for the same condition—rapid heartbeat and tachycardia are essentially the same thing. So you might find a poison listed under tachycardia and go to the main text and find rapid heartbeat listed instead. Nor are all symptoms listed for each poison, although most are. The section is organized by the different systems in the body.

VITAL SIGNS

BRADYCARDIA/SLOW HEARTBEAT OR PULSE

Antimony
Black locust
Catapres
Codeine
Curare
False hellebore
GHB
Inderal
Jimsonweed
Larkspur
Lily of the valley
Mandrake
Monkshood
Mountain laurel
Physostigmine
Pufferfish
Quinidine
Rhododendrum
Sodium pentathol
Tanghin
Water hemlock
Yellow jasmine

FEVER/HYPERTHERMIA

Adder
Aldomet
Anthrax
Aspirin
Atropine
Bacterial food poisoning
Belladonna
Benzodiazepene drugs
Brown recluse
Chloral hydrate
Cinchophen
Cobra
Copper
Corn cockle
Coumadin
Dilantin
Diquat
Epinephrine
Flagyl
Henbane
Iodine
Lasix
Lomotil
MAO inhibitor
Naphthalene
Nutmeg
Paraquat
Plague
Portuguese man-of-war
Potassium
    permanganate
Prolixin
Prozac
Spindle tree
Stelazine
Strychnine
Trinitrotoluene
Tularemia
Ventolin

HYPERTENSION/HIGH BLOOD PRESSURE

False hellebore
Foxglove
Ketamine
Phencyclidine
Preludin
Prolixin
Sinequan
Thyrolar
Ventolin

HYPOTENSION/LOW BLOOD PRESSURE

Akee
Aniline
Arsenic
Benzodiazepene drugs
Boric acid
Bromates
Caffeine
Cantharidin
Catapres
Cationic detergents
Chloral hydrate
Chlorophenoxy Herbi-
    cides
Cyanide
Dyphylline
Ethylene chlorohydrin
False hellebore
GHB
Haldol
Heroin
Hydrangea
Inderal
Insulin
Ipecac
Larkspur

Lasix
MAO inhibitor
Monkshood
Nitroglycerin
Norpramine
Norpramine
Opium
Panther mushroom
Paral
Peacock flower
Percodan
Phenol
Physostigmine
Plague
Potassium permanga-
    nate
Privet
Procaine
Quinidine
Quinine
Rhododendron
Sodium azide
Sodium pentathol
Sodium thiocyanate
Stelazine
Stingray
Tagamet
Thorazine
Trichloroethane
Trinitrotoluene
Turbarine
Tylenol
Vacor
Veronol

LOW BODY TEMPERA-TURE/HYPOTHERMIA

Chloral hydrate
Norpramine

Pufferfish
White snakeroot

Ammonia
Atropine
Baneberry
Belladonna
Bromates
Caffeine
Camphor
Cocaine
Common striped scor-
    pion
Cone shells
Croton oil
Cyanide
Deadly webcap
Digitoxin
Dyphylline
Elderberry
Epinephrine
Fool's parsley
Gold
Haldol
Hemlock
Henbane
Hydrangea
Insulin
Ipecac
Ketamine
MAO inhibitor
Nicotine
Norflex
Nutmeg
Paral
Paternoster pea
Phencyclidine

Prolixin
Sinequan
Smooth cap mushroom
Tansy
Thorazine
Turpentine

HEAD, EYES, EARS, NOSE, THROAT

Coumadin
Flagyl
Iodine
Lead
Preludin
Ventolin

Adder
Rhubarb

Acid
Adder
Ammonia
Cobra
Dimethyl sulfate
Fool's parsley
Hemlock
Jimsonweed
Methanol
Phenol

Adder
Rhubarb

Ambien
Atropine
Beaked sea snake
Belladonna
Benzodiazepene drugs
Betel nut seed
Botulism
Cinchona bark
Cobra
Dextromethorphan
Digitoxin
Dimethyl sulfate
Elavil
Epinephrine
False hellebore
Foxglove
Haldol
Henbane
Jimsonweed
Larkspur
Lasix
Librax
Meadow saffron
Methanol
Monkshood
Norflex
Nutmeg
Panther mushroom
Peacock flower
Phenergan
Quinine
Rattlesnake
Soman
Tabun
Tanghin
VX
Yellow jasmine

BREATH ODOR

Camphor

BURNING IN MOUTH

Aspirin
Atropine
Byrony
Camphor
Castor bean
Croton oil
Daphne
Diquat
Paraquat
Rhubarb
Silver nitrate

BURNING/IRRITATION IN NOSE

Chlorine
Hydrogen sulfide
Phosgene

BURNING IN THROAT

Aspirin
Bloodroot
Chlorine
Daphne
Meadow saffron

DEAFNESS/HEARING LOSS

Aspirin
Bromates
Cinchona bark
Mercury

DILATED PUPILS

Belladonna
Bloodroot
Cocaine
Cuckoopint

Henbane
Horse chestnut tree
Indian tobacco
Jimsonweed
Lily of the valley
Mandrake
Marijuana
Norflex
Norpramine
Phenergan
Prolixin
Tansy
Water hemlock
Yellow jasmine
Yew

DROOLING

Acid
Chlorine
Rhododendron
Soman
Tabun
Thorazine
VX

DROOPING EYELIDS

Beaked sea snake
Cobra
Rattlesnake
Yellow jasmine

DRY MOUTH

Atropine
Belladonna
Elavil
Inderal
MAO inhibitor
Norflex
Nutmeg
Preludin

Prolixin
Ventolin

FOAMING/FROTHING AT MOUTH

Chloramine-T
Tansy
Water hemlock

EYE BULGING

Thyrolar

EYE IRRITATION/ REDDENING

Chlorine
Dimethyl sulfate
Formaldehyde
Hydrogen sulfide
Oxalic acid
Phosgene
Marijuana
Sarin
Sodium azide
Soman
Tabun
Tetrachloroethane
Tularemia
VX

EYE PARALYSIS

Mandrake

EYE SPASMS

Ketamine
Phencyclidine
Quinidine

GUM SWELLING OR BLEEDING

Adder
Dilantin
Lomotil

Benzodiazepene drugs
Dilantin

Benzodiazepene drugs
Boric acid
Depakene
Meadow saffron
Radiation
Thallium

Lead

Atropine
Caffeine
Lasix

African milk plant
Ammonia
Beaked sea snake
Black hellebore
Dimethyl sulfate
Gold
Inocybe
Mercury
Tularemia

Mercury

Epinephrine
Heroin

Lomotil
Opium
Physostigmine
Soman
Tabun
VX

Cocaine

Dimethyl sulfate
Mountain laurel
Pyrethrin
Soman
Tabun
VX

Carbamates
Death camas
Inocybe
Lily of the valley
Mountain laurel
Organophosphates
Panther mushroom
Pufferfish
Silver nitrate

African milk plant
Arsenic
Barbados nut
Corn cockle
Daphne
Dimethyl sulfate
Flagyl

Oxalic acid
Prolixin
Trinitrotoluene
Tularemia

Dimethyl sulfate
Formaldehyde
Mountain laurel
Panther mushroom
Rhododendron
Soman
Tabun

Acid
Chlorine
Panther mushroom
Physostigmine

Aspirin
Cinchona bark
Elavil
Gila monster
Phenergan
Quinidine
Quinine
Valium

Diquat
Paraquat
Common striped
    scorpion

Cadmium

SKIN

ABNORMAL COLORATION
Acid
Aspirin
Potassium
   permanganate
Silver nitrate
Thallium

BLISTERS
African milk plant
Brown recluse
Byrony
Cantharidin
Common striped
   scorpion
Croton oil
Cuckoopint
Iodine
Savin

BRUISING
Coumadin

BURNS (INCLUDES CAUSTIC ACTION/ CORROSION)
Acid
Ammonia
Bromates
Cationic detergents
Chlorine
Chromium
Dimethyl sulfate
Oxalic acid
Phenol
Potassium
   permanganate

CLAMMY SKIN
Arsenic
Camphor

CYANOSIS
Bacterial food poisoning
Barbados nut
Boric acid
Carbamates
Castor bean
Colocynth
Elderberry
Heroin
Organophosphates
Pokeweed
Stingray

FINGERNAIL LINES
Thallium

FLUSHING/TURNING RED
Ammonia
Belladonna
Benzodiazepene drugs
Camphor
Cyanide
Hydrangea
Insulin
Lomotil
Nitroglycerin
Nutmeg
Persantine
Prolixin
Smooth cap mushroom
Ventolin

ITCHING
Albizia anthelmintica
Celandine
Prozac
Pyrethrin

JAUNDICE
Antimony
Arsenic
Atophan
Carbon tetrachloride
Coumadin
Deadly webcap
Death cap
Diquat
Elavil
Lepiota
MAO inhibitor
Naphthalene
Paraquat
Trinitrotoluene
Tylenol
White snakeroot

PALENESS/LOSS OF COLOR
Camphor
Epinephrine
Prolixin
Trinitrotoluene
Yew

PEELING
Acid
Acrylamide

RASH
Acrylamide
African milk plant
Aldomet
Antimony
Benzene
Benzodiazepene drugs
Boric acid
Brown recluse
Cantharidin

Catapres
Celandine
Coumadin
Formaldehyde
Iodine
Jimsonweed
Lily of the valley
Librax
Oxalic acid
Prolixin
Prozac
Pyrethrin
Smallpox
Tagamet
Tansy
Tetrachloroethylene
Trinitrotoluene
Turpentine

SCARRING/
DISFIGUREMENT
Acid

SWEATING
Adder
Akee
Amphetamine
Black widow
Caffeine
Camphor
Carbamates
Ecstacy
Ethanol
Inocybe
Insulin
Isopropanol
Larkspur
Lily of the valley
Methamphetamine
Monkshood

Oleander
Organophosphates
Panther mushroom
Prozac
Pufferfish
Rattlesnake
Sarin
Smooth cap mushroom
Sodium azide
Soman
Stingray
Tabun
Tetrachloroethylene
Ventolin
VX
White snakeroot
Yellow jasmine

INABILITY TO SWEAT
Thyrolar

HEART

CARDIAC ARREST
Acrylamide
Air embolism
Barium
Black hellebore
Bloodroot
Catapres
Cinchona bark
Cocaine
Dyphylline
Elavil
Ergot
Ipecac
Jellyfish
MAO inhibitor
Norflex

Oxalic acid
Paternoster pea
Percodan
Persantine
Procaine
Prolixin
Pufferfish
Quinine
Rhubarb
Scorpionfish
Star of Bethelehem
Stelazine
Stingray
Thyrolar
Valium
White snakeroot
Yew

CHEST PAIN (INCLUDES
TIGHTNESS)
Bloodroot
Cadmium
Carbon monoxide
Cone shells
Jellyfish
Larkspur
Monkshood
Persantine
Portuguese man-of-war

IRREGULAR HEARTBEAT
(INCLUDES PALPITA-
TIONS, LOUD HEARTBEAT,
AND OTHER HEART AND
PULSE IRREGULARITIES)
Amphetamine
Barium
Beaked sea snake
Belladonna
Benzodiazepene drugs

Caffeine

Common striped
   scorpion

Digitoxin

Dilantin

Dimethyl sulfate

Ecstacy

Elavil

Epinephrine

Flagyl

Flouroacetate

Foxglove

Gila monster

Methamphetamine

Nicotine

Nitrous oxide

Norpramine

Nutmeg

Phenol

Phosphorus

Preludin

Procainamide

Prolixin

Quinine

Sodium azide

Soman

Star of Bethelehem

Stingray

Tabun

Tanghin

Thorazine

Trichloroethane

Thyrolar

Tylenol

Ventolin

VX

AIRWAY AND LUNGS

AIRWAY IRRITATION (IN-
CLUDES MUCOUS MEM-
BRANE IRRITATION)

Acid

Boric acid

Cadmium

Carbon tetrachloride

Chromium

Formaldehyde

Phosphorous

Pyrethrin

Sodium azide

Tetrachloroethane

COUGHING

Acid

Ammonia

Anthrax

Black widow

Cadmium

Chlorine

Mercury

Oxalic acid

Paral

Petroleum distillates

Phosgene

Phosphine

Phosphorus

Plague

Potassium
   permanganate

Smallpox

Soman

Tabun

Tetrachloroethylene

Trinitrotoluene

Tularemia

Turpentine

Viral hemorrhagic fever

VX

INABILITY TO COUGH

Prolixin

Thorazine

INABILITY TO SMELL

Hydrogen sulfide

DIFFICULTY BREATHING

Anectine

Aniline

Anthrax

Barbados nut

Barium

Benzodiazepene drugs

Betel nut seed

Bivalve shellfish

Bloodroot

Camphor

Carbamates

Carbon monoxide

Cassava

Catapres

Chloral hydrate

Cobra

Codeine

Cone shells

Corn cockle

Curare

Cyanide

Dalmane

Death camas

Dimethyl sulfate

Diquat

Elderberry

Ethylene chlorohydrin

Flouroacetate
GHB
Gila monster
Heroin
Hydrangea
Inderal
Insulin
Ipecac
Isopropanol
Jellyfish
Lasix
Lomotil
Mercury
Mountain laurel
Nicotine
Norpramine
Opium
Organophosphates
Paral
Paraquat
Percodan
Persantine
Petroleum distillates
Phosgene
Phosphine
Physostigmine
Plague
Pokeweed
Pufferfish
Rattlesnake
Rhubarb
Rohypnol
Scorpionfish
Smooth cap mushroom
Sodium pentathol
Trichloroethane
Turpentine
Ventolin
Water hemlock

White snakeroot
Yellow jasmine

Atropine
Belladonna
Cinchophen
Epinephrine
Ethylene glycol
Lomotil
Paral
Soman
Tabun
VX

Ammonia
Aspirin
Cadmium
Chromium
Common striped
    scorpion
Epinephrine
Flouroacetate
Formaldehyde
Hydrogen sulfide
Lasix
Mercury
Oxalic acid
Petroleum distillates
Phosgene
Phosphorus
Prolixin
Quaalude
Sodium azide
Turpentine
Ventolin

Aspirin
Barium
Blue-ringed octopus
Byrony
Caffeine
Carbon monoxide
Chloramine-T
Chlorinated
    Hydrocarbons
Cinchona bark
Common striped
    scorpion
Corn cockle
Curare
Epinephrine
Ergot
Ether
Gila monster
Horse chestnut
Indian tobacco
Larkspur
MAO inhibitor
Meadow saffron
Monkshood
Nitroglycerin
Oleander
Phenol
Physostigmine
Procaine
Prolixin
Pyrethrin
Quinidine
Rhubarb
Sodium azide

Sodium pentathol
Soman
Tabun
Turbarine
VX
Water hemlock
Yellow jasmine

Anthrax
Benzodiazepene drugs
Chloral hydrate
Chromium
Gold
Oxalic acid
Phosphorous
Physostigmine

BLOOD

Antimony
Benzene
Boric acid
Cadmium
Dilantin
Naphthalene
Radiation
Rattlesnake

Aldomet

Atophan
Coumadin

Depakene
Plague

Aniline
Castor bean
Naphthalene
Turbantop

Adder
Aspirin
Atophan
Castor bean
Cinchona bark
Common striped
    scorpion
Cottonmouth
Coumadin
Cuckoopint
Lasix
Mercury
Paternoster pea
Potassium
    permanganate
Prolixin
Radiation
Savin
Smallpox
Viral Hemorrhagic Fever

GASTRO-INTESTINAL SYSTEM

Albizia anthelmintica
Ammonia
Anthrax

Aspirin
Baneberry
Barium
Bromates
Cadmium
Cantharidin
Carbon tetrachloride
Chlorophenoxy
    herbicides
Chromium
Cinchophen
Cobra
Cocaine
Corn cockle
Croton oil
Daphne
Deadly webcap
Death cap
Diquat
Ethylene chlorohydrin
Formaldehyde
Galerinas
Gold
Iodine
Iron
Isopropanol
Jellyfish
Lead
Lepiota
Lily of the valley
Lomotil
Meadow saffron
Mercury
Mountain laurel
Narcissus
Paraquat
Peacock flower
Phosphorous
Plague

Poinsettia
Portuguese man-of-war
Potassium
   permanganate
Privet
Rhubarb
Rotenone
Soman
Spindle tree
Star of Bethelehem
Stingray
Tabun
Thallium
Thyrolar
Turpentine
VX
Water hemlock
Yew

BLACK STOOL
Lead

BLOATING/FLUID RETENTION
Barbados nut
Benzodiazepene drugs
Lomotil

BLOODY DIARRHEA
Albizia anthelmintica
Baneberry
Boric acid
Colocynth
Coumadin
Croton oil
Daphne
Death cap
Galerinas
Iron
Lepiota

Meadow saffron
Moonseed
Oleander
Spindle tree

BLOODY STOOL
Coumadin

CONSTIPATION
Flagyl
Lomotil
Percodan
Preludin
White snakeroot

CRAMPS
Bacterial food poisoning
Barbados nut
Carbamates
Castor bean
Colocynth
Elderberry
Flagyl
Heroin
Organophosphates
Pokeweed
Stingray

DIARRHEA
Alkalis
Amphetamine
Antimony
Arsenic
Bacterial food poisoning
Barbados nut
Barium
Betel nut seed
Black hellebore
Black locust
Bromates

Byrony
Cadmium
Cantharidin
Carbamates
Chlorophenoxy
   Herbicides
Chromium
Cinchophen
Common striped
   scorpion
Copper
Digitoxin
Diquat
False hellebore
Flagyl
Foxglove
Galerinas
Gold
Horse chestnut
Inderal
Iodine
Iron
Jimsonweed
Lead
Mandrake
Naphthalene
Nicotine
Organophosphates
Paraquat
Paternoster pea
Phenol
Phosphorous
Plague
Poinsettia
Pokeweed
Preludin
Privet
Prozac
Quinidine

Radiation
Rhododendron
Silver nitrate
Sodium azide
Soman
Tabun
Tagamet
Tetrachloroethane
Thallium
Thyrolar
Tularemia
Turbantop
Turpentine
Viral hemorrhagic fever
VX
Water hemlock
Yew

DIFFICULTY SWALLOWING
Atropine
Beaked sea snake
Chlorine
Cobra
Curare
Jellyfish
Meadow saffron
Portuguese man-of-war

HUNGER
Akee
Insulin
Marijuana

NAUSEA
Akee
Ambien
Amphetamine
Antimony
Arsenic
Bacterial food poisoning

Baneberry
Barium
Benzene
Benzodiazepene drugs
Bivalve shellfish
Black widow
Botulism
Brown recluse
Byrony
Cadmium
Camphor
Cantharidin
Carbon monoxide
Carbon tetrachloride
Cassava
Castor bean
Catapres
Cationic detergents
Celandine
Chlorinated
    hydrocarbons
Cinchona bark
Cobra
Common striped
    scorpion
Copper
Corn cockle
Cuckoopint
Cyanide
Deadly webcap
Death cap
Depakene
Digitoxin
Dyphylline
Elderberry
Epinephrine
Ergot
Ethanol
Ethylene chlorohydrin

False hellebore
Flagyl
Foxglove
Gila monster
Hydrangea
Hydrogen sulfide
Inderal
Indian tobacco
Insulin
Ipecac
Isopropanol
Larkspur
Lasix
Lepiota
Lily of the valley
MAO inhibitor
Mercury
Monkshood
Naphthalene
Narcissus
Nicotine
Norflex
Nutmeg
Panther mushroom
Paternoster pea
Peacock flower
Percodan
Persantine
Petroleum distillates
Plague
Pokeweed
Preludin
Prolixin
Prozac
Quaalude
Quinidine
Radiation
Rattlesnake
Rhododendron

Rhubarb
Rotenone
Savin
Smooth cap mushroom
Sodium azide
Sodium pentathol
Soman
Spindle tree
Stingray
Tabun
Tanghin
Tetrachloroethylene
Tetrachloroethane
Thallium
Thyrolar
Trichloroethane
Turpentine
Tylenol
Vacor
VX
Water hemlock
Yew

PALE STOOL

Prolixin

SMOKING STOOL

Phosphorus

SMOKING VOMIT

Phosphorus

VOMITING

Akee
Alkalis
Ammonia
Amphetamine
Antimony
Arsenic
Atophan

Bacterial food poisoning
Baneberry
Barbados nut
Barium
Benzene
Betel nut seed
Bivalve shellfish
Black hellebore
Black locust
Black widow
Bloodroot
Boric acid
Botulism
Bromates
Brown recluse
Byrony
Cadmium
Caffeine
Camphor
Cantharidin
Carbamates
Carbon tetrachloride
Cassava
Castor bean
Cationic detergents
Celandine
Chlorinated
    hydrocarbons
Chlorophenoxy
    herbicides
Cinchona bark
Cinchophen
Cobra
Cocaine
Coumadin
Croton oil
Cuckoopint
Cyanide
Daphne

Deadly webcap
Death cap
Digitoxin
Diquat
Dyphylline
Elderberry
Epinephrine
Ergot
Ethanol
Ethylene chlorohydrin
False hellebore
Flagyl
Flouroacetate
Foxglove
Galerinas
Horse chestnut
Hydrangea
Inderal
Indian tobacco
Insulin
Iodine
Ipecac
Iron
Isopropanol
Larkspur
Lasix
Lead
Lepiota
Lily of the valley
Mandrake
MAO inhibitor
Meadow saffron
Mercury
Monkshood
Naphthalene
Narcissus
Nicotine
Nitroglycerin
Norflex

Oleander
Organophosphates
Panther mushroom
Paraquat
Paternoster pea
Peacock flower
Percodan
Petroleum distillates
Phenol
Phosphine
Phosphorous
Physostigmine
Plague
Poinsettia
Pokeweed
Preludin
Privet
Prolixin
Quaalude
Radiation
Rattlesnake
Rhododendron
Rhubarb
Rotenone
Savin
Silver nitrate
Smooth cap mushroom
Sodium azide
Soman
Spindle tree
Stingray
Tabun
Tansy
Tetrachloroethane
Thallium
Turbantop
Turpentine
Tylenol
Vacor

Ventolin
Viral hemorrhagic fever
VX
Water hemlock
Yew

Adder
Arsenic
Cantharidin
Chromium
Isopropanol
Petroleum distillates

LIVER AND KIDNEYS

Arsenic
Belladonna
Black widow
Bromates
Carbon tetrachloride
Ergot
Henbane
Iodine
Meadow saffron
Rhubarb
Savin
Silver nitrate

Brown recluse
Cantharidin
Castor bean
Chlorinated
    hydrocarbons

Coumadin
Deadly webcap
Naphthalene
Quinine
Savin
Turpentine

Atophan
Beaked sea snake
Coumadin
Flagyl
Prolixin

Deadly webcap
Jimsonweed
Lasix
Panther mushroom
Prozac
Savin
Soman
Spindle tree
Tabun
VX

Beaked sea snake
Boric acid
Cadmium
Carbon tetrachloride
Colocynth
Copper
Coumadin
Daphne
Deadly webcap
Dilantin
Ethylene glycol
Galerinas
Mercury
Mountain laurel

BOOK OF POISONS

Naphthalene
Oxalic acid
Phosphine
Privet
Rattlesnake
Rhubarb
Savin
Silver nitrate
Tansy
Tetrachloroethylene
Tetrachloroethane
Tylenol

LIVER DAMAGE

Albizia anthelmintica
Atophan
Boric acid
Cadmium
Carbon tetrachloride
Celandine
Cinchophen
Copper
Coumadin
Depakene
Dilantin
Ether
Formaldehyde
Galerinas
Iron
MAO inhibitor
Phosphine
Silver nitrate
Spindle tree
Tetrachloroethylene
Tetrachloroethane
Turbantop
Tylenol

LOSS OF BLADDER
CONTROL

Air embolism
Physostigmine

LOSS OF BOWEL CONTROL

Air embolism
Physostigmine

OLIGURIA (REDUCED
URINATION)

Aspirin
Atropine
Bromates
Carbon tetrachloride
Colocynth
Deadly webcap
Diquat
Elavil
Isopropanol
Lead
Naphthalene
Paral
Paraquat
Quinine
Savin

PAINFUL URINATION

Barbados nut

BENZODIAZ-EPENE DRUGS

Naphthalene
Turpentine

FLUIDS AND ELECTROLYTES

DEHYDRATION

Antimony
Aspirin
Byrony
Lasix

Nutmeg
Panther mushroom
Peacock flower
Radiation

MUSCULOSKEL-ETAL SYSTEM

BACK PAIN

Corn cockle

JOINT PAIN

Aldomet
Brown recluse
Tularemia

MUSCLE ACHES/PAIN

Aldomet
Anthrax
Copper
Fool's parsley
Hemlock
Plague
Tagamet
Tularemia

RIGIDITY/STIFFNESS

Atropine
Barium
Black widow
Camphor
Dilantin
Haldol
Thorazine
White snakeroot

WEAKNESS

Aldomet
Antimony
Arsenic

Barium
Benzodiazepene drugs
Bloodroot
Blue-ringed octopus
Carbamates
Chloral hydrate
Chlorophenoxy
    herbicides
Cobra
Corn cockle
Daphne
Deadly webcap
Death camas
False hellebore
Fool's parsley
Gila monster
Hemlock
Indian tobacco
Lasix
Lomotil
Meadow saffron
Norflex
Organophosphates
Oxalic acid
Paral
Passion flower
Percodan
Persantine
Petroleum distillates
Plague
Pokeweed
Prolixin
Pufferfish
Quinine
Radiation
Rattlesnake
Rhubarb
Smallpox
Sodium azide
Sodium thiocyanate
Soman
Stingray
Tabun

Thyrolar
Tularemia
Valium
VX
White snakeroot
Yellow jasmine
Yew

ENDOCRINE/ LYMPH SYSTEM

BLOOD SUGAR INCREASE/ DIABETES/ HYPERGLYCEMIA
Lasix
Vacor

BLOOD SUGAR LOSS/ HYPOGLYCEMIA
Akee
Dilantin
Inderal

SWOLLEN GLANDS
Dilantin
Plague
Tularemia

NEUROLOGICAL SYSTEM

AMNESIA
Mandrake

ATAXIA/STUMBLING
Acrylamide
Benzene
Benzodiazepene drugs
Caffeine

Cassava
Chloral hydrate
Cobra
Codeine
Death camas
Dextromethorphan
Elavil
Ergot
Ethanol
MAO inhibitor
Mercury
Panther mushroom
Percodan
Rohypnol
Rotenone
Tetrachloroethylene
Thorazine
Trinitrotoluene
Valium
Yellow jasmine

BRAIN DAMAGE
Nitrous oxide

CEREBRAL EDEMA/ BRAIN SWELLING
Aspirin
Boric acid
Dimethyl sulfate
Nitrous oxide

COMA
Akee
Ambien
Amphetamine
Aniline
Aspirin
Atropine
Belladonna
Benzene

Boric acid
Bromates
Byrony
Cantharidin
Cassava
Castor bean
Catapres
Cationic detergents
Celandine
Chloral hydrate
Chlorinated hydrocar-
    bons
Chlorophenoxy herbi-
    cides
Cinchona bark
Cinchophen
Codeine
Croton oil
Cuckoopint
Daphne
Deadly webcap
Death camas
Death Cap
Ecstacy
Epinephrine
Ergot
Ethanol
Ethylene chlorohydrin
Flouroacetate
GHB
Haldol
Henbane
Heroin
Hydrogen sulfide
Inderal
Indian tobacco
Insulin
Iron

Isopropanol
Jimsonweed
Lead
Lepiota
Lily of the valley
Lithium
Lomotil
LSD
Mandrake
Methamphetamine
Methanol
Mountain laurel
Nicotine
Nitroglycerin
Norflex
Norpramine
Opium
Paral
Percodan
Phenol
Phosphorus
Procaine
Pyrethrin
Rhododendron
Rohypnol
Savin
Silver nitrate
Sinequan
Sodium azide
Stelazine
Tetrachloroethane
Thorazine
Trinitrotoluene
Turbantop
Vacor
Valium
Yew

Akee
Ambien
Amphetamine
Aniline
Aspirin
Atropine
Belladonna
Benzene
Bromates
Byrony
Cantharidin
Cassava
Castor bean
Catapres
Cationic detergents
Celandine
Chloral hydrate
Chlorinated hydrocar-
    bons
Chlorophenoxy herbi-
    cides
Cinchona bark
Cinchophen
Codeine
Croton oil
Cuckoopint
Daphne
Deadly webcap
Death camas
Death cap
Ecstacy
Epinephrine
Ergot
Ethanol
Ethylene chlorohydrin

Flagyl
Flouroacetate
GHB
Haldol
Henbane
Heroin
Hydrogen sulfide
Inderal
Indian tobacco
Insulin
Iron
Isopropanol
Jimsonweed
Lead
Lepiota
Lily of the valley
Librax
Lithium
Lomotil
LSD
Mandrake
Methamphetamine
Methanol
Mountain laurel
Nicotine
Nitroglycerin
Norflex
Norpramine
Opium
Paral
Percodan
Phenol
Phosphorus
Procaine
Pyrethrin
Rhododendron
Rohypnol
Savin
Silver nitrate

Sinequan
Sodium azide
Stelazine
Tetrachloroethane
Thorazine
Trinitrotoluene
Turbantop
Vacor
Valium
Yew

CONVULSIONS/SEIZURES
Acrylamide
African milk plant
Ambien
Amphetamine
Aniline
Arsenic
Aspirin
Atropine
Baneberry
Barium
Belladonna
Benzene
Benzodiazepene drugs
Betel nut seed
Boric acid
Bromates
Byrony
Caffeine
Camphor
Cassava
Castor bean
Cationic detergents
Chlorinated hydrocar-
   bons
Cinchophen
Cobra
Cuckoopint

Cyanide
Daphne
Deadly webcap
Dimethyl sulfate
Dyphylline
Ecstacy
Elavil
Elderberry
Epinephrine
Ergot
Ethanol
Flagyl
Flouroacetate
GHB
Haldol
Henbane
Hydrangea
Hydrogen sulfide
Inderal
Indian tobacco
Iron
Jimsonweed
Larkspur
Lead
Lomotil
LSD
MAO inhibitor
Meadow saffron
Methamphetamine
Methanol
Monkshood
Moonseed
Mountain laurel
Narcissus
Nicotine
Norflex
Norpramine
Norpramine
Nutmeg

Oxalic acid
Panther mushroom
Paternoster pea
Persantine
Petroleum distillates
Phenol
Phosphorous
Physostigmine
Plague
Pokeweed
Procainamide
Procaine
Pufferfish
Pyrethrin
Quaalude
Rhododendron
Rotenone
Sarin
Savin
Scorpionfish
Silver nitrate
Sodium azide
Sodium thiocyanate
Soman
Spindle tree
Stelazine
Stingray
Strychnine
Tabun
Tansy
Thorazine
Trinitrotoluene
Turbantop
Turpentine
Ventolin
VX
Water hemlock
Yellow jasmine
Yew

DELIRIUM

African milk plant
Amphetamine
Brown recluse
Cinchophen
Corn cockle
Ethylene chlorohydrin
Foxglove
Horse chestnut
Inderal
Iodine
Jimsonweed
Lead
Mandrake
Meadow saffron
Phosphorus
Sodium pentathol
Tagamet
Tanghin
Tetrachloroethane
Trinitrotoluene

DIFFICULTY SPEAKING

Atropine
Blue-ringed octopus
Dilantin
Ethanol
Lithium
Mercury
Pufferfish
Thorazine
Yellow jasmine

DIZZINESS/VERTIGO

Aldomet
Ambien
Aniline
Arsenic
Aspirin

Baneberry
Barbados nut
Benzodiazepene drugs
Camphor
Carbon tetrachloride
Cone shells
Cyanide
Deadly webcap
Dextromethorphan
Elavil
Elderberry
Ethanol
Ethylene chlorohydrin
Flagyl
Gila monster
Hydrangea
Hydrogen sulfide
Jimsonweed
Lasix
Nicotine
Nitroglycerin
Norflex
Panther mushroom
Percodan
Persantine
Petroleum distillates
Phenergan
Phosphine
Preludin
Procaine
Prozac
Pufferfish
Sinequan
Stingray
Tagamet
Thorazine
Trichloroethane
Trinitrotoluene
Turpentine

Vacor
Ventolin
Yellow jasmine

DROWSINESS

Acrylamide
Aldomet
Barbados nut
Benzodiazepene drugs
Castor bean
Catapres
Chloral hydrate
Codeine
Dalmane
Dimethyl sulfate
Ethanol
GHB
Haldol
Jimsonweed
Librax
Norflex
Panther mushroom
Passion flower
Percodan
Phenergan
Prolixin
Prozac
Rattlesnake
Rohypnol
Sinequan
Sodium pentathol
Soman
Stelazine
Tabun
Thorazine
Tylenol
Valium
VX

DRUNKEN APPEARANCE

Ethylene glycol
Isopropanol
Methanol

EUPHORIA

Amphetamine
Benzene
Ecstacy
Heroin
Ketamine
Marijuana
Methamphetamine
Nutmeg
Opium
Phencyclidine
Preludin
Tetrachloroethylene
Yew

EXCITEMENT (INCLUDES
GIDDINESS)

Boric acid
Caffeine
Camphor
Cinchona bark
Codeine
Corn cockle
Ergot
Ethylene chlorohydrin
Ketamine
Larkspur
LSD
Monkshood
Phencyclidine
Procaine
Valium
Yellow jasmine

FLOATING SENSATION

Codeine

HALLUCINATIONS

Acrylamide
Ambien
Belladonna
Benzodiazepene drugs
Cocaine
Dextromethorphan
Ecstacy
Elavil
Flouroacetate
GHB
Henbane
Inderal
Ketamine
Lily of the valley
LSD
Magic mushroom
Marijuana
Meadow saffron
Nutmeg
Panther mushroom
Phencyclidine
Preludin
Sinequan
Valium
Ventolin

HEADACHE

Akee
Aldomet
Ambien
Aniline
Antimony
Benzene
Benzodiazepene drugs
Cadmium

Camphor
Carbon monoxide
Cinchona bark
Colocynth
Corn cockle
Cyanide
Deadly webcap
Dyphylline
Elavil
Elderberry
Ergot
Ethylene chlorohydrin
Flagyl
Foxglove
Haldol
Hydrangea
Hydrogen sulfide
Inderal
Jimsonweed
Lasix
Lead
Lily of the valley
Naphthalene
Nicotine
Nitroglycerin
Nitrous oxide
Norflex
Persantine
Phenergan
Phosphine
Phosphorus
Plague
Preludin
Prozac
Quinidine
Rohypnol
Smallpox
Sodium azide
Sodium pentathol

Soman
Tabun
Tagamet
Tanghin
Tetrachloroethylene
Thyrolar
Trichloroethane
Trinitrotoluene
Tularemia
Ventolin
VX
Yellow jasmine

Cocaine
Cottonmouth
Thyrolar

Caffeine
Lithium

Aniline
Aspirin
Benzodiazepene drugs
Boric acid
Bromates
Ketamine
MAO inhibitor
Marijuana
Passion flower
Phencyclidine

Aspirin
Benzodiazepene drugs
Bivalve shellfish
Flagyl

Librax
Preludin

Ambien
Tetrachloroethylene

Acrylamide
Cocaine
Cone shells
Ergot
Flouroacetate
Inderal
Larkspur
Monkshood
Procaine
Pufferfish
Rattlesnake
Rotenone

Beaked sea snake
Bivalve shellfish
Blue-ringed octopus
Botulism
Byrony
Cinchona bark
Cobra
Cone shells
Curare
Fool's parsley
Hemlock
Larkspur
Monkshood
Mountain laurel
Narcissus
Passion flower
Pavulon
Pufferfish

Rattlesnake
Rhododendron
Scorpionfish
Soman
Tabun
VX
White snakeroot

Ammonia
Amphetamine
Arsenic
Aspirin
Dextromethorphan
Ecstacy
Heroin
Horse chestnut
Jimsonweed
Lomotil
Methamphetamine
Paral
Preludin
Thorazine
Water hemlock

Acrylamide
Amphetamine
Caffeine
Camphor
Carbamates
Cassava
Chlorophenoxy
   herbicides
Cocaine
Common striped
   scorpion
Dilantin
Ecstacy

Elavil
Epinephrine
Ethylene chlorohydrin
Flouroacetate
Jimsonweed
Lasix
Lithium
LSD
Mercury
Methamphetamine
Nicotine
Norpramine
Organophosphates
Oxalic acid
Panther mushroom
Paral
Physostigmine
Pokeweed
Preludin
Procaine
Prolixin
Prozac
Pufferfish
Rotenone
Sodium thiocyanate
Strychnine
Thorazine
Thyrolar
White snakeroot
Yellow jasmine

Black locust
Castor bean
Inderal
Indian tobacco
Inocybe
Iodine

MAO inhibitor
Percodan

Acrylamide
Chloral hydrate
Codeine
Ethanol
Inocybe
Sodium azide

Acrylamide
Bivalve shellfish
Blue-ringed octopus
Common striped
   scorpion
Elavil
Ergot
Larkspur
Lasix
Lomotil
Monkshood
Quaalude

Adder
Boric acid
Camphor
Carbon monoxide
Cyanide
Dalmane
Ethanol
Ether
Formaldehyde
Inocybe
Ipecac
Mandrake
Oleander

Percodan
Persantine
Petroleum distillates
Rohypnol
Scorpionfish
Soman
Tabun
Trichloroethane
Turpentine
Veronol
VX

PSYCHIATRIC

Amphetamine
Atropine
Belladonna
Henbane
Preludin
Valium

Ambien
Amphetamine
Barium
Benzene
Caffeine
Camphor
Dyphylline
Elavil
Epinephrine
Insulin
Nutmeg
Phenergan
Preludin
Prozac
Sinequan

Sodium Azide
Stelazine
Thyrolar
Ventolin
Water hemlock

Lithium

Ambien
Benzodiazepene drugs
Flagyl
Haldol
Lomotil
Mercury
Preludin
White snakeroot

Phenergan

Akee
Amphetamine
Cadmium
Caffeine
Carbon monoxide
Common striped
   scorpion
Cottonmouth
Epinephrine
Flagyl
Lily of the valley
Mercury
Paral
Tetrachloroethylene

Elavil

Panther mushroom

Aldomet
Ambien
Phenergan

Tetrachloroethylene

Atropine
Camphor
Cocaine
Depakene
Dilantin
Ergot
Haldol
Ketamine
LSD
Nutmeg
Phencyclidine
Preludin
Procaine
Sodium thiocyanate

Marijuana

WHOLE BODY AND MISCELLANEOUS SYMPTOMS

Amphetamine

Antimony
Benzene
Benzodiazepene drugs
Cinchophen
Flagyl
Preludin
Prolixin
Prozac
Radiation

BURNING

Common striped
    scorpion
Larkspur
Monkshood
Oxalic acid
Phosgene
Radiation

CHILLS

Black widow
Brown recluse
Epinephrine
Insulin
Plague

COLD SENSATION

Black locust
Bloodroot
Ergot
Larkspur
Monkshood
Physostigmine

COLLAPSE (INCLUDES
FAINTING)

Adder
Alkalis
Ammonia
Boric acid

Bromates
Cantharidin
Carbon monoxide
Cationic detergents
Chloramine-T
Cinchona bark
Cottonmouth
Cyanide
Formaldehyde
Gila monster
Haldol
Inderal
Ipecac
Lead
Librax
Narcissus
Nitroglycerin
Peacock flower
Persantine
Physostigmine
Privet
Procaine
Radiation
Silver nitrate
Stingray
Thorazine
Trichloroethane
Vacor

FATIGUE

Aldomet
Ambien
Anthrax
Benzene
Elavil
Indian tobacco
Ipecac
Plague
Preludin

Radiation
Tagamet

HEAT SENSITIVITY/HOT
FLASHES

Lily of the valley
Thyrolar

INHIBITED DIGESTION

Paternoster pea

INSOMNIA

Ambien
Amphetamine
Benzodiazepene drugs
Caffeine
Dyphylline
Ecstacy
Elavil
Inderal
Mercury
Methamphetamine
Phenergan
Preludin
Prozac
Sarin
Trinitrotoluene
Ventolin

MENSTRUATION
IRREGULARITIES

Librax
Prozac
Savin

NECROSIS (DEAD TISSUE)

Alkalies
Brown recluse
Cobra
Cottonmouth

Dilantin
Ergot
Jellyfish
Phosgene
Phosphorus
Potassium
    permanganate
Rattlesnake
Scorpionfish

PAIN

Acid
Air embolism
Alkalis
Ammonia
Beaked sea snake
Chlorine
Cobra
Common striped
    scorpion
Gila monster
Haldol
Larkspur
Mandrake
Monkshood
Nutmeg
Rattlesnake
Scorpionfish
Stingray
Strychnine
Thallium

SENSITIVITY TO ALCOHOL

Catapres
Smooth cap mushroom

SEXUAL AROUSAL

Ecstasy

SEXUAL DYSFUNCTION

Aldomet
Elavil
Preludin
Prozac

SHOCK

Anthrax
Baneberry
Benzodiazepene drugs
Black locust
Cadmium
Copper
Insulin
Iodine
Lasix
Mercury
Moonseed
Portuguese man-of-war
Potassium
    permanganate
Rattlesnake
Silver nitrate
Yew

SUDDEN DEATH

Cyanide
Haldol
Hydrogen sulfide
Thorazine

SUICIDAL BEHAVIOR

Epinephrine
Prozac

SWELLING

Adder
Common striped
    scorpion
Portuguese man-of-war

Radiation
Scorpionfish
Smooth cap mushroom

THIRST

Atropine
Bloodroot
Camphor
Deadly webcap
Death cap
Iodine
Jimsonweed
Lepiota
Meadow saffron
Rattlesnake
Uterine bleeding
Tansy

WASTING AWAY

Lead
Phosphorus

WEIGHT GAIN

Elavil

WEIGHT LOSS

Boric acid
Cadmium
Jimsonweed
Prozac
Thyrolar

POISONS BY THE TIME IN
WHICH THEY REACT

The following index is based on the earliest times that symptoms will start to appear. In the descriptions of the toxins, you will see that there is actually a range of time in which one can expect to see symptoms. These times are hugely variable and will depend on a host of factors, but the following should get you into the appropriate time frame for your plot. Also, in many cases, symptoms will start, but death will occur much late—which can make for some interesting plot twists.

IMMEDIATE

Acid
Alkalis
Ammonia
Anectine
Benzene
Blue-ringed octopus
Boric acid
Botulism
Cadmium
Cantharidin
Carbon tetrachloride
Chloramine-T

Chlorine
Codeine
Common striped scorpion
Cone shells
Cyanide
Digitoxin
Dimethyl sulfate
Ecstacy
Epinephrine
Ether
Formaldehyde
Heroin
Hydrogen sulfide

Iodine
Ipecac
Jellyfish
Larkspur
Lily of the valley
MAO inhibitor
Marijuana
Mercury
Monkshood
Nitroglycerin
Oleander
Oxalic acid
Paral

Pavulon
Persantine
Phencyclidine
Physostigmine
Portuguese man-of-war
Procainamide
Quinidine
Quinine
Sarin
Scorpionfish
Silver nitrate
Sodium azide
Sodium pentathol
Sodium thiocyanate
Soman
Star of Bethelehem
Stelazine
Stingray
Tabun
Tanghin
Tetrachloroethylene
Tetrachloroethane
Turbarine
Turpentine
Ventolin
Veronol
VX

1 MINUTE

Ambien
Caffeine
Cyanide
Methamphetamine
Nitrous oxide
Prolixin

3 MINUTES

Atropine
Catapres
Cocaine

Flouroacetate
Mandrake
Peacock flower
Smooth cap mushroom

5 MINUTES

Adder
African milk plant
Air embolism
Bromates
Cobra
Copper
Iron
Magic mushroom
Naphthalene
Petroleum distillates
Potassium permanganate
Quaalude
Trichloroethane
Valium

10 MINUTES

Aniline
Cationic detergents
Cottonmouth
Croton oil
Dalmane
Isopropanol
Lasix
Phenergan
Privet
Pufferfish
Thorazine
Yellow jasmine

15 MINUTES

Barbados nut
Camphor
Dextromethorphan
Dilantin

Ecstacy
Elavil
Ethanol
GHB
Henbane
Lithium
Panther mushroom
Passion flower
Rattlesnake
Tagamet

20 MINUTES

Aldomet
Codeine
Betel nut seed
False hellebore
Foxglove
LSD
Rohypnol
Strychnine
Thyrolar
Trichloroethane
Water hemlock

30 MINUTES

Amphetamine
Antimony
Arsenic
Beaked sea snake
Benzene
Bivalve shellfish
Black hellebore
Chloral hydrate
Chlorinated hydrocarbons
Chlorophenoxy herbicides
Corn cockle
Curare
Depakene
Ethylene glycol
Flagyl

Formaldehyde
Hemlock
Inderal
Librax
Lomotil
Nicotine
Norflex
Percodan
Phenol
Phosgene
Pyrethrin
Sarin
Tylenol
Vacor

45 MINUTES
Daphne

50 MINUTES
Gila monster

1 HOUR
Barium
Black locust
Black widow
Bloodroot
Carbamates
Death camas
Dyphylline
Ethylene chlorohydrin
Indian tobacco
Inocybe
Lasix
Norpramine
Organophosphates
Preludin
Savin
Sinequan
Yew

2 HOURS
Akee
Brown recluse
Castor bean
Meadow saffron
Phosphorus
Pokeweed
Turbantop

4 HOURS
Aspirin

6 HOURS
Cinchophen
Death cap
Flouroacetate
Galerinas
Lepiota
Mountain laurel
Nutmeg
Rhododendron

8 HOURS
Botulism
Methanol

9 HOURS
Bacterial food poisoning

12 HOURS
Thallium

14 HOURS
Celandine

SEVERAL HOURS
Albizia anthelmintica
Baneberry
Belladonna
Byrony

Cadmium
Chromium
Cinchona bark
Colocynth
Cuckoopint
Dog mercury
Elderberry
Fool's parsley
Hydrangea
Jimsonweed
Moonseed
Narcissus
Paternoster pea
Poinsettia
Radiation
Rhubarb
Rotenone
Spindle tree
Tansy
Trinitrotoluene

1 DAY
Horse chestnut

2 DAYS
Anthrax
Paraquat
White snakeroot
Viral hemorrhagic fever

3 DAYS
Deadly webcap
Tularemia

SEVERAL DAYS
Atophan
Ergot
Smallpox
Tularemia

POISONS BY TOXICITY RATING

As mentioned in the introduction, the toxicity ratings are based on the amount needed for a fatal reaction. A rating of one means that so much would be needed to kill even a fictional victim that the substance is considered nontoxic. A rating of six means that a tiny bit will do the job on a healthy adult. Some substances, depending on how they are formulated, can be more or less toxic, and will appear more than once below.

TOXICITY RATING 2

Carbamates
Chlorinated hydrocarbons
Flagyl
LSD
Magic mushroom
Smooth cap mushroom
Turbantop

TOXICITY RATING 3

Aldomet
Bivalve shellfish
Caffeine
Carbamates
Chlorinated hydrocarbons

Chlorine
Dextromethorphan
Ethanol
Isopropanol
Librax
Marijuana
Nutmeg
Organophosphates
Panther mushroom
Poinsettia
Prozac

TOXICITY RATING 4

Adder
Akee

Albizia anthelmintica
Ambien
Ammonia
Aspirin
Benzene
Bivalve shellfish
Black widow
Bloodroot
Byrony
Cadmium
Carbamates
Cationic detergents
Celandine
Chlorinated hydrocarbons
Chlorophenoxy herbicides

Cinchona bark
Common striped scorpion
Corn cockle
Cottonmouth
Coumadin
Death camas
Depakene
Elderberry
Ethylene glycol
Fool's parsley
GHB
Iron
Lasix
Lomotil
Mandrake
MAO inhibitor
Naphthalene
Nitroglycerin
Organophosphates
Petroleum distillates
Phenergan
Pokeweed
Portuguese man-of-war
Pyrethrin
Rattlesnake
Rhubarb
Rotenone
Spindle tree
Stingray
Thyrolar
Tylenol
Ventolin

TOXICITY RATING 5
Acrylamide
Air embolism
Amphetamine
Aniline
Arsenic

Baneberry
Barium
Benzodiazepene drugs
Betel nut seed
Black locust
Boric acid
Bromates
Camphor
Carbamates
Carbon monoxide
Cassava
Chloral hydrate
Chlorinated hydrocarbons
Chlorine
Chromium
Cinchophen
Cocaine
Colocynth
Copper
Cuckoopint
Dalmane
Daphne
Death cap
Dilantin
Dog mercury
Dyphylline
Elavil
Ergot
False hellebore
Haldol
Henbane
Horse chestnut
Hydrangea
Inderal
Indian tobacco
Inocybe
Iodine
Ipecac
Lead

Lepiota
Lithium
Meadow saffron
Mercury
Methamphetamine
Methanol
Moonseed
Mountain laurel
Narcissus
Nicotine
Nitrous oxide
Norpramine
Opium
Organophosphates
Oxalic acid
Paral
Percodan
Persantine
Phencyclidine
Phenol
Phosgene
Phosphine
Physostigmine
Potassium permanganate
Preludin
Privet
Procainamide
Quaalude
Quinine
Radiation
Rattlesnake
Rohypnol
Sarin
Scorpionfish
Silver nitrate
Sinequan
Sodium azide
Sodium thiocyanate
Soman

BOOK OF POISONS

Stelazine
Tabun
Tagamet
Tansy
Tetrachloroethylene
Tetrachloroethane
Thallium
Thorazine
Trichloroethane
Trinitrotoluene
Turbantop
Turpentine
Vacor
Valium
Veronol
White snakeroot
Yellow jasmine

TOXICITY RATING 6

Acid
Adder
African milk plant
Alkalis
Anectine
Anthrax
Antimony
Atophan
Atropine
Barbados nut
Beaked sea snake
Belladonna
Bivalve shellfish
Black hellebore
Blue-ringed octopus
Botulism
Brown recluse
Cantharidin
Carbon tetrachloride
Castor bean

Catapres
Chloramine-T
Chromium
Cobra
Codeine
Cone shells
Cottonmouth
Croton oil
Curare
Cyanide
Deadly webcap
Digitoxin
Dimethyl sulfate
Epinephrine
Ether
Ethylene chlorohydrin
Flouroacetate
Formaldehyde
Foxglove
Galerinas
Gila monster
Hemlock
Heroin
Hydrogen sulfide
Insulin
Jellyfish
Jimsonweed
Larkspur
Lily of the valley
Monkshood
Norflex
Oleander
Organophosphates
Paraquat
Passion flower
Paternoster pea
Pavulon
Peacock flower
Phosphorus

Plague
Prolixin
Pufferfish
Quinidine
Rattlesnake
Rhododendron
Savin
Smallpox
Sodium pentathol
Star of Bethelehem
Strychnine
Tanghin
Tularemia
Turbarine
Viral hemorrhagic fever
VX
Water hemlock
Yew

BIBLOGRAPHY

Arena, Jay M., and Richard H. Drew. *Poisoning*. Springfield, Illinois: Charles C. Thomas, 1963.

Arnold, Happy. *Poisonous Plants of Hawaii*. Rutland, Vermont: Charles E. Tuttle, 1968.

Admiraal, P.V. *Justifiable Euthanasia: A Manual for Physicians*. Amsterdam: Netherlands Voluntary Euthanasia Society, 1981.

Ballantin, Bryan. *Current Approaches in Toxicology*. Bristol, England: Wright Publishers, 1977.

Bayer, Marc J., Barry H. Rumack, and Lee A. Wanke. *Toxicologic Emergencies*. Bowie, MD: R. J. Brady, 1984.

Beck, Aaron T., Harvey L. Resnick, and Dan J. Lettieri. *The Prediction of Suicide*. Bowie, MD: Charles Press Publishers, 1974.

Block, J. Bradford. *Signs and Symptoms of Chemical Exposure*. Springfield, IL: Thomas, 1980.

Boden, François F., and C.F. Cheinisse. *Poisons*. World University Library. Translated by Harold Oldroyd. New York: McGraw-Hill, 1970.

Browne, George, and C.G. Stewart. *Reports of Trials for Murder by Poisoning by Prussic Acid, Strychnia, Antimony, Arsenic and Aconitia*. London: Steven and Sons, 1883.

BOOK OF POISONS

Browning, Ethel. *Toxicology and Metabolism of Industrial Solvents.* London: Elsevier, 1965.

Burston, Geoffrey. *Self-Poisoning.* London: Lloyd-Luke Publishers, 1970.

Cassaret, Louis, and John Doull. *Toxicology: the Basic Science of Poisons.* 2nd ed. New York: Macmillan, 1980.

Cloudsley-Thompson, John L. *Spiders and Scorpions.* New York: McGraw-Hill, 1980.

Columbia Encyclopedia. 4th ed. New York: J.B. Lippincott, 1975.

Cooley, Lee Morrison. *Pre-medicated Murder.* Radnor, PA: Chilten Books, 1974.

Cooper, Marion R., and Anthony W. Johnson. *Poisonous Plants in Britain and Their Effect on Animals and Man.* London: H.M.S.O., 1984.

Cooper, Paulette. *Medical Detectives.* New York: David McKay, 1973.

Cooper, Peter. *Poisoning by Drugs and Chemicals, Plants and Animals.* 3rd ed. Chicago: Alchemist Publications, 1974.

Cumming, George. *Management of Acute Poisoning.* Springfield, IL: C.V. Mosby, 1961.

Curry, Allan S. *Poison Detection in Human Organs.* Springfield, IL: Charles C. Thomas, 1963.

Diechmann, William B. *Signs, Symptoms, and Treatment of Certain Acute Emergencies in Toxicology.* Springfield, IL: Charles C. Thomas, 1958.

Department of Justice. *Forensic Pathology, A Handbook.* July 1977.

Driesbach, Robert. *Handbook of Poisoning.* 11th ed. Los Altos, CA: Lange Medical Publications, 1983.

Duke, James. *Medicinal Plants of the Bible.* New York: Trade-Medic Books, 1983.

Ellenhorn, Matthew J. and Donald G. Barceloux. *Medical Toxicology.* New York: Elsevier, 1988.

Finkel, Asher J., Alice Hamilton, and Harriet Hardy. *Hamilton and Hardy's Industrial Toxicology.* 4th ed. Boston: John Wright, PSG Inc., 1983.

Forsyth, A. *British Poisonous Plants.* H.M.S.O., Bulletin No. 161, Ministry of Agriculture, Fisheries and Food, 1954.

Freiberg, Marcos, and Jerry G. Wells. *The World of Venomous Animals.* New Jersey: T.F.H. Publishers, 1984.

Goldfrank, Lewis R., et al. *Goldfrank's Toxicological Emergencies.* 3rd ed. Norwalk, CT: Appleton-Century-Crofts, 1986.

Goodman, Louis Sanford, and Alfred Gilman. *The Pharmacological Basis of Therapeutics.* 6th ed. New York: Macmillan, 1980.

Gosselin, Robert E., Harold C. Hodge, Roger P. Smith, and Marion N. Gleason. *Clinical Toxicology of Commercial Products*. 4th ed. Baltimore: Williams and Wilkins, 1979.

Graham, James, and David Provins. *The Diagnosis and Treatment of Acute Poisoning*. London: Oxford University Press, 1962.

Guyton, Arther C. *Textbook of Medical Physiology*. 6th ed. Philadelphia: W. B. Saunders, 1981.

Haddad, Lester M., and James F. Winchester. *Clinical Management of Poisoning and Drug Overdose*. Philadelphia: W. B. Saunders, 1983.

Hall, Jay Cameron. *Inside the Crime Lab*. Englewood Cliffs, NJ: Prentice-Hall, 1974.

Hanson, William, Jr., ed. *Toxic Emergencies*. New York: Churchill Livingstone, 1984.

Hardin, James W. *Human Poisoning From Native and Cultivated Plants*. Durham, NC: Duke University Press, 1969.

History of Anesthesia With Emphasis on the Nurse Specialist. Archives of the American Association of Nurse Anesthetists, 1953.

James, Wilma Roberts. *Know Your Poisonous Plants*. Healdsburg, California: Naturegraph Publishers, 1973.

Jensen, Lloyd. *Poisoning Misadventures*. Springfield, IL: Charles C. Thomas, 1970.

Kaye, Sidney. *Handbook of Emergency Toxicology*. 5th ed. Springfield, IL: Charles C. Thomas, 1988.

Kingsley-Levy, Charles. *Poisonous Plants and Mushrooms of North America*. Lexington, KY: Steven Green Press, 1984.

Lampe, Kenneth F., and Rune Gagerstrom. *Plant Toxicity and Dermatitis*. Baltimore: Livingston, 1968.

Lampe, Kenneth F. *AMA Handbook of Poisoning and Injurious Plants*. Chicago: American Medical Association, Chicago Review Press, 1985.

Le Riche, W. Harding. *A Chemical Feast*. New York: Methuen Publishers, 1982.

Lifflander, Matthew. *Final Treatment—The File on Dr. X*. New York: W.W. Norton, 1979.

The Lippincott Manual of Nursing Practice. Philadelphia: J.B. Lippincott, 1974.

Long, James W. *The Essential Guide to Prescription Drugs*. New York: Harper and Row, 1980.

Loomis, T.A. *Essentials of Toxicology*. Philadelphia: Lea and Febigen, 1968.

Lucas, George, and Herbert William. *Symptoms and Treatment of Acute Poisoning*. Toronto: Clark Irwin Publisher, 1952.

Lundy, John S., *Imagining in Time—Some Memories of My Part in the History of Anesthesia*. August 1997, AANA Archives Library.

Mair, George. *How to Die With Dignity*. Edinburgh; Scottish Exit, 1980.

Maletzky, B., and P.H. Blachly. *Use of Lithium in Psychiatry*. London: Butterworth's, 1971.

Matthew, H., and A.A. Lawson. *Treatment of Common Acute Poisonings*. Baltimore: Williams and Wilkins, 1967.

McCallum, John D. *Crime Doctor*. Vancouver, B.C.: Gordon Soules Book Publisher, 1978.

The Merck Manual. 13th ed. New Jersey: Merck, Sharp, and Dohme Research Laboratories, 1980.

Michael, Joshua B., and Matthew Sztajnkrycer. "Deadly Pediatric Poisons: Nine Common Agents that Kill at Low Doses." *Emergency Medical Clinics of North America,* 22, (2004) 1019–1050.

Miller, Ken and Andrew Chang. "Acute InhalationIinjury." *Emergency Medicine Clinics of North America,* Volume 21, Number 2. May 2003, W.B. Saunders Company.

Minton, Sherman A., Jr. *Venomous Reptiles*. New York: Scribner's and Sons, 1980.

Moeschlin, Sven. *Poisoning: Diagnosis and Treatment*. New York: Grune and Statton, 1965.

Morton, Julia F. *Plants Poisonous to People in Florida*. Miami: University of Miami Press, 1982.

Muenscher, Walter C. *Poisonous Plants of the United States*. New York: Macmillan Co., 1939.

North, P. *Poisonous Plants and Fungi*. London: Blandford Press, 1967.

Pammel, L.H. A *Manual of Poisonous Plants*. Cedar Rapids, IA: Torch Press, 1911.

Physician's Desk Reference. 34th ed. New Jersey: Medical Economics Co., 1980.

Picton, Bernard. *Murder, Suicide, or Accident*. New York: St. Martin's Press, 1971.

Plaidy, Jean. *A Triptych of Poisoners*. London: W.H. Allen, 1968.

Poisonous Plants of U.S. and Canada. New York: Prentice-Hall, 1964.

Poison, C.J., and R.N. Tattersal. *Clinical Toxicology*. 2nd ed. London: Pitman, 1969.

Proctor, Nick H., James P. Hughes, and Michael L. Fischman. *Chemical Hazards of the Workplace*. 2nd ed. Philadelphia: J. B. Lippincott, 1978.

Regenstein, Lewis. *America, the Poisoned*. Washington, D.C.: Acropolis Books, 1982.

Riley, Dick, and Pam McAllister. *Bedside, Bathtub, and Armchair Companion to Agatha Christie*. New York: Frederick Ungar Publishing, 1978.

Russo H., J. Bres, M. P. Duboin, and B. Roquefeuil. "Pharmacokinetics of Thiopental After Single and Multiple Intravenous Doses in Critical Care Patients." *Eur J. Clin Pharmacol* 1995, 49 (1-2):127–37.

St. Aubyn, Giles. *Infamous Victims: Notorious Poisoners and Their Poisons*. London: Constable Publishers, 1971.

Sax, N. Irving. *Dangerous Properties of Industrial Materials*. 4th ed. New York: Van Nostrand Reinhold, 1975.

Schmutz, Erwin M., and Lucretia Hamilton. *Plants That Poison*. Flagstaff, AZ: Northland Press, 1979.

Silverman, Milton, Phillip Lee, and Mia Leydecker. *Prescription for Death: The Drugging of the Third World*. Los Angeles: University of California Press, 1982.

Sittig, Marshall. *Handbook of Toxic and Hazardous Chemicals*. New Jersey: Noyes Publications, 1981.

Skoutakes, Vasilios A. *Clinical Toxicology of Drugs: Principals and Practice*. Philadelphia: Lea and Febigen, 1982.

Smyth, Frank. *Causes of Death*. New York: Van Nostrand Reinhold, 1980.

Soderman, Harry, and John O'Connell. *Modern Criminal Investigation*. 4th ed. New York: Funk and Wagnalls, 1973.

Stackhouse, John. *Australia's Venomous Wildlife*. New South Wales: Paul Hamlyn, 1970.

Taber, Clarence. *Taber's Medical Dictionary*. 10th ed. Philadelphia: F. A. Davis, 1965.

Thienes, C.H., and T.J. Haley. *Clinical Toxicology*. 4th ed. Philadelphia: Lea and Febigen, 1896.

Thompson, Charles, and John Samuel. *Poisons and Poisoning With Historical Aspects of Some Famous Mysteries*. London: H. Stysen, 1931.

Thorp, Raymond. *Black Widow*. Chapel Hill: University of North Carolina, 1985.

Trainor, D.C. *A Handbook of Industrial Toxicology*. London: Angus & Robertson, 1966.

Trevethick, R. *Environmental and Health Hazards*. New York: Heineman Medical Books, 1973.

Tu, Anthony T., ed. *Plant and Fungal Toxins*. Vol. 1, Handbook of Natural Toxins. New York: Marcel Dekker, 1983.

———. *Marine Toxins and Venoms.* Vol. 3, Handbook of Natural Toxins. New York: Marcel Dekker, 1988.

———. *Survey of Contemporary Toxicology.* New York: Wiley and Sons, 1980.

Vercourt, Bernard. *Common Poisonous Plants of East Africa.* London: Colliers, 1969.

Von Oettinger, Wolfgang. *Poisoning: A Guide to Clinical Diagnosis and Treatment.* Philadelphia: W.B. Saunders, 1958.

Webster's New Collegiate Dictionary, 9th ed.

Webster's New International Dictionary, 3d ed.

————. "A Fatal Overdose of Paraldehyde During Treatment of a Case of Delirium Tremens." *Journal of Forensic Science* 19 (1974):755–58.

"Diagnosis and Management of Food Borne Illness: A Primer for Physicians." MMWERecomm Rep 50(RR-2):1–69.

Achong, M.R., P.G. Fernandez, and P.J. McLeod. "Fatal Self-Poisoning With Lithium Carbonate." *Canadian Medical Association Journal* 112 (1975):868–70.

Aquanno, J.J., K.M. Chan, and D.N. Dietzler. "Accidental Poisoning of Two Laboratory Technologists With Sodium Nitrate." *Clinical Chemistry* 27 (1981):1145–46.

Backer, R.C., R.V. Pisano, and I.M. Sopher. "Diphenhydramine Suicide-Case Report." *Journal of the Annals of Toxicology* 1 (1977):227–28.

Baden, M.M., A. Blaustein, L.R. Ferraro, et al. "Sudden Death After Haloperidol." *Canadian Society of Forensic Science Journal* 14 (1981):70-72.

Bailey, B. "Fulminant Hepatic Failure Secondary to Acetaminophen Poisoning: a Systemic Review and Meta-Analysis of Prognostic Criteria Determining the Need for Liver Transplantation." *Crit Care Med* 31(1) 299–305.

Bednarczyk, L.R. "A Death Due to Levorphanol." *Journal of the Annals of Toxicology* 3 (1979):217–19.

Berger, R., G. Green, and A. Melnick. "Cardiac Arrest Caused by Oral Diazepam Intoxication." *Clinical Pediatrics* 14 (1975):842–44.

Bey Tareg, "Sarin Attack in the Tokyo Subway." *UICI* May 2005.

Bickel, M. H., R. Brochon, B. Friolet, et al. "Clinical and Biochemical Results of a Fatal Case of Desipramine Intoxication." *Psychopharmicology* 10 (1967):431–36.

Broughan, T.A., and R.D. Soloway. "Acetaminophen Hepatotoxicity." *Dig Dis Sci* (2000) 45: 1333–1558.

Bruce, A.M., and H. Smith. "The Investigation of Phenobarbitone, Phenytoin, and Primidone in the Death of Epileptics." *Medical Science Law* 17 (1977):195–99.

Caddy, B., and A.H. Stead. "Three Cases of Poisoning Involving the Drug Phenelzine." *Journal of Forensic Science Society* 18 (1978):207–8.

Catalfomo, P., and C. Eugster. "Muscarine and Muscarine Isomers in Selected Inocybe Species." *Helv Chim Acta* 53:848, 1970.

Christie, J.L. "Fatal Consequences of Local Anesthesia: Report of Five Cases and a Review of the Literature." *Journal of Forensic Science* 21 (1976):671–79.

Dantzig,PI "A New Cutaneous Sign of Mercury Poisoning?" *J Am Acad Dermatol*, O1-Dec-2003; 49(6);1109–11.

De Beer, J., A. Heyndricks, and J. Timperman. "Suicidal Poisoning by Nitrite." *European Journal of Toxicology* 8 (1975):247–51.

deGroot, G., R.A.A. Maes, C.N. Hodnett, et al. "Four Cases of Fatal Doxepin Poisoning." *Journal of the Annals of Toxicology* 2 (1978):18–20.

DiMaio, V.J.M., and J.C. Garriott. "Four Deaths Resulting From Abuse of Nitrous Oxide." *Journal of Forensic Science* 23 (1978):169–72.

Dinegman A,. and R. Jupa. "Chemical Warfare in the Iran-Iraq Conflict." *Strategy andTactics Magazine*, 1987:113-51-2, Professional, March 2005; 12–18.

Dunn, M.A., and F.R. Sidell. "Progress in Medical Defense Against Nerve Agents." *JAMA* 1989 262:649–52.

EiSohly, M.A., and S.J. Salamone. "Prevalence of Drugs Used in Cases of Alleged Sexual Assault." *J. Analytic Toxicol* (1999) 23:141–146.

Faulstich, H. "New Aspects of Amanita Poisoning." *Klin Wochesschr* 57:1143, 1979.

Finkle, B.S., K.L. McCloskey, and L.S. Goodman. "Diazepam and Drug-Associated Deaths." *Journal of American Medical Association* 242 (1979):429–34.

Garcia, MA et al. "Lead Content in Edible Wild Mushrooms in Northwest Sapin as Indicator of Environmental Contamination." *Arch Enrion Contam Toxicol* 34:330, 1998.

Giosti, G.V., and A. Canevale. "A Case of Fatal Poisoning by Gyromitra Esculenta." *Arch Toxicology* 33:49, 1974.

Gunderson, C.H., and C.R. Lehmann, F.R. Sidell, et al. "Nerve Agents: a Review." *Neurology* 1992:42:946–50.

Hansteen, V., D. Jacobsen, I.K. Knudsen, et al. "Acute Massive Poisoning With Digitoxin: Report of Seven Cases and Discussion of Treatment." *Clinical Toxicology* 18 (1981):679–92.

Henrickson, Robert G., and Jerris R. Hedges. "Introduction—What Critical Care Practitioners Should Know About Terrorism Agents." *Critical Care Clinics* 21 (2005) 641–652

Hettler, J. "Munchausen Syndrome by Proxy." *Pediatr Emerg Care* (2002) 18; 371–374.

Isbister, G.K. "Neurotoxic Marine Poisoning." *Lancet Neurological* 2005; 4(4):219–28.

Kaput, N. "Emergency Department Management and Outcome for Self-Poisoning Cohort Study." *Gen Hosp Psychiatry* 26(1):36–41.

Ketai, R., J. Matthews, and J. J. Mozden, Jr. "Sudden Death in a Patient Taking Haloperidol." *American Journal of Psychiatry* 136 (1979):112–13.

Knudson G. "Nuclear, Biological and Chemical Training in the U.S. Army Reserves: Mitigating Psychological Consequences of Weapons of Mass Destruction." *Mil Med* (2001) 166:63–65.

Koenig, K.L., and C. Boatright. "Derm and Doom: Common 'Rashes of Chemical and Biologial Terroristm." *ACEP Critical Decisions in Emergency Medicine* 2003; 17 (6) 1:11.

Koenig, K.L. "Advances in Local Catastrophic Disaster Response." *Acad Emerg Med* 1994:1:122–136.

Koenig, K.L., and R.G. Darling. "Bioterrorism: Is Smallpox a Real Threat or Just 'TV' drama?" Homeland Protection Agency.

Lee, K.Y., L.J. Beilin, and R. Vandongen. "Severe Hypertension After Ingestion of an Appetite Suppressant (Phenylpropanolamine) with Indomethacin." *Lancet* 1 (1979):1110–11.

McKay, C.A, M.G. Holland, and L.S. Nelson. "A Call to Arms for Medical Toxicologists: The Dose, Not the Detection Makes the Poison." *Int J Med Toxicol* (2003) 6:1.

McKenna, J.K. "Dermatologic Drug Reactions." *Immunol Allergy Clin North Am* 24(3):399–423.

Medical Management Guidelines for Nerve Agents. Ageny for Toxic Substances and Disease Register.

Michelot D., and B. Tobh. "Poisoning by Gyromitra Esculenta—A Review." *J Appl Toxicol* 11:235.

Mothershead, J.L., K. Tonst, and K.L. Koenig. "Bioterroism Preparedness: State and Federal Problems of Response." *Emerg Med Clin of North Am* 20(2) 477–500.

Newmark, Jonathan. "Nerve Agents." *Neurol Clinics* 23 (2005) 623–641.

Ohbu SW, Yamashina A, Takasuy N "Sarin poisoning on Tokyo Subway." *South Med J* (1997) 90:587–593.

Okumura T, Takasu N, Ishimatsu S, et al. "Report on 640 victims of the Tokyo Subway Sarin Attack." *Ann Emerg Med* 1996:28:129–35.

Pinson, C.W., et al. "Liver Transplantation for Severe Amanita Phalloides Mushroom Poisoning." *Am J Surg* 158:493.

Rabinowtch, I.M. "Acute Nitroglycerine Poisoning." *Canadian Medical Association Journal* 50 (1944):199–202.

Raginsky, B.B., and W. Bourne. "Cyanosis in Nitrous Oxide Oxygen Anesthesia in Man." *Canadian Medical Association Journal* 30 (1934):518–22.

Reingold, I.M., and I.I. Lasky. "Acute Fatal Poisoning Following Ingestion of a Solution of DDT." *Annals of Internal Medicine* 26 (1947):945–47.

Rives, H.F., B.B. Ward, and M.L. Hicks. "A Fatal Reaction to Methapyrilene." *Journal of American Medical Association* 140 (1949):1022–24.

Schou, M., A. Amdisen, and J. Trap-Jessen. "Lithium Poisoning." *American Journal of Psychiatry* 125 (1968):520-27.

Sehmer, "Mercury in Seafood." *CMAJ* 167(2) 122–124.

Smith, N.J. "Death Following Accidental Ingestion of DDT." *Journal of American Medical Association* 136 (1948):469–71.

Standefer, J.C., A.N. Jones, et al. "Death Associated With Nitrite Ingestion: Report of a Case." *Journal of Forensic Science* 24 (1979):768–71.

Stevens, H.M., and R.N. Fox. "A Method for Detecting Tubocurarine in Tissues." *Journal of Forensic Science Society* 11 (1971):177–82.

Su, John R. "Emerging Viral Infections." *Clin Lab Med* 24 (2004) 773795.

Suchard, Jeffrey. "Chemical and Biological Weapons." *UICI* May 2005.

Usubiaga, J.E., J. Wikinski, R. Ferrero, et al. "Local Anesthetic-Induced Convulsions in Man." *Anesthesia Annals* 45 (1966):611–20.

Vetter, J. "Toxins of Amanita Phalloides." *Toxicon* 36:13 1998

Volcheck GW. *Immunol Allergy Clin North Am* 24(3):357–71.

Wikinski, A., J.E. Usubiaga, and R.W. Wikinski. "Cardiovascular and Neurological Effects of 4000mg Procaine." *Journal of American Medical Association* 213 (1970):621–23.

Wiley, J.F., "Difficult Diagnoses in Toxicology: Poisons Not Detected by the Comprehensive Drug Screen." *Pediatr Clinics of North Am* (1991) 38:725–737.

Yokoyama K., A. Yamada, and M. Nobuhide. "Clinical Profiles of Patients With Sarin Poisoning After the Tokyo Subway Attack." *Am J Med* 1996; 100–586.

Botulism, CDC Briefs, 2002.

GLOSSARY

ABORTIFACIENT: A chemical that induces abortion or labor.

ACETYLCHOLINE: A chemical produced by the autonomic nervous system (ANS) to assist transmission of nerve impulses.

ACIDOSIS: A disturbance in the acid-base level of the body in which there is an accumulation of acids. Metabolic acidosis can happen in diabetes, renal disease, or with intake of acids or acid salts. Impaired liver function can also cause this. Symptoms of metabolic acidosis are apathy, irritability, delirium, and dehydration. Respiratory acidosis is acidosis resulting from retaining more carbon dioxide than is being given off. Symptoms of respiratory acidosis are light-headedness, fainting, and fast heartbeat. Both forms can lead to death.

ACUTE: Happening quickly; sudden onset; demanding urgent attention within minutes, hours, or days.

ADRENERGIC BLOCKERS: Chemicals that inhibit the flow of transmitters.

ADENOPATHY: Enlargement of the lymph nodes. (*Adeno* = glands; *pathy* = disease study.)

ALKALOSIS: An alkaline condition of the blood. Two common types are respiratory, usually caused by hyperventilation (breathing too quickly); and metabolic (cardiac), caused by acid loss during extreme vomiting.

ALKYLATING AGENT: A chemical frequently used in the chemotherapy treatment of cancer.

ALOPECIA: Hair loss, often as a result of disease or chemicals.

ANAPHYLAXIS: (Or anaphylactic shock.) Reactions during an allergic crisis, as with multiple bee stings or drug allergies, that occur swiftly and include increased irritability, a sensation of the throat closing off, difficulty breathing, cyanosis (blue coloring of the skin due to lack of oxygen), sometimes convulsions, and unconsciousness. Death results from spasm of the muscles in the diaphragm. People who have hay fever, asthma, and hives (urticaria) are thought to be more susceptible to these reactions. They can also be caused by badly matched blood transfusions, certain medications, or anything else to which the body is hypersensitive.

ANEMIA: A severe decrease in the number of red blood cells that can carry oxygen. Symptoms are pallor of the skin and mucous membranes, shortness of breath, palpitations of the heart, soft systolic murmurs, lethargy, and fatigability.

ANGINA: A constricting pain in the chest area. Historically: a sore throat from any cause.

ANOREXIA: A psychological process in which the victim refuses food and wastes away. The patient dies, usually of cardiac complications. Karen Carpenter, the singer, is a famous case.

ANOXIC: (*A* = without; *oxic* refers to oxygen.) Lack of oxygen or no oxygen or suffocation.

ANTICHOLINERGIC: A chemical that blocks the actions of certain nerves.

ANTICOAGULANT: Prevents the clotting of blood (an example is warfarin).

ANTIEMETIC: Something that prevents vomiting, nausea, or both.

ANTIPYRETIC: An agent used to reduce fever.

ANURIA: (*A* = without; *uria* = urine.) Anuria refers to a lack of urine output or total failure of the kidneys to produce. A patient who is anuric will soon die.

APHASIA: The inability to speak or be understood through speech, usually occurring after a stroke or other accident.

APNEA/APENIC: Temporary cessation of breathing, as in sleep apnea.

ARRHYTHMIA: An irregularity of the heartbeat.

ASPIRATE: To inhale material into the lungs.

ATAXIA: Jerky, involuntary movements.

ATROPHY: The wasting away of muscle or ability through lack of use.

AUTONOMIC NERVOUS SYSTEM (ANS): The nervous system controlling involuntary bodily functions.

BRADYCARDIA: Slow heartbeat.

BRONCHIAL DIALATOR: Something that opens up the bronchial tubes.

BRONCHIOSPASM: Uncontrollable cough or contractions of the bronchi.

BUBONIC PLAGUE: An illness caused by the bacterium *Yersinia pestis*. So named because of the enlargement and blackening of the glands in the groin, axillae, or other parts. Also known as the Black Death of the Middle Ages.

CALCIUM CHANNEL BLOCKER: Drugs that prevent calcium from passing through biologic membranes. These agents are used to treat hypertension, angina pectoris, and cardiac arrhythmias; examples include nifedipine, diltiazem, verapamil, amlodipine.

CARDIAC ARREST: (Also cardiac collapse.) The heart stops.

CARDIAC GLYCOSIDES: Drugs like digitalis, which increase the forced contraction of the heart.

CARDIOVASCULAR COLLAPSE: When the heart stops working and the veins collapse as no blood flows.

CATATONIA: Psychiatric disorder characterized by periods of physical rigidity and immovability.

CATECHOLAMINES: Body chemicals produced in response to stress.

CATHARTIC: A laxative or cleansing chemical. Castor oil is one example.

CENTRAL NERVOUS SYSTEM (CNS): The brain and spinal cord.

CEREBRAL EDEMA: Brain swelling due to increased volume of fluid.

CEREBRAL VASCULAR ACCIDENT (CVA OR CV): A stroke as result of rupturing a blood vessel rather than a clot blocking a blood vessel.

CHEYNE-STOKES RESPIRATION: An irregular cycle of breathing that occurs near death. Breathing is at first slow and shallow and then increases in rapidity and depth; then it decreases, stopping for ten to twenty seconds before repeating the same pattern. Defined by Scottish physician John Cheyne and Irish physician William Stokes in the late eighteenth century.

CHOLINESTERASE: An enzyme needed in the body for smooth nerve-muscle function. Also called acetylcholinesterase. Without cholinesterase the muscle fibers are in constant stimulation, as in the disease myasthenia gravis.

CHRONIC: Happening over a prolonged period of time; usually over several weeks, months, or years.

CLONIC-TONIC CONVULSIONS: A spastic alternation of relaxation and contraction of muscles.

COLONIC: A high enema going as far as the intestine. Health faddists have them on a regular basis, but their worth is doubtful.

CONGESTION: Presence of an abnormal amount of fluid in the vessels or passages of a part or organ. See also *edema*.

CYANOSIS: A blue tinge of nails, face, and toes from lack of oxygen in the blood.

CYTOTOXIC: injuruious or deadly to cells, as in chemotherapy.

DELIRIUM: An altered state of consciousness, consisting of confusion, distractibility, disorientation, disordered thinking and memory, defective perception (illusions and hallucinations).

DEPRESSANT: An agent that suppresses a bodily function or nerve activity. A cerebral depressant affects the brain and makes the patient seem slower and dull. Large doses of depressants produce sleep or unconsciousness.

DERMAL: Refers to skin.

DERMATITIS: Irritation of skin; seen as red, chapped, and possibly peeling skin. Often a result of allergy (contact dermatitis.)

DIAPHORESIS: Damp, clammy skin.

DIURETIC: A drug that increases the amount of urine excreted (for example, Lasix).

DIPLOPIA: Double vision.

DEEP VEIN THROMBOSIS (DVT): Clots in the veins of the extremities.

DYSPHAGIA/DYSPHAGY: Difficulty in swallowing.

DYSPHONIA: Altered voice.

DYSPNEA: (*Dys* = pain or difficulty; *pnea* = breathing.) Air hunger, or difficult and painful breathing.

ECCHYMOSIS: The purple discoloration of the skin commonly known as a black-and-blue mark.

EDEMA: An accumulation of an excessive amount of watery fluid in cells or intercellular tissues, causing swelling. Often when people stand for a long time, ankles swell. This can be an indication of heart or lung problems. (See also *congestion*.)

ELECTROCARDIOGRAM (EKG): The electrical impulses of the heart measured by machine.

ELECTROLYTE: A balance of chemicals made up of acids, bases, and salts; found in the blood.

ELIXIR: A clear, hydro-alcoholic liquid taken orally. Elixirs may contain flavoring substances. Used as vehicles for the active medicinal agents. True elixirs must have an alcohol base. Some medications (such as Dimetapp) call themselves elixirs but have no alcohol.

EMETIC: A substance that encourages vomiting, like syrup of ipecac.

ENDOGENOUS: Originating or produced within the organism or one of its parts.

ENTERAL: Within the intestine or absorbed by the intestine; eaten. (As opposed to *parenteral*, taken in through means other than the digestive tract, such as intravenously.)

EPIDERMAL: Relating to skin (epidermis).

ESOPHAGEAL SPASM: Uncontrolled contraction of the esophageal muscles, causing painful or forceful releasing of gas after swallowing food.

ESOPHAGUS: The portion of the digestive canal between the pharynx and stomach.

EXPECTORANT: An agent that increases bronchial secretions and facilitates their expulsion.

EXTRAPYRAMIDAL SYNDROME (EPS): A group of symptoms sometimes related to stroke or to side effects of medications. These include drooling, slurring of words, abnormal gait, dry mouth, blurred or double vision, stiffness of muscles, and involuntary movements of face and tongue (tardive dyskinesia), causing difficulty in speech.

FASCICULATION: Involuntary contractions or twitchings of groups (fasciculi) of muscle fibers. A coarser form of muscular contraction than fibrillation.

FATTY INFILTRATION: Increased deposits of fat in the organs that interfere with their function.

FIBRILLATION: Rapid contractions or twitchings of muscle fibers that can prevent the heart from beating.

FIRST RESPONDERS: The first on the scene, often firefighters or police officers.

FLEXOR MUSCLES: Muscles that bend, as opposed to muscles that extend.

GASTROENTERITIS: Inflammation of the stomach and bowels, causing severe stomach cramps, bloody diarrhea, nausea, and vomiting.

GASTRIC LAVAGE: Pumping the stomach.

GASTROINTESTINAL UPSET: Stomachache, gas, bloating, nausea, vomiting, diarrhea.

HEATSTROKE: A severe and often fatal illness produced by exposure to excessive environmental high temperatures. Characterized by headache; vertigo; confusion; hot, dry skin; and a slight rise in body temperature; in severe cases, very high fever, collapse, and coma.

HEMATURIA: Blood in the urine.

HEMATEMESIS: (*Hema* = blood; *emesis* = vomiting.) Vomiting of blood.

HEMOLYTIC: Describes something that destroys red blood cells.

HEPATIC: Associated with the liver.

HEMODYNAMIC: The physical aspects of blood circulation.

HEMOLYSIS: The breakdown of red blood cells, which releases hemoglobin into the blood.

HEMOPTYSIS: Sudden coughing up of blood.

HEMORRHAGE: To bleed.

HEMORRHAGIC FEVER: A viral disease characterized by hemorrhages from body orifices. (See chapter twelve, Biological, Chemical, and Radiological Weapons.)

HEMORRHAGIC SHOCK: Shock resulting from acute blood loss, characterized by hypotension; tachycardia; pale, cold, and clammy skin; and oliguria.

HEPATITIS: Liver disease.

HYPERFLEXION: Bending of a limb or part beyond the normal limit.

HYPERTENSION: High blood pressure; any variation above 150/100.

HYPERTHERMIA: Fever.

HYPOTHERMIA: Occurs when the body reaches any temperature below normal range.

HYPOTENSION: Low blood pressure; any variation below 100/60.

HYPOXIA: Oxygen hunger short of suffocation. Some signs: confusion; euphoria; delirium; vomiting; irregular breathing; abrupt rise or drop in blood pressure; faint, irregular pulse going from rapid to slow; damp, clammy skin; cyanotic skin; and pupils dilated and fixed.

HYPERPYREXIA: Body temperature above 106 degrees F.

HYPERVENTILATION: Breathing at a fast rate, as in hysteria.

INFILTRATE: A localized, ill-defined opacity seen on an X-ray.

INNERVATE: To stimulate a part of a nerve or an organ and make it respond.

INSULIN SHOCK: Severe hypoglycemia produced by administration of insulin. Manifestations include sweating, tremor, anxiety, vertigo, and diplopia, followed by delirium, convulsions, and collapse.

INTENTION TREMOR: Involuntary movement of muscles. Can be slight or pronounced.

INTRAMUSCULAR (IM): An injection given into the muscle.

INTRAVENOUS (IV): Medication and fluid going directly into the vein.

INTUBATION: Insertion of a tube into the nose or mouth for anesthesia or control of breathing.

LASSITUDE: Weariness, fatigue, grogginess.

LEUKOPENIA: An abnormal decrease of white blood cells.

LD_{50}: The lethal dose of a poison that will kill 50 percent of those exposed.

MEDIASTINUM: A septum between two parts of an organ or a cavity.

MENINGITIS: Inflammation of the membranes of the brain or spinal cord.

MIOSIS: Small, pinpoint pupils.

MITRAL STENOSIS: Narrowing of the mitral valve opening.

MONOAMINE OXIDASE INHIBITORS/ MAOI: Antidepressants, popular in earlier years, but used less today because of the dangerous reactions they cause with other drugs.

MYDRIASIS: Abnormal dilation of the pupil of the eye.

MYOCARDIAL INFARCTION: Heart attack caused by blockage of the artery supplying nutrients to the heart.

MYOTONIA: A temporary rigidity that occurs after a muscle contraction.

NARCOSIS: Stupor.

NECROSIS: The death and decay of tissue.

NERVINE: Something that acts as a nerve sedative or decreases the irritability of the nerves.

NEUROPATHY: Any disease that causes degeneration of the nerves.

NEUTROPENIA: Abnormally small numbers of neutrophils (a type of white blood cell) in the circulating blood.

NEUROPIL: Nerve network that makes up the grey matter of the brain.

NICOTINIC: Relating to the stimulating action of acetylcholine.

NYSTAGMUS: Constant. involuntary movement of the eyeball.

OLIGURIA: A condition in which the kidneys do not produce the amount of urine necessary to remain healthy.

OLIPNEA: Infrequent respiration.

ORTHOSTATIC HYPOTENSION: A sudden fall in blood pressure as one stands up rapidly from a prone position.

OVER THE COUNTER (OTC): Medications that can be purchased without a prescription, like most cold medicines.

PALLIATIVE: A treatment that addresses symptoms without curing the underlying disease.

PALSY: Uncontrolled shaking or spasms.

PARANOIA: Mental disorder characterized by the presence of delusions—often involving being followed, poisoned, or harmed by other means—in an otherwise intact personality.

PARASYMPATHETIC NERVOUS SYSTEM: Controls the smooth muscle function.

PARENTERAL: Introduced into the system in ways other than by the gastrointestinal tract; for example, intravenously. (Compare to *enteral*.)

PARESTHESIA: An abnormal sensation, as in numbness, prickling, or tingling of the skin, without external cause.

PERCUTANEOUS ABSORPTION: (*Per* = through; *cutaneous* = of or relating to the skin.) The absorption of drugs, allergens, and other substances through unbroken skin, as in topical application.

PERISTALSIS: The movement of food through the intestine, characterized by waves of alternate circular contraction and relaxation, which propel contents onward.

PERITONEAL DIALYSIS: Removal from the body of soluble toxins and water by transfer across the peritoneum, utilizing a dialysis solution. It is a reverse osmosis through the membranes of the walls.

PERITONEUM: The lining of the abdominal cavity, which contains the stomach, liver, spleen, kidneys, and other organs.

PERITONITIS: Infection of the peritoneum.

PETECHIAL: Small, red, rashlike spots or hemorrhages that appear on the skin or organs. usually indicating a lack of oxygen to the organ.

PLEURAL EFFUSION: Increased fluid in the pleural space; can cause shortness of breath by compression of the lungs.

PER OS (PO): By mouth (Latin). Used in prescriptions.

POLYURIA: Urination of far greater frequency than considered normal.

POSTICTAL: An altered state of consciousness following a seizure.

PROGNOSIS: Predicted outcome of a disease or incident.

PRONE: Lying facedown.

PSYCHOSIS: A mental and behavioral disorder causing gross distortion or disorganization of a person's mental capacity; affective response; and capacity to recognize reality, communicate, and relate to others.

PSYCHOTROPIC: Capable of affecting the mind, emotions, and behavior; denoting drugs used in the treatment of mental illnesses.

PTOSIS: A sinking down of an organ (as in drooping of the eyelid—blepharoptosis).

PULMONARY: Related to the respiratory system.

PULMONARY EDEMA: Fluid accumulation and buildup in the lungs.

PURGATIVE: Any agent that causes the evacuation of the bowels. A cathartic.

PURGE: To evacuate or eliminate.

PURULENT: Containing, consisting of, or forming pus.

PUTREFACTION: Decomposition and liquification of body parts or other protein, usually associated with a horrendous smell and gas by-products.

RALES: Abnormal sounds from the lungs made by the thickening of mucus in the chest.

RENAL: Kidney, or associated with the kidneys.

RESPIRATORY ARREST: Cessation of breathing.

RESPIRATORY DEPRESSION: A slowness of breathing or the inability to take a deep breath.

RETICULAR ACTIVATING SYSTEM (RAS): Part of the brainstem reticular formation that plays a central role in the organism's bodily and behavioral alertness.

RHINORRHEA: Runny nose.

SAPONIN: An unabsorbable glycoside contained in the roots of some plants. These can be mixed to form a watery solution that causes vomiting, diarrhea, and other irritating symptoms if taken internally.

SEPTIC SHOCK: Shock associated with infection that has released large quantities of toxins into the blood.

SEPTICEMIA: Systemic disease caused by the spread of microorganisms and their toxins into the blood; formerly called blood poisoning.

SHOCK: A sudden physical or biochemical disturbance that results in inadequate blood flow and oxygenation of an individual's vital organs.

SHORTNESS OF BREATH (SOB): Inability to catch one's breath or take full breaths.

STRIDOR: A harsh, high-pitched sound during inhalation or exhalation.

STRICTURE: A narrowing or stenosis of a hollow structure or tube.

STROKE: There are two different types of stroke. One is the thrombotic stroke, or blockage of the blood vessels in the brain. The other is a CVA or cerebral vascular accident, caused by blood vessels breaking and bleeding into the brain.

SUBCUTANEOUS: Under the skin.

SUPINE: Lying faceup.

SYMPATHETIC SYSTEM: The part of the autonomic nervous system that controls the breathing, heart rate, and other nonpurposeful movements within the body that occur without our being acutely aware of them. Also called the parasympathetic nervous system.

SYNAPSE: The space between two nerve endings in which nerve transmitters travel.

SYNAPTIC RESISTANCE: The ease or difficulty with which a nerve impulse can cross a synapse.

TACHYCARDIA: Quickened heartbeat; racing pulse.

TETANIC CONVULSIONS: Spasm-like convulsions associated with the disease process of tetanus.

THROMBOTIC STROKE: Formation or presence of a thrombus (blood clot); clotting within a blood vessel, which may cause infarction of brain tissues supplied by the vessel.

TINNITUS: Ringing in the ears.

UNIVERSAL PRECAUTIONS: (In full, Universal Blood and Body Fluid Precautions) A set of procedural directives and guidelines published in August 1987 by the Centers for Disease Control and Prevention (CDC) (as *Recommendations for Prevention of HIV Transmission in Health-Care Settings*) to prevent parenteral, mucous membrane, and nonintact skin exposures of health care workers to bloodborne pathogens. In December 1991, the Occupational Safety and Health Administration (OSHA) promulgated its Occupational Exposure to Bloodborne Pathogens Standard, incorporating universal precautions and imposing detailed requirements on employers of health care workers, including engineering controls, provision of protective barrier devices, standardized labeling of biohazards, mandatory training of employees in universal precautions, management of accidental parenteral exposure incidents, and availability to employees of immunization against hepatitis B.

UREMIA/UREMIC POISONING: An excess of urea and other nitrogenous waste in the blood as a result of renal failure; can be relieved by dialysis.

VASCULAR/VASO: Referring to veins.

VASODILATOR: A drug or chemical that widens the circumference of the veins.

VENTRICULAR FIBRILLATION: Ventricles are chambers in the heart. Fibrillation occurs when the muscle tissue no longer works in unison.

VENULES: Small blood vessels between the veins and capillaries.

VERTIGO: A sensation of spinning or of a whirling motion; dizziness.

WMD: Weapons of mass destruction

ZOONOSIS: An infection or infestation shared in nature by humans and other animals.

INDEX

A

acetaminophen, 151–152

acid, 224–225

acidosis, 345

acrylamide, 225–226

acute poisoning, 9–10

adder, 119–121

administration of poisons, methods of, 295–299

adrenaline, 185–186

African coffee tree, 69

African coral snake, 125

African milk plant, 97–98

air embolism, 202–203

akee, 76–77

albizia anthelmintica, 98

alcohol
   grain, 254–256
   rubbing, 45–46
   wood, 240–241

Aldomet, 197–198

alkaline corrosives, 32–34

alkalosis, 345

allergies, 284–286

Amanita family of mushrooms, 105–110

Ambien, Ambien CR, 163

American nightshade, 73–74

ammonia, 34–35

ammonium hydroxide, 34–35

amphetamine, 250–252

amphibians, 131–132

anaphylaxis, 346

Indian krait, 124

Indian paint, 92

Indian tobacco, 88–89

industrial poisons, 224–248

ingested poisons (swallowed), 297–299

inhaled poisons, 295–296

injected poisons, 296–297

inky cap mushroom, 114

inocybe mushroom, 112–113

inorganic salts, 32–34

insane root, 99–100

insect repellants, 52

insecticides, 215–220

insulin, 207–209

insulin shock, 350

iodine, 191–192

ipecac, 89–90

iron, 44–45

isopropanol, 45–46

isopropyl alcohol, 45–46

ivy bush, 73

J

Jack-in-the-pulpit, 92–93

Jacob's ladder, 60–61

Jamestown weed, 59–60

jellyfish, 139–141

Jericho rose, 62–63

jimsonweed, 59–60

Joplin, Janis, 257

K

kerosene, 46–47

ketamine, 261–262

kidneys, poisons affecting, 318–319

king cobra, 123

king puff adder, 120

knockout drops, 163–164

koli, 69

kraits, 122, 124

L

LaFarge, Marie, 16

lambkill, 73

lancehead, 127–128

larkspur, 94–95

Lasix, 194–195

Lassa fever, 272–273

laudanum, 153–154

laurel, 73

laxatives, 52

lead, lead compounds, 237–239

lepiota mushroom, 108

lethal injection, 161

lethal poisons, 9–10

levintine viper, 120–121

lewisite, 275

Librax, 174

lidocaine, 159–160

lily of the valley, 60–61

listeria, 36–38

lithium, 174–175

liver, poisons affecting, 319

lizard, Mexican beaded, 130–131

lobelia, 88–89

locoweed, 75–76

locust, 91–92

Lomotil, 209–210

Lorfan, 155

loveapple, 78–79

LSD, 258

lungs, poisons affecting, 312–314

lye, 32–34

M

Madame LaFarge, 16

magic mushroom, 113–114

mambas, 123–124

mandrake, 78–79

man-of-war, Portuguese, 141–142

Marburg virus, 272–273

marijuana, 258–259

Marsh, James, 16

mass hysteria, 286–287

maypop, 81

meadow saffron, 72–73

medical treatment, changes in, 11–12

membrane absorption, poisoning by, 297

mercury, 239–240

mercury levels, in fish, 136

meth, 250–252

methanol, 240–241

Mexican beaded lizard, 130–131

Mickey, Mickey Finn, 163–164

mole death, 28–30

monkshood, 61–62

monoamine oxidase inhibitors (MAOI), 182–183, 351

monosodium glutamate (MSG), 50–51

Monroe, Marilyn, 161

Monvoisin, Catherine, 15

moonseed, 79–80

morphine, 153–154

moth balls, moth flakes, 46

mountain adder, 120–121

mountain laurel, 73

mountain mahogany, 79

mouse-nots, 28–30

mouth, poisons affecting, 307–309

mugwort, 90

muscle relaxation drugs, 183–188

musculoskeletal system, poisons affecting, 319–320

mushrooms, 103–115

muskrat weed, 58

myocardial infarction, 351

N

naphtha, 46–47

naphthalene, 46

narcissus, 95–86

narcotic analgesics, 152–157

necrosis, 351

neocinchophen, 149–150

nerve agents, 276–281

neurological system, poisons affecting, 320–327

nicotine, 217–218

nightshade, 55–56

nitroglycerin, 195–196

nitrous oxide, 158–159

Norflex, 150–151

Norpramine, 175

nose, poisons affecting, 307–309

nuclear bomb, 282–283

nutmeg, 80–81

O

ocean-dwelling creatures, 136–145

octopus, 137–138

oleander, 62–63

opium, 260–261

ordeal bean of Madagascar, 66–67

Orfila, Matthew J.B., 16–17

organophosphates, 218–219

oxalic acid, 241–242

oxybenzene, 47–48

oxycodone, 154–155

P

paint thinner, 46–47

panther mushroom, 108–110

Paral, 165–166

paralysis, poisons causing, 325–326

paranoia, 351

paraquat, 221–222

parasol mushroom, 108

passion flower, 81

paternoster pea, 63–64

Pavulon, 186

Paxil, 180–181

peacock flower, 96

pepper spray, 282

Percodan, 154–155

Permital, 176

Persantine, 196–197

pesticides, 213–223

petroleum distillates, 46–47

phencyclidine (PCP), 261–262

Phenergan, 210

phenic acid, 47–48

phenobarbital, 166–167

phenol, 47–48

phenyl hydroxide, 47–48

phenylic acid, 47–48

phosgene, 242–243, 276

phosphine, 243

phosphorus, 243–244

physic nut, 54–55

Physostigmine, 187

pie plant, 82

pigeonberry, 73–74

pilocarpine, 187

plague, 268–269, 347

ABOUT THE AUTHORS

SERITA STEVENS: As a registered nurse specializing in forensics, Serita has studied poisons for many years and also assisted numerous screenwriters and novelists in writing medically correct material for their stories. An award nominated author, she has thirty-two books out. Her most recent one, *The Forensic Nurse* (St Martin's Press) is scheduled to go into TV production. Currently she is working on a true crime book that she helped solve. She and her family live in Los Angeles' San Fernando Valley with cats Othello, Caesar, Shakespeare, Marky Twain and dogs Pupperazzi (who hounds her) and Sophie. Her Web sites are www.seritastevens.org and www.nursingtheevidence.com.

ANNE LOUISE BANNON: A freelance journalist and contributing editor for *Homeland Protection Professional* magazine, her work has also been seen in *Emergency Physicians Monthly, WineMaker, Wines & Vines, On Direct TV, Catholic Parent* and in newspapers across the country. She is also the author of the mystery novel *Tyger, Tyger.* A semi-retired parent (the kid is away at college), Anne lives in Southern California with her husband and (at last count) two dogs and two cats. Her Web site is www.annelouisebannon.com.